To my children—
Sara, Matt, and Andy

Contents

Preface

Bertram Hartnett, recounting his many years as both a judge and practicing attorney, recently noted that many laypersons are confused by the judicial process, viewing the American legal system in strictly mechanical terms. Instead, Judge Hartnett declares, we must realize that "lawyers and judges are not cogs in a computer mechanism. They are thinking, unthinking beings with all the frailties of the human condition."[1] The importance of the individual judge and his or her interaction with attorneys and other members of the courtroom work group is a concept that has been eloquently argued for over 60 years. The legal realists led by Jerome Frank and Morris Cohen as well as the perceptive writing of Justice Benjamin Cardozo established the foundations of a behavioral approach to the study of law that attacks the legalistic and mechanical analyses of judicial decision making. Cardozo's *The Nature of the Judicial Process* was the apotheosis of this new and enlightened approach to comprehending the realities of our nation's legal system.

Borrowing from Freudian psychology as well as other early social science theories, Cardozo explained that a judge's legal decisions are only partially determined by the relevant precedents and statutes. Cardozo wrote that "the directive force of a principle may be exerted along the line of logical progression; this I call the rule of analogy or the method of philosophy; along the line of historical development; this I call the method of evolution; along the lines of the customs of the community; this I call the method of tradition; along the lines of justice, morals and social welfare, the mores of the day, and this I call the method of sociology."[2]

Predating Cardozo's ground-breaking analysis by five years, C. G. Haines in 1916 presented his research findings from an examination of New York City magistrates in 17,000 cases argued before them. From these statistics Haines concluded that "something else besides the law and the facts was motivating some magistrates' decisions."[3] He went on to state that in his view appellate court justices, such as members of the United States Supreme Court, were influenced more by their personal,

---

[1]Bertram Hartnett, *Law, Lawyers, and Laymen* (New York: Harcourt Brace Jovanovich, 1984), 13.

[2]Benjamin Cardozo, *The Nature of the Judicial Process* (New Haven: Yale University Press, 1921), 30.

[3]Charles Haines, "General Observations on the Effects of Personal, Political and Economic Influences on the Decisions of Judges," *Illinois Law Forum* 17 (1922): 96.

social, and economic beliefs than by the words of the Constitution or earlier precedents.[4]

Judges and Lawyers: The Human Side of Justice is a book that continues the intellectual tradition of Frank, Cardozo, and Haines. It is an examination of the professional behavior of judges and lawyers that reinforces and emphasizes Judge Hartnett's belief that these critical legal actors are not merely performing their professional functions as "cogs in a mechanical process" but are bringing the unique amalgamation of their personalities and life experiences to bear upon their legal responsibilities. The best way for the reader to understand the unique perspective utilized in this volume is to briefly review the major topics that will be covered. The book begins with a description of the law school experience, stressing its important role as a critical socializing agent for the legal profession. Chapter 2 offers a social-psychological portrait of judges and lawyers, providing a demographic description of each group as well as an overall personality assessment. Chapter 3 examines the lawyer's working environment. This chapter illustrates the variety of workplaces, ranging from the often bare-bones operations of a solo practitioner to the opulent surroundings of the large corporate law firms. Chapter 4 focuses on the lawyer's primary tasks such as litigating, negotiating, counseling, and drafting. Much of the chapter is devoted to describing the unique relationship that exists between lawyer and client. Chapter 5 discusses the most significant ethical problems facing lawyers and evaluates efforts to regulate the profession by such groups as the American Bar Association.

The second half of the book turns to the judiciary as Chapter 6 studies selection, training, and socialization of our nation's judiciary. Chapter 7 describes the working environment of judges, focusing on the courthouse as well as the members of the courtroom work group. This chapter also attempts to indicate the wide diversity of judicial environments as all major types of judicial settings are analyzed, from the chaotic operations of the lower municipal courts processing thousands of cases to the more elegant and thoughtful collegial deliberations of appellate courts. The variety of judicial responsibilities are presented in Chapter 8. These range from adjudicative and administrative duties to negotiating and opinion-writing functions. Chapter 9 turns to the strains and hardships of judging. A brief analysis of the most common complaints of judges as well as an examination of the problem of judicial misconduct and its regulation are the major issues in this final chapter.

Because the large majority of textbooks examining the American legal system have chosen to emphasize the jurisprudential (philosophical), historical, legalistic, procedural, and structural approaches, they have therefore minimized the humanistic and social-psychological perspective adopted in this volume. Several of the topics covered, such as judi-

---

[4]Ibid. p. 106

cial socialization, legal misconduct, and the working environment, are rarely discussed in other textbooks. I believe that my extensive research and professional experiences during the past 20 years have provided an excellent background for completing this unusual textbook. During this period I interviewed over 500 judges and lawyers and spent countless hours in courtroom observations in 15 cities across the country. By supplementing these experiences with a thorough review of relevant legal and social science literature, this book offers the reader continuous opportunities to hear the actual voices of judges and lawyers as they attempt to carry out their professional responsibilities within the confines of their diverse working conditions.

ACKNOWLEDGMENTS

I would like first to thank the countless number of judges and lawyers who have allowed me to intrude into their chaotic world, observing their professional behavior and selflessly sharing their many thoughts and insights. Without their assistance this volume could never have been completed. The following individuals deserve special thanks for their many kindnesses and support extended to me over the years: Richard Max Bockol, Judge George Nicola, Judge Marvin Halbert, John Paul Ryan, Robert Lipscher, Professor Fred Cohen, Professor David Neubauer, and Professor George Cole. In addition, professors Cole and Neubauer were among the people who reviewed draft versions of this manuscript. I would like to thank all of these reviewers, including Milton Heumann, Rutgers University; Herbert Jacob, Northwestern University; and Albert P. Melone, Southern Illinois University.

I would also like to thank my eternally loyal colleagues in the political science department at Drew University as well as my special student assistants who provided much needed help in the preparation of this volume—Chip Miller and Addie Harchik. Finally, I wish to express my deep gratitude to Dick Welna of Scott, Foresman, without whose perseverance and encouragement this volume would never have seen the light of day, and the wonderful editorial assistance received from Claire Caterer, Catherine Woods, and Lauren Silverman at HarperCollins.

Paul Wice

Chapter
1

Law School and Early Socialization

*D*espite the diversity of work experiences (many of which will be described in subsequent chapters), nearly all of our nation's 600,000 lawyers share a common socialization experience—attending and graduating from one of the approximately two hundred law schools presently in operation in the United States. Although there are clearly discernible differences between the social and intellectual climates of these various law schools, there remains nevertheless a broad commonality of experience. This chapter will examine both the formal and informal aspects of the socialization process. The concluding section of the chapter will analyze the socialization process as it affects the law school graduate's initial work experience. The first position, as will be seen, serves as a critical socializing institution, emerging as a type of modern-day apprenticeship, providing those pragmatic professional lessons that are frequently omitted from the more theoretical and scholarly law school experience.

THE LAW SCHOOL EXPERIENCE

Current Enrollment Trends

Since the early 1960s, the legal profession has become an increasingly popular career choice. Table 1.1 indicates the fairly consistent growth pattern in law school enrollment as nearly 130,000 students are currently attending law school. The greatest spurt in attendance occurred during the turbulent period extending from the late 1960s through the mid-sev-

1

Table 1.1   LEGAL EDUCATION AND BAR ADMISSION STATISTICS 1965–1986

Year	Total Enrollment[a]	Women Enrolled[b]	First Year	LSAT Taken	LSDAS Completes[c]	JD or LLB Awarded	New Admissions to the Bar
1965–1966	59,744	2,537	24,167	44,905		11,507	13,109
1966–1967	62,556	2,678	24,077	47,110		13,115	14,644
1967–1968	64,406	2,906	24,267	49,756		14,738	16,007
1968–1969	62,779	3,704	23,652	59,050		16,077	17,764
1969–1970	68,386	4,715	29,128	74,092		16,733	19,123
1970–1971	82,041	7,031	34,289	107,479		17,183	17,922
1971–1972	94,468	8,914	36,171	119,694	80,364	17,006	20,485
1972–1973	101,707	12,173	35,131	121,262	81,913	22,342	25,086
1973–1974	106,102	16,760	37,018	135,397	85,999	27,756	30,879
1974–1975	110,713	21,788	38,074	133,546	83,100	28,729	30,707
1975–1976	116,991	26,737	39,038	133,316	82,243	29,961	34,930
1976–1977	117,451	29,982	39,996	128,135	78,717	32,597	35,741
1977–1978	118,557	32,538	39,676	127,760	81,366	33,640	37,302
1978–1979	121,606	36,808	40,479	115,284	72,529	33,317	39,086
1979–1980	122,860	38,627	40,717	112,466	76,669	34,590	42,756
1980–1981	125,397	42,122	42,296	107,373	79,669	35,059	41,997
1981–1982	127,312	44,986	42,521	118,565	82,636	35,598	42,382
1982–1983	127,828	47,083	42,034	111,620	82,145	34,846	42,905
1983–1984	127,195	47,980	41,159	104,621	72,900	36,389	41,684
1984–1985	125,698	48,499	40,747	95,129	70,001	36,687	42,630
1985–1986	124,092	49,050	40,796	91,921	68,000[d]	36,829	42,450

[a]Enrollment figures courtesy of the ABA's *A Review of Legal Education in the United States*, Fall, 1985. Total enrollment includes post-JD and "other" programs.

[b]The number of women enrolled includes women in JD, post-JD, and "other" programs.

[c]An "LSDAS Complete" is a person who has subscribed to the Law School Data Assembly Service, who has a reportable LSAT score, and whose transcripts have been summarized by LSDAS.

[d]Estimated.

Source: The Official Guide to U.S. Law Schools (Newtown, Pa.: LSAC/LSAS, 1987). 9.

enties, when students turned away from the imagined crass world of big business to the more socially relevant vocation of law, which seemed to offer the greatest opportunity for correcting the unacceptable injustices of American society. These sentiments resulted in law school enrollments catapulting from 62,000 in 1968 to over 101,000 in 1972, an increase of nearly 60 percent in just 4 years. Even though the rate of increase has declined and appeared to reach a plateau in the past 10 years (1978–1988) as interest in business careers (especially investment banking) achieved greater popularity, law schools still exhibited modest gains. As a matter of fact, during the academic year 1987–1988, with the frightening collapse of the stock market in October of 1987, students again moved away from business toward careers in law. A *New York Times* article (April 1, 1988) reported a 15 percent rise in applicants over the previous year, the first such notable increase since the late 1970s. (Most of the prestigious law schools were experiencing a 25 percent jump in applicants.) Explanation for the rapid rise, according to the article, "ranged from the stock market collapse which may have tarnished the allure of a career on Wall Street to 'L.A. Law,' a television show which glamorizes the lives of upscale lawyers."[1]

Law schools are obviously quite concerned with these figures, and when enrollment statistics appeared to stagnate during the mideighties, as Wall Street reached its peak of desirability, nervous law school administrators tried to analyze the depressing figures. Edward Fiske reported in July of 1986 that enrollment figures to the nation's 175 accredited law schools declined by 25 percent from its peak year of 1982 (70,000 applicants) to only 52,000 for the fall of 1986. Legal educators attributed the decrease to a wide range of causes, including the following: (1) a perceived glut of lawyers; (2) growing interest in alternative fields such as computer science and business; (3) the declining image of the profession; (4) the evaporation of student idealism, replaced by self-interest concerns; and (5) a general backlash against the hordes of people going to law school in the 1960s and 1970s.[2]

Given the somewhat erratic enrollment figures for the past 10 years, it is difficult to predict if the number of law students will continue to expand exponentially. Nevertheless, if one takes the longer view, the legal profession will continue to be an attractive vocation for many undergraduates, and most law schools, especially those with strong regional and national reputations, will have little trouble filling their classrooms. Why has the law continued to attract so many students? A 1980 report sponsored by the American Bar Association (ABA) examined this question and offered the following range of answers: (1) prestige and high earnings; (2) intellectual interest in law study and legal work; (3) traditional image of the lawyer as a professional dedicated to ideals of service, high ethical standards, and problem solving; (4) function of law as a mechanism for distributing rights, power, and influence among different social groups; and (5) external reasons such as the advancement of a nonlegal career, influence of significant others, and lack of opportunity to pursue a first choice field.[3]

Stated in more basic terms, the ABA offered the tautological conclusion that students went to law school because they wanted to become lawyers. One of the most frequently quoted books on the topic is Warkow and Zelan's study *Lawyers in the Making* contrasting law students who valued making money and helping others with nonlawyers who placed greater emphasis on originality and creativity, avoidance of a high-pressure working environment, and a willingness to sacrifice a boom or bust career for job security and steady, yet slow, progress.[4]

Have these motivating factors changed during recent years? Are they modified by the law school experience? Much attention was paid to the first question by social scientists during the late 1960s and mid-1970s as college students were depicted as evolving from socially concerned, politically active individuals who often wished to use their degrees to work in public-interest law firms into hedonistic, materialistic young adults who were the precursors of today's generation of "yuppies." They sought employment in large corporate law firms and the legal departments of private financial institutions and corporations where they could be assured of earning a comfortable salary, which could easily stretch to six figures within five to ten years. Carl Auerbach compared these two generations of law students and was surprised to find only modest decreases in the number practicing public-interest law.[5] Auerbach believes that the decline could be at least partially explained as a logical by-product of the overall shrinkage in federal funding for poverty law clinics nationally. Turning to the second question, James Hedegaard's exhaustive study of Brigham Young University law students failed to disclose any pattern of shifting career interests. His research, in fact, concluded that the general pattern of career interest in the law seems to have been firmly established in most of the sample by the time the students entered law school.[6]

1 L, Scott Turow's fascinating description of his first year at Harvard Law School appears to illustrate a trend away from the more public and esoteric aspects of the law and toward greater student interest in corporate law and other specializations that are associated with lucrative salaries.[7] This process may simply be part of the maturing process for all students in their early twenties, especially those who enter law school with little preconceived notions about what areas of the law they would eventually wish to select as a specialty.

The enrollment decision by the law school admission's office is based primarily on two criteria: the undergraduate grade point average as reflecting academic performance and the score on the Law School Admissions Test (LSAT) administered by the Educational Testing Service (the same Princeton-based organization that administers the Scholastic Aptitude Tests to high school seniors and a wide range of additional tests for admissions to graduate and professional schools). The LSAT attempts to measure a student's potential for law school by testing verbal skills and reasoning abilities. Although the exam has never been found to be significantly related to success in law school,[8] it nevertheless does provide an alternative measurement beyond the undergraduate scholastic average, thereby helping to control for the relative quality and difficulty of each applicant's undergraduate academic program. Although such additional factors as letters of reference and extracurricular activities may be considered in borderline decisions, admissions directors will candidly admit that the overwhelming majority of decisions are primarily influenced by the two quantitative measures of undergraduate grades and LSAT scores.

Similar to other aptitude tests developed by the Educational Testing Service, the LSAT has been criticized as being culturally biased. David White, writing for the National Conference of Black Lawyers, conducted an extensive investigation of the issue and concluded that college grades are a much better predictor of law school success than LSAT scores and have "considerably less discriminatory impact against minority applicants."[9] It is rather difficult to definitively conclude predictability of LSAT scores or assess the magnitude of their possible cultural bias, but it does seem clear that as long as the sizable number of students continue to apply to law school (a 300 percent increase in 20 years), quantitative measures such as grades and LSAT scores will be the primary selection criteria. These numerical measures allow for easier admissions decisions by establishing clearly defined cutoff points and reserving for an admissions committee only the few difficult borderline candidates where additional "qualitative" criteria may be considered. As part of this strategy of dealing with the massive number of applicants and the small admissions staff, many law schools have generally eliminated the opportunity for applicants to have personal interviews.

Typology of Law Schools

In contrast to most professions such as medicine and clinical psychology, which maintain extremely high admissions standards at *all* of their approved professional schools, American law schools utilize a wide variety of admissions standards from the very selective to those with virtually open admissions for anyone who can afford the tuition. Despite the efforts of the ABA to raise admissions standards and tighten the requirements for professional approval, the diversity persists. There are nearly 175 ABA-approved institutions, with another 30 to 40 nonapproved degree-granting law schools licensed in their respective states. Typically, a graduate of a nonapproved ABA school may take the bar exam and practice in *only* that specific state. For example, if one graduated from San Fernando Valley College of Law (one of several non-ABA-approved law schools currently operating in California), he or she would only be allowed to take the California bar and practice solely in California. If this person wished to move and practice in another state, he or she would not only have to take another bar exam, but, in all likelihood, the law degree would not be recognized since it was from an unapproved school. This could therefore mean that one would have to enter a new law school and begin working toward the degree, this time in an ABA-approved institution. Thus, although admission to these unapproved law schools may be very easy, with nearly all candidates gaining acceptance, nevertheless one is running the risk of limiting one's future professional life to only that state where the degree was granted. The *Official Guide to United States Law Schools*, published by the Educational Testing Service in cooperation with the ABA and the Association of American Law Schools (AALS), warns prospective students about these unapproved law schools: "Before enrolling you should carefully consider the limitations that result from obtaining a degree from these unapproved programs. You should carefully review the implications of your decision and enroll only if it is clear that such a school will provide adequate legal training and that employment possibilities will not be unduly restricted after graduation."[10]

As was already noted, even the ABA-approved law schools possess widely disparate admissions standards. It is therefore the essence of the "admissions game" for the law school applicant to select a law school to which he or she can be reasonably sure to gain acceptance. Another consideration is the location of the law school and certain other special features such as a commitment to clinical education or a heavy emphasis on some specialized area of the law. Nevertheless, the typical applicant generally tries to get into the best law school—"best" being operationally defined as having the highest standards.

One of the most common typologies employed for classifying law schools is suggested by the *Official Guide to U.S. Law Schools*, which divides schools on the basis of their geographic orientation, working down from national law schools to state and, finally, local ones at the bottom. (All three categories, however, are superior to any of the unapproved schools, which are all strictly "local" in orientation.) The distinction between national, state, and local may also be viewed as euphemisms for law schools of varying quality and selectivity. The national law schools select only the top students who apply from all over the country, whereas the regional schools attract good but not great applicants, and local law schools are left with those students who have not been admitted to the two higher levels.

The highest-quality national law schools require LSAT scores in the ninetieth percentile and above, with nearly A-quality undergraduate averages. Although any listing of top law schools is highly subjective and influenced by personal bias, the list in Table 1.2 of the top 12 with regard to both academic quality and employment value was recently compiled as the result of an extensive survey of law school deans.

Table 1.2   TOP U.S. LAW SCHOOLS

Academic Quality	Employment Value
1. Harvard	Harvard
2. Yale	Yale
3. Stanford	Columbia
4. Michigan	Stanford
5. Chicago	Michigan
6. Columbia	Chicago
7. Berkeley	Virginia
8. Penn	Penn
9. Virginia	NYU
10. NYU	Berkeley
11. Georgetown	Georgetown
12. Duke	Duke

Source: "Rankings of the Top Schools," Juris Doctor
(December, 1976): 17.

The schools listed in Table 1.2 contain few surprises since they are probably among the finest overall educational institutions in the country, possessing excellent undergraduate, graduate, and professional programs. Other schools frequently listed close to the top 12 and noted by several of the deans in this survey include Cornell, Texas, Northwestern, UCLA, Wisconsin, North Carolina, and Vanderbilt. In addition to attracting students from wide geographic areas, these schools are national because their curriculum does not concentrate on the laws of any specific jurisdiction, and even more significantly, the school's prestigious reputation allows its graduates to gain employment with the best law firms throughout the country.

The second category of law schools is more regional in nature, with several having a statewide orientation. This group of schools may also be difficult to enter, requiring LSAT scores above the seventy-fifth percentile and a minimum grade point average of B plus. These schools, frequently the top public institutions in their respective states, include the University of Illinois, Rutgers University, University of Georgia, University of Colorado, and the University of Arizona. Other regional schools may also be private, maintaining fairly high admissions standards and serving an extended regional area. Examples of this genre include Boston College and Boston University in the East, Emory and Tulane in the South, and Washington University and Notre Dame in the Midwest. These schools also utilize a national perspective in terms of their teaching emphasis, but the majority of their students both originate and eventually practice within the same geographic region as the law school.

The final group comprises the largest number of schools and has been characterized as "local." Although admissions standards of these schools are perceptibly below the national and regional schools, their varying standards make it difficult to generalize. Some local schools even attempt to maintain a national perspective in their teaching although most realize that the overwhelming majority of their students will practice locally and therefore feel obligated to stress the laws of their own state. Examples of these local law schools are Seton Hall in New Jersey, University of Baltimore in Maryland, Stetson University in Florida, Mercer University in Georgia, and Pepperdine University in California. Approximately one hundred schools qualify as local, all having ABA approval. The majority are private institutions, and those operating in large cities frequently offer evening and part-time programs.

Does the type of law school one attends make a difference? Given the abundance of lawyers competing for business, is it critical that one attend either a national or regional law school? In a later section we will discuss that the large, prestigious law firms do in fact limit themselves to applicants from only the very best law schools. These highly selective, very well paid positions, however, affect only 1–2 percent of each year's graduating class. For the large majority of remaining positions, applicants are accepted from a broad range of law schools. The hiring partners are frequently more interested in how well one did rather than the quality of law school attended. Thus a law review member or honor graduate from a regional or local school may fare better in the job market than someone from a more prestigious school who graduated in the middle of his or her class. Other factors affecting the applicant's chances may be the intern experience, the quality of the placement office, and alumni commitment to helping recent graduates. Local schools such as Seton Hall and Duquesne have developed reputations as maintaining an excellent placement record through the dedication of alumni in Northern New Jersey and Western Pennsylvania, at least equaling the efforts of more notable regional schools (i.e., Rutgers and the University of Pittsburgh) with which they are often in direct competition. Finally, the personality and unique background characteristics of each applicant, when combined with the special requirements for a particular job opening, can also be a critical factor influencing the hiring decision. As a closing note on law school reputation and its import to one's career, most lawyers agree that its significance declines the longer one practices. Thus, after the first or possibly second job, potential employers are much more interested in the type of lawyer the applicant has become than in which school he or she attended.[11]

The Curriculum

American legal education was initially based on the British model and continued as a type of apprenticeship system until after the Civil War.

An aspiring lawyer in the 1800s would work with an established lawyer, with whom he would "read the law." This meant observing what the lawyer did, researching decisions, copying legal documents, serving process papers, and reading a select group of treatises such as Blackstone and Coke.[12] Gradually, the novice attorney would be able to abandon the mentor and open a private practice, initially depending primarily upon referrals from the lawyers who had assisted him during the apprenticeship period. It was not until the 1870s that law schools began to emerge as formalized educational programs, usually associated with a major university. Robert Stevens credits this development as growing out of the prevalent "middle class urge to get ahead through structured education," as well as the growing dissatisfaction with the apprenticeship model.[13] This period, from the 1870s to the close of the nineteenth century, also witnessed the legal profession becoming a boom industry. Under the leadership of Christopher Columbus Langdell at Harvard, law school was now accepted as an appropriate topic for university education.[14]

The law school curriculum today still reflects the abandonment of the apprenticeship system, replacing it with a more scholarly and theoretical approach. The debate over whether law schools have erred by overemphasis on scholarship and deemphasis on practical skills has continued throughout the twentieth century. This controversy was succinctly characterized by Associate Justice Robert Jackson of the United States Supreme Court in a speech at Stanford Law School nearly 40 years ago and still rings true today: "If the weakness of the apprenticeship system was to produce advocates without scholarship, the weakness of the law school system is to turn out scholars with no skills of advocacy."[15] The American emphasis on scholarship with only a minimal exposure to practical training makes our system unique in the world. In Canada, for example, in the Province of Ontario, all law school graduates are required to complete a 12-month clerkship followed by a 6-month teaching program of practical training, lectures, and tutorial groups. The responsibility for the entire postgraduate program is vested in the bar association. Jerome Kramer, in an article in the *National Law Journal* (January 9, 1989), comments that the "educational and training requirements in the civil law countries of Europe are similar, ranging from tutorial and internship training after law school for one year in France to as much as two and a half years in West Germany . . . while Eastern bloc socialist countries have even longer periods ranging from three to five years in Czechoslovakia and Poland."[16] Kramer concludes that the American system could profit by returning to a more practical, tutorial type of instruction. He finds that "our typical law schools are still using the same methodology and except for frills at the expense of substance, the curriculum has not changed much since the turn of the century. This in the face of a revolution in the way law is practiced and the virtual abandonment of formerly classic areas of practice to lay persons and agencies."[17]

How valid are these complaints by Kramer and others concerning the unchanging nature of the law school curriculum? Despite a proliferation of diverse elective courses during the last two years and the growing number of clinical experiences offered, the basic law school curriculum—those courses required during the first year and a half—has barely changed during the last 50 years. In comparing my program at Vanderbilt Law School in 1964 with current course requirements, not only at Vanderbilt but at nearly all ABA-approved law schools, there were virtually no changes. It is also interesting to note that the essential law school curriculum is comprised of similar requirements in schools of significantly varying repute and prestige. Scott Turow, describing his first year at Harvard, was enrolled in exactly the same courses I had taken at Vanderbilt 15 years earlier and that were also required in the Cumberland School of Law, Samford University in Alabama in 1989. This typical program includes the following courses:

Torts (two semesters)

Constitutional Law (one semester)

Criminal Law (one semester)

Property (two semesters)

Civil Procedure (two semesters)

Contracts (two semesters)

Legal Research (one semester)

As the student enters the second year, the number and type of required courses begin to vary, but generally law schools will require students to take courses in Professional Responsibility (more generally entitled "The Legal Profession"), Income Tax, Corporations, and Evidence, while also either encouraging or requiring participation in a Clinical Law Program. The remainder of the second- and third-year curriculum is comprised of a wide range of elective course offerings stretching from Administrative Law to Wills, Trusts, and Estates. Table 1.3 captures the diversity of elective offerings by presenting the upperclass courses from Cornell Law School.

In addition to the formal courses offered during the final two years, many students also become involved in clinical programs, as well as the increasingly popular part-time work experience with law firms. The latter opportunity frequently leads to full-time employment and especially during the third year may occupy 20 hours a week of the student's time. Beyond the potential for subsequent employment, these part-time jobs are especially tempting to financially strapped students who need the money these jobs provide. Dean Kramer of Tulane, in a recent examination of the topic, discovered several well-placed and industrious law students who had earned in excess of $40,000 during their three years in law school. (This also includes summer employment.)[18] Dean Kramer discovered, however, that the allure of these vocational opportunities can distract students from their law school obligations. Troubled by the negative impact of these part-time jobs, Dean Kramer offers a plea for the intellectual advantages of undistracted study. Nevertheless, candid law school administrators interviewed by Kramer acknowledged that the attraction of these jobs is more than merely financial and is clearly a reaction to the "repellent quality of upper-class education, the drive to obtain an early foothold in the competitive job market, and the more dubious pleasure of being a law firm gofer."[19]

In reviewing the overall scheme of courses taken, especially the diverse offerings during the final two years, one may be perplexed by what constitutes a legal education. It seems clear that the first year is geared toward making the student "think like a lawyer," while obtaining the very basic writing and research skills. Additionally, a none-too-subtle socializing process (described later in greater detail) shapes each student. The legal writing course and moot court experience are the first-year courses that prepare the student for entry into the profession. And all first-year professors are quite aware of their critical role in this developmental process, not merely through course content but also through the manner in which they conduct their classes, their style of dress, and form of interpersonal relationships with their colleagues.

Beyond the few required courses, the remaining elective subjects that dominate the last two years simply offer the student a smorgasbord of topics from which to sample, hopefully locating one or two substantive fields in which to pursue a vocational interest. Thus when law firms come to interview, advertising for openings in tax, real estate, or some other specialty, the student will have an idea of which type of law would be most interesting. Without developing some area of interest, the opportunities for interviewing and ultimately receiving an offer of employment would be impossible. The last two years of elective courses, therefore, perform the important task of giving direction to an otherwise undecided and inexperienced law student about to embark on a legal career.

Is this really what law schools should be doing—the socializing, intellectualizing, and specializing functions? This question has troubled both the bar and legal educators for many years. The answer is greatly dependent on whom you ask. For example, law students who have been surveyed evaluate their legal education from the perspective of how it has contributed to their career development. A recent study by Leonard

Table 1.3   ELECTIVE COURSES AT CORNELL LAW SCHOOL

Upperclass Courses		Problem Courses and Seminars	
Fall	Credit Hours	Fall	Credit Hours
Administrative Law	3	Children's Rights	3
Antitrust Law	3	Comparative Public Law of the United	
Banking Law and Regulation	3	States and the United Kingdom	3
Commercial Law	3	The Constitution and the Schools	3
Comparative Law	2	Constitutional Theory	3
Corporations	4	Law and Medicine	3
Evidence	3	Law, Science, and Technology	3
Federal Income Taxation	4	Legal Aid I*	4
Freedom of Expression	3	Legal Aid II*†	4
History of the Common Law	2	Organized Crime Control	3
International Law	3	The Role of Communities	3
Land-Use Planning	3	Securities Regulation, Corporate	
Law and Social Science	3	Finance, and the Public Corporation	3
Law, Society, and Morality	3	Selected Problems of International	
The Legal Profession	3	Economic Law	3
Negotiation for Lawyers	2	Social Security Law	3
Patents, Copyrights, and Trademarks	3		
Real Estate Transfer and Finance	3	**Spring**	
Taxation of Corporations and Shareholders	3	American Legal Theory	3
Taxation of Partnership Income	2	Church and State	3
Trial Advocacy	3	Constitutional Law and Political Theory	3
Trusts and Estates I	4	Contemporary Legal Theory	3
		Family Law Clinic	3
Spring		Law and Economics Seminar	3
		Legal Aid I*	4
Administrative Law	3	Legal Aid II*†	4
Admiralty	3	Legislation	3
American Indian Law	3		
Antitrust and the Health Care Industry	2	**Writing Requirement**	
Commercial Law	3		
Conflict of Laws	3	Before graduation every student must satisfy
Constitutional Remedies	2	a writing requirement by taking (1) a problem
Corporations	4	course or seminar of three credit hours that
Criminal Procedure	3	contains a substantial writing component and
Debtor-Creditor Law	4	(2) an additional writing course, either (a)
Environmental Law	3	another problem course or seminar (of two or
Evidence	3	three credit hours) or (b) two credit hours of
Fact Investigation and Discovery	3	supervised writing. Satisfactory completion of
Family Law	3	Legal Aid I or II, election to the editorial board
Federal Courts	4	of the *Cornell Law Review* or of the *Cornell*
Federal Income Taxation	4	*International Law Journal,* or submission of
The First Amendment	3	satisfactory briefs in at least two upperclass

Table 1.3 (*cont.*)

Upperclass Courses		Problem Courses and Seminars
Spring	Credit Hours	Writing Requirement
International Business Transactions	3	Moot Court competitions satisfies the second, but not the first, writing requirement.
International Taxation	3	
Interviewing and Counseling	3	In a three-hour problem course or seminar
Labor Law	3	that satisfies the first writing requirement, the
The Law of Mergers and Acquisitions	3	student is expected to produce high-quality
The Legal Profession	3	legal writing, requiring substantial effort. The
Securities Regulation	3	form, nature, and length of the written work
Trial Advocacy	3	may be highly variable, but its preparation
Trusts and Estates II	2	involves extensive faculty supervision, criticism, review, and, when appropriate, rewriting. Attention is given to structure.

*These courses fulfill the second writing requirement only; all other problem courses and seminars satisfy either of the two requirements (see below for a discussion of the writing requirement).

†Runs throughout the year and must be elected in both semesters.

Source: Cornell University Law School Bulletin (1987–88): 19.

Baird of 1600 recent law graduates found that significant numbers were dissatisfied with their law school preparation for advocacy skills.[20] Baird's overall conclusion, presented in Table 1.4, declared that law schools had in general "prepared them reasonably well. However, when it came to specifics, many of them considered several aspects of their law school training to be inadequate and in need of improvement."[21]

Frances Zemans and Victor Rosenbloom also explored this issue and found that in their survey of the Chicago bar, the practitioners irrespective of law school attended were quite critical of law schools. They viewed law schools' neglect of certain professional skills as simply a reflection of the inappropriateness of formal schooling to such training. These areas of competence would have to be acquired after graduation.[22]

In concluding this discussion of law school curriculum, the following eloquent summary of legal education offered by Thomas Shaffer and Robert Redmount in their treatise entitled *Lawyers, Law Students, and People* is offered: "American legal education is a portentious, extensive, recondite enterprise. . . . We find that, despite the myths and the movies, law teaching does little more than the most obvious things for its students. It is a sometimes clever, often boring, initiation rite for the legal profession; and it serves up reams of information about the law. It is a ritual in a library."[23]

Table 1.4 RATINGS OF ADEQUACY OF LEGAL TRAINING BY LAWYERS IN
DIFFERENT TYPES OF ACTIVITIES FOR THE SPECIALTIES MOST
IMPORTANT IN THEIR WORK
(Answers expressed as percentage of group replying)

	Views of Training in Law School			
Group and Specialties	Not Useful	Somewhat Useful	Very Useful	Had no Training
Solo practitioners				
General practice	12.5	47.9	25.0	14.6
Trial and litigation	16.7	42.9	26.2	14.3
Family law	12.8	46.2	23.1	18.0
Real estate	10.5	50.0	21.1	18.2
Criminal law	13.8	34.5	31.0	20.7[a]
Small-firm lawyers				
General practice	14.1	49.5	16.2	20.2[a]
Trial and litigation	14.7	48.4	21.1	15.8
Real estate	15.3	44.7	18.8	21.2[a]
Family law	15.9	48.9	14.8	20.5[a]
Trusts and estates	12.2	52.7	17.6	17.6
Large-firm lawyers				
Corporate law	10.4	42.9	26.0	20.8
Trial and litigation	8.8	45.6	25.0	20.5
Real estate	10.6	38.3	23.4	27.7[a]
Commercial law	12.3	36.8	26.3	24.6[a]
Tax law	15.0	47.5	22.5	15.0
Lawyers in judicial branch[b]				
Criminal law	7.7	69.2	23.1	
Trial and litigation	8.3	75.0	16.7	0
Family law	0	72.7	27.3	0
Personal injury (plaintiff)	10.0	70.0	20.0	0
General practice	0	66.7	33.3	0
Lawyers in executive/legislative—city, county, state				
Trial and litigation	7.1	48.2	21.4	23.2
Criminal law	11.1	41.7	16.7	30.6[a]
Administrative law	6.2	48.2	23.5	22.2
Municipal law	6.5	47.8	19.6	26.1
General practice	8.8	52.9	17.7	20.6
Work in executive/legislative—federal				
Administrative law	5.9	45.1	30.4	18.6
Trial and litigation	7.0	39.5	37.2	16.3
Criminal law	8.3	41.7	33.3	16.7
Other	5.0	40.0	35.0	20.0
Constitutional law	7.4	42.6	33.3	16.7
Legal educators				
Trial and litigation	15.8	47.4	10.5	26.3[a]
Administrative law	13.3	46.7	20.0	20.0[a]
Real estate	25.0	50.0	12.5	12.5[a]

Table 1.4 (cont.)

Group and Specialties	Views of Training in Law School			
	Not Useful	Somewhat Useful	Very Useful	Had no Training
Self-employed in business				
Real estate	15.4	30.8	15.4	28.5[a]
Trial and litigation	16.7	33.3	33.3	16.7[a]
General practice	20.0	40.0	10.0	30.0[a]

[a]"Not useful" plus "Had no training in this" response by one-third of those rating.

[b]Small numbers of lawyers rated each skill, so the percentages should be interpreted cautiously.

Source: Leonard Baird, "A Survey of the Relevance of Legal Training to Law School Graduates," Journal of Legal Education 29 (1978): 293. Copyright 1978. Reprinted with permission of the publisher.

Life in the Classroom

Beginning with its introduction into the Harvard Law School by Christopher Columbus Langdell, who eventually became its preeminent dean from 1870 to 1895, law schools have utilized the case method of instruction. Although captured in its most extreme and intimidating form by the feared Professor Kingsfield in the movie The Paper Chase, the case method is the most common form of instruction in the introductory series of law school courses. It is designed to teach the student to carefully read and comprehend a series of appellate court decisions, and then be able in class to answer penetrating questions designed to ensure that the class has in fact grasped the legal essence of the assigned case and is able to evaluate the judge's reasoning process as well as the overall import of the decision.

Facing the Socratic method from the student's perspective is usually a frightening experience, regardless of the intellectual benefits derived and the hopefully benign indifference of the professor who merely wants to impart knowledge, albeit in a rather circuitous and oftentimes befuddling manner. In order to prepare for class, law students must read and "brief" three to four cases per course. Therefore approximately 12 briefs are to be completed for the next day. A brief is a summary of the facts, issues, and reasoning in the assigned case. The brief assists the student in attempting to answer the professor's probing questions. Although class participation rarely counts toward the grade, the ability to answer these inquiries can either win the respect and admiration of classmates or sink the student into deep despair for several days. With no feedback concerning performance until final exams at the end of the semester, first-year students attach grave significance to their class performance. Since they may be called upon only a handful of times in each class due to the typically large class size—first-year sections usually run between 50 and 100 students per course—students are even more desirous of impressing the professor (or at least not totally humiliating themselves).

Despite its prevalence, especially in first-year courses, the case method has recently come under heavy fire. The major weakness according to most critics is the narrowness of its focus. By concentrating solely on the legal reasoning in appellate decisions, the case method prevents the law student from grasping the broader social and political context affecting the court's opinion. Willard Hurst, in his classic work *The Growth of American Law*, elaborates on this limitation by writing that "the case method isolated the study of law from the living context of society . . . he [the law student] needs some appreciation of the balance of power within the community, the clash of interests, and the contriving of economic institutions, as all these influenced and were influenced by the effort to order society under law. But all of this so far as law school was concerned the student was made aware only incidentally."[24] Another renowned legal scholar, Lawrence Friedman, attacked Langdell's case method approach more succinctly yet in even more graphic terms by describing this supposed science of law as being analogous to geology without the rocks, leaving only a "dry, arid logic, divorced from society and life."[25]

Other critics believe that the case method has a serious deleterious effect upon the overall quality of instruction in law school classrooms and frequently alienates many students. A recent analysis of American law schools by David Margolick concluded that the case method was the single leading cause for dissatisfaction among law students. Margolick described contemporary usage of the case method as resulting in "bewildering hour long digressions, choreographed by professors in which students are customarily asked to apply strictly legal reasoning to explain what may have been a seat of the pants decision or to reconcile two essentially irreconciliable decisions. . . . A few student logicians find the process stimulating and invariably dominate class discussions. The tedium is further aggravated by the deliberate narrowness of class discussions."[26]

The major proponents of continued usage of the case method appear to be found disproportionately among law school administrators and segments of the faculty. From a somewhat cynical perspective, it is easy to understand why law school administrators and teachers endorse the present system. It allows for the economic advantage of having large classes with few instructors as well as permitting the instructor to maintain absolute control over the classroom. One professor when recently questioned as to why the system persists despite rampant criticism candidly responded: "The present structure is very congenial to us [the faculty], it really is. We're not indifferent to the fact that our students are bored but that to one side, law school works pretty well for us."[27]

It should be remembered that the case method is not used in every law school course, and additionally, not every professor utilizing it tried to emulate Professor Kingsfield by traumatizing his students. As already noted, it is primarily used during the first-year courses, whereas upper-level electives often resemble graduate school seminars with small discussion groups and intensive research projects. The group of law school professors who entered the profession since the 1970s seems to have opted for a more low-pressure teaching style, more willing to generate and tolerate students' ideas and beliefs. The erosion of the Socratic style may also be a by-product of greater teacher concern for student feelings. Most younger professors appear to be empathetic toward the frustrations of students who are either unable or unwilling to take part in the highly structured dialogue and, therefore, increasingly turn to more straightforward, traditional lectures providing the information directly to the students.

Given the lack of consensus among law school faculty toward the utility of the case method, and the willingness of some professors to perpetuate the continued psychological cold war with students, a variety of teaching styles has developed. Schaffer and Redmount's analysis of the law student's classroom experience has created the following typology of teaching styles:

1. *The Accepting Style:* Teachers take their cues from student interest and development. They accept feelings and ideas, and they encourage and praise.
2. *The Probing Style:* The teacher emphasizes interrogation and criticism, which has developed from the Langdell case method. The teacher asks questions, gives directions, criticizes, and justifies personal authority.
3. *The Lecture Style:* The teacher gives the facts or opinions about content and procedure, expresses personal ideas and asks rhetorical questions.[28]

Directly related to the overall dissatisfaction with the case method style of instruction is a second major problem area of grave concern to students: the virtual absence of faculty-student relationships. The chronically high student-faculty ratios are obviously the prime cause of this problem, but unfortunately little has been done to reduce the imposing class size. Several critics, such as Harvard's David Kennedy, believe the problem is caused more by the professor's attitude than sheer numbers. He describes the classroom as being "a place of collective terror where the student knows himself to be defenseless before a person who has demonstrated a desire to hurt him."[29] Most students define the problem in less emotional terms, simply criticizing faculty for being so inaccessible and disinterested in either their personal or professional problems. Carl Auerbach found in his survey of law students that 84 percent believed *no* professor was taking special interest in their academic progress and 71 percent felt there was no faculty member to turn to for advice. Additionally, 72 percent believed that none of their professors was or would be taking a personal interest in helping them obtain a job after graduation.[30]

In *1 L,* Scott Turow clearly describes the difficulty of gaining access to a professor,

> It was frequently impossible to get to the faculty. After class there was that cattle show, 15 or 20 people clustered about the teachers, the brownnosers and the shouters and a few people who'd resolved not to miss a single faculty word . . . as well as a number of students who had sincere questions that had seemed too minor or personal to disturb the whole section with during class. To visit professors in their offices was even trickier. Frequently they were out and if your problem was small you were reluctant to make an appointment.[31]

This negative passage does not mean that law professors are totally inaccessible, for even someone as critical as David Kennedy admits that faculty can be reached and reward such contact with warmth and openness, even going so far as to "bind up the lacerations inflicted in public minutes or an hour before, and add a word of encouragement which is like a laying on of hands."[32]

Overall, legal education in the United States appears to be earning passing grades in its ability to teach young law students how to think like a lawyer through the case method and other rather traditional modes of instruction. But as Frances Zemans and Victor Rosenbloom, as well as several others, have discovered, "not a single one of the interpersonal skills was acquired through formal education."[33] Psychiatrist Bernard Diamond goes so far as to blame both the case method and the insensitive role model offered by legal educators as encouraging future lawyers to be just as impersonal with their own clients once they begin practicing.[34]

Informal Socialization

The preceding description of the law school experience focused entirely on the formal socialization process in which the faculty and administrators devoted their efforts to developing analytical abilities and introducing substantive material directly related to the practice of law. Beyond these formal boundaries, however, the law student must also undergo an informal socialization into the mores and folkways of the profession. Thus, not only must the student learn how to "think like a lawyer" but also how to "behave like one."

There are many aspects to the informal socialization process ranging from developing an ideological perspective that is professionally acceptable to learning how to interact with clients and colleagues in a lawyer-like demeanor. It is generally assumed that law students, as a result of undergoing their professional training, become increasingly conservative, business oriented, with a declining concern with social reform. Scott Turow described this attitude change as leading to one of the most painful aspects of his law school experience, causing previously held values and beliefs to be challenged and exposed. Students learn that for every argument there is a counterargument, and there is rarely such a thing as the "right answer" to a problem. Turow concludes that as a result of law school, the idealist becomes the technocrat and the do-gooder strives only to do well.[35]

Additional philosophical changes noted by students of legal socialization include decreasing interest in humanistic concerns. James Himmelstein, who has been the director of the Project for the Study and Application of Humanistic Education in Law, believes that law schools not only "fail to provide guidance to students about the human interactions crucial to responsible lawyering, but traditional legal education can even destroy the appreciation of human dimensions with which students enter."[36] Himmelstein and others argue that as a result of the way law students are treated by the faculty, they soon become tyrannical and dictatorial in their treatment of their clients, "objectifying" both the client and the client's problem. The ABA's 1971 Carrington Report on Legal Education also pointed an accusatory finger at law professors whose relationship with students "has tended to reinforce such aggressive, authoritarian and dependent traits as may be present in those choosing careers in law."[37]

Not all research into the socialization process agrees that such significant attitude changes are occurring as a result of the law school experience. Howard Erlanger and Douglas Klegon, for example, found that "although some changes in attitude are found, they are much smaller than suggested in recent critical literature in legal education."[38] Outside pressures such as the job market and the maturation process can also have an important impact upon one's ideals, as students become married, have children, and incur weighty debts during this tense three-year period.

A second area of informal socialization that occurs during law school is learning how to behave like a lawyer. This means that law students by looking to their professors or other role models, including their own idealized versions, attempt to act like lawyers. I discovered early in my first year, as did Turow at Harvard, that law students begin to dress in three-piece suits and utter highly stylized legalistic phrases. Students soon interact with one another in what is obviously their preconceived lawyerlike handshakes and other affectations. Even outside of the classroom, the posturing continues as a pseudogregariousness sweeps over all social interaction. As a result of clerking experiences, clinical programs, and part-time work, law students are able to expand and hasten this informal socialization process as a greater variety of role models are observed.

One final area of change is the emotional transformations, not all of them positive, that often occur during the law school years. The classroom pressure, the absence of positive feedback, and deep-seated insecurity combine to push many students to the brink of emotional and/or physical collapse. Turow comments that he had "never seen more manifest anxieties in a group of persons under normal circumstances than is visible in first year law students. . . . As the year went on I learned there were many 1 L's [first-year Harvard law students] who felt they'd tilted a little, many of them in more severe and painful ways than I had. I know of at least one suicide attempt in my class and there were more people than I can count who confided that they'd been driven through the door of the psychiatrist's office for the first time in their lives by the experience of being a Harvard 1 L."[39]

Most students recover from the trauma of what James Elkins terms law school's "transformative rite of passage." In a fascinating study of the psychological dimensions of the socialization process, Elkins examined student journals that candidly described the intense experience of these students. He discovered that the words *tension, stress, apprehension, anxiety, doubt, fear, intimidation, terror,* and *impending doom* were the most oft-repeated phrases used to describe their emotional condition during this period.[40] Most law students seemed to feel they were on an emotional roller coaster, alternating between periods of extreme confidence and utter despair. The incessant demands, coupled with a teaching style that constantly threatened the student's sense of self-worth, forced students to deal with their emotional polarities. Elkins discovered that the most successful students, psychologically speaking, were able to compartmentalize their unpleasant law school experiences, learning how to "maintain dual lives: one dominated by the public life with the legal persona and a private/personal self that must be shielded from the law school."[41] This struggle to maintain such a bifurcated existence, consciously separating private from professional, will be a mode of existence throughout the careers of most lawyers and will be described in future chapters. The failure to establish such an effective division can be equally disastrous in the post–law school years.

Not everyone makes the successful psychological adjustments just described. Research by Carrington and Conley at the University of Michigan indicates that approximately one out of seven law students drops out emotionally and intellectually, most without formally withdrawing from school. The study discovered that alienation was the most important factor driving the law student away from his or her classmates, with the disengagement being not so much hostile as turned off. These students were often the least sure of why they entered law school and became increasingly displeased with the entire experience.[42]

Reform Efforts

Law schools have attempted to be responsive to the wide-ranging criticism described in earlier sections of this chapter. Although changes are rarely made quickly or radically, there are nevertheless ongoing discussions and plans for improving the quality of the law school experience. One of the most controversial movements directed toward reforming legal education is the Critical Legal Studies (CLS) organization. This is a rather loosely knit organization of law school faculty that was created in 1977 at a meeting in Madison, Wisconsin. In the succeeding decade members have continued to hold annual meetings, and its membership has risen to 350. Although their numbers represent a small percentage of the total number of law faculty, they disproportionally come from the more prestigious law schools, and through their access to the top law journals and reviews they have been extremely effective at publicizing their message. Although they fail to have a clear-cut agenda of reforms, the major thrust of their position is to attack the traditional law school belief in teaching that "the law is a body of more or less neutral principles [which] when applied to real life disputes produce results that are more or less consistent and more or less derived from considerations of justice rather than power."[43] The "Crits" (as members of the CLS group are called) reject this premise and argue that rather than being neutral principles, the laws and decisions of the courts clearly favor certain economic and social arrangements that are neither inevitable nor just. Additionally, the law is much more inconsistent and malleable in the hands of the judiciary so that similar cases may produce differing results depending on the ideology of the judge and the system he or she represents. Thus the Crits attempt to debunk the supposed apolitical nature of law and show it for what they believe it really is: an instrument to enforce the political ideology of those individuals currently controlling the judicial branch of government and representing the status quo.

One of the difficulties in understanding more clearly what the CLS movement represents is that it appears to be much more preoccupied with demystifying and critiquing the present legal system and the way it is explained to law students than with establishing its own positive agenda of specific proposals. Currently, CLS members are able to achieve limited success in reaching the outside world by publishing critical articles and engaging in political debates with their colleagues. Many law school administrators are upset by the Crits and echo the sentiments of Duke University Law Dean Paul Carrington, who wrote in 1984 that "in an honest effort to proclaim the need for revolution, nihilist teachers [his name for the Crits] are more likely to train crooks than radicals," and he further urged that law schools stamp out the CLS movement entirely.[44] The tension between the Crits and their detractors is seen most clearly in tenure decisions involving CLS supporters. The current dilemma in choosing a new dean at Harvard offers the most prescient test of CLS strength as three professors sympathetic to the movement are on the six-person screening committee.

As might be expected, the CLS movement has generated the creation of new opposition groups, espousing counterproposals supporting the traditional concepts of the judicial system. The most noteworthy of these anti-CLS groups is the Federalist Society formed in 1982 by a small number of conservative and libertarian law students. Their credo espouses the principle "that the state exists to preserve freedom, that the separation of governmental powers is central to our constitution and that it is emphatically the province and duty of the judiciary to what the law is, not what it should be."[45] Since its founding, the Federalist Society has spread to 75 law schools. The national organization is headed by Eugene Meyer and sponsors an annual symposium while also running a speaker's bureau that brings prominent legal scholars who support its position to law school campuses across the country. It is still a rather small organization but is tightly knit and offers an interesting and articulate counterpoint to the CLS movement.

Beyond the rather esoteric reforms advocated by the Crits and Federalists, most of the efforts at improving American law schools have been of a much more pragmatic nature. One of the most persistent areas of reform has been the continued effort to provide law students with greater technical skills. According to studies by Ronald Pipkin for the American Bar Foundation, students are desirous of creating a more "practical curriculum" in which greater attention would be paid to teaching certain necessary legal skills. It is still unclear exactly to which legal skills the students refer, but it is clear that they want a "greater emphasis on communication skills (including counseling and interviewing), ability to negotiate and arbitrate, ability to investigate the facts of a case, or a proficiency at oral advocacy."[46]

The necessity for developing legal skills among graduating law students was also the concern of the bar as indicated in a recent article in the *National Law Journal* that urges law schools to model themselves more on the European style. This would provide for law schools to emphasize scholarship and then coordinate with the bar to develop a rigorous apprenticeship or intern program under the control of the organized bar. The article concludes that if the legal profession is "to enhance our level of competence and concurrently our image, it is essential for the bar in this country to reassert control over our requirements for admission to the bar and to establish a bar-controlled and supervised skills program."[47]

It has been clear for some time that law firms specifically and the bar in general are disappointed with the type of preparation their new associates receive in law school. From a strictly economic point of view, it is extremely costly for these firms to expend time and energy to train and supervise new attorneys. It is therefore in their best interests to shift as much of the cost as possible back to the law schools or to the creation of alternative institutions that would provide transitional training for recent graduates. These specialized training programs could be modeled after existing masters of law graduate programs in tax, patent, and labor law. Because of his special concern with improving the lawyer's advocacy skills, former Chief Justice Warren Burger also urges the creation of special institutes.

Restructuring law school curricula to better achieve heightened lawyer competency has been of concern to the bench and bar for nearly a decade. Its most publicized manifestation was a series of recommendations from the Devitt Committee to the Judicial Conference in 1979. The following recommendations were then unanimously approved, although the law schools have been slow to implement them:

1. Recommend to the ABA that it consider amending its law school accreditation standards to require that all schools provide courses in trial advocacy, including student participation in actual or simulated trials taught by instructors having litigation experience.
2. Create a special committee of the conference to oversee and monitor on a pilot basis an examination on federal practice subjects, a trial experience requirement, and a peer review procedure, in a selected number of district courts that indicate a desire to cooperate in any or all of the programs mentioned.
3. Recommend to the district courts generally that they adopt student practice rules and support continuing legal education programs on trial advocacy and federal practice subjects and encourage practicing lawyers to attend.[48]

Two additional reform issues are on a much more theoretical plane than the more pragmatic topics just discussed. First is the continuing concern in the post-Watergate era with lawyer's ethics. This requires an expanded role for law schools in ensuring that these perplexing issues will be given the necessary attention. Scott Turow, in a recent article entitled "Law School v. Reality," argued that these moral concerns of the bar presently receive scant attention. He concluded that "the most profound and troubling questions in the practicing lawyer's life involve matters of ethics and they deserve scrutiny not as part of some course required as an afterthought and taken as students are dragging themselves out the door, but as part of the first year curriculum."[49]

The second problem area is improving student-faculty relations. Although fewer law professors are modeling themselves after the *Paper Chase*'s Kingsfield or Turow's Perini, the legendary contracts professor, there still appears to be a problem of accessibility. Especially from the students' perspective, law professors continue to offer little personal assistance in their professional development. Although there is scarce tangible evidence of law schools successfully bridging the chasm between professor and student, there is an increasing number of faculty who are addressing the problem publicly. Professor David Kennedy of Harvard Law School has been one of the most persistent critics of his colleagues and offers the following analysis of the problem: "The faculty as a group, make much of their own atomization. . . . One of the first and most lasting impressions that many students have of the law school is that teachers are either astoundingly intellectually self-confident or just plain smug. It is hard for the students not to wince at the air of magisterial self-satisfaction with which professors tend to approach questions they know little about. No amount of brilliance justifies this pose."[50]

Maybe if there were more serious problems facing American law schools, placing them on the brink of either fiscal or professional collapse, legal educators could be motivated toward taking more viable steps toward correcting the numerous problems recounted in this chapter. Or possibly, these criticisms are merely the habitual complaints of legal gadflies who always are finding some minor imperfection in an otherwise fairly competent institution. On the other hand, it is just as feasible that these problem areas are so deep-rooted that only the most radical and penetrating type of surgery can resuscitate this quietly suffocating institution. With the absence of more obvious signs of debilitation, the motivation for urgent and radical reforms will likely remain dormant despite the persistent murmurings of a minority of critical voices.

Law School Honors

Law school grades are based, especially in the first year, entirely on final exams. For those students achieving the highest grades in their class (usually reserved for the top 10 percent), they are invited to join the law review: a publication of scholarly articles and case notes that is edited and produced by these top students. Making law review, which usually occurs after completion of the first year, is the highest honor earned by a law student and can be an extremely influential factor in obtaining a desirable clerking opportunity or a lucrative job offer. It also means a great deal of additional work—at least 20–30 hours a week—beyond the regular courseload and is done without academic credit. In the 1970s there was an effort to democratize entrance onto the review, reducing its meritocratic basis by allowing people to "write on." This meant that any student, regardless of grades, who could impress the staff with superior writing ability would be offered a position. Today most schools have decided to maintain the traditional selection criterion of superlative grades but have allowed for a limited percentage of the class to "write on" in open competition.

AFTER LAW SCHOOL: EARLY CAREER DEVELOPMENT

The second section of this chapter will offer a brief examination of the difficult early years in a lawyer's professional life when he or she faces the job market for the first time, confronts the menacing bar exam, and begins the initial work experience attempting to move from associate to partner status. Let us begin this exploration into a lawyer's early career development with a discussion of the initial confrontation with the job market.

Facing the Job Market

Law schools have become increasingly involved in the law student's quest for the first job. Placement offices working closely with prospective law firms, governmental agencies, corporations, and other potential employers provide critical assistance to law students seeking employment. In contrast to previous years, the employment process begins as early as the first semester of the student's second year as law firms begin to invade law school campuses interviewing students for possible summer employment between the second and third year (although a small number of students are able to begin summer jobs after the first year). Firms generally indicate the area of specialization they desire but often are rather vague, realizing that most students have not had the opportunity to develop much understanding of very many fields of law. These summer experiences, besides paying the law student an impressive salary that can help to defray the staggering cost of a legal education, permit both the law firm and the law student to see if they might eventually be a good match for full-time employment following graduation. Although no empirical studies have established exactly what percentage of law students ultimately join the firm or agency that initially offered them summer employment, it is imagined to be a significant figure since law firms have continued to utilize such summer programs, for at least the past decade, with increasing popularity.

The law firms, governmental agencies, and other potential employers begin their on-campus interviews in late fall and hope to make their final decisions early in the second semester. The competition between firms often becomes quite intense as top candidates are flown all over the country to be wined and dined in the hopes of obtaining their summer services, and possibly full-time employment following graduation. After completing the summer internship, the law firms will review the students' potential for future positions and notify them during their final year.

For those students who either did not enjoy their summer experience or who were not acceptable to the firm, as well as those students who had chosen not to enter the second-year internship program at all, the final year of law school is dominated by the search for a full-time job. The fall is again marked by a large number of potential employers interviewing at the law school, with finalists for each position being transported to the firm or agency for followup interviews and a closer inspection. By the third year students have taken a wide enough selection of courses to have a sense of what type of law they wish to practice. Through conversations with their fellow students and practicing attorneys as well as their experiences during part-time legal jobs, third-year students may also have some definite preferences regarding the size and type of firm, public versus private employment, geographic location, and a possible alternative career in a nonlegal field. This last option was very popular recently as many law school graduates opted for the quick profits of investment banking. Tamara Levin reported this trend for the *New York Times* in the summer of 1986, writing that "despite the fact that investment banking offers a far less secure future than law, the prospect of doing deals holds great allure for law students who don't know exactly what doing a deal involves."[51] The competition for several years between investment banks and law firms for the top law school talent succeeded in driving up starting salaries at the best Wall Street firms to approximately $80,000 a year. This boom period, however, ended abruptly in October of 1987 with the collapse of the stock market, and the current crop of law school graduates have turned away from the insecure world of investment banking, at least temporarily.

As an alternative to beginning the practice of law immediately after graduation, many of the top students may choose a clerking opportunity. Thus, for one year (or possibly extended to a second year in a limited number of courts), a graduate can work for a judge as a law clerk. This typically entails assisting an appellate court judge in the conduct of legal research associated with the deciding of important motions or the writing of the final opinion. Clerking for a judge is an honor that increases with the prestige of the court. The top law school graduates, therefore, compete for a clerkship on the United States Supreme Court while the top graduates from regional schools may be selected by their state appellate court justices.

Much research has been devoted to the question of whether the law school experience shapes or alters the ultimate career goals of the law student. Although there does not seem to be a definitive answer to this question, it is clear that some change does occur. Craig Kubey's research into the modification of career orientations of law students in California is fairly representative of the literature on this subject. His survey disclosed that students were slightly less idealistic than when they arrived. This change in idealism was manifested through a perceptible decline in the percentage of students wishing to become public-interest lawyers or some other related public sector position, between the first and third year. Table 1.5 presents the changes in attitude by these law students surveyed by Kubey in 1975 in terms of their perceived future employment. Kubey conjectured that the changes were not caused by any spe-

Table 1.5   SURVEY OF UNIVERSITY OF CALIFORNIA—DAVIS LAW STUDENTS (1975)
FUTURE EMPLOYMENT PREFERENCES

Students in the University of California at Davis law school class of 1975 were surveyed at the beginning of their first and third years by Craig Kubey, a member of that class. Davis is one of the four law schools of the University of California. As a small law school founded in 1966, Davis is still unknown by some lawyers. It has high enrollment of minorities and women (on entrance, the class of 1975 was 37.9 percent minority and 27.3 percent female), small classes, young professors, relatively relaxed student-faculty relations, a strong clinical program, and a student-written law review. Its weaknesses, as indicated by the article, are those of the typical law school.

Table 1.5 (*cont.*)

The first year of the survey, 166 (or 91 percent) of the class of 182 responded. The third year, it was answered by 129 (or 85 percent) of the by-then 151 who were also members of the class two years before. All responses have been converted to percentages of the total respondents for each year. The questions appear exactly as they were on the original questionnaires.

1. Which is most likely to be your employer (a) one year after graduation and (b) ten years after graduation, respectively?

	After one year		After ten years	
	% first year	% third year	% first year	% third year
Self	1	4	29	28
Office of 1–9 lawyers	22	13	20	27
Office of 10–29 lawyers	4	10	2	10
Office of 30–49 lawyers	1	0	0	2
Office of 50 lawyers or more	1	2	0	0
Local government	10	17	0	1
State government	14	8	2	2
Federal government	12	19	8	2
Small business firm	2	0	3	0
Large corporation	2	1	2	1
Other (fill in)	10	12	7	5
Don't know	21	15	25	22

2. Which is most likely to be your occupation (a) one year after graduation and (b) ten years after graduation, respectively?

	After one year		After ten years	
	% first year	% third year	% first year	% third year
Civil trial lawyer	7	9	2	14
Corporate lawyer	3	2	2	2
Criminal defender	7	3	8	5
Criminal prosecutor	3	12	1	1
"Movement" lawyer	8	5	8	6
Poverty lawyer	16	8	5	2
Public-interest lawyer	13	9	14	9
Tax lawyer	1	2	1	4
General practitioner not covered above	8	11	10	20
Government lawyer not covered above	7	12	4	3
Law professor	1	1	4	3
Businessman	1	1	2	3
Politician	0	0	6	2
Other (fill in)	6	11	6	11
Don't know	20	13	27	15

Table 1.5 (*cont.*)

3. If you intend to practice law at any time, what is your prime motivation for such intention?

	% first year	% third year
Alleviate social problems	32	20
Can be successful at it	4	9
Enjoyable	11	19
Help individuals	25	14
High income	3	5
High social status	2	2
Intellectual challenge	12	9
Other (fill in)	10	9
Don't know	1	12

Source: Craig Kubey, "Three Years of Adjustment: Where Your Ideals Go," *Juris Doctor* (December, 1976): 34.

cific law school experience but rather an inevitable by-product of the maturation process. Students simply grew older, incurred family and financial responsibilities that gently coerced them into more traditional law firm positions in the private sector. He also notes that there has been a significant decline in the number of public-interest opportunities available, especially at the federal level.[52]

It must also be noted that one reason law school may not be such an influential force in restructuring a student's professional aspirations is that there is a self-selection process at work in which those students initially opting for a law career in the 1980s were most likely business oriented as undergraduates. Scott Turow describes this phenomenon with regard to his first-year class at Harvard in the following quote: "Over three-fourths of the members of each HLS class practice with private firms at one time or another. Things just seem to push that way. Some students arrive with a strong interest in business law, and others develop it in school. And there is a still larger number who come to feel over time that their obligations as attorneys are simply to represent the clients who call on them without making an extensive ethical scrutiny of either the clients or themselves. For those students, the money, the power, the training, the quality of practice all make joining the big firms inevitable."[53]

Bar Exam

Following graduation, the beginning lawyer must surmount a greatly feared obstacle before officially starting to practice law: technically, this means before the graduate can appear before a state or federal court and legally represent a client. This hurdle is the state bar exam, a grueling test that measures the individual's knowledge of his or her state's laws (and in most jurisdictions also requires passage of a multistate exam with more general questions). The difficult exam lasts several days as each state constructs and grades its own version. The test is dominated by fairly specific, substantive inquiries into a wide range of legal topics. Since most law schools do not design their courses with the bar exam in mind nor emphasize the law of only one particular jurisdiction, nearly all law students must take a special course to prepare for the bar exam. This course is usually taken the summer after graduation from law school and typically runs for 6–8 weeks. The course is often a series of taped lectures by experts on the various topics to be covered in the exam.

The bar exam is a feared rite of passage, but the majority of students pass it the first time with the national average fluctuating near 70 percent. Some states have reputations for having more rigorous standards and flunking higher percentages, but even these jurisdictions rarely fail more than 50 percent. If the exam is not passed, it may be attempted additional times (the limit varies according to state law), but since it is usually given only twice a year, this may mean a difficult limbo period for the beginning lawyer until he or she has official credentials. For those unfortunate individuals who never pass the bar exam, there may still be employment involving law-related activities such as legal research, title searches, and office management. However, without the official status of state certification through passage of the exam, there are extremely limited opportunities and a rather low pay ceiling.

The First Five Years: Early Career Socialization

Historically, the American legal profession has made a clear-cut choice favoring education of lawyers within the academic confines of law schools rather than continue with the original apprenticeship model borrowed from England, and still at least partially implemented in nearly all European countries. Earlier sections of this chapter presented strong arguments from both the bench and the bar that our graduating law students are gravely in need of skills training most readily obtained through an apprenticeship system. Even the recent law school graduates themselves, as shown in Table 1.6, complain about the inadequacy of law school preparation with regard to the most basic skills required for professional competency.

What then happens to the beginning practitioner as he or she commences a professional career? If the law schools have failed to provide law graduates with adequate instruction in basic lawyering skills, as the research seems to indicate, where and how do young lawyers gain this crucial knowledge? In their comprehensive analysis of Chicago lawyers, Frances Zemans and Victor Rosenbloom point to the following alternative sources outside a lawyer's formal legal training: (1) observation or

Table 1.6   LAW SCHOOL PREPARATION FOR PRACTICE

Skills and Areas of Knowledge	Percent Respondents Indicating Insufficient Attention in Law School[a]	Percent Respondents Indicating Can Be Taught Effectively in Law School
Fact gathering	65[b]	66[c]
Capacity to marshal facts and order them so that concepts can be applied	—	87
Instilling others' confidence in you	72	17
Effective oral expression	64	74
Ability to understand and interpret opinions, regulations, and statutes	—	96
Knowledge of the substantive law	—	95
Legal research	—	98
Negotiating	84	35
Drafting legal documents	79	84
Understanding the viewpoints of others to deal more effectively with them	62	42
Ability to synthesize law	—	89
Getting along with other lawyers	68	16
Knowledge of theory underlying law	—	98
Letter writing	74	50
Knowledge of procedural law	—	91
Financial sense	72	32
Interviewing	78	48
Writing briefs	—	93
Opinion writing	57	84
Knowledge of political science, psychology, economics, sociology	59	32
Accounting skills	65	71

[a]Includes data for only those skills and areas of knowledge that more than 50 percent of the bar think received insufficient attention in law school.

[b]Percentages based on *N*'s ranging from 492 (interviewing, accounting skills) to 517 (fact gathering).

[c]Percentages based on *N*'s ranging from 437 (ability to synthesize law) to 488 (drafting legal documents).

Source: Frances Zemans and Victor Rosenbloom, "Preparation for the Practice of Law—The Views of the Practicing Bar," *American Bar Foundation Research Journal* (1980): 20.

advice from other lawyers in the same firm, (2) observation or advice from other lawyers not in the same firm, (3) repeated personal experience, and (4) personal study of the area.[54] From this description it clearly appears that although we may not formally title it as such, we may in fact utilize a quasi-apprenticeship system in this country in order to provide the practical education that law school generally seems to ignore. Young lawyers, especially those working in law firms but most likely also including those working in governmental agencies and corporation legal departments, all receive an informal education from their colleagues during their first years of practice. Chapter 3, which examines the various working environments, will describe this process in greater detail, with special emphasis on describing the difficult path from associate to partner, but at this point it is important for the reader to firmly grasp the fact that a quasi-apprenticeship system is alive and functioning. And without such a system, regardless of its rather unstructured form, the beginning practitioner would be totally unprepared for facing the most basic professional challenges of providing competent service for his or her first clients.

The necessity for serving an apprenticeship under the tutelage of more senior attorneys in a firm, agency, or corporation raises the perplexing question of how then does a young lawyer, who wishes to begin as a solo practitioner, learn the critical skills necessary to competently serve future clients. From my research with litigators, which I believe replicates the studies of Carlin and others, the answer is that it simply cannot be done. After reviewing the career patterns of a current group of solo practitioners, virtually every one started out either with a firm, governmental agency, or under the personal tutelage of an older lawyer who served as a mentor. It was only after a sufficient period of time had passed, usually several years, when the young lawyers' level of self-confidence combined with a sufficient degree of frustration with their initial job, to force them "out of the nest" and into solo practice.[55]

Let us now move on to Chapter 2, where we will examine the legal profession by providing a group portrait of both judges and lawyers.

NOTES

1. "Law School Applications Up Sharply," *New York Times*, 1988, April 1, sec. II, p. 7.
2. Edward Fiske, "Law Schools Turn to Competing to Win Students," *New York Times*, 7 July 1986, sec. I, p. 1.
3. *Law Schools and Professional Education* (Chicago: American Bar Association, 1980), 17.
4. Seymour Warkow and Joseph Zelan, *Lawyers in the Making* (Chicago: Aldine Publishing, 1965).
5. Carl Auerbach, "Legal Education and Some of Its Discontents," *Journal of Legal Education* 34 (1984): 52.
6. James Hedegaard, "The Impact of Legal Education: An In-depth Examination of Career Relevant Interests, Attitudes and Personality Traits among First-Year Law Students," *American Bar Foundation Research Journal* (1979): 793–868.
7. Scott Turow, *1 L* (New York: Penguin Books, 1977).
8. Paul Miller, "Personality Differences and Student Survival in Law School," *Journal of Legal Education*, 19 (1967): 460.
9. David White, "An Investigation into the Validity and Cultural Bias of the LSAT," in *Towards a Diversified Legal Profession*, ed. David White (San Francisco: National Conference of Black Lawyers, 1981), 67.
10. *Official Guide to U.S. Law Schools*, 18.

11. Paul Wice, *Criminal Lawyers* (Beverly Hills, Calif.: Sage Publications, 1978) and Martin Mayer, *Lawyers* (New York: Harper & Row, 1967).
12. *Law Schools and Professional Education,* 22.
13. Robert Stevens, *Law School: Legal Education in America from the 1850's to the 1980's* (Chapel Hill: University of North Carolina Press, 1983), 22.
14. Ibid.
15. Jerome Kramer, "Scholarship and Skills," *National Law Journal* (January 9, 1989): 15.
16. Ibid.
17. Ibid.
18. Lisa Green Markoff, "All Work and Little Study Worries Officials and Placement Directors," *National Law Journal* (December 12, 1988): 3.
19. Ibid.
20. Leonard Baird, "A Survey of the Relevance of Legal Training to Law School Graduates," *Journal of Legal Education* 29 (1978): 293.
21. Ibid. p. 294
22. Frances Zemans and Victor Rosenbloom, "Preparation for the Practice of Law—The Views of the Practicing Bar," *American Bar Foundation Research Journal* (1980): 29.
23. Thomas Schaffer and Robert Redmount, *Lawyers, Law Students, and People* (Colorado Springs: Shepards, 1977), 13.
24. James Willard Hurst, *The Growth of American Law* (Boston: Little, Brown, 1950): 265–266.
25. Ibid.
26. David Margolick, "The Trouble with American Law Schools," *New York Times Magazine,* 22 May 1983, 22.
27. Ibid.
28. Thomas Schaffer and Robert Redmount, "Legal Education: The Classroom Experience," *Notre Dame Lawyer* 52 (1976): 199.
29. David Kennedy, "How the Law School Fails," *Yale Review of Law and Social Action* 1 (1970): 71.
30. Auerbach, "Legal Education," 49.
31. Turow, *1 L,* 124.
32. Kennedy, "How the Law School Fails," 73.
33. Zemans and Rosenbloom, "Preparation for Practice of Law," 250.
34. Bernard Diamond, "Psychic Pressure: What Happens to Your Head," *Juris Doctor* (December 1976): 40.
35. Turow, *1 L,* 3.
36. James Himmelstein, "Reassessing Law Schooling," *New York University Law Review* 53 (1978): 533.
37. Ibid. p. 534.
38. Howard Erlanger and Douglas Klegon, "Socialization Effects of Professional School," *Law and Society Review* 33, no. 1 (1985): 31.
39. Turow, *1 L,* 154.
40. James R. Elkins, "Rites of Passage: Law Students Telling Their Lives," *Journal of Legal Education* 35 (1985): 31.
41. Ibid. p. 44.
42. Paul Carrington and James Conley, "The Alienation of Law Students," *Michigan Law Review* 75 (1977): 889.
43. Louis Menard, "Radicalism for Yuppies," *New Republic* 194 (March 17, 1986): 20.

44. Leslie Helm, "Radical Rumblings Shaking up Law Schools," *Business Week* 2 June 1988, 116.
45. Charles Bork, "Battle for the Law Schools," *National Review* 38 (September 26, 1986): 44.
46. *Law Schools and Professional Education*, 44.
47. Kramer, "Scholarship and Skills," 16.
48. *Law Schools and Professional Education*, 12.
49. Scott Turow, "Law School v. Reality," *New York Times Magazine*, 18 September 1988, 74.
50. Kennedy, "How the Law School Fails," 72.
51. Tamara Levin, "Leaving Law School for Wall Street," *New York Times Magazine*, 10 August 1986, p. 14.
52. Craig Kubey, "Three Years of Adjustment: Where Your Ideals Go," *Juris Doctor* (December, 1976): 34.
53. Turow, *1 L*, 95.
54. Zemans and Rosenbloom, "Preparation for the Practice of Law," 26.
55. Wice, *Criminal Lawyers*, 82.

Chapter
2

A Group Portrait: Judges and Lawyers

Who then are the thousands of attorneys who have successfully survived their law school experience and passed the bar exam as described in the preceding chapter? This chapter answers this question by providing a group portrait of the legal profession, first focusing on lawyers and then moving on to a description of judges. In addition to providing a demographic description of each group with special attention devoted to minority members, this chapter will also analyze the prestige and status of the profession and conclude with a brief assessment of their respective personality types.

Although subsequent chapters (especially Chapter 4 on the art of lawyering and Chapter 7 on the variety of judicial work environments) will discuss the great diversity in legal and judicial behavior and workplaces, the emphasis in this chapter will be on modal types of backgrounds and personalities. It should not be thought, however, that judges and lawyers cluster too tightly within these descriptive parameters. A continuing theme throughout this book is for the reader to grasp the wide variation in professional styles adopted by judges and lawyers. Lawyers are continually forced to develop their practices in new areas as they are forced to confront the ever-widening array of problems facing our society. Let us now turn to the legal profession and examine recent demographic trends affecting its current period of dynamic growth.

LAWYERS: A GROUP PORTRAIT

An Expanding Profession: Recent Demographic Developments

Lawyers, according to Frances Zemans and Victor Rosenbloom, play a nearly ubiquitous part in American life. They discovered that "almost two-thirds of the adult population have consulted a lawyer at least once about a personal nonbusiness legal problem."[1] With the growth of the public sector in general and the expansion of governmental regulation, these two researchers from the American Bar Foundation recently concluded that the legal profession has become involved in every aspect of American life.

Barbara Curran, also writing for the American Bar Foundation, has provided the most definitive documentation of the extraordinary recent growth of the legal profession. Her study, entitled *The Lawyer Statistical Report: A Statistical Profile of the U.S. Legal Profession in the 1980's*, found that in 1950 there were fewer than 250,000 lawyers in the United States, but by 1980 the lawyer population had increased to over half a million and projected that if this rate of growth continues we will have 750,000 lawyers by 1989 and over a million by the mid-1990s. Beyond this startling linear growth in total number of attorneys, Curran also discovered the presence of several noteworthy changes in the demographic composition of American lawyers, such as the growing proportion of women and continued decrease in the median age. Additionally, employment patterns have also perceptively modified as "the proportion of lawyers engaged in the private practice of law has declined and the proportion of lawyers working in other employment settings has risen."[2]

Terrence Halliday has traced the demographic transitions of the American legal profession over a much longer period of time (1850–1980) and concluded that "the growth experienced since the 1970's is without precedent for the previous 140 years."[3] Consistent with findings of the Curran report, Halliday also noted significant increases in the number of women attorneys and a perceptible regional shift in the ratio of lawyers to population with the eastern states declining while the Pacific states have been increasing. Figure 2.1, from Halliday's historical study illustrates graphically the change in the ratio of lawyers to population from 1850 to 1980.

Law Professor Richard Abel has also investigated recent transformations of the American legal profession and concluded that the trend toward a less and less homogeneous group has produced a sharply bifurcated profession, stratified into "two hemispheres divided by backgrounds, clients, functions, structures, rewards, and associations."[4] Abel finds the solo practitioner at the base of the hierarchy, becoming

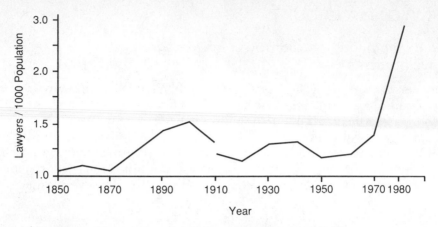

Figure 2.1 Ratio of lawyers to population: U.S., 1850–1980. [*Source:* Terrence C. Halliday, "Six Score Years and Ten: Demographic Transitions in the American Legal Profession, 1850–1980," *Law and Society Review* 20 (1986): 57. Reprinted by permission of the Law and Society Association.]

more permanently entrenched in this "hostile economic environment" while large firms, growing in size and prominence, are found at the apex. He concludes his article pessimistically, noting that as the heterogeneity increases within the legal profession, the ensuing stratification is likely to cause racial and gender tensions that are likely to lead to discriminatory practices.[5] Abel's explanation for all of these trends, even those with probable negative long-term effects on the profession, is the erosion of the gatekeeping function of the American Bar Association that has led to the excess supply of law graduates and heightened competition both within and outside the profession.

A Demographic Description

Given the rapid growth and possible transformation of the legal profession, how may the current group of lawyers be demographically described? A recent survey (1986) by the *American Bar Association Journal* found the typical attorney to be a male, 38 years of age, earning $65,000 a year, and working in an eight-person law firm. Table 2.1 shows that the majority of lawyers engage in civil trial practice, concentrating in business and corporate law.

Approximately two-thirds of the lawyers in this country, according to Curran, are presently in private practice with the large majority being in small firms of less than six lawyers. Although 25 percent of the lawyers working in law firms were employed in large firms with over 20 attorneys, such firms numbered just over 1000 nationally and comprised less than 3 percent of the total number of firms.[6] Beyond law firms, Curran's 1980 statistical report discovered "that approximately equal proportions were working in private industry (10 percent) and in govern-

Table 2.1   AREAS OF WORK[a]

Civil Trial Practice	53%
Business and Corporate	44
Real Property	40
Personal Injury	33
Family Law	26
Estate Planning	33

[a]Note many lawyers practice in several areas of the law.

Source: Nancy Blodgett, "A Look at Today's Lawyer." Reprinted with permission from the Sept. 1, 1986, issue of the ABA Journal (p. 47), the Lawyer's Magazine, published by the American Bar Association.

ment (9). Four per cent were employees of educational institutions, legal aid, public defender, private associations (ie. unions and trade associations), or other special interest organizations. The remaining 5% of the lawyer population was retired or otherwise inactive."[7]

Minority Lawyers: Issues of Gender and Race

As the ABA's demographic portrait indicated, the legal profession is overwhelmingly white and male, but one of the greatest developments of the past two decades has been the extraordinary increase in the number of women and blacks entering the legal profession. The meteoric rise in the number of women entering the field of law is graphically illustrated in Figure 2.2, which is taken from the Curran study of American lawyers in the 1980s. Up until the early 1970s women constituted less than 4 percent of the lawyers in this country, but with the rise of the feminist movement and a general lessening of gender bias, by 1983 women comprised 38 percent of the law school admissions. This has meant an increase in absolute figures from about 5500 female lawyers in 1951 to an estimated 83,000 in 1984.[8]

Beyond the dramatic rise in law school admissions, an even more important issue is what happens to these female attorneys following graduation. As shown in Figure 2.3, which compares male and female employment, women are much less likely to engage in private practice while being more likely to work for public agencies at all levels of government.

Given the highly stratified nature of the American legal profession in terms of prestige, wealth, and other measures of status, where will the new generation of women attorneys be distributed across the professional landscape? If one believes that large firms cluster at the upper end of the profession, then the figures presented in Figure 2.3 paint a

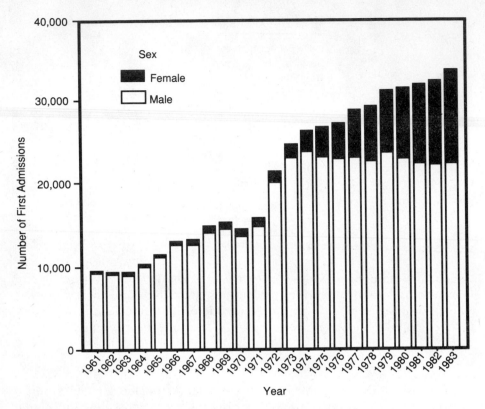

Figure 2.2 Number of first admissions by year and sex. [*Source:* Barbara Curran, *The Lawyer Statistical Report: A Statistical Profile of the U.S. Legal Profession in the 1980's* (Chicago: The American Bar Foundation, 1985), 34. Copyright 1985. Reprinted with permission of the publisher.]

somewhat pessimistic picture for the upcoming generation of female attorneys. Richard Abel describes a trend in women selecting salaried employment disproportionately in the public sector that places them in the very group of lawyers out of touch with the small cohort of elderly white men governing the ABA at both state and national levels.[9]

For those women who choose private practice, there seems to be a preference for either solo practice or relatively small firms. One of the major reasons for this has been the frustrating experience of those women who did initially join large law firms and found themselves unable to move out of associate status. Many thought that making partner was never a viable option for a woman. The Hudson discrimination case

Figure 2.3 (*right*) 1980 Lawyer specialization by sex. [*Source:* Barbara Curran, *The Lawyer Statistical Report: A Statistical Profile of the U.S. Legal Profession in the 1980's* (Chicago: The American Bar Foundation, 1985), 39. Copyright 1985. Reprinted with permission of the publisher.]

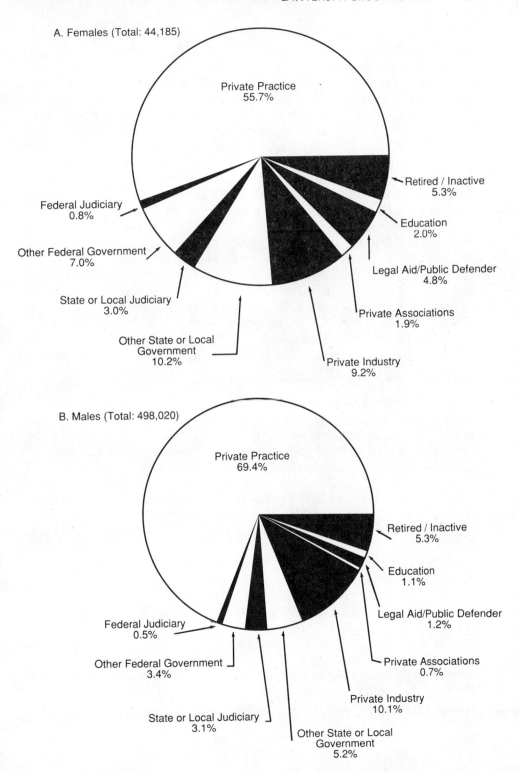

A. Females (Total: 44,185)

Private Practice
55.7%

Retired / Inactive
5.3%

Federal Judiciary
0.8%

Education
2.0%

Other Federal Government
7.0%

Legal Aid/Public Defender
4.8%

State or Local Judiciary
3.0%

Private Associations
1.9%

Other State or Local
Government
10.2%

Private Industry
9.2%

B. Males (Total: 498,020)

Private Practice
69.4%

Retired / Inactive
5.3%

Education
1.1%

Legal Aid/Public Defender
1.2%

Federal Judiciary
0.5%

Other Federal Government
3.4%

Private Associations
0.7%

State or Local Judiciary
3.1%

Private Industry
10.1%

Other State or Local
Government
5.2%

against the large Atlanta law firm of King and Spaulding in 1984 did sound a clear-cut warning in its ruling that partnership decisions do come under protection of the federal antidiscrimination laws.[10] Nevertheless, the number of female partners is miniscule, and as Cynthia Epstein explains in the following quote, the structure of the profession and the nature of men and women make it extremely unlikely that the numbers will radically change in the near future: "Belonging, the sense of being an insider at ease with colleagues and clients—no matter what kind of practice a woman engages in, the prejudice and practices that have kept law a male profession for so long make such a feeling rare for the woman lawyer. . . . It is one thing to be employed and even paid well, and another to be a true working partner."[11]

In recent years several books and a multitude of articles have been written on the unique difficulties faced by women attorneys. There is general agreement in all of these works that there is a discernible bias against women attorneys, and it surfaces not only in the promotional policies described in the previous paragraphs but frequently occurs in the courtroom as well. Sexual stereotyping by both judges and male adversaries is the most obvious manifestation of this bias. William Eich describes many examples of gender bias in the courtroom in a recent article that finds the judge at the heart of the problem. Although many judges plead ignorance to such charges, Eich argues that "their thoughtless remarks which can range from the seemingly innocuous habit of calling a woman lawyer by her first name, while referring to her male counterparts as 'Mr.' or calling her sweetheart and making direct reference to her physical appearance are not flattering to a woman who wishes to be simply evaluated on professional competence and not her sexuality."[12] Compounding the problem even more is the feeling expressed by many women attorneys that, despite lengthy and distinguished professional careers, there is a persistent presumption of incompetence. Louise Lamothe, an attorney for over 15 years, complained in a recent *ABA Journal* article that she bitterly resents having to "prove my competence over and over again."[13]

What can women attorneys do to overcome these biases and professional disadvantages? Rosabeth Kantor, writing for the *Harvard Women's Law Journal*, offers the following advice: " 'Be professional at all times; don't allow yourself to be treated as a token. Form women's support groups to give each other positive job related help. Competence counts and you should be willing to take risks. Stick your neck out and ask someone for help.' "[14]

The prognosis does seem positive for women attorneys as their numbers mount. No longer will they be so isolated as to be viewed as mere tokens. With expanded opportunities, women should move into the mainstream of the profession, not only at the associate level but ultimately as partners in major law firms. The American Bar Association has recently taken a rather strong stand against sex discrimination and gender bias in both courtrooms and law firms exemplifed by the passage of the following resolutions:

1. Recommending that state and federal education programs for judges include a separate course on the role of the judge in keeping a courtroom free from sex and race bias.
2. Adopting a goal to promote full and equal participation by minorities and women in the legal profession.
3. Supporting the Civil Rights Restoration Act of 1985 to require institutions that receive federal funds to prohibit discrimination in all programs.[15]

As a closing comment on the current condition of women attorneys, two recent articles in the *New York Times* chronicle interesting trends. The first notes that there are a growing number of women in their forties and older who are entering law schools, usually after they have raised their families or pursued alternative careers. Although age is not the liability in law that it is in most other professions, the article contends that nevertheless, these women can expect to have a very difficult time landing the job they want—a problem shared by all of their fellow classmates who are entering a nearly glutted job market.[16] The second article describes the recent trend of dissatisfied women attorneys abandoning the profession. Their disillusionment with the profession, after being swept up in the activism of the 1970s, plus the extremely competitive and overcrowded job market, have convinced a growing number of women that the profession is not what they hoped it would be. As one woman stated, she refused to pay the professional dues of late nights, lost weekends, and family neglect. Exact demographic evidence of the magnitude of this movement was not provided in the rather impressionistic article that was mainly a series of quotes from disappointed women whose decision to leave the law has been a positive one.[17]

The second major minority group, black attorneys, have had recent professional experiences that appear to parallel those of women lawyers. Both groups have felt the sting of discrimination and yet are witnessing marked increases in their numbers. Throughout past decades, blacks accounted for barely 1 percent of the nation's lawyers; however, beginning in the early 1970s, their numbers have grown to where black law students presently comprise 10 percent of the law school enrollment. Despite these gains in enrollment and a decade of affirmative action initiatives, there continues to be evidence of discrimination. An ABA (1985) panel holding hearings on racial barriers in the legal profession listened to more than 80 witnesses complain about problems in education, placement, and promotion. The major area of the law that was most frequently condemned was large corporations who continue to withhold their legal business from minority attorneys. The ABA itself was the frequent target of criticism because of its "inaction and ongoing insensitivity."[18] Although there is a general consensus among the current bar leadership that the plight of black attorneys is improving, the following rather bleak conclusions reached 17 years ago by a *Howard Law Journal* study appears to be still valid today: "Prospects of having a rewarding career [for black law students] were dimmed by the realization that white bar associations excluded blacks, judges and juries often discriminated against blacks, private firms discriminate against blacks, and opportunities for advancement were extremely limited. It is surprising that the small number of black lawyers is not even smaller."[19]

Where then do black lawyers go after graduation? In the past few decades there has been a clear movement away from private practice toward government and corporate positions. Table 2.2 presents the results of a 1979 survey of 11,000 black lawyers conducted by the Equal Employment Opportunity Commission that clearly indicates this direction toward the public sector. These figures contrast sharply with the results of recent studies of white lawyers that showed 60–70 percent in private practice and only 20 percent in government service.[20] Only 13.6 percent of black attorneys were in private practice with nearly 40 percent working in some type of governmental position.

J. Clay Smith believes that the employment trends presented, especially the shift from the private to the public sector, are attributed to two primary influences: " 'First, more and more blacks have been attending predominantly white law schools. Some of these students after being exposed to different legal philosophies and living in a more prosperous era do not have any desire to return to the black community to do time representing the poor. Second, established white law firms have not hired blacks in substantial numbers although they have begun to seek outstanding black law graduates as associates.' "[21]

Smith's second point was validated by a 1981 *National Law Journal* survey that found only 30 black partners in the nation's 50 largest firms (over 150 lawyers). These blacks comprise 0.5 percent of the firms' 4,271 attorneys. The figures improve slightly at the associate level (2.4 percent) and have been showing modest gains in recent years, but it still appears nearly impossible for a black to move into partnership status in these large firms.[22]

Table 2.2   CATEGORIES OF EMPLOYMENT
HELD BY BLACK LAWYERS (1979)

Private practice	13.6%
Public-Interest law firms	4.5
Corporations (legal and nonlegal)	20.9
Federal or state government lawyers	31.8
Law teachers	2.7
Federal or state judges	3.6
Nonlegal jobs (or unemployed)	22.7

Source: Geraldine Segal, *Blacks in the Law* (Philadelphia: University of Pennsylvania Press, 1983), 215.

One possible response to the seemingly discriminatory practices of large white law firms has been for blacks to establish their own firms. In New York City *The Manhattan Lawyer* recently reported that there are 25 minority firms citywide, although the largest has only 10 attorneys. Most of the firms offer general practices serving individual clients and small businesses. The few that have corporate finance and commercial litigation experience complain that their opportunities are limited and presently have difficulty attracting "mainstream clients." The ABA has recognized the unique problem of these minority firms and has implemented an experimental project called The Minority Counsel Demonstration Program, aimed at diverting a significant amount of work from corporate businesses to these firms. Despite these good intentions one of the partners in a minority firm was quoted as complaining about the magnitude of this assistance, describing it as "crumbs off the table," although he did acknowledge it will help to feed associates and begin to build a practice.[23]

As a concluding comment, it should be noted that the problem of discrimination by the larger white male-dominated law firms toward minorities has been in existence for many years and historically has been directed at many other groups besides blacks and women. Historian Jerrold Auerbach in his critical examination of the legal profession chronicles the antisemitism and general hostility of the WASP-dominated ABA and professional elite. He described the 1925 efforts of the Pennsylvania bar to change the state's admission requirements to maintain "the honor and dignity of the profession"—a euphemism for keeping out ethnic and religious minorities. Auerbach concludes that "although the tide of bigotry and hostility has lessened and become less obvious, there has been continued a subtle and professional antipathy toward these types."[24]

Location

Lawyers are similar to most other professions in terms of personal preferences for regions of the nation where they would prefer to establish their practices. Thus, some sections of the country such as the South and Midwest and generally rural areas everywhere, find themselves with a scarcity of available legal assistance. In contrast, major urban areas on both coasts possess a glut of lawyers. Since most large firms as well as the corporations and institutions that act as clients are frequently located in cities on the East and West coasts, it is not surprising to find this imbalanced demographic trend. Twenty-five percent of the total number of attorneys are in California and New York, while another six states add 30 percent more attorneys, thereby placing half of the nation's lawyers in just eight states.[25] Barbara Curran's 1980 statistical study of the profession reported similar findings although not quite so dramatic. She discovered 76.6 percent of the nation's lawyers being employed in urban areas.[26] The most thorough analysis of migratory patterns of lawyers over time is Terrence Halliday's article on demographic transitions of the pro-

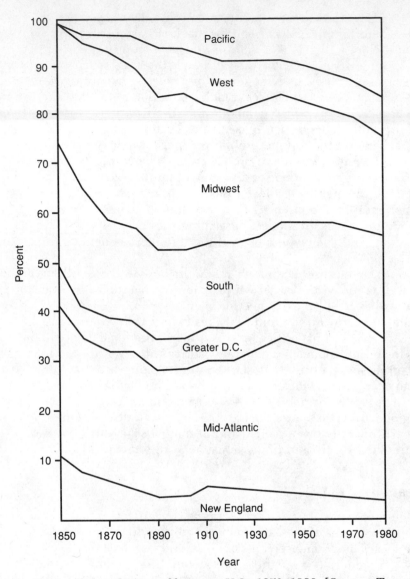

Figure 2.4 Regional distribution of lawyers, U.S., 1850–1980. [*Source:* Terrence C. Halliday, "Six Score Years and Ten: Demographic Transitions in the American Legal Profession, 1850–1980," *Law and Society Review* 20 (1986): 58. Reprinted by permission of the Law and Society Association.]

fession from 1850 to 1980. Figure 2.4 chronicles the regional distribution of lawyers during this 130-year period. He found a decline in the lawyer population of New England and the Mid-Atlantic states although the greater Washington, D.C., area has maintained a steady growth. The Pacific states display the most noticeable proportional gain.

Table 2.3   NET ANNUAL INCOME
(1978): CRIMINAL LAWYERS

$10,000–25,000	23%
26,000–40,000	16
41,000–55,000	14
56,000–70,000	9
71,000–85,000	3
86,000–100,000	7
Over 100,000	16

Source: Paul B. Wice, *Criminal Lawyers* (Beverly Hills, Calif.: Sage Publications, 1978), 109.

Economic Rewards

One of the major beliefs of the general public is that all lawyers earn impressive salaries and enjoy lavish lifestyles. As we shall see in subsequent portions of this book, the legal profession is highly diverse and so when one examines median and mean salary figures, these statistics blur the very wide disparity between lawyers at both ends of the economic spectrum. In conducting a study of criminal lawyers ten years ago, I found significant differences in income even within the same field of legal specialization. The typical criminal lawyer in the sample of 200 earned a gross income of $80,000, and wound up with a net profit (actual annual income) before taxes of approximately $35,000–$40,000. Table 2.3 from this study illustrates the income distribution figures for this national sample.

Arthur Anderson conducted a survey of New Jersey lawyers for the state bar association and found major differences between the incomes earned by solo practitioners and those earned by partners in law firms employing over five lawyers. While 40 percent of the solo practitioners earned less than $30,000 a year, 40 percent of the partners in the firms earned between $50,000 and 100,000 a year. The survey suggested that lawyers in large firms worked harder or at least billed clients more assiduously than legal loners. (The average solo lawyer billed 960 hours in 1984 compared with 1240 hours in the firms with two–five lawyers and 1670 hours in larger law firms.)[27] A survey conducted by the *ABA Journal* of 500 of its readers discovered their average incomes to be $121,000, but serious methodological questions concerning the representativeness of the sample cloud the validity of these findings. Another survey also conducted by the ABA of a select group of its readership in 1986 found that the mean income was $64,000 compared to an average income figure of $104,625.[28]

The most commonly cited proof of the soaring incomes earned by lawyers is the highly misleading starting salaries of first-year associates at the leading Wall Street firms. In 1986 Cravath, Swaine and Moore announced that it was raising its starting salaries to $65,000 a year, an amount that was soon matched by the other major New York firms. Officials at Cravath explained the $12,000 hike in salary over the previous year as a way of stemming the tide of law school graduates choosing more lucrative careers in investment banking. Another reason offered was that the previous year had been quite busy, and, given a high attrition rate in the associate ranks, there was a need to fill a large number of positions.[29] Tempering the law student's excitement at the possibility of receiving such a lofty salary is the fact that only a very few graduates (less than 1 percent) will be able to break into the ranks of these highly selective Wall Street firms. As one moves into other cities across the country, starting salaries at even the largest firms lag $15,000–$20,000 a year behind the New York leaders.[30]

The constant rise in lawyers' salaries has not been without its negative side, and according to a recent *New York Times* article, the legal profession, remembered by some older lawyers as a civilized vocation, has become an extremely competitive business. As one partner in a major New York firm commented: "With five floors in the CitiCorp Building and a couple of thousand mouths to feed, we don't have the luxury of giving one of my favorite clients a break on his bill." Peter Megargee Brown, an esteemed partner at another established New York firm lamented the change in style and retired from practice rather than take part in the rat race. He noted sadly that "as law firms have grown and expenses have risen faster than the ability to collect fees, there is much less time to develop excellence, to develop quality of work. It's a deep crisis in the history of the American law firm."[31]

Peter Pashigian has traced the rise in the number of lawyers and their increased income in this country during the past 50 years. His economic and historical analysis concludes that the legal profession has followed the general rise in real income in the nation as a whole and experienced parallel periods of economic prosperity in the 1920s and 1960s. He was surprised, however, to discover that law schools in terms of their enrollments lagged behind the increase in demand for lawyers.[32]

Prestige and Status: Public Perceptions

Earlier sections of this chapter documented the remarkable growth of the legal profession as law school enrollments continued to expand. What is the appeal of the profession to so many undergraduates? Obviously, the economic rewards just presented and the comparative ease of entry contribute heavily to its popularity, but what about the prestige factor? Ironically, that seems to be on the decline, at least to the degree that at the 1988 ABA convention, a special study group was formed to combat what one lawyer described as America's newest favorite pastime: "lawyer bashing." The essence of these negative attacks on the legal profession is stereotyping lawyers as greedy, money grubbers who live off the problems of others.

Despite the obvious decline in lawyer prestige, many people persist in holding the profession to its traditional lofty position. The National Opinion Research Center at the University of Chicago has been calculating prestige scores for various professions and has determined that lawyers score in the high 80s (86 in 1947, 87 in 1963, and 85 in 1979) out of a possible 100. They trail physicians, who are the highest-scoring occupational group with a score of 93, by only a handful of prestige points.[33] Another well-respected social science study of occupational prestige conducted by Donald Treiman in 1977 also placed lawyers quite high with a score of 75.7 that can be compared with doctors at 81.5, college professors at 78, airline pilots at 70, nurses at 61, and insurance agents at 44.[34] Comparing American lawyers with those of other nations, Richard Abel finds that we have recently suffered slight declines in prestige due most likely to the ease of entry and lack of self-regulation that has permitted the previously acknowledged growth rate to continue at its accelerated pace, especially during the past two decades.[35]

In contrast to the vagaries of prestige and status enjoyed by the legal profession, its public image appears to be in a more precipitous state of decline. This confusing picture is made even cloudier by the paradoxical combination of awe and contempt with which the general public seems to regard lawyers, generally. Zemans and Rosenbloom have captured the reasons for this puzzling position in their important book *The Making of a Public Profession,* noting that "although criticism of lawyers takes many forms, underlying most of it is a feeling that law has become curiously dissociated from justice, that lawyers look more to private gain from advocacy of the interests of their clients than to the public good."[36]

Jon Waltz took a more historical approach in his analysis of the unpopularity of lawyers in America. He believes that Watergate set in motion a new wave of criticism by the general public. Among the members of the bar swept up in this 1973 scandal in addition to President Richard Nixon (himself a lawyer) were such key figures as Spiro Agnew, Charles Colson, John Dean, John Ehrlichman, Donald Kalmbach, Gordon Liddy, John Mitchell, and Donald Segretti. Waltz went on to conclude that the profession deserves a large part of the criticism, especially attacks upon its overly conservative nature and its persistence in operating "a racist, sexist club." Some lawyers deserve criticism because they are incompetent, and Waltz believes that their self-defined, self-regulating monopoly over dealing with professional conduct, totally excluding any public interference, has contributed immeasurably to the larger society's frustration and anger toward them.[37]

Part of society's disillusionment with the legal profession may in fact be caused by the lofty and inflated position that we have previously awarded to it. When the "mystique of lawyers" becomes punctured by such events as Watergate or other well-publicized examples of legal incompetence, the public often overreacts and attacks the profession more aggressively and passionately than fairness and logic would dictate. This discussion concludes with an eloquent explanation by David Riley as to why the public reaction to lawyers has often been so negative:

> Lawyers stride across our social landscape with one hand toward the sky and the other in the gutter. . . . But if we are to have social peace that is more than fleeting, we will have to haul our impractical ideals of justice and charity down from the sky as we reach for them with our feet cemented in the ground. We will need not a mystique about our ideals, but a workable belief in them as practical standards thoroughly livable in our everyday lives.[38]

Specialization and Stratification

In its discussion of the overall prestige of the legal profession, the preceding section purposefully neglected examination of the heterogeneous nature of the bar and the resulting variation in status between types of lawyers specializing in particular areas of the law. The major reason for the highly diversified nature of the American bar is an extensive specialization process, and the resulting varying levels of status. This specialization has been a feature of the American legal profession for many years. Karl Llewellyn recognized its prevalent form in 1933 and commented that " 'the bar is in this country almost a meaningless conglomeration. What we have is lawyers, by the tens of thousands— individual lawyers without unit of tradition, character, background or objective; as single persons, many of them powerful; as a guild inert beyond easy understanding.' "[39] Bar associations and other leaders of the legal community have continued to deny the existence of such professional diversity, hoping to convince the public in the timeliness of the mythical "omni-competent practitioner." Recent studies by John Heinz and Edward Laumann have refuted this misleading myth, replacing it with an empirical description of a highly fragmented profession, sharply divided into two divergent hemispheres. Table 2.4, from one of the Heinz and Laumann studies of legal specialization and prestige, lists both the variety of legal specialties as well as their relative rank orders of prestige.

Why has specialization occurred? The increasing complexity of the law, which continues to expand exponentially through the years, is probably the most significant factor. It is simply too difficult for a lawyer to maintain competence in numerous diverse fields of law. The clients likewise demand specialized expertise, and, as Zemans and Rosenbloom have noted, this has generated the need for greater efficiency in the face of rising demand for legal services. Recent surveys presently estimate that nearly three-fourths of urban lawyers identify themselves as specialists.[40]

The major variable influencing the type of legal specialty and, as we shall see, its prestige rating (which in turn has created our highly stratified legal profession) is the type of clientele served. Henry Glick be-

Table 2.4   HIGHEST AND LOWEST RANKED
LEGAL SPECIALTIES IN TERMS
OF PRESTIGE

Top 10 (1–10)	Bottom Ten (21–30)
Securities	Criminal (prosecution)
Tax	General Family (paying)
Antitrust (defendants)	Criminal Defense
Patents	Consumer (creditor)
Antitrust (plaintiffs)	Personal Injury (plaintiffs)
Banking	Consumer (debtor)
Public Utilities	Condemnations
General Corporate	Landlord-Tenant
Probate	Divorce
Municipal	General Family (poverty)

Source: Edward Laumann and John Heinz, "Specialization
and Prestige in the Legal Profession: The Structure of Deference," American Bar Foundation Research Journal No. 1
(Winter, 1977): 155.

lieves that an important reason for this linkage between client and status
is because "the law is a much more fluid profession (in contrast with
doctors) where a lawyer's skills in business law often are very difficult
to separate from his or her personal contacts and social status. . . . Low
status lawyers have no high status contacts and represent clients who
pose a direct threat to social, economic, and political elites."[41]

In addition to the type of clientele, social scientists have identified
a variety of secondary variables that may influence the prestige differences between the areas of specializations. One of the most commonly
noted is the size of the firm, which is obviously associated with the type
of clientele, since the larger firms tend to represent businesses and corporations whereas small firms and solo practitioners typically represent
individuals. Interestingly, the size of a lawyer's income was found to
have little relation to his or her status. Highly successful criminal lawyers or negligence specialists whose incomes surpass six figures are still
unable to command the professional respect of their colleagues who represent corporations. Heinz and Laumann partially explained the basis
for this surprising lack of relationship, stressing that legal specialties associated with personal suffering such as divorce work or personal injury
"lose social standing as a result; that prestige within the profession is
directly proportional to the degree to which the specialty facilitates the
conduct of corporate enterprise and that the varying prestige of the specialties is likely to affect the political and professional power of the lawyers who practice in them and to influence the patterns of recruitment
of lawyers into law practice."[42]

Recruitment patterns also fit into the systematic development of a stratified bar. Thus, the type of lawyers gaining entrance to the more prestigious areas of the law are nearly always from the nation's most renown law schools. And although there is only a modest correlation between the quality of legal education and a lawyer's socioeconomic status, the law firms who dominate the top-ten prestige fields of law identified in Table 2.4 are almost uniformly white Anglo-Saxon Protestants.[43]

One factor limiting the development of a stratified and highly specialized bar is the size of the community. Joel Handler and others have found that in rural areas and smaller towns general-practice lawyers still flourish, and the presence of legal specialists is an infrequent occurrence. Handler also noted that background variables, such as quality of legal education and socioeconomic status, seem less important as city size decreases.[44]

Summarizing the findings on the stratification issue, it appears that there is a pattern of prestige rankings that divides the legal profession into two clearly definable categories: those with specialties serving big business and large institutions are at the top while those representing individual interests reside at the bottom. Although the ranking of legal specialization is on a continuum rather than falling neatly within these two idealized groups, nevertheless there is little interaction between the various specializations, which cluster around either half of this dichotomy. This facet of professional behavior was clarified by Heinz and Laumann when they wrote that "lawyers in fields that enjoy similar levels of prestige within the profession will be more likely to associate with one another than will lawyers from fields with widely differing prestige."[45]

What are the consequences of this sharply divided legal profession? Richard Abel believes that the divisive trend will continue as divisions of race, gender, age, and class structure of practice will make it increasingly difficult for the legal profession to present a united front. Thus, with the inevitable clashes between these various self-interest groups within the profession, lawyers will be unable to be governed effectively by a single association, and any attempts at self-regulation and advancement will be doomed to failure.[46] Although Abel's predictions may be more pessimistic than most, the legal profession does acknowledge that specialization and ensuing tensions have had a debilitating effect upon the legal community's ability to present a united front to an increasingly disenchanted public.

Overall Personality Assessment

Thus far this chapter has described the legal profession in broad sweeping demographic and social terms, neglecting the unique psychological attributes of the individual attorney. While there is obviously a wide variety of personality types practicing law, this section will discuss the modal personality characteristic associated with the legal profession as well as present a brief taxonomy of personality types I have personally observed during several previous research endeavors.

Given the difficulty in defining and assessing the lawyer's personality, it is not surprising that so little research has been done on this perplexing topic. Two exceptions to be briefly reviewed are Walter Weyrauch's study of the personality of German lawyers and my own work on criminal lawyers. Weyrauch interviewed approximately 130 German lawyers in the early 1960s. His sample included judges, law professors, and a control group of laymen in addition to practicing attorneys. He described his sample as including "a sizable number of malcontented misfits and disgruntled individuals, many of whom were thought to be ill-equipped to establish normal human relationships."[47] Weyrauch's overall description was rather negative as he found most lawyers were overconcerned with their personal status and "appeared more concerned about the esteem of their colleagues and superiors than about their clients . . . They were inclined to be jealous, susceptible to flattery, easily irritated and offended and fussy about details of form and style."[48]

Combining my work on criminal lawyers with a review of the literature, there appear to be three substantive qualities present in the lawyer's modal personality. The first is a strong ego, often manifested by an extroverted demeanor; second is an aggressive or contentious dispositon; and third is a skeptical or cynical nature. The first two traits are clearly related to the lawyer's litigating and negotiating functions as well as the adversarial nature of the American legal system. Being egotistical and extroverted are character traits frequently associated with actors, and it was interesting to find so many of the criminal lawyers I interviewed to be former Thespians. (A few were still actively engaged in amateur productions.) The ability to act and deceive an audience as to one's true feelings is critical for any litigator to possess to convince the jury of the rightness of a client's cause.

Turning to the second trait—an aggressive and contentious disposition—David Riley, writing on the mystique of lawyers, characterized this tendency as an occupational hazard that often led to such unpleasant associated traits "as being arrogant, deceitful and punitive." Riley quoted a University of Chicago Law School dean who warned the wives of first-year law students: "Your husbands are going to change; their personalities will become more aggressive, more hostile, more precise and more impatient."[49] In my research I discovered the roots of this aggressiveness in the early athletic experiences of many of the sample who had thrived in competitive sports. Many of the lawyers, despite growing paunches, still attempted to remain active in some form of competition. One West Coast lawyer was an active rugby player on the top amateur team in the nation while another wrestled regularly in the police department gym. The most impressive example of this continuing competitive drive was found in New York City, whose Lawyers Basketball League has 3000 participants on 200 teams vying for division championships. The league has even gone so far as to hire Peter Grean, a former tax litigator, as the executive director, a full-time position necessitating the abandonment of his practice.[50]

The third character trait is a skeptical or cynical nature. This also is the likely by-product of operating within an adversarial legal system but is also a requisite disposition given the propensity for clients to hide, shade, distort, or simply ignore unpleasant or damaging facts concerning their case. Leonard Eron and Robert Redmount discovered that law schools facilitate, and even encourage, the development of a cynical disposition. There also appears to be little following graduation that does not reinforce this inclination to be skeptical and overly cautious.[51]

In addition to these three personality traits, most lawyers are also trained to be articulate problem solvers, and, while these are primarily technical attributes, they are tools of the mind that are critical to a lawyer's professional success. Lawyers therefore can be characterized as not only being in possession of above-average intellects, but they are constantly forced to utilize their intellectual capabilities to the fullest, often reaching to the optimal level of their mental capacity in order to satisfy their clients and successfully combat worthy adversaries.

JUDGES: A GROUP PORTRAIT

The second half of this chapter begins with a social-psychological description of American judges. The final portion of the chapter will attempt to construct a workable classification scheme based on the diverse styles of professional behavior. This section therefore parallels the first half of this chapter, which provided a demographic portrait of our nation's lawyers.

Demographic Description

The typical American trial judge may be demographically described as a white male in his mid-forties who graduated from law school approximately 20 years ago. He has been a judge for approximately eight years. The majority of trial judges come directly from private practice with a broad range of legal specialties being represented.[52] Appellate judges, at both the federal and state levels, are slightly older and may have held a previous judicial office but are generally similar demographically, with the overwhelming majority being white Anglo-Saxon male Protestants.

To gain a clearer vision of the background from which our nation's judiciary emerges (which may provide clues as to both their future decision-making predilections as well as determining the optimally effective route to judicial selection), three background variables will be examined: prior work experience, prior political activity, and socioeconomic background. Tables 2.5 and 2.6 summarize how state supreme court justices and federal court appointees (with the exception of the U.S. Supreme Court) are divided within each of these three categories of background characteristics. Table 2.5 presents an interesting comparison of

Table 2.5   BACKGROUND CHARACTERISTICS OF STATE SUPREME COURT JUSTICES

	1961–1968 (percentage, $N = 441$)	1980–1981 (percentage, $N = 300$)
Race and Sex		
Female	—[a]	3.1
Nonwhite	—	0.6
Religious Affiliation		
High-status Protestant[b]	38.8	29.9
Low-status Protestant	41.5	30.3
Catholic	16.1	23.9
Jewish	3.6	11.6
Other	—	4.2
Localism		
In-state birth	74.6	78.1
In-state undergraduate school	73.9	69.5
In-state law school	64.6	69.0
Possesses Bachelor's Degree	57.8	80.0
Democratic Party Affiliation	57.4	67.0
Government Career Experience		
Prosecutor	51.5	21.5
Legislator	19.3	20.2
Previous judicial	57.8	62.9
Other	—	39.2
Average No. Years Practiced Law	—	14.5

[a]Dashes indicate that no data are available.

[b]High-status Protestant denominations include Episcopalian, Congregationalist, Presbyterian, and Unitarian. These are conventional categories and were used by Canon.

Sources: Data for the 1960s are based on a recalculation of data reported in Bradley C. Canon, ''The Impact of Formal Selection Process on the Characteristics of Judges: Reconsidered,'' *Law and Society Review* 6, No. 4 (May 1972): 575, 579–593. The table is reprinted from Henry R. Glick and Craig F. Emmert, ''Stability and Change: Characteristics of State Supreme Court Judges,'' *Judicature* 70, No. 2 (Aug.–Sept. 1986): 107–112. Copyright 1986. Reprinted with permission of the publisher.

Note: Missing data are excluded from the calculations in this table.

state court judges surveyed first in 1961–1968 by Brad Canon and then 20 years later by Henry Glick and Craig Emmert.[53] Table 2.6 indicates the background characteristics of federal court appointees from 1977 to 1984 and was compiled by Sheldon Goldman for *Judicature.*

Table 2.5 indicates that state supreme court justices tend to follow a rather predictable route toward appointment in terms of their employ-

Table 2.6   BACKGROUND CHARACTERISTICS OF FEDERAL COURT APPOINTEES

	Reagan (first term) % N	Carter % N	Ford % N	Nixon % N	Johnson % N
Gender:					
Male	90.7%	85.6%	98.1%	99.4%	98.4%
	117	173	51	178	120
Female	9.3%	14.4%	1.9%	0.6%	1.6%
	12	29	1	1	2
Ethnicity or race:					
White	93.0%	78.7%	88.5%	95.5%	93.4%
	120	159	46	171	114
Black	0.8%	13.9%	5.8%	3.4%	4.1%
	1	28	3	6	5
Hispanic	5.4%	6.9%	1.9%	1.1%	2.5%
	7	14	1	2	3
Asian	0.8%	0.5%	3.9%	—	—
	1	1	2	—	—
ABA ratings:					
Exceptionally well qualified	6.9%	4.0%	—	5.0%	7.4%
	9	8	—	9	9
Well qualified	43.4%	47.0%	46.1%	40.2%	40.9%
	56	95	24	72	50
Qualified	49.6%	47.5%	53.8%	54.8%	49.2%
	64	96	28	98	60
Not qualified	—	1.5%	—	—	2.5%
	—	3	—	—	3
Party:					
Democratic	3.1%	92.6%	21.2%	7.3%	94.3%
	4	187	11	13	115
Republican	96.9%	4.9%	78.8%	92.7%	5.7%
	125	10	41	166	7
Independent	—	2.5%	—	—	—
	—	5	—	—	—
Past party activism:	61.2%	60.9%	50.0%	48.6%	49.2%
	79	123	26	87	60
Religious origin or affiliation:					
Protestant	61.2%	60.4%	73.1%	73.2%	58.2%
	79	122	38	131	71
Catholic	31.8%	27.7%	17.3%	18.4%	31.1%
	41	56	9	33	38
Jewish	6.9%	11.9%	9.6%	8.4%	10.7%
	9	24	5	15	13
Total number of appointees	129	202	52	179	122
Average age at appointment	49.6	49.7	49.2	49.1	51.4
Occupation:					
Politics/government	3.2%	—	8.3%	4.4%	10.0%
	1	—	1	2	4
Judiciary	61.3%	46.4%	75.0%	53.3%	57.5%
	19	26	9	24	23

Table 2.6 (*cont.*)

	Reagan (first term) % N	Carter % N	Ford % N	Nixon % N	Johnson % N
Large law firm					
100+ partners/associates	—	1.8%	—	—	—
	—	1	—	—	—
50–99	3.2%	5.4%	8.3%	2.2%	2.5%
	1	3	1	1	1
25–49	6.4%	3.6%	—	2.2%	2.5%
	2	2	—	1	1
Moderate size firm					
10–24 partners/associates	3.2%	14.3%	—	11.1%	7.5%
	1	8	—	5	3
5–9	6.4%	1.8%	8.3%	11.1%	10.0%
	2	1	1	5	4
Small firm					
2–4 partners/associates	—	3.6%	—	6.7%	2.5%
	—	2	—	3	1
Solo practitioner	—	1.8%	—	—	5.0%
	—	1	—	—	2
Professor of law	16.1%	14.3%	—	2.2%	2.5%
	5	8	—	1	1
Other	—	1.8%	—	6.7%	—
	—	1	—	3	—
Experience:					
Judicial	70.9%	53.6%	75.0%	57.8%	65.0%
	22	30	9	26	26
Prosecutorial	19.3%	32.1%	25.0%	46.7%	47.5%
	6	18	3	21	19
Neither one	25.8%	37.5%	25.0%	17.8%	20.0%
	8	21	3	8	8
Undergraduate education:					
Public-supported	29.0%	30.4%	50.0%	40.0%	32.5%
	9	17	6	18	13
Private (not Ivy)	45.2%	50.0%	41.7%	35.6%	40.0%
	14	28	5	16	16
Ivy League	25.8%	19.6%	8.3%	20.0%	17.5%
	8	11	1	9	7
None indicated	—	—	—	4.4%	10.0%
	—	—	—	2	4
Law school education:					
Public-supported	35.5%	39.3%	50.0%	37.8%	40.0%
	11	22	6	17	16
Private (not Ivy)	48.4%	19.6%	25.0%	26.7%	32.5%
	15	11	3	12	13
Ivy League	16.1%	41.1%	25.0%	35.6%	27.5%
	5	23	3	16	11

Source: Sheldon Goldman, "Reaganizing the Judiciary," *Judicature* 68 (April/May, 1985): 318, 324. Copyright 1985. Reprinted with permission of the author.

ment history. They typically begin work in a moderate-size firm and then enter public life either as a prosecutor or legislator, and finally serve briefly as a trial court judge. Roughly two-thirds of the judges surveyed appear to have followed this path, with a brief stopover for many at an intermediate appellate court.[54] The great majority of state trial judges, who were surveyed by John Paul Ryan and his colleagues at the American Judicature Society, came directly to the bench from private practice with no clearly discernible fields of specialization being disproportionally represented.[55] Lawrence Baum does believe that there is a perceptible difference between trial judges and appellate judges in terms of the relative success of their previous law practice. He argues that trial court judges come from a broader cross section of less successful private practitioners while the appellate bench typically has judges who left more successful practices and were more likely to have worked in larger law firms.[56]

As previously noted the only category of prior practice noticeably present in the background of over one-third of the judges surveyed is work in a prosecutor's office. What impact does such prosecutorial experience have on the objectivity of criminal court judges? My recent national studies of the urban criminal courts indicated that approximately one-third of the judges I observed in the past 15 years (this is from a sample of nearly 150 judges in 15 cities) visibly favored the prosecution, while the remaining two-thirds were responsibly neutral. Several judges were discovered to be making an obvious effort to ensure that the defendant received a fair trial, with a sizable minority even going so far as to favor the defense. When questioned about this seemingly ironic position, the judges often replied that their prior experience had hardened them to many prosecutorial maneuvers they found distasteful and brought to mind the adage that "familiarity may breed contempt."[57]

Turning to federal court appointees, Sheldon Goldman's definitive work concludes that about 40 percent were previously members of a state court while a large number were U.S. magistrates or bankruptcy judges. Goldman was surprised to find a declining number of former U.S. attorneys (federal prosecutors), a position that had previously been a direct stepping-stone for many federal judges. The remaining 50 percent of the federal appointees were in private practice just prior to taking the bench, with a wide variety in the size of their previous firms. Focusing solely on the federal appeals court, one striking finding is that nearly 60 percent of all Reagan appointees (as well as over 50 percent of Ford, Nixon, and Johnson selections) were already serving in the judiciary at the time of appointment, most usually serving on a federal district court (16 out of 19 Reagan appeals court nominees were elevated from the district courts). It seems clear that the Reagan administration felt most comfortable selecting federal court judges who had already established clear track records on the bench with their judicial philosophy self-evident through their written opinions.[58] This trend was also apparent in his selection of Supreme Court justices as all five of the Reagan nominees had prior judicial experience.

The second category of background characteristics involves the judges' prior political activity. Although this issue will be examined in greater detail in Chapter 6, a brief discussion of their partisan political affiliation and their political activity will be offered. As a broad generality, the partisan political affiliation of the nation's judges reflects the dominance of the Democratic party at state and local levels, while recent Republican control of the presidency is mirrored in an increasing number of Republican federal court appointments. Craig and Emmert discovered that two-thirds of the state supreme court justices were Democrats, and Goldman identified 90 percent of the federal judges appointed by Reagan, Ford, and Nixon as Republicans.[59] His research also indicated that more than 60 percent of the federal judges nominated between 1977 and 1984 had records of prominent political activism in a political party (and it may also be assumed that many others were probably involved in party politics in a more limited capacity). This finding appears consistent with the limited amount of research relating to the political activism of state judges. One frequently cited case study conducted in California in the 1960s estimated that 70 percent of the state's judiciary described themselves as having been politically active.[60]

Given the political nature of the selection process (see Chapter 6), it is not surprising that so many judges have been politically active. Even where the appointment process is utilized, and merit selection emphasized, it is still politicians making these decisions. What better way to gain the attention of those political figures responsible for judicial selections than to be politically active? Gaining the favorable attention of the public officials who choose judges is, therefore, the most common characteristic shared by all members of the bench. This has led to the oft-repeated quip describing judges as lawyers who once knew the governor.

The third category of background characteristics relates to the social and economic circumstances from which the American judiciary emerges. It is the overwhelming conclusion from all of the surveys that judges are selected from a very narrow and restricted socioeconomic pool. As a group judges most typically come from families of greater than average wealth and status. There does seem to be a slight trend in recent years toward broader representation of all types of socioeconomic backgrounds, this being especially true for judges serving on trial courts. Nevertheless, the patterns of judges evolving primarily from families of above-average status continues and is an inevitable product of the advantages that relative wealth and high social status confer. Ryan found a direct link between generations and concluded that although individuals may not be born to be judges, "some start with a decided advantage by virtue of the visibility of their family names in social, legal, or political circles."[61]

Minority Judges

As noted in Chapter 1, there has been a meteoric rise in the number of women and blacks enrolling in law schools during the past decade. Thus far, however, their presence has not been felt in the judiciary at either the state or federal levels, although there has been a barely perceptible trend in this direction and several ground-breaking appointments have recently been made. The fact, however, that a woman was not named to the U.S. Supreme Court until 1981 provides uncontrovertible proof of this country's historical reluctance to admit women to the bench. Even in New Jersey, which has been characterized as operating one of the nation's more progressive court systems, a woman was not named to its highest court until 1982.

Today only 2 percent of our nation's 27,000 judges are female, and if we look back 20 to 30 years the figure shrinks to less than 1 percent. Examining the backgrounds of women judges serving at the state level, Susan Carbon in 1980 described the typical female judge as being 48 years of age, having been on the bench 6 years. She was likely to be a white Democrat with a liberal political orientation. She had attended a quality private law school, had previously been employed with a small firm, and only slightly involved in politics. Most women judges sit on courts of limited jurisdiction in a medium-sized city, with declining numbers at the appellate level. Table 2.7 shows what factors women judges believe facilitated their appointment to the bench. It controls for the varying types of selection processes, although it is clear that prior professional experience was most important.

The greatest strides toward selecting increased numbers of women to the bench occurred during the Carter administration on the federal courts. He named more women to the federal courts than had served under all previous administrations. His creation of special selection panels with a strong commitment toward affirmative action was the primary reason for this increase, but with the Reagan administration's dissolution of the panels, the percentage of women selected slipped back to pre-Carter levels. Elaine Martin recently investigated the women on the federal bench, and the findings of her study, which focused primarily on the Carter administration, are presented in Table 2.8. Women still comprise only 8 percent of the federal judiciary even after the Carter appointments, but their strong liberal commitment as well as their mere presence on the court may have important policy implications.

Turning to the topic of black judges, the first question is how many are there? Although the numbers may be on the rise, they still comprise only 4 percent of the nation's judiciary. A recent survey by the Coalition of Concerned Black Americans found that this small group was concentrated in the nation's largest urban court systems. They discovered that more than one-half of the nation's black judges were found in six major cities: New York, Chicago, Washington, Detroit, Philadelphia, and Los

Table 2.7 FACTORS WOMEN BELIEVE FACILITATED THEIR SELECTION AS A JUDGE (BY METHOD OF SELECTION[a])

	Partisan Elections (N=62)	Nonpartisan Elections (N=53)	Governor with Commission (N=91)	Governor without Commission (N=85)	Overall Percentage (N=368)
Prior professional experience	50%	51%	64%	60%	58%
Being a woman[b]	32	43	65	62	51
Acquaintance with political leaders	37	38	48	55	44
Active in bar association work[b]	24	28	50	46	38
Endorsement of interest groups[b]	29	55	35	29	35
Accepting visible cases as a lawyer	27	32	34	20	27
High-quality campaign[b]	66	66	6	8	25
Endorsement of political parties[b]	37	28	13	27	20
Worked in political campaigns	23	15	19	22	18
Law school attended	11	11	21	20	17
Held public office	18	17	12	22	16
Well-known family name	18	21	8	11	13
Held party office	7	6	3	9	7
Well-financed campaign[b]	7	25	3	4	7

[a]Judges selected by legislators, judges, and executive officers other than governors (excluding the "overall percentage" column) are omitted from this table.

[b]p < .05.

Source: Susan Carbon, Pauline Houlden, and Larry Berkson, "Women on the State Bench," Judicature 65 (December/January, 1982): 300. Copyright 1982 American Judicature Society. Reprinted with permission of the publisher.

Angeles. Even in these cities blacks are underrepresented in the judiciary when compared with their relative proportion of the local population. In New York, for example, with a black population of 30 percent, only 10 percent of the city's judiciary are black.[62] (When one compares the proportion of black judges to the percentage of black defendants that constitute the court's clientele, the degree of underrepresentation is even more significant.)

Is there any preferred system that permits potential black judges a relatively better chance to reach the bench? Research by the American Judicature Society indicates that the appointive rather than elective systems are more favorable toward creating a more racially balanced bench. One explanation for this phenomenon is that since most local elections

Table 2.8 CHARACTERISTICS OF WOMEN
JUDGES APPOINTED BY
PRESIDENT CARTER (N = 40)

Occupation at time of appointment	
Politics/government	10.3%
Judiciary	53.8
Large law firm	7.7
Moderate law firm	12.8
Solo or small firm	5.1
Academic	10.3
Undergraduate school	
Public	51.3
Private	30.8
Ivy League	17.9
Law school	
Public	48.7
Private	25.6
Ivy League	25.6
Prior experience	
Judicial	59.0
Prosecutorial	35.9
Neither	35.9
Party activism	15.4
Religion	
Protestant	35.9
Catholic	5.1
Jewish	20.5
Unknown	38.5
Race	
White	82.1
Black	17.9
Median Age	46 years

Source: Elaine Martin, "Women on the Federal Bench: A Comparative Profile," *Judicature* 65 (December/January, 1982): 309.

for the judiciary are conducted on an at-large basis (rather than electoral districts), racial minorities historically have fared poorly in these city-wide contests as their bloc-voting power is diluted over the expanded electoral terrain. The record of the federal courts, especially during the Carter years, also shows how the appointive process can be utilized to bring greater numbers of blacks to the bench. President Carter was able to significantly alter the racial balance of the federal courts through his aggressive affirmative action program. Nearly 14 percent of Carter's appointments to the federal district courts were black, another 7 percent being Hispanic. These 42 minority judges will serve life terms, and although President Reagan has markedly decreased the number of minority judges (only one black judge appointed during his first term), nevertheless the impact of the Carter appointees will be felt for many years to come.[63]

In any discussion of altering the racial composition of the judiciary, especially through the conscious efforts of an affirmative action program, it is often feared that selection standards may be lowered. Although little research has been done on this very sensitive and complex issue, a recent study by Thomas Uhlman discovered that there were virtually no differences between the background and qualifications of black and white trial judges. The black judge met, and frequently surpassed, the informal standards of white colleagues. Ironically, this situation may have created a wide chasm between the black judge whose elevation to the inner circle of the "legal establishment" may place him or her out of touch with less successful black lawyers. Some argue cynically that if a black is selected for the judiciary he or she must be acceptable to the white legal community, which means that only "safe" blacks have a chance of becoming judges. Given the presence of such outspoken black judges as Bruce Wright in New York and George Crockett in Detroit, there are many exceptions to this supposed trend.[64]

What are the implications for racial minorities presently utilizing the courts of the apparent underrepresentation of minority judges? Because of the absence of empirical research addressing this question, and as the following list of reasons convincingly argues, the race of a judge appears to bear little importance to the defendant and his or her accuser. Most people who are in the throes of a trial seem to have more weighty concerns than simply the race or ethnic background of the judge. Especially in criminal matters, where the likelihood is that the defendant and the judge will be coming from sharply divergent socioeconomic backgrounds, the mere fact of racial similarity looms as a very minor factor drawing the two parties together. Given the miniscule number of cases (both criminal and civil) that actually go to trial, the overwhelming majority of individuals will experience only fleeting contact with a judge, and therefore the issue of race fails to have much of an opportunity to impress itself upon the court's clientele.[65]

It must be acknowledged, however, that other members of the community beyond the plaintiffs and defendants are concerned with the underrepresentation of racial minorities within their city's judiciary. It is the symbolic nature of this oversight by the white power structure that has proven so distasteful to the leadership of the minority groups. This frustration is likely to be part of a larger feeling of powerlessness felt by our nation's racial minorities, but since the judicial system has played so important a part in their efforts to achieve equal justice as promised by the Constitution, it is a crucial concern in a critical institution. Without an opportunity to place increasing numbers of minority group members into judgeships, blacks and Hispanics will continue to grow more distrustful of the quality of justice dispensed by our courts. This can ultimately lead to a decline in the legitimacy of the local court system, threatening the very social and political fabric of the community.[66]

Status and Prestige

As discussed in Chapter 1, lawyers in general have maintained a fairly high status ranking, despite recent declines, and judges as a subset of the legal profession have consistently held even higher prestige rankings without the recent fluctuations. According to Donald Treiman in his work on occupational prestige, judges scored approximately 80—five points higher than lawyers. Scores were broken down by the level of court and ranged from a Supreme Court justice at 85 to a municipal court judge at 77.[67] It is interesting to find that judges have continued to sustain such high scores despite growing dissatisfaction with the nation's judicial system. The judicial process is frequently criticized as a slow-moving, cumbersome administrative system whose ultimate decisions are too lenient and generally unpopular with large segments of the population. Nevertheless, the public seems capable of distinguishing between a flawed institution mired in its day-to-day machinations and the rather elevated status it projects in its more idealized form.

This paradoxical situation probably is a by-product of both the wishful thinking and ignorance of the public. From the perspective of the layman, the life of a judge continues to be one of elevated status and privilege. It is viewed as a highly respected profession offering the opportunity to pursue altruistic aims while enjoying a comfortable salary and enviable working conditions. The public imagines the judge arriving at a specially designated parking space a few feet from the courthouse entrance in time for the leisurely commencement of courtroom business at ten o'clock. Upon entering the courthouse, doors are held and deference is extended, as the judge moves toward his or her chambers, exchanging morning salutations with a seemingly endless line of well-wishers. The royal treatment extends into a spacious, elegant office as a secretary brings already sorted correspondence along with a cup of coffee. A law clerk also is ready for the judge's morning appearance as legal memos, schedules, and other bits of critical information are officiously presented. Following a perusal of the morning paper and a brief ordering of the day's business, the judge is helped on with his or her robe and strides purposefully into the courtroom where the bailiff announces the arrival and demands immediate subservience.

Once in the courtroom, wearing the impressive robes and sitting above all other participants, the judge's power and status reach even greater heights. Lawyers, defendants, witnesses, the courtroom audience, all stand in awe, carefully trying to curry his or her favor. After a two- to three-hour morning session, the judge breaks for lunch, which the office staff has obtained and is ready in the judge's chambers. By two o'clock the judge has returned to the courtroom, where he or she will eloquently orchestrate the proceedings for the next two hours. Following a conclusion of the day's business, the judge will return briefly to chambers to catch up on the latest mail and gossip, and by five o'clock has returned to the chauffeur-driven car and heads back to a palatial residence to dine and socialize with entertaining personalities. The summers mean two-month vacations and shorter working days. The winters are interrupted by professional meetings in the Caribbean and long weekends in Vermont.

The pleasant and productive professional life just described is a far cry from reality for many judges, especially those assigned to the trial courts in large cities. The working environment of our nation's judges will be described in Chapter 7, and their reactions to these conditions will be analyzed in Chapter 9. Complaints about their working conditions, relatively low pay (in comparison to other members of the legal profession), administrative tedium, and irritating political involvements will be discussed in both of these chapters. It should be clarified, however, that even the judges themselves can be somewhat inconsistent and waver between the negative and positive aspects of their jobs. On the whole, most judges interviewed and observed were positive about most aspects of their lofty position and enjoyed the responsibilities and challenges inherent in their profession.

Idealized Personality Traits

The importance of the judge's character was noted at the turn of the century by German sociologist Eugen Ehrlich who warned that "there is no guaranty of justice except the personality of the judge."[68] This volume offers further documentation as to the critical importance of the judge's personality in influencing the quality and style of justice being dispensed in our nation's courtrooms. It, therefore, becomes extremely important for both the layman about to elect a judge or the politician about to appoint one to consider what type of person would develop into the best judge.

In my earlier research on criminal lawyers, I was able to describe a persistent modal personality, dominated by strong egos and an aggressive/combative nature. Judges, however, appear to possess such a wide range of personality traits that it is almost impossible to generalize about a typical judicial personality. The only persistent characteristic that did emerge is that like criminal lawyers felony court judges possess strong egos that are usually manifest in a high degree of self-confidence. Their experience as lawyers, and even more importantly as litigators, as well as the heavy responsibilities inherent in resolving difficult issues, make the presence of a strong ego and self-confident attitude necessary occupational requirements. It almost becomes a self-fulfilling prophecy that such types of individuals are attracted to, and eventually reach, the bench.

Much has been written about what characteristics would be necessary for the ideal judge. One of the most frequently quoted lists is offered by Bernard Shientag in an address nearly 50 years ago to the Association of the Bar of the City of New York. He described the "Eight Cardinal Virtues of Being a Judge," which included the following: independence, courtesy and patience, dignity, open-mindedness, impartiality, thoroughness and decisiveness, compassion, and social consciousness.[69] Some experts offer a much simpler formula for judicial success such as Supreme Court Justice Byron White who stated that a judge should simply be "reasonably intelligent, reasonably industrious, and reasonably honest."[70]

Another approach to the dilemma is to work backward by first selecting a group of outstanding judges, assessing their personality traits, and then use them as the idealized qualities. Judge John Noonan made such an effort in his attempt at understanding what makes a judge great as he examined the lives of six famous judges: Sir Edward Coke, Francis Bacon, John Marshall, Oliver Wendell Holmes, Benjamin Cardozo, and Louis Brandeis. He found that all of his choices were "highly intelligent, not in abstract terms but their intelligence was manifested in their sense of style and in retentive memories, keen perceptions, the ability to analogize, to make distinctions, to marshall data, to grasp relationships and to bring fact and theory together. In short, their intelligence as manifested, was that peculiarly appropriate to the legal profession."[71] (Other character traits examined by Noonan, such as fortitude, temperance, and prudence, were first established in Aristotle's *Ethics* and have been identified along with "justice" as cardinal virtues.)

A recent attempt to define desirable traits for our nation's judges appeared in the *Judge's Journal* and was entitled "What Makes a Good Appellate Judge." The Honorable Ruggero Aldissert of the Third Circuit of the U.S. Appellate Court opened the article with the following list:

1. The quality of fairness, justness, and impartiality.
2. The twin values of devotion and decisiveness.
3. The quality of clear thought and expression.
4. The quality of professional literacy.
5. The quality of institutional fidelity.
6. The quality of political responsibility (understanding that the legislature and executive have primary responsibility to fashion public policy).[72]

One would be hard pressed to find fault with any of these groups of attributes that combine to form an ideal judge. Actually, anyone who possesses even a few of these laudatory characteristics would be a welcome addition to the bench. These attributes simply provide a useful set of idealized guidelines for describing the type of individual we would like to have sitting in our nation's courts.

Taxonomy of Judicial Personalities

As the previous section noted, there does not appear to be a model personality for all judges. This is a likely by-product of the wide variety of judicial positions ranging from a rural justice of the peace to a United States Supreme Court justice. The diversity is also compounded by the wide range of personality types attracted to both the bench and bar. Thus, despite widespread analysis of what types of character traits we would like to see in our judges, in fact, as they attempt to deal with the complex and challenging cases before them, a highly divergent array of personality types is apparent.

Let us now examine the variety of judicial behavior in action. The following series of character sketches are the product of the nearly 20 years of personal courtroom observations and are designed to illustrate the rich diversity of judicial styles that are to be found within the legal system today. I have given each of the four judges a shorthand label that seems to capture the essence of his or her judicial style: the routinizer, the educator, the humorist, and the advocate.

The Routinizer   In this large Midwestern city, the frigid weather and rising unemployment rate appear to be producing a staggering number of skid-row alcoholics. This results in a steadily increasing number of arrests of downtrodden individuals charged with being "drunk and disorderly." In order to minimize the impact of this sizable group of defendants, the court administrator has designated one of the criminal court judges to conduct a morning "drunk court." With the accent on speed, the judge is able to dispose of 50–75 cases prior to assuming his regular responsibilities 20 minutes later at ten o'clock. The judge is able to accomplish this speedy processing of defendants by handling all of the guilty pleas (which constitute well over 90 percent of the cases) by combining the defendants into small units for sentencing.

In sad groups of twos and threes, the inebriates try to listen attentively to the judge's litany, which concerns the court's acceptance of the guilty pleas. Since most of the defendants are repeat offenders, they are well versed in the entire procedure and patiently wait for the quickly revolving wheel of justice to spin them once more out into the chilly winter air. With vague promises of staying sober, finding a job, or most commonly leaving town (and thereby becoming a problem for some other city), these social outcasts are led out of the courtroom. The judge rarely lifts his head from behind the steep pile of case folders, as he sips morning coffee while accepting the guilty pleas, and noting each case disposition in the appropriate folder. The judge's impatience with the rare defendant confused by the proceedings or unwilling to plead guilty was readily apparent. This case would be rescheduled for later in the week, and the defendant would be hurriedly led back to the detention facility.

The judge seemed almost without personality, except for the isolated outbursts of displeasure with recalcitrant defendants. Otherwise, he appeared like an automaton or a foreman on an assembly line, cranking out cases as if they were drive shafts. Peering up at the large clock to his right, working against the ten o'clock deadline, he deftly shuffled through the paperwork and the defendants associated with it. The message was clear, do not tamper with the mechanized process. For those who failed to comprehend this message, they could expect harsh words from the judge and face the maximum penalty of the law.

The Educator   Believing in the necessity for educating the public, especially school-age children, this judge from a large Eastern city invited school classes to sit in and observe his courtroom in action. Fortunately, he has been provided with an ample-sized facility in the city's historic courthouse, and the judge reserves large areas of the room for his "pupils." Despite the noble ends, the judge's educative endeavors did seem to generate some serious problems. The judge continually annoyed both prosecutor and defense counsel by pausing in the middle of proceedings to carefully explain a point of law to the class in attendance. Although the judge is restricted to nonjury cases, the attorneys appeared unnerved by the interruptions and delays.

On one occasion, the attorneys did seem justified in their consternation as the judge appeared to have carried his "courtroom classroom" too far. The case involved a man accused of assaulting his girlfriend. The outcome of the case was wholly dependent on whether the version of the events in question of the victim or defendant was to be believed. Following cross-examination of both parties, the judge turned to a class of sixth graders (about 30 in number) and asked by a hand vote which party was to be believed. The majority of the students accepted the woman's version. The judge stated his agreement with their perceptions and found the defendant guilty. The defendant, who had watched the judge's behavior in wide-eyed disbelief, became irate at the court's decision and had to be restrained by his attorney and two bailiffs, while the judge calmly terminated his lecture to the class on how the judicial process works. It was just another class/case for this judicial educator.

The Humanist   Although judges may appear to process cases in an assembly-line style, as described earlier, sacrificing individual attention for speed and efficiency, many judges of the criminal courts make a conscious effort never to go so rapidly as to lose their concern for the constitutional rights of the individual defendants appearing before them. One judge, observed in the far West, exhibited such care and unwillingness to allow his judicial decisions to be affected by heavy caseloads. Both the prosecutor and defense counsel were visibly frustrated by the judge's attention to detail and snail-like pace. Their eyeballs would frequently roll skyward as the judge dwelled for what seemed an eternity on a seemingly obvious point involving a blatantly guilty defendant.

Despite the judge's lack of popularity with other court officials, he continued his careful and sometimes plodding ways. I observed him in the fall of 1981 when it appeared that this careful scrutiny may have saved an innocent man from accepting an unjustified guilty plea on the questionable advice of his seemingly unconcerned attorney. The defendant, who spoke only halting English, felt embarrassed to ask for an interpreter. He initially stepped before the judge, all too willing to accept the advice of his attorney to plead guilty to a lesser charge. It was only after the judge questioned the defendant as to the certainty of his plea did the language problems begin to become apparent. Once an interpreter was obtained, the judge spent the next hour questioning the defendant as to what had actually happened during the time of the original incident that led to his arrest. At the conclusion of the testimony, the judge was convinced of the defendant's innocence and moved for a new trial, rejecting the defendant's initial guilty plea, and instead accepting a new plea of not guilty with some advice to the prosecutor that he was contemplating dropping the charges entirely. This judge may be an exception and this case may be even more remarkable and unique, but it did happen and there are many more judges who refuse to compromise their constitutional obligations to the pressures of caseloads and efficiency.

The Advocate It seems ironic to most observers of the criminal courts to have the judiciary criticized by the public for being too liberal and too kindly disposed toward criminals. Most of the judges within the criminal courts have prosecutorial inclinations (and in many instances, professional experience as well), and if they are to be accurately criticized, it should be on the grounds of being too "hard" rather than too "soft" on the defendants before them. Judges were found to vary greatly in the degree to which they adopted the prosecution bias, but one judge observed during a visit to a large southern city illustrated one of the most extreme set of prosecution orientations discovered in all of my travels.

The case involved one of the city's underground newspapers and its possible relationship to some terrorist activities that included the bombing of the local police station. The editor of the paper, a long-haired flower child who was clearly a throwback to the radicals of the Vietnam War protest movement, was being both evasive and somewhat belligerent toward the young prosecutor while he was attempting to cross-examine her. The judge, sensing the prosecutor's tentative approach, and also aware of his lack of experience in cases of this type, quickly became an active participant in the cross-examination, and soon took over the questioning of the defendant entirely. The antagonistic attitude of the judge toward the young editor, who refused to back down or show any deference toward the judge, was reflected in his acerbic and aggressive style of questioning. He even went so far as to comment to the jury his conclusion that the defendant was not a very truthful individual. The frustrated defense counsel made countless objections, but could only insist that all the judge's antics be recorded by the stenographer and all of his objections preserved for the obvious appeal. His only recourse was to try and build a record of the judge's prejudicial behavior for an appeal, for it soon became apparent that he had little chance of victory at the trial level.

These four judges and the highlighted incidents serve primarily as examples of the varied styles and personalities of the urban court judiciary. They were purposefully selected to challenge the simplistic vision of judicial behavior held by most of the public. But how much diversity does actually exist between, and even within, our judicial system? How great an influence can the broad range of judicial personalities, as well as the personalities of other important members of the courtroom work group (i.e., prosecutors, defense attorneys, bailiffs, court clerks, etc.) have upon the operation of these courts? It is hoped that the remainder of this book will contribute toward a greater understanding of this complex question.

NOTES

1. Frances Zemans and Victor Rosenbloom, *The Making of a Public Profession* (Chicago: American Bar Foundation, 1981), 2.
2. Barbara Curran, *The Lawyer Statistical Report: A Statistical Profile of the U.S. Legal Profession in the 1980's* (Chicago: American Bar Foundation, 1985), 3.
3. Terrence C. Halliday, "Six Score Years and Ten: Demographic Transitions in the American Legal System, 1860–1980," *Law and Society Review* 20 (1986): 53.
4. Richard Abel, "The Transformation of the American Legal Profession," *Law and Society Review*, 20 (1986): 6.
5. Ibid. p. 16.
6. Curran, *Lawyer Statistical Report*, 51.
7. Ibid. p. 12.
8. Ibid. p. 39.
9. Abel, "The Transformation of the American Legal Profession," 13.

10. Karen Berger Morello, *The Invisible Bar: The Woman Lawyer in America* (New York: Random House, 1986), 219.
11. Cynthia Epstein, *Women in Law* (New York: Basic Books, 1981), 265.
12. William Eich, "Gender Bias in the Courtroom: Some Participants are More Equal Than Others," *Judicature* 69 (April/May, 1986): 339.
13. Nancy Blodgett, "I Don't Think Ladies Should Be Lawyers," *American Bar Association Journal* (Dec. 1, 1986): 48.
14. Rosabeth Kantor, "Reflections on Women and the Legal Profession: A Sociological Perspective," *Harvard Women's Law Journal* 1 (1978): 1.
15. Blodgett, "I Don't Think Ladies Should Be Lawyers," 49.
16. Sharon Johnson, "Women Over 40 Choosing Law," *New York Times*, 2 Oct. 1985, sec. C, p. 1.
17. Judy Klemesrud, "Women in the Law: Many Are Getting Out," *New York Times*, 9 Aug. 1985, p. A14.
18. David Margolick, "Bar Group Is Told of Racial Barriers," *New York Times*, 16 Feb. 1985, sec. 1, p. 15.
19. Jerome Shuman, "A Black Lawyers Study," *Howard Law Journal* 16 (1971): 230.
20. Curran, *Lawyer Statistical Report*, 51.
21. Geraldine Segal, *Blacks in the Law* (Philadelphia: University of Pennsylvania Press, 1983), 216.
22. Ibid. p. 216.
23. Jeffrey Maclin, "Minority Firms Struggle for Business and Talent," *Manhattan Lawyer* (May 24, 1988): 1.
24. Jerrold Auerbach, *Unequal Justice* (New York: Oxford University Press, 1976), 128.
25. Harry Stumpf, *American Judicial Politics* (New York: Harcourt Brace Jovanovich, 1988), 182.
26. Curran, *Lawyer Statistical Report*, 243.
27. "New Jersey Surveys Lawyers," *New York Times*, 23 June 1985, sec. 1, p. 34.
28. Nancy Blodgett, "A Look at Today's Lawyer," *American Bar Association Journal* (Sept. 1, 1986): 47.
29. Tamara Levin, "At Cravath, $65,000 to Start," *New York Times*, 18 April 1986, sec. D, p. 1.
30. Ibid.
31. Tamara Levin, "A Gentlemanly Profession Enters a Tough New Era," *New York Times*, 16 Jan. 1983, sec. 3, p. 1.
32. A. Peter Pashigian, "The Number and Earnings of Lawyers—Some Recent Findings," *American Bar Foundation Research Journal* (Winter, 1978): 51.
33. Zemans and Rosenbloom, *Making of a Public Profession*, 3.
34. Donald Treiman, *Occupational Prestige in Comparative Perspective* (New York: Academic Press, 1977), 1.
35. Richard Abel, "Comparative Sociology of the Legal Profession," *American Bar Foundation Research Journal* (Winter, 1985): 59.
36. Zemans and Rosenbloom, *Making of a Public Profession*, 3.
37. Jon R. Waltz, "The Unpopularity of Lawyers in America," *Cleveland State Law Review* 25 (1976): 144.
38. David Riley, "The Mystique of Lawyers," in *Verdicts on Lawyers*, ed. Ralph Nader and Mark Green (New York: Thomas Crowell, 1976), 93.

39. Edward Laumann and John Heinz, "Specialization and Prestige in the Legal Profession: The Structure of Deference," *American Bar Foundation Research Journal* No. 1 (Winter, 1977): 155.
40. Zemans and Rosenbloom, *Making of a Public Profession*, 76.
41. Henry Glick, *Courts, Politics, and Justice* (New York: McGraw-Hill, 1988), 74.
42. Laumann and Heinz, "Specialization and Prestige," 209.
43. John Hagan, Marie Huxter, and Patricia Parker, "Class Structure and Legal Practice: Inequality and Mobility Among Toronto Lawyers," *Law and Society Review* 22, no. 1 (1986): 9.
44. Joel Handler, *The Lawyer and His Community* (Madison: University of Wisconsin Press, 1967).
45. Laumann and Heinz, "Specialization and Prestige," 59.
46. Abel, "Comparative Sociology," 24.
47. Walter O. Weyrauch, *The Personality of Lawyers* (New Haven: Yale University Press, 1964), 24.
48. Ibid. p. 249.
49. Riley, "Mystique of Lawyers," 90.
50. "Basketball League Summons 3,000 Players to Court," *Manhattan Lawyer* (Feb. 16, 1988): 26.
51. Leonard Eron and Robert Redmount, "The Effect of Legal Education on Attitudes," *Journal of Legal Education* 9, no. 4 (1957): 431.
52. John Ryan with Allan Ashmore, Bruce Sales, and Sandra Share-DuBow, *American Trial Judge* (New York: Free Press, 1980), 124.
53. Harry Stumpf, *American Judicial Politics* (New York: Harcourt Brace Jovanovich, 1988), 180.
54. Stumpf, *American Judicial Politics*, 181.
55. Ryan, *American Trial Judge*, 124.
56. Laurence Baum, *American Courts: Process and Policy* (Boston: Houghton Mifflin, 1986), 126.
57. Paul Wice, *Chaos in the Courthouse* (New York: Praeger Publishing, 1985), 4.
58. Sheldon Goldman, "Reaganizing the Judiciary," *Judicature* 68 (April/May 1985): 323.
59. Ibid. p. 318.
60. Baum, *American Courts*, 124.
61. Ryan, et al., *American Trial Judge*, 129.
62. "A Preliminary Report of the Experiences of the Minority Judiciary in the City of New York," *Howard Law Review* 18 (1975): 495.
63. Goldman, "Reaganizing the Judiciary," 319.
64. Thomas Uhlman, "Race, Recruitment, and Representation: Background Differences Between Black and White Trial Judges" *Western Political Quarterly* 30 (December, 1977): 469.
65. Wice, *Criminal Lawyers*, 97.
66. This point has been echoed by such critics as Richard Quinney, Richard Abel, and Richard Schwartz in their analysis of the American justice system.
67. Donald Treiman, *Occupational Prestige in Comparative Perspective* (Orlando, Fla.: Academic Press, 1977), 5.
68. Bernard Shientag, *The Personality of the Judge* (New York: Association of the Bar of the City of New York, 1944).

69. Ibid.
70. Elmer M. Gunderson, "Jurisprudential Character: The Typology of James David Barber in a Judicial Context," *Southwestern University Law Review* 13, no. 3 (1983): 396.
71. Hon. John T. Noonan, "Education, Intelligence and Character in Judges," *Minnesota Law Review* 71 (May 1987): 1124.
72. Ruggero Aldissert et al., "What Makes a Good Appellate Judge," *Judges Journal* 22, no. 2 (Spring 1983): 14.

Chapter
3

The Lawyer's Working Environment: Firm and Profession

*T*his chapter examines the working environment of the practicing attorney. Although lawyers who specialize in litigation may spend a significant amount of time in court, this chapter limits its analysis to the law firm; a discussion of the courthouse will be reserved for Chapter 7. Following a brief description of the major categories of working environments (large firms, legal clinics, small firms and lawyers in association, solo practitioners, public agencies, and corporation legal departments), special attention will be devoted to large corporate firms and solo practitioners because of their heightened public image. The final section of the chapter will be devoted to an analysis of the role of the organized bar as it attempts to influence professional behavior.

DESCRIPTION OF TYPES OF FIRMS BY SIZE

Large Corporate Firms

Two important characteristics of large law firms are of paramount importance in understanding their current position within the legal profession: (1) large law firms have a significance that far outweighs their rather meager numbers and (2) these firms have experienced a dramatic growth both in size and prestige in the last half of the twentieth century. Arbitrarily defining large law firms as those employing more than 50 attorneys, there are presently only approximately 300 firms satisfying this operational definition, employing less than 20,000 lawyers out of over 600,000 practicing attorneys.[1] James Stewart, being even more selective, in his highly regarded study of what he termed "the nation's blue chip corporate firms," believed that only 3000 lawyers were employed in these elite firms.[2] Table 3.1 offers a representative sampling of ten of these "elite corporate law firms," indicating their size, location, and key clients.

In addition to their size and remarkable recent growth, large corporate law firms are also identified by their clientele, which are the nation's major economic institutions: banks, corporations, insurance companies, and a miscellany of powerful financial enterprises. These large firms are able to attract powerful corporate clients because of their ability to solve complex legal problems, drawing upon extremely competent specialists in widely diverse areas of the law. Typical fields of specialization include antitrust, patents, business tax, securities, real estate, public utilities, banking, and labor. The firm is usually organized into sections based on the various areas of speciality with a litigation department ready to assist any case that faces the likelihood of going to trial. The success of these firms is described succinctly in a 1981 American Bar Association (ABA) Task Force report on the role of the lawyer in the 1980s that concluded that "because of the greater number of lawyers and support services, large firms are able to compete successfully against smaller firms through the economies of scale and a full service approach."[3]

It should also be noted that these large corporate firms have not only grown in the size of their legal staff but have also expanded into the operation of branch offices in major American cities as well as important foreign capitals such as London, Paris, Cairo, and Tokyo. As might be expected, the most common location for a new branch is Washington, D.C., where nearly every major corporate firm presently maintains a modest operation specializing in keeping an eye on what the federal government is doing in areas that could possibly have an impact on one of their clients.

As a final point, all large firms are divided into partners and associates. The partners are the more experienced members of the firm who share the risks and profits while making the critical management decisions. The associates are the younger lawyers who have joined the firm earning annual salaries and who, after surviving several years (usually between five and eight) of intense competition, hope to become partners. The overall staffing pattern is described as a pyramid design in which a small group of powerful partners preside over a large number of associates. James Stewart describes the financial relationship created by the imbalance between partners and associates as being a major factor in producing the firm's immense profitability: billing clients for associates' work at rates that far exceed associates' salaries.[4]

Table 3.1 THE ELITE CORPORATE LAW FIRMS

Name	Location	Size	Date Founded	Key Clients	Notes
Cravath, Swaine & Moore	New York	213	1819	IBM, CBS, Chemical Bank	The archetype of elite corporate firms
Davis Polk & Wardwell	New York	230	1849	ITT, LTV, Morgan Guaranty	Long known as the top "white shoe" firm
Debevoise & Plimpton	New York	154	1931	Chrysler, Prudential	A relative newcomer; strong in corporate
Donovan Leisure Newton & Irvine	New York	185	1929	Mobil, Westinghouse	Litigation strength, firm's standing threatened by Kodak
Kirkland & Ellis	Chicago	290	1908	Standard Oil (Indiana)	Awesome reputation in litigation
Milbank, Tweed, Hadley & McCloy	New York	211	1860	Chase Manhattan, the Rockefellers	Preeminent in trusts and estates
Pillsbury, Madison & Sutro	San Francisco	245	1865	Standard Oil (California)	The established West Coast firm
Shearman & Sterling	New York	341	1860	Citibank, United Technologies	The ultimate banking firm
Simpson Thacher & Bartlett	New York	211	1884	Manufacturers Hanover, Gulf & Western	On the rise; strong banking and corporate
Sullivan & Cromwell	New York	215	1897	Exxon, General Foods, GE	The quintessential business practice

Source: James B. Stewart, Partners (New York: Simon and Schuster, 1983). 14. Copyright 1983 by James Stewart.

Legal Clinics

In terms of size the next largest category of law firm is the legal clinic (also referred to in more derogatory terms as a legal supermarket). These offices began to appear in the mid-1970s following such Supreme Court decisions as *Bates* v. *Arizona Bar*, which gave lawyers a constitutional right to advertise their prices for specified legal services, and *Goldfarb* v. *Virginia State Bar*, which held that bar association minimum fee schedules violated federal antitrust laws. Through effective advertising campaigns and the heavy use of paralegals at the early stages of a client's case, these clinics were able to handle a large volume of cases at very reasonable prices. Most of the legal clinics are fairly large in terms of the total number of employees, but they are usually organized into a large number of neighborhood branches, maximizing their accessibility to a basically middle-class market. The clinics specialized in uncomplicated legal problems that could be handled primarily by standard forms filled in by trained paralegals. Typical areas of work include wills, personal bankruptcy, divorce, negligence, and traffic offenses that could lead to a loss of driving license.

Although these legal clinics are still looked down upon by state and national bar associations, they have been able to carve out a niche in working and middle-class communities for families who cannot afford the services of most law firms, which charge a minimum of $50–$75 an hour and rather stiff fees for even the most perfunctory services. Recent developments in the expansion of legal clinics have been their success in joining with tax-return preparing operations as well as entering the prepaid legal services field with trade unions. Most lawyers working in these clinics do not seem to be achieving great financial success, but bringing improved legal services to a frequently neglected middle class is a matter of great pride to all clinic practitioners.

The most authoritative report on legal clinics was completed by a special committee of the American Bar Association, and despite the possibility of biased research, their survey of 84 clinics offered the following list of seemingly reasonable conclusions:

1. Legal clinics were defined as a law firm that offers routine legal services for reasonable fees and seeks a high volume of work.
2. The average income in 1980 for the clinics was $93,000.
3. Although nearly all clinics used standardized forms, they were not necessarily high volume operations, averaging only 300 cases per clinic.
4. They advertised in the yellow pages and with a weekly or daily newspaper, spending an average of less than $6000 on advertising during 1980.
5. They were usually opened with the lawyers' own funds and are presently owned by one or two lawyers with less than 10 years of experience.

6. There was such a tremendous variety in the ways that the legal clinics functioned and the rewards they received, it is very dangerous to base too much upon the average/median findings reported in this rather limited survey.[5]

Midsized Firms

Halfway between the large corporate law firms with over 50 lawyers handling complex cases and representing powerful economic institutions and the struggling solo practitioner fighting for survival, one finds a large percentage of lawyers working in modest size law firms. According to John Heinz and Terrence Halliday in their comprehensive survey of the Chicago bar, over one-third of the city's lawyers work in these midsized firms. Given the wide range in the number of attorneys as well as diverse operating procedures, it is difficult to generalize about midsized firms, although there are a few overall characteristics that appear applicable to the entire category. Similar to the large corporate firms, midsized firms also divide their staff between the newly hired associates earning annual salaries and the partners who make the major decisions and divide up the firm's profits. In contrast to the larger firms representing wealthy institutional clients on a wide range of legal problems, the midsized firm tends to specialize and limit itself to a handful of legal areas. Such firms prefer to offer a reputable product in a selected area rather than spreading themselves too thin. Recent terminology refers to these midsized firms as "boutique firms" specializing in such areas as admiralty law, entertainment law, or real estate. These firms often are dependent on referrals from other midsized firms whose clients have developed unusual legal problems which they are ill-equipped to handle. John Flood in his 1985 survey of the American legal profession noted that one apparently unsolvable problem facing the specialty firm is growth. He comments that if "the firm has determined that a particular number of lawyers is the optimum size of the firm, it will be difficult to hire new associates, for they can have no expectation of becoming a partner. The problem may cause such firms to split into even smaller entities to allow for future growth."[6]

A recent phenomenon in many cities observed during my research on private criminal lawyers was to discover groups of lawyers being "in association," sharing office, secretarial, and library space, yet each working independently. Although these attorneys in association may be technically "solo practitioners" simply sharing space without sharing profits, nevertheless it creates the physical appearance of a midsize law firm. Thus, given the perplexing taxonomic difficulties of placing lawyers in association in a specific grouping, they are simply described here as a fairly common innovative scheme among urban lawyers who prefer the economic advantages of a group environment while still preserving the independence of their individual practices.

Solo Practitioners

According to the previously cited study of Chicago by Heinz and Halliday, nearly 20 percent of the city's lawyers were solo practitioners. Jerome Carlin, also analyzing Chicago, credited with the most complete examination of solo practitioners in his book entitled *Lawyers on Their Own*, offers the following description of this rather beleaguered practitioner: "Finding himself on the lowest rung of the status ladder of the profession, with little or no chance of rising, his practice restricted to the least remunerative and least desirable matters and beset by competition from lawyers and laymen alike, the individual practitioner is frequently a dissatisfied, disappointed, resentful, angry man."[7]

The solo practitioner can be sharply contrasted with the large or even midsized firm on several levels, but the most striking is probably the type of clients and type of cases he or she handles. The solo practitioner represents individuals and, if on a rare occasion he or she does have a business client, it is usually a small neighborhood enterprise. Given the type of client, the solo practitioner is involved in civil and criminal legal problems affecting middle-class Americans. Buying a house, drawing up a will, being injured in an accident, divorcing a spouse, declaring bankruptcy, or being arrested for drunk driving represent the normal range of cases handled by these hard-working individuals. Given the financial limitations inherent in these types of cases and the difficulties of competing with larger firms, the solo practitioner is at the bottom of the legal profession both in terms of annual salary and overall status. The status problem, which is more complex than simply earning less money, is related to the generally less distinguished law school educations of so many solo practitioners. Often coming from a working-class background, unable to attend a more prestigious (and typically more expensive) law school, these solitary lawyers usually attend local law schools (described in Chapter 1), often during the evening or on a part-time basis. In the recent past many of these solo lawyers were discriminated against by the larger law firms, which were controlled by white, Anglo-Saxon Protestants. Although much of the more blatant discrimination has abated, economic realities still handicap a large percentage of these first-generation urban ethnic attorneys in their efforts to break into the major corporate firms.

Despite the overall increase in the number of law school graduates during the past 20 years, the number of solo practitioners has experienced a serious decline. Every year more of these individuals are unable to survive economically, in most instances joining midsized firms or governmental agencies (although several simply choose to abandon the law entirely). In my own work on private criminal lawyers completed in 1978, the large majority of whom were either solo practitioners or working in association with a handful of other attorneys, I discovered that there were approximately half the number practicing this specialty compared to 1960. For those young law school graduates interested in criminal law, nearly everyone opted for either the public defender's or the district attorney's office rather than the much riskier option of private practice.[8]

Governmental Agencies

Returning again to the work of Heinz and Halliday in Chicago as well as the broader national study by Curran noted in Chapter 1, it is clear that during the past 25 years public agencies have experienced noteworthy increases in the number of lawyers being hired. Although only approximately 15 percent of the legal work force currently is employed by a public agency, this represents a nearly 200 percent increase in the past three decades.[9] Although working in large firms continues to attract many law school graduates, the increasing number of black and women attorneys entering the job market prefer the opportunities offered in the public sector. This may be a result of both the prior history of racial and sexual discrimination in corporate firms as well as the current difficulties in achieving partnership facing all associates. Public agencies, therefore, provide job security without the intense competitive pressure found in larger firms as associates battle one another for the select few partnership positions. After hearing "horror stories" about the pursuit of partnership, detailing 80-hour work weeks with tedious cases for undesirable clients under tyrannical and insensitive partners, it is not surprising that so many recent law graduates have decided to turn away from the enticing salaries of large firms choosing the more secure life of public service.

The public agencies not only provide greater job security, but in recent years their salaries have become increasingly respectable. Although obviously no match for starting salaries at large corporate firms, they are often close to the money offered at midsized firms and usually above that found in the smaller firms. Additionally, young lawyers in government may be given greater responsibility and gain both wider and quicker professional experiences. This is especially true for those lawyers interested in litigation who can almost immediately gain important trial experience working for public defender agencies and district attorney offices. It should also be noted that given these early opportunities for sharpening legal skills, many young lawyers begin their careers with government expecting to stay for only a brief period of time before moving on to a private law firm. Current wisdom seems to indicate that private firms are desirous of hiring young attorneys who have developed perceptible professional skills as a result of their governmental working experience.

House Counsel in Private Corporations

Growing at an even faster rate than lawyers joining the public sector is the significant increase in the number of lawyers presently being hired to work in the legal departments of private corporations. Current statistics place 20 percent of our nation's attorneys working for these large businesses, a figure that has nearly doubled in the past decade.[10] One authority estimates that the number of staff attorneys has increased by 400 percent in the past 25 years, and another reports that currently in-house law departments are growing twice as fast as law firms.[11]

Why has such a remarkable increase occurred in such a short period of time? In her recent study of salaried lawyers at work, entitled *Lawyers for Hire*, Eve Spangler explains this growth as being primarily the result of the staggering cost of privately retained counsel. In general, "it is estimated that the cost of legal work done in house is 35 to 50 percent less than the cost of comparable work referred out."[12] Beyond the important monetary considerations, changes in the legal and economic environment of the corporation are also responsible for the altered and expanded role of corporate counsel. The board chairman of a large corporation explains these developments in an article in the *American Business Lawyer* by stating: "Years ago legal activity was remedial, not preventative; it was sporadic not so continuous; less demanding as to deadlines, more controllable by counsel's ingenuity. Today the old kind of work is still there but it doesn't predominate. . . . Thus the most active companies now require—or are best served by—the constant availability of counsel who is informed on a day to day basis of the company's activities and directions."[13]

The traditional role of a corporation legal department was typically that of a specialist, its members utilizing their technical expertise as lawyers to solve specific problems handed to them by their corporate superiors. These assignments often involved detailed work on contracts, acquisitions, patents, and tax issues. Although still bound to their superiors within the corporation, nevertheless, these legal departments today are being given broader responsibilities; and, when they do interact with outside law firms, they are no longer forced to take a backseat, but dominate the interaction and control the final judgment.

ANATOMY OF A LARGE FIRM

In this section a rather detailed examination of one type of legal working environment will be presented. Although both the large corporate firm discussed here and the solo practitioner discussed next have been briefly described in the previous section, it is believed that they both merit more extensive analysis. Both of these working environments, despite the polarity of their relative positions among the variety of legal environments just described, capture the public's imagination as representing the two quintessential forms of law practices. Additionally, social scientists and legal researchers have also been principally concerned with each of these extreme workplaces. Therefore, the availability of information, combined with the heightened public interest, has convinced me to devote supplemental space to these two types of law practices. Let us first turn to the large corporate law firm.

Physical Description

The popular television show "L.A. Law" has done much to glamorize the corporate law firm. Housed in a gleaming tower above a sparkling, vibrant city, the offices combine the latest technological advances (fax machines, high-powered computers, etc.) with the height of creature comforts in terms of stylish offices offering breathtaking views of the city. Assisted by a phalanx of attractive, dedicated, and omnipresent support staff, these corporate lawyers appear to inhabit an ideal workplace environment. Popular literature also contributes to the glorification of the Wall Street practice, through the works of Louis Auchincloss and others. The following excerpt from the recent best-selling novel by Tom Wolfe, *Bonfire of the Vanities*, does an excellent job capturing the feel of these elitist institutions:

> Dunning, Spongit and Leach occupied four floors of a skyscraper on Wall Street, three blocks from Pierce and Pierce. When it was built it had been the very latest in the 1920's modern style. But now it had the grimy gloom that was typical of Wall Street. . . . Modern interiors had been caked with 18th century English paneling and stocked with 18th century English furniture. . . . Freddy's office was done, the way Judy talked about doing apartments. It looked like something from one of those abominable magazines . . . burgundy velvet, oxblood leather, burled wood, brass and silver bibliolots.[14]

Most large corporate law firms are located near the clients they serve, which means in close proximity to a city's financial center. In New York City they are clustered throughout Wall Street; in Chicago they are found along LaSalle Street; and in Los Angeles it is the Century City area. These large firms are identified by the names of several of their most preeminent partners who may even be deceased. In the parlance of the legal community they refer to each other by just the first two names. Thus, in New York City, the prestigious firm of Paul, Weiss, Rifkind, Wharton and Garrison is noted among insiders as simply Paul, Weiss. Because it is such a rare honor to be a name partner and in order to eliminate the potential conflict by adding new names or dropping old ones, the firms generally maintain the names of the founding partners. Thus, even though Sullivan and Cromwell has been headed by such prominent figures as John Foster Dulles and Arthur Dean, it still maintains its original identification.

Since the large corporate firms may contain well over 100 lawyers with at least an equal number of support staff (secretaries, paralegals, computer operators, etc.), they often have to occupy several floors of a building. The entrance to the firm typically admits one to a large reception area where an attractive individual directs clients to the proper attorney. If a client's attorney is temporarily occupied, he or she is directed to the waiting room adjacent to the reception area. This is an impressive room filled with elegant yet comfortable furniture. A wide array of reading material is made available. If the firm occupies several floors, the myriad of offices are linked together by a complex of stairways and a maze of hallways. In addition to the numerous offices, the firm usually maintains a substantial law library, imposing conference rooms, and increasingly larger duplicating and computer facilities.

As might be expected, the office space is allocated on the basis of status, with senior partners meriting the largest rooms with the most favorable views. Younger members have the smallest offices, with the more senior associates being bestowed the privilege of having their own secretary rather than being dependent on the central secretarial pool. The beginning associate is often placed in a large room (the "bull pen") with several other attorneys and may spend the first year in these undistinguished communal quarters. Irwin Smigel's classic study of the Wall Street lawyer describes the distribution of offices in the following terms: "It is allocated on the basis of custom and status. The size, location, and decor of a room become to a law firm what generals' stars and sergeants' stripes are to the army. They are symbols of status; they tell the newcomer how to behave; they make relationships easier because they provide clues to status. They also are rewards for service and success."[15]

The Law Firm Work Group

A large law firm is similar to a military force with clearly delinated lines of power, its organizational chart resembling a pyramid with lines of authority flowing down from the senior partners at the narrow pinnacle through junior partners, permanent associates, senior associates, junior associates, paralegals, and finally the secretaries and other support staff at the broad base. Each member of the law firm's work group will now be described, moving in ascending order from the base up toward the senior partners at the apex.

Legal secretaries and support staff often earn higher incomes than their functional equivalents in nonlegal positions, but most feel that the constant pressure, obsessive attention to detail, and total subservience to the whims of their employer more than justify their wages. Although many lawyers may boast of the loyalty and longevity of a particular secretary or other support person, in reality there is a frustratingly high turnover rate as might be expected by the rather difficult working conditions. Inadequate and incompetent secretarial help is one of the most frequently heard complaints from most members of a law firm. The office manager, who is responsible for the day-to-day administrative concerns of the firm, is constantly in search of new secretaries to satisfy his or her demanding and disgruntled employer. Most secretaries leave because they believe they are inadequately paid given the demands of the job. One lawyer recently admitted the disruptive effect caused by the firm's unwillingness to pay another $5 a week: "That's absolutely insane. There's such a disruption when you lose a secretary. We can lose damn near that person's salary in billing time by just not having a good secretary."[16]

Nearly every large firm employs an office manager to ensure that all phases of the nonprofessional operation of the firm run smoothly. Although the office manager may not be a lawyer, she or he does have some power over lawyers, especially the younger associates. Smigel points out that in several of the firms he studied the office manager doubles as the managing clerk and can give the beginning associates their assignments.[17] He or she is, however, on a rather short leash since the office manager's authority is directly controlled by the executive committee of the firm. The office manager is therefore given those "housekeeping functions" with which most lawyers do not wish to be bothered. Whatever power he or she does possess is related to control over certain quality-of-life issues that can make an attorney's professional existence more comfortable. Decisions over who receives the talented new secretary or the intelligent paralegal or even mundane decisions related to the distribution of office furnishings, equipment, and supplies can give the office manager the upper hand in dealing with the associate staff. Conflicts are resolved by reporting the difficulty to the managing partner or the firm's executive committee, and these senior attorneys always have the final say.

Within the past decade a new group of specialists have been added to the law firm's work group. These are the paralegals, who are usually college graduates who have attended six-month or one-year paralegal institutes where they have received extensive training in conducting legal research. Paralegals fall into two general categories: legal advocate and legal assistant. Legal advocates are usually found in either a legal clinic or legal services agency. They work independently of the lawyer, consulting directly with clients and client groups, providing representation for clients at administrative hearings at those agencies that authorize lay representation.[18] Legal assistants, on the other hand, are found in private law firms and work closely with and under the supervision of an attorney, providing cases for litigation, working on technical problems, analyzing and documenting facts, and researching legal issues.

Early in the development of the paralegal worker, it was hypothesized by some that these intelligent, trained paraprofessionals could be used in law firms to replace junior associates, especially in the performance of nonlegal chores previously delegated to them. This has not occurred since associates are in possession of a three-year legal education and are designated for possible partner status if they prove successful during their highly competitive trial run. Additionally, many paralegals view their jobs as only temporary way stations before deciding exactly what they really wish to do with their lives. Many paralegals use the experience to determine if they should pursue a career in the law. Contributing to the disillusionment of the paralegal's existence and the brevity of his or her career is the tedious nature of the responsibilities involved. As one disappointed paralegal disclosed to journalist Paul Hoffman in his survey of Wall Street firms: "As for the work, it's a lot of garbage—compiling bound volumes, the permanent collection of documents in each case; digesting testimony; culling through corporate files for relevant documents—nothing that requires great talent. If we're doing nothing we're sent to accounting or proofreading."[19]

Just above the support staff and paralegals are the associates. These are the youngest members of the firm who hope to impress the managing partners and eventually be offered a partnership position. They typically must remain in this tentative and rather insecure associate position for five to ten years before a decision is rendered. Associates are a clearly distinguishable class of lawyers within the firm because they are paid an annual salary, they can be fired, they do not participate in the management of the firm, and do not share directly in its profits and losses. They often characterize themselves as lackeys and wage slaves, but the possibility of achieving partnership is an enticement that has drawn them eagerly into the competition. An initial inducement into becoming an associate in a large firm is the impressive starting salary. Currently (1988) law school graduates joining the top New York firms can expect starting wages in the range of $75,000–$82,000 a year. Even in less affluent cities, large firms now pay $50,000 a year and more to 25-year-old lawyers fresh out of law school. Despite the high wages and the potential for even greater wealth if partnership status is achieved, the professional life of an associate is filled with uncertainty and trepidation. The core of the problem is the realization among each new group of associates hired by a firm that only a limited number of them will eventually be offered a partnership. Current estimates indicate that only one out of every four associates hired will survive the competition and receive a partnership offer. Given the high qualifications necessary to even be selected as an associate, the amount of work and brains necessary to successfully gain partnership is both mind-boggling and frightening. Eighty-hour workweeks, ceaseless attention to detail, continual subservience to the whims of insensitive and sometimes tyrannical partners soon take their toll on all but the strongest candidates. The abysmal treatment has often resulted in many competent young attorneys dropping out of the competition, forcing many large firms to realize that retention of quality associates is a serious problem. David Bradlow, describing the changing legal environment of the 1980s, identifies retention as a critical issue and comments that "compensation is not enough: law firm associates are often susceptible to problems of low morale and alienation. The best way to counter this is for supervising attorneys to take a personal interest in the careers of the younger members; giving praise for a job well done, and constructive, non-threatening criticism when there is room for improvement. Unfortunately these fundamentals of human interaction are more observed in the breach than in the observance, and at great cost."[20]

The discussion in Chapter 1 indicated the inadequate preparation most students receive in law schools in terms of lawyering skills. Thus, law firms must play a special role in educating their young associates. This is usually accomplished through a "mentoring" system in which the associate serves a type of quasi-apprenticeship with a specific partner who assists the associate in skill development and professional socialization. This includes not only training in substantive areas of the law but also includes training in the use of office routines and forms. Initially the associate is placed under the intensive supervision of one of the senior partners who will assign specific tasks. First assignments are typically research projects that require work reminiscent of law school seminars. Preparing memoranda on increasingly more challenging subjects will continue at whatever pace the associate appears capable of mastering, tempered by the experience and demands of the mentor. The objective at the end of a successful apprenticeship is for the associate to have developed into a reliable and productive colleague. Eve Spangler reports that once the associate has passed beyond the apprenticeship stage "supervision is converted into consultation" and they "begin to work with increased autonomy . . . handling small matters on their own. . . . Eventually they become members of the teams handling the largest and most sophisticated deals and cases in the office—When this happens in an orderly progression, associates can expect to be made partners."[21]

It should be noted that there are status differences among associates as they fall within a rather well-defined hierarchy. Erwin Smigel divides associates into permanent, senior, middle, and junior levels. The permanent ones are further subdivided into two categories: "those with relatively high status in the firm and those who are regarded as failures."[22] The first group is composed of lawyers who have been denied partnership for some reason unrelated to their lawyering skills but are retained by the firm because of some special competence and are given secure, well-paid positions. The "failures" are used to do routine work and are often simply biding time until they can obtain a position with another firm. They are barely a step above the paralegals in terms of status and are in a rather shaky position in terms of continued employment. Senior, middle, and junior associates can be categorized mainly on the basis of length of time with the firm.

The final group of participants in the large corporate firm are the partners who manage and control its operation. Probably the most important responsibility reserved to the partners is the dividing up of the profits at the end of the year. This process, usually controlled by the senior partners or some type of executive committee, is termed "hacking the pie." After subtracting the operating expenses (such as the rent of the office space and the annual salaries of associates and support staff) from the gross income generated from the billing of clients, the remaining profits must then be divided among the partners. Tough decisions over the relative worth of each partner are debated late into the night as the executive committee or managing partners must weigh each lawyer's value to the firm. Complicating these difficult decisions is the varying ways in which a partner can prove valuable to the firm. Some partners, nicknamed "rainmakers," specialize in being able to attract new clients. Their abilities may be more evident on the golf course or squash court than in the courtroom. Other partners may be effective litigators or brilliant drafters of documents. Some may even be invaluable in helping manage the firm, training associates, or mastering some narrow area of the law demanded by one important client. Ranking the relative worth of all of these highly diverse skills is a perplexing job that junior partners must simply delegate to their more experienced seniors and hope for a fair distribution. Eventually, if they stay with the firm, and continue to maintain the respect of their colleagues, the younger partners will eventually be elevated to the executive or managing committee and be able to directly influence these crucial salary decisions.

In contrast to the associates who are engaged in a continuing struggle to gain partnership, the partners are able to operate with a significant amount of autonomy. Eve Spangler clarifies this prized independence by writing: "As long as partners bring money into the firm, they enjoy enormous freedom in almost all aspects of work: client selection, case staffing, scheduling, billing, travel, continuing legal education."[23] Of course, simply becoming a partner does not mean the end of pressure, long hours, and many of the other frustrations that may have plagued the corporate attorney from the time he or she joined the firm. The same drive that powered the successful lawyer through the apprenticeship will continue to spark his or her performance as a partner. Conflict and friction with colleagues over the proper share of the pie and competition for representing the firm's more prestigious clients will most likely continue throughout a lawyer's professional career. Additionally, pressure from clients who have their own priorities and deadlines can also contribute to the tension-filled career of these attorneys. One junior partner in a large New England firm recently described these client-generated pressures in the following statement: "I've had the experience when I've had two deals that had to be done by Friday, and even if I stay here 'round the clock,' I can only get to so much of each of these deals. You could work at this firm every night and every weekend and never run out of work."[24]

Just as the associates can be subdivided into several categories, falling into a definite pecking order, partners may also be classified into several hierarchical groups. At the bottom are the junior partners who have recently been elevated to their esteemed position. Although they share in the firm's profits, they usually have no voice in deciding how the money is to be distributed. At the next level are the senior partners who often have a voice in determining the formula for salary allocations and may be called upon to make capital contributions to the firm. Martin Mayer in his popular book on the legal profession offers the following stylized description of a typical senior partner:

> He spends several hours each day on the telephone and takes most of the rest of the information he needs from pieces of paper. He is never in a trial court. . . . He rarely gathers information himself; though he browses advance sheets . . . his time is too precious to be wasted by close study of the kind done in a library and it is of course out of the question that he should ever interrogate anyone below a policy-making level in a client organization. Every once in a while an old client may have a personal problem which the senior partner will explore personally, otherwise his information is largely the product of staff work.[25]

At the apex of the partners group may be a managing or executive committee that in the larger firms is assisted by a managing partner. Depending on the size of the firm, this managing partner may devote one-fourth of all of his or her time to firm management. Responsibilities of a managing partner may include making decisions in the areas outlined in the following list:

1. Development and implementation of the strategic plan.
2. The marketing plan, including defining the service line, target markets, and communication program.
3. The number of attorneys and the ratio of associates to partners.
4. The recruitment and training program for associates.
5. Departmental structure and the selection of department heads.
6. Billing and collection procedures.
7. Establishing and maintaining quality controls.
8. Level of automation.[26]

The firm's executive committee, which typically consists of five to ten of the most respected senior partners, is charged generally with preparing reports designed to guide the entire firm. This elite group meets once or twice a month to ponder broad policy issues affecting the firm such as expansion of branch offices, possible merger with smaller firms, and future hiring policies. Although some firms may still be controlled and directed by a handful of powerful senior partners, it is much more common today to utilize some type of executive committee to act as an overseer for the firm and settle critical matters and disputes.

Unique Characteristics

This concluding section on large corporate law firms will briefly review their unique characteristics, noting how the current legal environment may be modifying their traditional features. The first characteristic is their hierarchical structure, usually pyramid in shape with a plethora of associates at the base and a select group of senior partners controlling the action from the apex. Smigel adds that the top of the pyramid may also be "divided vertically into departments based on various important legal specialties or by clients and finally around the 'Big Case.'"[27]

Robert Nelson, who has just completed a major reanalysis of large firms, argues that Smigel's work is gradually slipping out of date as large law firms are evolving from a traditional to a more bureaucratic organization. Nelson finds both the impetus and the paradigm for this transformation in the modern corporation and its legal needs. He writes that "routine corporate matters were taken over by inside counsel, forcing law firms to move into more novel areas of specialization. Also the firm's relationship with its corporate clients changed from a continuous broad-ranging coverage to a series of ad hoc, case by case relationships between one corporation and several law firms. The rise of the role of internal counsel (corporate legal departments) has been credited with causing this shift in control over legal affairs from the law firm to the corporation."[28]

A second unique feature of large corporate firms, especially as a reaction to contemporary economic pressures, is the movement toward specialization. Also related to the increasing role of in-house counsel in corporations, specialized services that cannot be matched by legal departments is the optimal strategy for economic survival. Although firms have traditionally used specialization as a tool for achieving increased efficiency, it is imperative that large firms today be able to provide full service to clients faced with an expanding range of complicated problems. Another current trend related to the drive for specialization is the increased acquisition and merger offers from large firms to highly specialized well-positioned smaller firms.

The third feature, the manic pursuit of partnership by overworked associates, is a characteristic that has been present in large law firms for many years and is likely to only become more frenetic. It is somewhat ironic that the highly seductive starting salaries, which now top $75,000 a year with Wall Street firms, are being blamed for contributing to the financial decline of these same firms who must then be even more prudent in whom they admit into partnership five to ten years into the future. Thus, the spiraling costs of these attractive salaries will only serve to drive up the already intense competition for the declining number of partnership vacancies. Related to this greater caution in signing on associates for lifetime partnership tenure are two interesting trends that may help in circumventing these difficult decisions. First has been the perceptible movement among many large firms to retain growing numbers of attorneys as "permanent associates" rather than be forced into an "up-or-out" decision regarding partnership. Law firms have attempted to implement a permanent associate program by guaranteeing greater security and higher salaries to these young lawyers. In a way it is a benefit for attorneys who do not wish to leave a prestigious law firm to remain in its employ, despite the likelihood that they would never have been offered a partnership.

The second trend is toward increased "lateral hiring." This means that firms are more willing today to offer partnership status and a respectable share of the profits to experienced attorneys from other firms. This policy represents a radical shift from the traditional view (first developed at Sullivan and Cromwell at the turn of the century) that all promotions are to be internal, and no one is to be brought into the "law firm family" from the outside. Proponents of lateral hiring argue that it is better to go after a proven attorney whose area of specialization will be of great assistance to a firm, either replacing someone, or indicating a shift by the firm into a new area of expertise.

There are many books and articles written advising the young attorney on how best to pursue partnership. Most agree that the successful candidate must first be able to prove he or she can handle the work. Second, the associate must not only fit in with the firm but, even more critically, show that he or she can get along with the clients. The third, and often characterized as the most effective strategy since so many associates seem capable of satisfying the first two, is for the young lawyer to hook up with a prominent member of the firm who will become a "rabbi" or mentor. Inevitably, the other senior partners will observe the trust bestowed upon the associate by one of their respected colleagues and will likewise begin to form a positive opinion. It is almost a case of "greatness by association." Paul Hoffman, in his account of life in the Wall Street firms, adds a fourth element to the equation that unfortunately may be out of the associate's control. This is simply "the luck factor," which Hoffman describes in the following comment: "Finally there's the element of luck. A new associate may have the ill-fortune to get assigned to doing a routine research or to a dead-end case where he never gets a chance to demonstrate his abilities and attract the attention of an influential partner. He may get caught up in a mammoth antitrust action only to find that the firm has no place for him once the case is concluded. . . . The luck can run the other way—and a smart associate can angle the odds in his favor."[29]

The fourth, and final, unusual feature of large firms is their ability to maintain branch offices, not only around the nation but more recently expanding into foreign marketplaces. Ever since the New Deal many Wall Street firms began to operate branches in Washington, D.C., as a courtesy to their clients who were becoming increasingly affected by federal legislation. By the 1950s Joseph Goulden reported in his book, *The Superlawyers,* that such firms as Mudge, Rose found it an economic necessity to maintain a D.C. branch.[30] The trend has continued although many large firms fear that the branches may begin to develop a life of their own and and eventually split off from the parent, taking clients with them.[31] Nevertheless, a recent survey in the *National Law Journal* finds the trend toward expansion still growing. Figure 3.1 offers visual

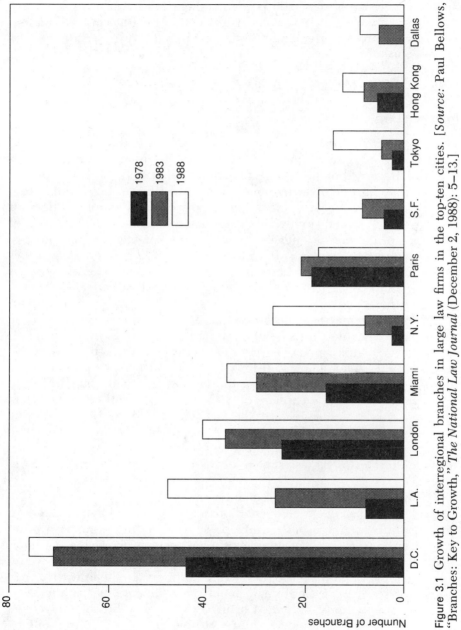

Figure 3.1 Growth of interregional branches in large law firms in the top-ten cities. [*Source:* Paul Bellows, "Branches: Key to Growth," *The National Law Journal* (December 2, 1988): 5–13.]

evidence of this growth in interregional branches as the number of branch offices of the largest firms has jumped in ten years from 295 to 899—an increase of over 200 percent. The article also documents the spread of branches into various world capitals with Tokyo, London, Paris, and Cairo experiencing the greatest popularity.[32]

THE SOLO PRACTITIONER

Introduction

At the opposite extreme from the imposing offices of the large corporate firms is the solo practitioner, whose modest accommodations stand in sharp contrast. Although the public may still believe that the solo practitioner occupies a noteworthy position in the American legal profession, empirical studies depict a beleaguered and steadily declining collection of attorneys. National surveys indicate that approximately 20 percent of the legal profession is engaged in individual practice. Since most of those solitary practices reside in small or midsized communities, it is in the large urban areas where the percentage of solo practitioners has declined most precipitously. Young lawyers have clearly decided to join midsized firms, governmental agencies, and corporation legal departments instead of pursuing an individual practice. Contrasting the urban and small-town solo practitioners, the larger the city the greater likelihood of a specialized practice in such areas as family, negligence, criminal, and real estate. The small-town lawyer appears to continue to be more of a generalist, representing individuals in a wide range of legal problems. This may be explained by the paucity of fellow attorneys in the more rural areas, especially the absence of midsized firms offering a specialized practice. If a complex case does arise, the small-town solo practitioner often seeks out a larger firm in the region who can provide the technical assistance necessary for competent representation.

It was noted earlier in the chapter that solo practitioners represent individuals and an occasional small business in contrast to organizations and institutions that usually are represented by the larger law firms. Whatever type of legal problem faces middle-class Americans, it is most likely that they will be represented by an individual attorney. The most common areas of law covered by solo practitioners are the following: real estate, personal injury, criminal, bankruptcy, divorce, wills, and basic business transactions. Jerome Carlin adds another broad area of endeavor that is of a quasi-legal nature. He found that his sample of Chicago practitioners devoted a large amount of time to what he termed "brokerage activities." Carlin described these endeavors as being a middleman between a client and other lawyers. Because of the solo practitioner's narrow area of expertise and deference to more competent specialists, Carlin notes that this referral system is inevitable and unfortunately quite expensive for the client.[33]

Physical Description

Just as Tom Wolfe provided an excellent description of the impressive offices of a large Wall Street firm, his novel *Bonfire of the Vanities* also provides a wonderful portrait of the law offices of a modestly successful solo practitioner: "On the 4th floor of an old cast iron building, Sherman walked down a corridor with a dingy tile floor. . . . Sherman opened the door and found himself in a tiny and surprisingly bright glassed in vestibule tended by a Latin woman who sat behind a glass partition. A glass door led to a larger even brighter space with white walls. The lights overhead were so strong Sherman kept his head down. Just ahead, on the floor, he could make out a couch. The base was made of white formica. Pale tan leather cushions were on top of it. Sherman sat down and his tailbone immediately slid forward."[34]

Although not wishing comparison to the eloquent description just offered by Mr. Wolfe, I would like to add my observations of the solo practitioner's working environment. The following description was part of my national study of private criminal lawyers, the large majority of which were solo practitioners:

Just as the income levels of the criminal lawyers varied greatly so did their offices. At the meager end of the spectrum were one-room offices in rundown buildings. There would be a noticeably absent secretary, and the office would be locked when the lawyer was in court. An answering service would be utilized to record phone calls. At the opposite end of the continuum were the opulent offices, lavishly furnished, and located in splashy new highrises on prestigious avenues such as Wilshire Boulevard in Los Angeles. . . . The typical office had a secretary who greeted the visitor as he stepped off the elevator or entered the office. There would be a small wood-paneled waiting room with enough modern furniture to seat three or four clients. Behind the receptionist would be a typing pool of two or three secretaries. Once admitted to the inner sanctum, one would find three to four individual offices and a small law library with an even smaller supply room dominated by a coffee-making device. Brown would be the predominant color in nearly every office with blue being a distant second. The lawyer's office would have an impressive desk, functionally designed. There would usually be a sofa in the background which never seemed to be used and two or three chairs for clients, strategically placed around the lawyers' desk. It was interesting to note that most lawyers took great care in how their offices were decorated and even devised certain strategies geared toward maximizing their client relationships. One New Orleans lawyer stated that he made it a point not to display any academic degrees and forced his partners to do the same. His reasoning was the degrees frequently intimidated the clients and made them uneasy. By replacing these symbols of academic achievement with happy, warm paintings, he thought he could more readily break down the wall between client and lawyer. Another strategy was noted by a Philadelphian, who had the lowest chairs and tables in any of the offices visited. With soft lighting and beige and bone-colored rugs and furniture, the visitor was almost put to sleep. He thought that by relaxing and soothing the client, he would have the best chance of developing an open working relationship.[35]

Advantages and Disadvantages of Solo Practice

Being a solo practitioner provides many unique opportunities and advantages but also contains many serious limitations. Turning first to the positive attributes, the most frequently stated advantage is the great freedom. You are able to control your work pace, select your clients, and make all decisions without deference to anyone else's preferences outside of your own. Many solo practitioners started their legal careers in law firms or bureaucratic agencies and obviously bridled over the numerous constraints inherent in such institutions. Certain types of individuals temperamentally are not suited to following orders and therefore gladly choose private practice, regardless of whatever financial consequences may ensue (and they usually do experience a loss of revenue).

Solo practitioners I have interviewed added other advantages that also contrasted with the professional life in a law firm. They usually enjoyed representing individuals rather than institutions and described themselves as "more person-oriented." They also disliked long involvement in a handful of complex cases, preferring instead a wider variety of short-term cases that could be clearly resolved in a few weeks or months. One also had the feeling that they thought they were capable of providing a service to the local community by assisting in the legal woes of their clients. Large firms do engage in limited pro bono work, but one rarely senses a concern for local problems since many of their clients may come from distant and varied regions of the country.

Beyond the inevitable absence of wealthy clients, there are several additional disadvantages facing the individual practitioner. One practical problem is the limitation on the types of cases and clients. Complex antitrust matters, corporate mergers, and other cases involving large financial institutions and private corporations cannot be satisfactorily handled by a single attorney. Even cases in which the solo practitioner is defending an individual against some powerful economic concern such as a bank or insurance company, there are serious difficulties in being able to provide competent legal assistance. Facing an adversary represented by a large law firm means tackling a team of talented specialists who are probably backed by expert witnesses, the latest technical resources, and a diverse range of support services. Although some attorneys enjoy romanticizing these David and Goliath confrontations, the odds may be so stacked against the solo practitioner that he or she cannot in good conscience believe that he or she has a chance for victory. Certain types of cases may simply not be within the province of most solo practitioners. Also, resources such as an extensive law library, fax machines, and the latest in computer services are the kinds of operating costs easily absorbed by large firms but usually beyond the financial capabilities of most individual attorneys.

Carlin also noted another difficulty facing solo practitioners that he terms "lay competitors." He writes that "practically all areas of practice—but principally in the real estate, business, and will-probate-estate fields—certain institutions or occupational groups perform critical functions with regard to the various matters or transactions involved."[36] Banks are one example of prominent institutions that have recently become involved in a variety of areas, such as probate, which were formerly reserved for attorneys.

One final disadvantage relates to the logistical problem of being the isolated representative of the client. In essence, the solo practitioner is like a doctor on 24-hour call; whenever a client may need advice he or she believes the attorney should be available. Obviously, also like a physician, a solo practitioner can occasionally have another lawyer cover for him or her (e.g., for a two-week summer vacation). However, like the doctor and patient, the lawyer must convince the client that he or she can be counted upon whenever an emergency occurs. If this hand-holding security-blanket type of service is not provided, the solo practitioner may be faced with the loss of a client.

THE ORGANIZED BAR AND PROFESSIONAL ASSOCIATIONS

Many lawyers, especially those associated with large law firms, expend a significant amount of energy as members of state, local, and national bar associations. The major national organization for the legal profession is the American Bar Association. There are also 50 state bar associations as well as a large number of local groups. Additionally, lawyers may join organizations limited to special fields of law such as the Trial Lawyers Association. These professional associations are not social groups (although they do hold conventions that contain social affairs as part of the festivities). They are instead committed to improving the performance and image of the legal profession. Therefore, the concluding portion of this chapter will briefly discuss the functions and performance of these professional organizations serving the American bar. Since the ABA, as the preeminent national organization for attorneys, so overshadows its state and local counterparts and plays such a major role in judicial selection and the development of ethical codes, this brief analysis will concentrate primarily on this group.

Historical Development

Organizing American lawyers has not been an easy task. Although there were clamorings throughout the eighteenth and nineteenth centuries by members of the bar to develop improved educational standards, tighten admission requirements, and develop workable disciplinary standards and procedures, it was not until the 1870s that the first coherent efforts to organize American lawyers were initiated. Harry Stumpf reports that the first local effort occurred in February of 1870 when a group of New York lawyers calling themselves "the decent part of the profession" met to form the Association of the Bar of the City of New York, and the movement to organize soon spread across the country.[37] Eight years later 75 lawyers met in Saratoga, New York, to form the American Bar Association. However, its growth was slow, and by 1900 it appeared to be little more than a tight-knit social circle, comprised of only a handful of elite lawyers from corporate firms.

From the beginning the ABA maintained a consistently conservative bias, appropriately reflecting the ideology of both its white upperclass membership as well as its financially successful clients. Professor Edward Corwin caustically describes the organization as growing out of the ashes of the *Munn* v. *Illinois* decision and soon becoming "a sort of juristic sewing circle for mutual education in the gospel of laissez-faire."[38] The ABA's persistent criticism of liberal government policies and its tampering with the economy began with a series of attacks on the Sherman Antitrust Act during the early 1920s and reached its peak during Franklin Roosevelt's New Deal, when the entire package of reform legislation was aggressively attacked.

During the past 25 years, the ABA has appeared to mellow, being less strident in its conservatism and more willing to assume moderate positions on many issues, presenting a more cautious and carefully reasoned response. This development is probably due to the continued increase in membership, which now exceeds 300,000, representing nearly half of the entire profession. With such a large and diverse membership, the reflexive social Darwinists of earlier generations who formulated ABA policy are in a minority, and the association has been significantly democratized. It should be noted, however, that these ideological changes are of fairly recent vintage. The association was not even willing to admit blacks into its membership until 1956!

Lack of Representation

Beyond the just noted regrettable history of racism, the ABA has faced complaints from much larger sections of the bar, charging that the association fails to adequately represent the entire profession. The leadership of the ABA, which controls its politics and vocalizes its directives, is dominated by representatives from elitist law firms who represent the financial institutions of this nation. Government attorneys, solo practitioners, law professors, and many more progressive or liberal-thinking attorneys are either not members of the ABA or are not part of its ruling hegemony. The research of John Heinz and Terrence Halliday clearly shows how the deep-rooted division between the ABA leadership and large groups of disgruntled attorneys merely reflects the continuing chasm within the profession. Historian Jerrold Auerbach places the legal profession's fragmentation within the context of our society's broader development. He endorses Karl Llewellyn's still valid assessment that "the best talent of the bar will always muster to keep Ins in and to man the barricades against the Outs."[39] Auerbach goes on to blame the adversary system as providing an easy means for guaranteeing the continued dominance of the more powerful law firms who also control the direction of the ABA. He explains how the Darwinian model is not so fairly applied to the legal process because "the adversary process was hardly value free when access to counsel was determined by wealth or when the interests of those likely to be affected by the outcome of negotiation or litigation were unrepresented in the neat two-sides division of adversary proceedings."[40]

It is obvious that the ABA is more than a trade association for lawyers. It clearly represents the interests of certain types of lawyers: typically those from large firms who represent major financial institutions. Mark Green, working with the Ralph Nader Study Group on the Legal Profession, describes how the association's policies are closely related to the economic interests and political preferences of its leadership and their clients in the following quote: "It will take up issues like presidential succession, firearms control or even marijuana but not the distribution of wealth and income or the high cost of lawyers. It spends untold hours attacking a handful of disruptive lawyers but fails to study the dilatory tactics of big corporate firms."[41]

For the large number of attorneys who do not feel adequately represented by the ABA and are in sharp disagreement with many of its policy positions, they have been unable to create and sustain a viable rival organization at the national level. The National Lawyers Guild comes closest to espousing a minority viewpoint, but it does not possess the numerical strength to offer a challenge. There have also been national organizations for particular types of attorneys who have been historically unrepresented by the ABA such as women and blacks, but the narrowness of their constituency prevents them from evolving into a broad-based alternative.

There have been instances, however, at the local level where a rival bar group can successfully challenge an older, more traditional association. The Chicago Council of Lawyers, which was founded in 1969 and grew out of the social ferment of the 1960s, is a good example. Michael Powell recently described its evolution "as a reformist group with a small and relatively homogeneous membership, and lacking strong ties to powerful institutions. . . . By aggressively supporting positions at odds with those of the more established bar associations and thus providing the media, the public, and legislators with an alternative viewpoint, the Council contributes to shattering the myth of a unified profession and to the demystification of professional authority."[42]

Major Functions of the Organized Bar

The organized bar performs many important tasks beyond the social interaction at annual conventions and the issuance of periodic policy statements from its leaders directed to both the profession and the public. The most important task bestowed upon the bar may be its role in the selection of judges. Whether this is done formally by a committee on judicial qualifications as is used by the federal government or less formalized pronouncements at the local level where certain candidates are endorsed by the organized bar, it can play a critical role in the judicial selection process. (Chapter 8 offers a more detailed description and analysis of this process and the impact of the organized bar.)

A second area of responsibility, also of considerable importance, is the role of the organized bar in developing and implementing codes of professional behavior. The ability of the legal profession to control and discipline its membership has become of increasing concern to the public as the instances of professional misconduct appear to be growing. The current disciplinary proceedings have been loudly criticized both because of the infrequency of their use and the rather blatant class bias inherent in their proscriptions. The Nader and Green report concluded that the bar association disciplinary proceedings have been an embarrassment and near total failure. In 1972 they discovered that only 357 lawyers across the entire country had been disciplined during that 12-month period. This penalized group represented less than 0.01 percent of the nation's 380,000 lawyers (practicing in 1972). They also found that less than one complaint in 100 results in any penalty.[43]

Turning to the second criticism, several commentators have pointed to the rather obvious we/they mentality inherent in the codes of behavior. It is apparent that the senior members of major law firms have dictated to the rest of the profession, especially the less fortunate members of the metropolitan bar, what should be the standards for acceptable professional behavior. Historian Auerbach describes the class-conscious bias of bar association ethical codes in the following quote: "A cluster of canons pertaining to acquiring an interest in litigation, stirring up litigation, and division of fees, almost exclusively effecting the activities of struggling metropolitan solo lawyers. They did not apply to the conduct of firm members or securely established practitioners who formulated them."[44] The ABA has been sensitive to these types of criticisms and adopted a new Code of Professional Responsibility in 1969, but despite the more modern style, it still emphasized the same issues as the older canons.

The organized bar has also been active in two other important areas of professional concern: regulating the requirements for entrance into the profession and providing for the necessary continuing education of lawyers throughout their careers. Although the power to control admissions into the profession originated as a public concern, by the early 1920s with the steady growth of the organized bar, it slowly evolved into a bar association prerogative as various requirements were imposed. In 1921 the ABA required at least two years of college and a three-year law degree prior to taking a bar exam. By 1978, 36 states were requiring a bar applicant to be a graduate of an ABA-approved law school. The control over the bar exam itself, the final hurdle, has been placed in the hands of the National Board of Examiners, thereby removing any taint of bar association interference and hopefully ensuring the desired aura of objective professionalism. Each state presently maintains fairly close public regulation of its own bar examination. Howard Abadinsky describes the typical bar examination as having "twenty to thirty questions requiring the candidate to analyze hypothetical cases and set forth proposed solutions and the applicable laws. The exam usually lasts two or three days."[45]

NOTES

1. John Flood, *The Legal Profession in the U.S.* (Chicago: American Bar Foundation, 1985), 10.
2. James B. Stewart, *Partners* (New York: Simon and Schuster, 1983), 14.
3. *Report of the Task Force on the Role of the Lawyer in the 1980's* (Chicago: American Bar Association, 1981), p. 5.
4. Stewart, *Partners*, 15.
5. ABA Special Committee on the Delivery of Legal Services, *Legal Clinics: Merely Advertising Law Firms* (Chicago: American Bar Association, 1981), 48.
6. Flood, *Legal Profession*, 16.
7. Jerome Carlin, *Lawyers on Their Own* (New Brunswick, N.J.: Rutgers University Press, 1962), 168.
8. Paul Wice, *Criminal Lawyers* (Beverly Hills, Calif.: Sage Publications, 1978), 219.
9. John Heinz and Terrence Halliday, "Diversity, Representation and Leadership in an Urban Bar," *American Bar Foundation Research Journal* (1976): 717.
10. "A New Corporate Power Base—The Legal Department," *Business Week*, 9 April 1984, 66.
11. Eve Spangler, *Lawyers for Hire* (New Haven: Yale University Press, 1986), 70.
12. Ibid. p. 71.
13. Ibid.
14. Tom Wolfe, *Bonfire of the Vanities* (New York: Farrar, Strauss, Giroux, 1987), 288.
15. Irwin Smigel, *The Wall Street Lawyer* (Bloomington, Ind.: Indiana University Press, 1973), 209.
16. Spangler, *Lawyers for Hire*, 50.

17. Smigel, *The Wall Street Lawyer*, 245.
18. Helen Brown, "The Paralegal Profession," *Howard Law Journal* 19 (1976): 117.
19. Paul Hoffman, *Lions in the Street* (New York: New American Library Signet, 1973), 134.
20. David Bradlow, "The Changing Legal Environment: The 1980's and Beyond," *American Bar Association Journal* (December 1, 1988): 73.
21. Spangler, *Lawyers for Hire*, 46.
22. Smigel, *The Wall Street Lawyer*, 230.
23. Spangler, *Lawyers for Hire*, 46.
24. Ibid. p. 41.
25. Martin Mayer, *The Lawyers* (New York: Harper & Row, 1966), 306.
26. Bradlow, "Changing Legal Environment," 76.
27. Smigel, *The Wall Street Lawyer*, 225.
28. Robert L. Nelson, *Partners with Power: The Transformation of the Large Law Firm* (Berkeley, Calif.: University of California Press, 1988), 8.
29. Hoffman, *Lions in the Street*, 130.
30. Joseph Goulden, *Superlawyer* (New York: Weybright and Talley, 1972), 242.
31. John Heinz and Edward Laumann, *Chicago Lawyers: The Social Structure of the Bar* (New York: Russell Sage Foundation, 1982), 370.
32. Paul Bellows, "Branches: Key to Growth," *National Law Journal* (December 2, 1988): S-13.
33. Carlin, *Lawyers on Their Own*, 208.
34. Wolfe, *Bonfire of the Vanities*, 380.
35. Wice, *Criminal Lawyers*, 130–131.
36. Carlin, *Lawyers on Their Own*, 142.
37. Harry Stumpf, *American Judicial Politics* (New York: Harcourt Brace, 1988), 256.
38. Mark Green, "The ABA as Trade Association," in *Verdicts on Lawyers*, ed. Ralph Nader and Mark Green (New York: Crowell, 1976), 4.
39. Jerrold Auerbach, *Unequal Justice* (New York: Oxford University Press, 1976), 307.
40. Ibid. p. 280.
41. Green, "ABA as Trade Association," 17.
42. Michael Powell, "Anatomy of a Counter-Bar Association: The Chicago Council of Lawyers," *American Bar Foundation Research Journal* (1979): 501.
43. Green, "ABA as Trade Association," 48.
44. Auerbach, *Unequal Justice*, 42.
45. Howard Abadinsky, *Law and Justice* (Chicago: Nelson-Hall, 1988), 66–67.

Chapter
4

The Art of Lawyering and Its Diversity

N ow that we have completed our description of the lawyer's working environment, what types of services does an attorney provide for his or her clients? In an effort to answer this basic question, this chapter will first describe the basic functions and services provided by the legal profession and conclude with an overview of several of the specialties that lawyers have developed. Although we have previously discussed the varying levels of status and prestige associated with each field of law, the emphasis here will be on the substantive aspects of each of the subfields. Let us now turn first to the four major functions performed by members of the legal profession.

MAJOR FUNCTIONS

Most students of the legal profession have agreed with Martin Mayer when he divides a lawyer's professional activities into four major functions: litigating, negotiating, drafting, and advising. This section will therefore be divided into these four categories in addition to a brief discussion of a small group of minor tasks that an attorney may on occasion also be required to perform.

Before moving on to a detailed examination of each of the four major functions of an attorney, it should be first noted that most lawyers believe their overriding professional activity is that of a problem solver. Based on the several hundred interviews I conducted with attorneys during the past 20 years, nearly all the lawyers deeply believed that their most important ability was their talent for unraveling a client's seemingly complex legal problem and ultimately being able to advise him or her on a reasonable course of action. This expertise is developed primarily through a lawyer's postgraduation professional experiences, although a unique law school education does provide a foundation. Whether the difficulty is economic, social, personal, governmental, or a combination of several areas, the lawyer takes pride in his or her capacity for cutting through the emotional and often barely relevant presentation of the client's problem and finally being able to succinctly state the legal issue and its possible ramifications. Maureen Cain describes this process as "translating" and also believes that it is the primary function of the attorney.[1] After sorting through the client's explanation of the problem, the lawyer must then "translate" this mass of information into legal terms, that is, boil down the client's dilemma into a definable legal issue. Once the attorney has calmed down the client and presented the essence of the legal problem, the lawyer can begin to analyze and advise the client.

James Freund, who has written several books attempting to demystify the American legal system and explain it to the layman in comprehensible terms, also believes that the lawyer's main task is to make sense out of a "sprawling and messy" justice system that appears chaotic and confusing. Freund finds the best lawyers to be those who are able to deal with this chaos and "who thrive on ambiguity."[2] If there is one critical attribute that the successful lawyer must possess in his or her frenetic professional life, Mark McCormack (another attorney/author attempting to explain the legal profession to the general public) believes it is an ability to perform with "grace under pressure."[3] McCormack concludes his treatise on the legal profession with a further elaboration on this point: "What allows skilled lawyers—and can allow all of us—to function under great duress is the ability to strike a balance between commitment and detachment."[4] The competent lawyer must be able to be a zealous advocate for a client's best interests, while at the same time be intellectually objective in evaluating the strength of a case. The ability to maintain this delicate balance in pressure-filled situations is what distinguishes the lawyer from nearly all other professions.

Why is the practice of law so messy and difficult? James Freund offers a convincing set of reasons in the following list:

1. Fact patterns are rarely clear-cut. Some facts point one way, some another; others just are not available and the lawyer must do without.
2. Things are rarely black and white; whether a statute has been violated, for example, is open to contradictory interpretations.
3. Deals are complex; every transaction has multiple facets to consider. Lawsuits are enormously complicated, with truckloads of documents, endless depositions, and hyperactive motion practice.

4. The practice of law is basically a people business. But people don't behave in predictable patterns. Motivations aren't always clear; communication may be lacking.[5]

It is true that much of a lawyer's practice may be fairly straightforward and repetitive in nature so that the previous depiction of the complexity and confusion of the lawyer's professional life might appear to be exaggerated. The uncontested divorce between a childless couple, the uncomplicated purchase of a home, or the simple construction of a will are typical legal problems facing most middle-class Americans. Nevertheless, the majority of a lawyer's time is spent in resolving the perplexing and upsetting legal problems that have just been described. Let us now turn to a more detailed examination of the major functions performed by lawyers as they attempt to deal with their client's challenging and diverse problems. It should be noted that although lawyers have become increasingly specialized in recent years, most attorneys are nevertheless still called upon to perform not just one, but a combination of tasks. Thus, the competent private criminal lawyer must not only be an effective litigator but also be able to shrewdly negotiate a plea settlement if the case merits such a resolution.

Litigating

It is ironic that the very skill the public most commonly associates with the art of lawyering is, in fact, the least utilized of the four major functions discussed in this chapter. Although litigation may allow the lawyer to present a wide range of lawyering skills such as piercing cross-examination of witnesses, persuasive argumentation, and perceptive selection of jurors, only a small percentage of lawyers, estimated to be between 10 and 20 percent, actually devote the majority of their time to litigation and are willing to describe themselves as trial attorneys or litigators.[6] The majority of attorneys in the United States almost never venture into a courtroom, other than to file a legal notice with a clerk of the court. The unexpected discrepancy between reality and the public's misperception is most likely due to the mass media's depiction of lawyers as primarily litigators. There is also a heightened public interest and concern in highly publicized cases that wind up in the courtroom, although approximately 90 percent of all civil and criminal suits are resolved through negotiation without any trial occurring.[7]

It is interesting to note that because of the increasing rarity of trials and the growing complexity of the laws and procedures affecting the processing and arguing of cases, litigation has evolved into a legal specialization in which only a few practitioners have excelled. In most law firms there are a designated group of attorneys who will handle the firm's litigation while the majority of the remaining attorneys develop substantive areas of expertise. Further, many litigators have narrowed themselves to trial work in specific areas of the law such as criminal, accident, or divorce. Martin Mayer in his comprehensive volume on the legal profession offers the following list of reasons why litigation has evolved into such a specialized activity, attracting declining numbers of young attorneys:

1. The rising costs of litigation make it an option for only the most affluent client.
2. Certain fertile sources of litigation have been either legislatively eliminated or radically altered, that is, no-fault auto insurance, no-fault divorce, and workmen's compensation.
3. The continued decline of the generalist attorney who is likely to be at increasing disadvantage against the litigation specialist with his or her vast experience and time-tested resources.
4. Fifty years ago a young attorney could make a mark based upon courtroom performance; but today academic credentials serve as the necessary prerequisites for entry into the nation's most prestigious law firms. Additionally, litigation skills are often unnecessary in serving the most important clients in these firms and therefore are no longer critical for career development such as achieving partnership status.[8]

The trial lawyer must not only possess skills related to a successful performance during the trial, but must also be able to operate effectively during the lengthy pretrial period. It is during the extended time prior to the actual trial that the litigator must exhibit skill in obtaining necessary information from witnesses through depositions and discovery. Additionally, trial lawyers must be able to maneuver their cases through various pretrial appearances and conferences where critical motions will be argued and a broad range of procedural requirements satisfied. Because of the diverse range of professional obligations, both before and during the trial, the effective litigator must combine a number of seemingly contradictory legal skills and personality traits that are rarely found in a single attorney. First, the trial attorney must be a convincing performer, able to sway both the judge and jury to his or her point of view. This may require an actor's temperament and a gift of self-deception, as well as polished communication skills and the ability to think quickly on one's feet. Many litigators believe that they must be able to convince a judge and/or jury of a strong commitment to their clients' positions because, as so many lawyers warn, "before one can set out to persuade others, you must convince yourself—you cannot very well keep your tongue in your cheek while you are talking."[9] Secondly, the litigator must be able to organize and retrieve massive amounts of information concerning the specific case. This requires the attorney to become an instant expert not only on his side of the dispute but also on the adversary's point of view. In his autobiography, *My Life in Court*, Louis Nizer describes in fascinating detail his complex filing system that, after countless hours of out-of-court preparation, allows him to effectively cross-examine hostile witnesses: "I prepare my cross-examination notes by writing out the questions on the left side of the page. On the right I fill in the exact answer that the witness has made previously at the examinations before trial. If he has given several versions, I write out each with a page reference to the examination minutes. If he has changed his testimony, I add his changed testimony in a different colored ink. When he testifies at the trial on direct exam I write in his latest answers to the same subject matter in still a different colored ink. . . . The result is a set of notes in red, blue, and green ink representing the witnesses' various answers in all their refinement."[10]

A third quality of a competent litigator is the ability to be both an aggressive and feared adversary while still being able to adroitly negotiate when necessary. By having established a reputation as an effective litigator, the trial attorney may best serve his or her client by negotiating from a position of strength, thereby achieving an exceptional monetary settlement in a personal injury case or a highly favorable plea bargain in a criminal matter.

All three of these demanding skills indicate that the competent litigator must not only be a convincing extrovert in the courtroom but must also possess extremely cerebral skills in preparation for a successful performance. Since most individuals are rarely able to combine such disparate skills of public and private competence, it is no wonder that the litigator is such a respected and unique member of the legal profession.

Negotiating

As previously noted, approximately 90 percent of both civil and criminal lawsuits are settled prior to trial. It is true that a successful litigator is often a successful negotiator since his or her reputation in the courtroom can serve to facilitate the settlement process. Nevertheless, negotiating requires its own unique blend of talents and tactics. McCormack defines the negotiating process broadly as involving "the mediation between competing interests, with an eye toward a mutually profitable, face-saving, and whenever possible, relationship-preserving result."[11] He characterizes negotiations as falling into three categories: cooperative, adversarial, and hostile. The cooperative negotiation occurs when both parties' interests are fairly similar, and it is understood that there is a mutual desire to resolve the matter. The negotiations, therefore, usually involve only emphasis and details, rather than basically contradictory perspectives. The difference between adversarial and hostile negotiations is both more subtle and more critical than the cooperative style. The best example of adversarial negotiations is the bargaining that goes on between labor and management. Although both sides are involved in a "zero sum game" where one side's loss is the other's gain, these still remain professional adversaries, not personal enemies, who are likely to need each other in the future if larger gains are to materialize for both sides. In those rare instances involving hostile negotiations, one side's rights have clearly been violated before negotiations begin, and a tough, nonconciliatory attitude is appropriate. Hostage negotiations offer a good example of this third category, which is typically a one-time confrontation.[12]

What combination of skills are required for an attorney to be an effective negotiator? One skill that is essential and is noted by most commentators on the subject is the lawyer's capacity to objectively evaluate the strengths and weaknesses of both his or her client's case and the adversary's position. This should permit a realistic determination of how much of a client's interests may be prudently surrendered in return for comparable concessions by the other side. A second skill is the necessary poise and assurance to convince an adversary of the strength and reasonableness of the client's position. This may mean the lawyer must resist certain ego-driven assumptions that only his or her own brilliance and clout can achieve the desired result. And closely related is the third trait of avoiding grandstanding histrionics designed to impress a client but that actually only serve as an impediment to the negotiations, and are likely to adversely effect a client's best interests in the long run.[13]

Tactics in negotiations are often described in terms of leverage. Like two boys balancing on a see-saw, neither one can exert his full weight or the ride will be over. One important tactical maneuver a good negotiator should employ that is noted by most experts is to always allow an opponent some room for saving face. Forcing an adversary into a corner will likely provoke an irrational response that will lead to a breakdown in negotiations. Freeman and Weihofen offer a concise group of tactical strategies that are relied upon by effective negotiators:

1. Give help to get help: logrolling.
2. Use ambiguity, uncertainty, silence, and delay.
3. Employ a "good lawyer–bad lawyer" team. The good lawyer gains empathy; the bad lawyer exercises the clout and insists on hard terms.
4. Start with or quickly surrender the peripheral items; small bargains show reasonableness.
5. Set up and control the agenda.
6. Make false demands, bluffs, threats; even use irrationality; but tactics are only means to an end. Never let the opponent take control.[14]

The successful negotiator has a wide choice of strategies to utilize, but if a settlement is to be achieved the attorneys on both sides must act selflessly and professionally, placing their clients' best interests above personal considerations. Because of the delicacy of the skills involved in successful negotiations as well as the extended periods of time involved in both preparation and actual discussions, it is not surprising to find negotiators among the most highly paid group of practitioners.[15]

Drafting

Most legal scholars believe that the lawyer's drafting function is the most intellectually challenging. By composing a document designed to stand the test of time, the legal draftsperson must consider every conceivable future contingency in order to provide a client with the desired protection. Like an insurance policy, the business contract, will, or prenuptial agreement must protect the client from future harm.

In contrast to litigating and negotiating, which require a lawyer to assist a client facing an immediate legal problem, the drafting of documents (and to a lesser extent the advising of clients) is a preventive skill. If successful, the documents drafted by the attorney will keep the client out of the courthouse. Mayer believes this skill has the greatest societal significance. He explains that "communal life in a modern society rests upon pieces of paper that tell people their rights, privileges, powers, and immunities, duties, liabilities and disabilities. When challenged, these pieces of paper—wills, trusts, agreements, mortgages, deeds, certificates of incorporation, leases, agreements to purchase or to sell, warrants and so forth—must stand up. The lawyer assures that they will."[16]

Mayer's description of the drafting function clearly indicates the lawyer's pivotal role in preserving the stability of our nation's economic life, at both the personal and corporate level. As governmental involvement has expanded into wider areas of public concern, lawyers have also been involved in the drafting of relevant legislation. Thus lawyers' drafting skills will be affecting both the public and private sectors of our society. How do lawyers provide competent service in so demanding an area of the law? Fortunately for most lawyers, the documents they are called upon to draft are frequently highly repetitive so that reliable forms have been developed that permit attorneys to simply fill in the details of the specific transaction on the applicable "boiler plate" format. Most wills, trusts, and real estate transactions fall into this rather predictable pattern, making them both simple and profitable exercises for most attorneys. Even the majority of commercial transactions have become routinized through adoption of the Uniform Commercial Code in all states.

Unfortunately, not all transactions are of this routine nature, and when large businesses engage in contractual negotiations, both sides will utilize large teams of attorneys specializing in the drafting of corporate mergers and other complex business dealings. The final product can be a document running hundreds of pages designed to cover every possible emergency. Before the contract is agreed upon by all parties, the careful preparation of the document, which typically involves a word-by-word analysis, can stretch to many thousands of billable hours for each of the law firms. Despite the costly expense, however, if the document can provide long-term security to all parties and thereby avoid future litigation, it is thought to be well worth the price.

How do lawyers successfully draft documents that prove secure and acceptable? Mark McCormack offers the following advice as a result of his experience drawing up documents for a large corporate law firm: try to keep the document concise, consistent, and simple. The real challenge, McCormack found, was to avoid the trap of excessive legalese and to try and accomplish the very difficult task of ensuring that the document would be both complete in its coverage of all contingencies while also being sufficiently clear so that all parties can easily comprehend the other's position.[17]

Counseling

Although attorneys may be required to advise clients during litigation and negotiation, it is primarily a preventive skill. Clients typically ask for an attorney's advice prior to engaging in questionable behavior. It is true that advice must still be provided after the fact, and legal repercussions leading to possible litigation may necessitate even more astute counsel, but the counseling function is still best categorized as a preventive measure. As our discussion of large law firms in Chapter 3 noted, the senior partners specialize in providing the counseling function. Important clients assume that the firm's senior partners, as the result of their lengthy and distinguished careers, are most likely to provide the type of sage advice desired.

This advice may not be cheap. As Joseph Goulden recounts in his book on the powerful world of the great Washington law firms, *The Superlawyers,* even the most cursory piece of advice can be extremely costly. Goulden offers the following anecdote involving "Superlawyer" Clark Clifford to illustrate the staggering cost of legal advice: "There is a story, perhaps apocryphal, of the corporation general counsel in the Midwest who asked Clifford what his company should do concerning certain tax legislation. After several weeks Clifford responded, 'Nothing,' and enclosed a bill for $20,000. Unaccustomed to the Clifford style, the general counsel testily wrote that for $20,000 he certainly was entitled to a more complete explanation of the recommendation. He got it. 'Because I said so,' Clifford said in letter two and billed the corporation for another $5,000."[18]

Although the Clark Clifford story is an extreme example, advice from senior partners can be expected to be not only costly but usually well worth the price when one considers the stakes involved in most large corporation business decisions. A reliance on a trusted attorney's acquiescence or rejection of a possible business endeavor can involve the possible loss of millions of dollars. Therefore, paying the lawyer a shockingly high five-figure fee for one or two lines of advice may not be so incomprehensible.

It should be noted that in many instances the advice being offered is not in the blunt, abbreviated form just noted in the Clark Clifford example. It is more common for the advice to be in the form of a lengthier, more detailed recommendation, the product of careful and hopefully exhaustive legal research. Additionally, most corporate clients whose business decisions often necessitate legal judgments usually hire law firms on a retainer basis, paying a handsome annual fee rather than paying for a series of ad hoc and very expensive recommendations on an individual basis.

Most commentators believe the most difficult aspect of the counseling function is being able to provide intelligent advice regardless of whether it supports the client's intentions. Lawyers are relied upon to be objective and courageous. Experienced lawyers warn that one must be very sensitive to the client's psyche as well as his or her legal problems. One rather jaundiced view went so far as to recommend "not telling my client what to do; I tell them how they can do what they want to do. There's always a legal way to achieve any legitimate purpose."[19] This quote appears to verge on the type of arrogance lawyers may be accused of when they are placed on a lofty pedestal as unchallenged experts. Most lawyers are in agreement with Mark McCormack's prudent counsel on this issue when he writes that "many of us [lawyers] spout off advice rather lightly, but we receive advice with the utmost seriousness. We remember where the advice comes from and if it turns out to be bad, we remember whom to blame! Advice . . . carries with it accountability and advice that in the long run is shown to have been self-serving is one of the surest ways to breed ill will."[20]

Secondary Activities

Beyond the four primary lawyering functions (litigating, negotiating, drafting, and advising), attorneys may also be required to perform a variety of additional tasks. Although the secondary tasks about to be examined do not represent an exhaustive list of all remaining lawyering activities, they are generally acknowledged to be among the five functions most commonly practiced beyond the four primary tasks. The first of these secondary functions is legal research. This is the effort by attorneys and their staff to investigate the facts of a case and to then analyze their findings in terms of relevant statutes and precedents. This involves the taking of depositions, subpoening, and interviewing witnesses as well as consulting with expert witnesses. The ability to effectively interview a witness and construct meaningful questions for a deposition are critical skills in developing the factual basis for making subsequent legal judgments. Because of the close personal involvement of clients in their own legal predicaments, their testimony may be biased and of questionable validity. The attorney must therefore be able to generate alternative sources of information that will hopefully be more reliable and allow for a more objective assessment of a client's position.

Lawyers may also have to act as a broker for the client in dealing with third parties. This quasi-legal function requires that the attorney possess a keen business mind and an up-to-date awareness of reliable, high-quality business associates. The lawyer in his capacity as a broker must unite his or her client with either other clients or outside parties who can provide the necessary services, materials, or financial backing. These brokering services often require the arranging of meetings between clients and third parties as well as assisting in negotiations to effectuate agreements between the client and others.

A third type of activity does not demand the intellectual challenge of the first two but can prove critical to a client's interests if neglected. This task is the filing of documents with the appropriate institutions at the required time. Although this may seem a rather mundane responsibility, it is nevertheless something to which attorneys devote a great deal of time and care. Failure to file legal documents with a court or other governmental agency by the requisite date and in the specified manner can eliminate a client's chances for legal redress regardless of the strength of his or her position. We will see in the next chapter that one of the major sources of malpractice suits against lawyers is the failure to file a document by the required date. Thus, inattention to these seemingly petty details may not only cost the errant attorney a lucrative client but can also result in a malpractice suit that can be even more damaging, affecting a lawyer's reputation as well as the pocketbook.

Public relations may seem like an irrelevant concern for the practicing attorney, but as Quintin Johnstone and Dan Hopson point out in their comprehensive study of the legal profession, *Lawyers and Their Work,* in certain instances it can be an important aspect of a lawyer's responsibilities. Presenting a client in the best possible light involves the development and emphasis on the positive attributes of the party(ies) being represented. This projection may be directed at the general public or more likely toward a smaller group of concerned and/or effected individuals.[21] An excellent example of the significance of the public relations function is the recent Alaskan oil spill by the Exxon tanker *Valdez.* The attorneys for Exxon have been engaging in a continuing series of public relations maneuvers to defuse the public's anger toward the oil company as a result of the accident that has wreaked such environmental damage to the Alaskan coastline.

The fifth and final secondary function of attorneys is to provide emotional support for the client. Although many lawyers may downplay the importance of this function and dislike having to spend time performing "hand-holding" responsibilities, it is still perceived by most as an essential part of their professional services. Just as many physicians may lack empathetic bedside manners, lawyers may also be deficient in their capacity to appear sympathetic toward their client's plights. Nevertheless, attorneys practicing matrimonial, criminal, and personal injury (plaintiffs) law are keenly aware of the necessity of providing support and reassurance to their clients. The need for such assistance is recognized by attorneys not only for its humane aspects but equally for its more pragmatic impact upon improving lawyer-client relations. These improved relations can often result in smoother pretrial preparation as well as providing better assistance during the actual trial.

In my research on the private practice of criminal lawyers, the importance of emotional support for the defendant was a prominent topic of discussion. Abraham Blumberg argued that the defense attorney's role in the cooling-off process of preparing the defendant for his or her likely conviction was a crucial part of an attorney's task and directly related to his or her chances of collecting the fee. On the other hand, many criminal lawyers agreed with a New Orleans attorney who "believed that most defense attorneys were overly concerned with the psychological well-being of their clients. He felt that the defendant of today had very little remorse over his criminal activity and was entirely result oriented. He was therefore completely disinterested in having his lawyer adopt any quasi-psychiatric role designed to help him maintain a cool psyche."[22]

PRETRIAL ACTIVITIES

Although we have seen in our previous examination of the major professional functions of an attorney that the preparation for litigation and the actual courtroom performance may be activities reserved for only a minority of American lawyers, they are nevertheless functions that exemplify the art of lawyering to most laypersons. Additionally, most of the more important political and social issues of concern to the general public are frequently resolved through litigation. All of these reasons, therefore, necessitate the following review of the major pretrial and courtroom activities of a lawyer. There has been a conscious effort to avoid an overly technical and legalistic analysis of these varied responsibilities. Instead, I hope to convey the basic tasks the trial attorney must perform at critical junctures in the litigation process.

Collecting the Facts: Investigations and Depositions

When a client initially consults with an attorney, he or she will usually describe in great detail the perceived predicament that has necessitated the visit. It is from this typically rambling discourse, which may contain many irrelevant asides, prejudicial statements, and blatant inaccuracies, that the attorney must begin to unravel not only what the client wishes to accomplish but also determine the specific legal issues that will likely determine the resolution of the client's dilemma. Once the attorney has clearly defined the crux of the legal conundrum facing the client, he or she must begin to investigate both the legal precedents and factual evidence relevant to the case. The legal research necessary to determine the most recent germane legal precedents and statutes is a fairly straightforward process in which attorneys and their staff (paralegals, interns, law clerks, etc.) turn to the law library to consult legal treatises, annotated codes, state and federal reporters, and any other useful resource. More perplexing as well as time consuming is the attorney's efforts to substantiate critical aspects of a client's allegations. This will require researching reliable documentation as well as interviewing individuals whose testimony will contribute to the verification of the client's perceptions. The attorney may either personally or with the assistance of paralegals, law clerks, or trained investigators begin to interview potential witnesses and other persons who can shed light on the client's case. To ensure that the individuals being interviewed appreciate the seriousness of the matter as well as committing them to a legally binding set of responses, witnesses are questioned through the use of depositions. The questions, which are carefully framed prior to the interview by the attorney, are answered and recorded with the witness swearing before a third party, such as a notary public, that all of the information is accurately transcribed.

Discovery

On the basis of the legal analysis as well as the completion of the factual investigation supporting the client's position, the attorney has one-half of the information collected that will be critical to his or her case. It is now through the process of discovery that an attorney can learn what his or her adversary believes to be the legal and factual basis of the case. Up to now our discussion of the pretrial investigation has been restricted to the client and the supporting witnesses, but given the nature of the adversary system, both attorneys must also be cognizant of the strengths and weaknesses of their protagonist's case. If the confrontation between both parties cannot be resolved amicably, they must resort to using a judicial tribunal that will serve as neutral arbiter and decide the controversy. Even when a jury is used to settle factual questions as well as the ultimate decision, the judge must still remain in the center of proceedings in order to assist the jury and ensure that both parties follow the required evidentiary and procedural rules established by the local jurisdiction.

To assist both sides in reaching a pretrial settlement as early as possible, as well as ensuring that there will be no surprise witnesses or submission of last minute evidence unknown to the other side, the federal and state courts have developed discovery procedures that require both sides to disclose the essential facts of their respective cases. This usually means a list of potential witnesses as well as copies of depositions, interrogations, and any relevant documentation. Each attorney can therefore become as familiar with his or her adversary's case during the pretrial period as he or she is of the client being represented.

Discovery also enables each attorney to have a clearer idea of the strength of his or her own case as well as gaining clearer insight into the reliability of his or her client and supposedly friendly witnesses. Defense attorneys were found to depend a great deal on discovery procedures that would grant them access to police reports, witness statements, and other pertinent data. Armed with this information, the attorney can confront a client with the prosecution's uncontested evidence. Hopefully, this will spark a client's memory or at least indicate how much information the lawyer actually has. This realization may aid the client in disclosing complete information to ensure the best possible defense.

Since discovery can be so easily abused, attorneys for both sides are urged to adopt a reasonable attitude in pestering the court for frivolous discovery motions requesting reams of information. Such requests can also annoy opposing counsel and eliminate or at least decrease the possibility of reaching a reasonable pretrial settlement. James Freund issues a warning to young lawyers concerning pretrial discovery skirmishing by writing that "busy judges become easily irritated by discovery applications; moreover rulings by jurists unfamiliar with the complexities of a case may not help either side. You and your adversary are in the best position to work out sensible solutions to discovery disputes—with a consequent saving of time and your client's money."[23]

Research has indicated that as the magnitude of the case increases, the efficiency of the discovery process seems to decline. Personal injury suits and criminal cases are probably the best examples of cases where the use of discovery is optimally effective. It was, however, pointed out by Wayne Brazil in his extensive study of discovery practices in Chicago that in even these smaller cases one side is vulnerable to economic pressure from opponents with more substantial resources.[24] The most serious problems appear to occur in the more complex cases. In one of the most horrendous examples of discovery abuse, the 1979 IBM antitrust case that dragged on for years, prosecutors examined more than 30 million documents and asked for 5 million more. The case was ultimately dismissed. In a less extreme example from a more typical commercial lawsuit, Peter Greenberger of New York's Weil, Gotschal and Manges estimates that these disputes often involve 10 to 15 parties with 400-page interrogatories filled with 2800 questions. Greenberger estimates the cost for obtaining this information to be in excess of $300,000, assuming that the junior associates will be billing their work at only $50 an hour.[25]

The courts have been quite upset by the misuse of discovery and its role in the delay of cases. In 1983 the U.S. Supreme Court implemented the following four rules of civil procedure in order to reform the chaotic pretrial conditions:

1. To try to have judges intervene to bring cases to quicker settlement.
2. To make it more difficult for lawyers to extend suits with frivolous or overzealous motions and pleading.
3. To keep discovery proportionate to the case.
4. To impose sanctions against abusers of discovery.[26]

Although these reforms were positively received in the federal courts, they have not had the expected results. Additionally, even though they served as models for possible state adoption, they were not implemented in very many jurisdictions and have therefore had only limited success reducing the growing incidents of discovery abuse and the related problem of unmanageable case backlogs leading to unacceptable periods of court delay.

Preparing for Trial

Following the lawyer's investigation into the facts of a client's case as well as learning through discovery the strength of the adversary's position, both sides are ready to either settle the case or proceed to trial. In the vast majority of cases a settlement is achieved. This is the product not only of both sides rationally assessing their chances of ultimate victory but also through the effective negotiations between the attorneys representing the disputing parties. The negotiation skill was discussed earlier as one of the lawyer's most fundamental professional activities. Given the high percentage of cases resolved in this manner, it is a skill that must be utilized frequently and effectively.

Since attorneys can never be certain which cases will be resolved through negotiation and which will eventually go to trial, they must prepare for the possibility of trial even though the odds are against it. The pretrial period, which has become increasingly drawn out and may stretch to several years in some states, is recognized by trial lawyers as a period in which a lawsuit's preparation will greatly determine whether the case will be won or lost. Mark Dombroff, writing in the *National Law Journal*, emphasizes this point by stating: "Skillfully taken depositions, extensive document discovery and the ability to put everything together into a scenario that either proves or disproves a case . . . typically marks the successful litigator. . . . The key to winning lawsuits is preparation. Not only preparation to ensure the successful outcome of the pretrial process but the preparation needed to ensure the successful outcome of the trial."[27]

Most jurisdictions have formulated a variety of pretrial conferences before a judge that will hopefully make effective use of the lengthy period of time awaiting trial. These may simply be informal conferences where the judge attempts to coerce a possible settlement by bringing the adversaries together and informing them of how he or she believes the dispute may best be resolved that will be mutually beneficial to all parties. Given the seemingly endless variety of pretrial motions that may be made by either party, many jurisdictions have adopted the use of omnibus motion conferences in which all of the pretrial motions must be made. This has been an effective reform in streamlining the procedures and reducing the number of dilatory motions.

COURTROOM PERFORMANCE

Despite the statistical infrequency of trials and the importance of adroit pretrial maneuvering, the reputation of most lawyers is determined by their courtroom performance. This section of the chapter will briefly describe the most critical aspects of this culminating phase of the legal process.

Selection of Jurors

The initial question facing an attorney about to begin a trial is whether to have a client's fate decided by a judge or jury. Most defense counsels in criminal cases opt for a jury trial since it is mathematically favorable to only have to create "reasonable doubt" in the mind of one of the twelve jurors, which will result in a hung jury and lead to a mistrial. In personal injury cases the plaintiff (the injured party) usually chooses a jury in the belief that jury members may be more sympathetic toward the injured party and therefore more liberal in their assessment of damages than a judge. In both criminal and negligence cases defense counsels are more inclined to choose a nonjury trial if they contemplate a rather complex, legalistic defense that may confuse the jury. Another reason a nonjury trial is chosen is if the lawyer believes the defendant's appearance on the witness stand is necessary and is not likely to make a positive impression upon a jury. This might be caused by the defendant's physical appearance or the especially heinous nature of the supposed behavior.

Once an attorney has chosen a jury trial, the challenging and often time-consuming task of jury selection—referred to as the voir dire—will begin. In states where lawyers are allowed to ask most of the questions (rather than the judge), such as New York, the voir dire is estimated to account for 40 percent of the trial's time. In jurisdictions that follow the federal model allowing the judge to ask nearly all of the questions, jury selection accounts for only 20 percent of the time.

How important is jury selection to the eventual outcome of a case? Although there are widely divergent views on this question, the majority of attorneys believe that it is a critical factor in the final disposition of the case. A small minority of lawyers, however, believe that too much emphasis has been placed on the voir dire. They believe that the skill of the attorney and the facts of the case are the critical factors influencing the resolution of a lawsuit. One skeptical San Francisco lawyer with a successful defense practice stated that "any twelve are okay. I rarely use up my challenges. All I look for are obvious signs and let my common-sense intuition guide the way."[28]

For most attorneys careful attention is paid to the selection process and a concentrated effort is made to predict as accurately as possible

how potential jurors are inclined to vote. These lawyers assume that
a jury's verdict is likely to be influenced not only by the admissible
evidence presented during the trial but also by jurors' preexisting
biases. They are also affected by the legally irrelevant and inadmissible
information that invariably filters into every judicial proceeding despite
the judge's best efforts. In recent years an entire industry has grown
around the need to assist attorneys in the calculated selection of the maximally sympathetic group of jurors. One of the best known of these organizations that has been assisting lawyers for over a decade is Litigation
Services, which has conducted in-depth interviews with more than
14,000 actual and surrogate jurors throughout the United States. Based
on these interviews, this company has framed basic concepts of juror
psychology that it believes are very helpful to any lawyer in preparing
for trial. They conclude that in a "typical case, jurors are often faced
with overwhelming complexities. They must consider many legal and
behavioral issues, absorb many facts, and act quickly to simplify these
to a manageable level. Jurors do this by establishing a few premises consistent with their attitudes and beliefs. They then employ these premises deductively, consistent with their personalities, attitudes and
beliefs."[29]

Most lawyers rely upon their own intuitive hunches developed
through trial experience rather than employing the high-tech services of
organizations such as Litigation Services. Recent interviews with prosecutors in New York City noted a preference for blue-collar workers,
older more conservative jurors, and citizens with long-established roots
in the community. Assistant District Attorney William Hoyt summarized
his preferred juror as simply being "someone who has the guts to con-
vict."[30] Defense counsel, on the other hand, desired jurors who were
seen as compassionate, tolerant of deviant lifestyles, and employed in
some type of creative or humanistic profession as opposed to a scientist
or businessperson.[31] The range of guidelines utilized by lawyers varied
widely, although the term *rapport* was repeatedly mentioned, and a conscious effort was made during the voir dire to discover the presence of
racism and prejudice among the jurors. Since no one is likely to admit
to being a racist or bigot, it is difficult to directly uncover such attitudes.
Charles Traylor, an experienced Colorado attorney, recommends the use
of the following line of obtuse questions which may partially uncover a
prejudiced juror:

> Are you acquainted with the activities of the (SLA) (B'Nai Brith) or the John
> Birch Society? Do you believe that organization is doing a good job? Are
> you familiar with Father Berrigan? Heard him speak? Have you ever taken
> part in a protest march or a sit-in demonstration? What is your opinion of
> these activities?[32]

Interaction with the jurors does not end with the completion of the
voir dire. Many lawyers realize that the eyes of the jury are critically
examining the attorney throughout the trial and in fact he almost re-

places the client in the mind of many jurors as the individual whose credibility must be assessed. Recent research indicates that juries carefully evaluate an attorney's credibility on the basis of their estimation of his expertise, trustworthiness, and dynamism. A recent *Time* magazine article described how some attorneys have turned to drama coaches to assist them in making a maximally effective presentation to the jury, although Jerry Coughlan of the National Institute for Trial Advocacy warns that "if a lawyer overplays and comes across as an actor, then credibility is lost."[33]

Witnesses and the Art of Cross-Examination

A large part of any trial is the lawyer's examination of witnesses, both friendly and hostile. Friendly witnesses are presented by the attorney in order to substantiate and emphasize significant elements of a client's position. These witnesses are selected by an attorney and coached prior to their courtroom appearances in order to maximize the effectiveness of their testimony. These witnesses will initially face direct examination by the lawyer whose questioning will carefully develop the desired information to the judge and jury. Attorneys will also attempt to prepare these supportive witnesses for the expected cross-examination from the opposing counsel. Their objective is to be able to anticipate and thereby negate the effects of the hostile cross-examination.

Interrogating the opposition's witnesses who will be attempting to present damaging evidence is accomplished through cross-examination—a quintessential skill for the litigator. The basic objective of cross-examinations noted by Bailey and Rothblatt, in their treatise on the fundamentals of advocacy, is to either discredit the direct examination and testimony of witnesses against a client or to clarify or amplify testimony favorable to a client. These authors then go on to recommend the following strategies designed to achieve these objectives: (1) show that the witness is incompetent as to the events he or she claims to have observed; (2) show that the passing of time and suggestion of others have colored or distorted recollection of the facts; (3) indicate contradictions in the testimony; (4) induce the witness to admit uncertainty as to statements made directly; and (5) expose bias or prejudice and thereby impeach his or her character.[34]

To accomplish the objective on cross-examination, it is critical for the attorney to be extremely well prepared and be able to anticipate the answers from both friendly and hostile witnesses. Litigators emphasize the importance of knowing the answer to every question about to be asked. The worst thing that can happen to an attorney is to be surprised by a witness's response. It is also recommended that questions should be narrowly drafted so as to avoid offering the witness an opportunity to evade the intended answer. The successful cross-examiner must maintain tight control over the questioning process, being sure to plug all escape routes. Legendary West Coast litigator Jake Ehrlich offered the following advice on how to ensure this client control: "There is no point in giving a witness an opportunity to add facts which further probing may recall to him. The lawyer is not always smarter than the witness and the witness who is honest and who is obviously trying to tell the truth as he understands it, has the jury on his side. Personally, I never cross examine unless it is absolutely necessary."[35]

Beyond the careful preparation of witnesses and comprehensive understanding of an opponent's case, lawyers must select a cross-examination style. In determining a particular style of cross-examination, each attorney must develop a rapport with the witness that is most consistent with his or her overall personality. In facing an adversary's witness, the lawyer must be careful not to be overly aggressive because this can easily gain sympathy for the witness and antipathy toward the lawyer in the minds of the jurors. Defense attorneys I have interviewed were nearly unanimous in urging attorneys to tailor their cross-examination style to their natural demeanor and disregard the emotional and theatrical approach typified in the movies or on television. Many lawyers felt that by intelligent planning one could conduct a devastating cross-examination while still appearing to be a pleasant person.[36] One can be much more effective by surprising the hostile witness, calmly questioning him or her and maneuvering obliquely until the trap has been set and the witness is unexpectedly forced to compromise his or her credibility.

Dealing with Adversaries

Given the adversarial nature of the American legal system, one of the most important decisions to be made by an attorney is how to deal with the opposing counsel. James Freund believes the first question an attorney beginning a lawsuit should ask himself or herself is, What attitude should I adopt in this case to best serve my client's interest? The entire tone of the adversarial relationship should be established as early as possible. The attorneys have two basic choices: antagonistic or amicable. Although clients may prefer their lawyer to adopt a bellicose style, Freund and other experienced attorneys discourage utilizing the antagonistic posture. Freund argues that "it's rather rare for one litigator to be able to dominate another, requiring a certain weakness of spirit in the latter isn't typical of the breed. In fact, a contentious posture frequently just serves to make the other lawyer madder than hell—much like a red cape waved in front of a bull. And that won't help you down the road when—inevitably—you'll need the other lawyer's cooperation."[37]

The ability to work with opposing counsel is especially critical during the early stages of a lawsuit. A reasonable disposition is especially important during pretrial discovery where much time is spent negotiating for the exchange of documents, interrogatories, and depositions. If attorneys adopt hostile attitudes at this early stage, the opportunities for effective discovery are severely limited. This could result in lost opportunities for early settlement that could prove beneficial to both sides.

Judges are also irritated by overly contentious lawyers whose bickering over discovery applications prolongs pretrial proceedings and embroils the judge in what he or she perceives to be petty, dilatory, and unprofessional conduct. Although clients may encourage lawyers to be aggressive and even unyielding, in the long-run it may prove costly, both in terms of time and money. Once the trial begins, it is often necessary for both attorneys to appear to be enthusiastic adversaries, but even in the heat of courtroom combat, attorneys should maintain control and realize when their behavior has exceeded acceptable limits, threatening the credibility of their position.

It is generally recognized that the tone of relations with a hostile adversary will often be influenced by the ongoing needs of the client. Adversaries may have to deal with one another in future situations, so care must be exercised not to jeopardize either current or contemplated business transactions. Similarly, litigation with a particular governmental agency is necessarily affected by the likelihood that the client will remain under that organization's regulatory control in the years ahead.

It is interesting to note that in recent years there has been a trend among several prestigious trial attorneys to adopt increasingly aggressive tactics that have been journalistically labeled "Rambo litigation," a legal version of "playing hardball." This style was recently defined by respected Chicago defense lawyer Philip Corboy as when a lawyer "is personally antagonistic or insistent on all of the procedural rules being followed. . . . A really hardball player will make you prove the obvious or travel across the country to take a deposition you could just as easily take in town."[38] Most attorneys view such excessive aggressiveness as simply an ultimate weapon to be utilized only when provoked or necessitated by a desperate situation. Other factors affecting the use of hardball techniques might be the acceptability of such behavior patterns to the local legal culture and how likely the lawyers are to confront each other again in the near future. Thus it is more likely to find lawyers engaging in Rambo tactics in New York and Chicago with their enormous pool of attorneys and reputation for aggressive lawyering than in smaller towns in the South and Midwest where such behavior is likely to appear offensive. Although lawyers who regularly play hardball may blame their choice of style on client pressure, New York attorney Robert Fiske believes that "there are few clients who like that macho image and style of lawyering and want to see it adapted across the board. Most don't and would rather look at your track record."[39]

LAWYER-CLIENT RELATIONS

This section moves from the technical, procedural, and tactical responsibilities of the trial attorney before and during litigation to the more generalized professional obligations and problems inherent in lawyer-client relations. The topics to be covered range from the ways in which clients are obtained to recent developments in improving the availability of legal services to a wider group of possible clients.

Obtaining Clients

The obvious point of departure for any discussion of lawyer-client relations is the critical, yet often puzzling, question of how clients select a particular attorney. Similar to other professions, such as medicine, people in need of a lawyer's services do not merely flip randomly through the yellow pages until a name strikes their fancy. The choice is made difficult for the layperson because, despite the recent lessening of professional restrictions against lawyer advertising (a topic to be examined in greater detail in Chapter 5), there is virtually no public information available to prospective clients concerning the professional reputations and specialized expertise of either individual lawyers or their firms.

The question of how to obtain clients has deeply concerned lawyers for many years and has generated numerous articles and books devoted to answering the question. In 1955 Claude Rowe published a volume containing the responses of 1500 lawyers in a national survey attempting to resolve this issue. The following represent a brief sample of some of those lawyers surveyed.

1. You know and I know that getting law business isn't because of special ability or talent. Negligence cases come through policemen, firemen, nurses, matrons, hospital attendants, deputy sheriffs.
2. Acquaintances are the main source. You get one, he sends another.
3. Friendships, publicity, and recommendations.
4. From meeting people. At lunch someone you meet gives you a case or brings you one later. Meet 1,000 or 100, you are going to get some clients.
5. It depends on the reputation you build up. Also according to the class of people you deal with, whether wealthy or working.
6. From insurance companies, associations, organizations. I am a politician so I get to meet a lot of people socially.[40]

Attacking the issue more systematically, Bertram Harnett recently wrote that getting legal business depends on four factors: lawyering presence, exposure, goingness, and luck. The following statements more clearly defines each of these factors.

1. Lawyering presence is a combination of the appearance to the client of legal talent, determination, and the inspiration of confidence.
2. Exposure means displaying your lawyering presence to potential clients. Reputation is a form of exposure both within the profession and to the public at large.
3. Goingness relates to exposure. Being in practice, working daily, seriously, openly, exposes the lawyer to legal business.
4. The fortuities of personal fortune, rich family and friends, and social and business connections are all lucky incidents. So is being in the right place at the right time.[41]

Based on my interviews with nearly 300 defense attorneys as well as reviewing the exhaustive research on this question, the lawyer's reputation emerges as the most important variable influencing attorney selection. Prospective clients will learn of a respected attorney with skills relevant to their special problem through conversations with friends, family, or business associates who have utilized the same lawyer in similar circumstances. Given the high degree of legal specialization, a large number of lawyers are forced to refer their clients to a particular specialist when a problem arises outside their own area of expertise. How does a lawyer establish the type of reputation that will attract future clients? The following lengthy quote from my work on criminal lawyers illustrates the complexity and confusion surrounding this perplexing process:

> It seemed paradoxical that in a profession where nearly all of the members work in virtual isolation, they [the local lawyers] are still able to rank and list all of their fellow criminal lawyers in terms of competence and showmanship. It was amazing to find that in each city, so many of these solo or isolated practitioners could reach similar opinions concerning colleagues whom they so rarely observed. Whether these rankings are accurate is impossible to say because of their subjective nature, but because of their consistency and the degree to which they are believed, they can be a crucial factor in a criminal lawyer's ability to achieve a successful practice. The basis for these judgments seemed derived mainly from hearsay evidence from a few lawyers who had observed the subject in action in the courtroom, as well as evaluations offered by prosecutors, judges, bailiffs, reporters, and assorted courthouse regulars who had opportunities to watch the entire bar in operation.[42]

With increasing numbers of attorneys and law firms competing for business among a limited number of desirable clients, several firms have begun to engage in serious marketing efforts not only to attract new clients but also ensure that their present group of clients do not depart. A recent article in the *National Law Journal* investigated new techniques devised to improve servicing of current clients and discovered that several law firms are using a new tactic entitled the "responsible partner" concept that has many advantages over the traditional billing-partner system. The firm selects a specific partner for a particular client and assigns the following responsibilities: (1) understanding the client's business or situation and objectives; (2) ensuring that the client's needs are being met to his or her satisfaction; (3) identifying the client's needs for services in other areas and informing the client of the firm's capabilities in these new areas; and (4) keeping informed on all matters in which the firm is rendering service to the client. In other words the designated partner is responsible not only for providing quality service but also for developing a quality relationship with the client.[43]

In concluding this discussion of how lawyers obtain clients, a statement by James Freund summarizes the essence of the problem: "I have a feeling that the days of landing clients on the thirteenth tee are largely behind us (if indeed they ever existed), although it's clearly worthwhile to enlarge your circle of friends and acquaintances—spreading bread on the water, so to speak. Nowadays, however, clients come to a lawyer because they've heard good things about him or her professionally, or they've witnessed the lawyer in action representing another client. If you give efficient, intelligent service, the word is going to get around. So we tell our young people not to worry too much about *how* to go about attracting business; we say 'Do a first-rate job and the clients will seek *you* out.' "[44]

Art of Client Handling

Once a client has selected a lawyer, a rather complicated professional relationship develops, sometimes involving a power struggle over who is in charge. The style of client handling may be affected by the legal specialization or more basically by the personality and attitude of the attorney. Bertram Harnett examined both factors and found first of all that litigators are much less concerned with their client's feelings than lawyers specializing in business and personal affairs who see the client on a long-range basis and must take the client's personal needs into more daily account. Harnett then describes two extreme handling styles: the "terrorizer" and the "soother." The terrorizer is described as scaring clients by depicting the possible dire consequences of their legal plight and intimidating them into submission while the "soother" minimizes the seriousness of the problem, hoping to generate an atmosphere of tranquility and optimism.[45]

As might be expected, there are often major struggles between lawyers and clients as to who is in charge of the case. Lawyers argue that they possess the necessary technical expertise unavailable to the layperson while the client counters with the claim that since the client is the one ultimately affected, he or she should have the final say in any decision. Mark McCormack, author of the controversial book *The Terrible Truth About Lawyers*, argues in favor of the client, writing: "Remember, when you're the client, you're the boss, even if sometimes it doesn't feel that way. Your lawyer should be accountable to you in whatever reasonable form *you* are comfortable with."[46] McCormack believes it is especially important in business deals where it is more likely the client has a clearer sense of what he or she wishes to accomplish for the lawyer to be kept "from meddling in situations where the legal approach just isn't appropriate . . . and when lawyers try too hard to apply their smarts to issues that are really business issues, the terrible truth is that they sometimes end up seeming not so smart at all. In situations like that, it is the client's responsibility to let the attorney know when to back off."[47]

Although research into the question of who dominates the lawyer-client relationship is extremely limited, Carl Hosticka did complete a fascinating study of public service lawyers on this topic. His report, which is based on a nine-month survey, concluded that the lawyer was clearly in control: "They [the lawyers] almost always directed the conversation, paying less attention to the client's story than in filling out forms. The lawyers asked the questions and interrupted the client's responses . . . the lawyers did not seem so much uncaring as overworked."[48] From my personal observations as well as literature review, it appears that Hosticka's conclusions regarding lawyer dominance are generally valid when the client is an infrequent user of legal services. However, for those clients, such as wealthy businesspersons, who must utilize attorneys on a regular basis, they are much more likely to challenge their attorney's judgment and maintain significant influence over their legal dealings.

Beyond the debate over whether the client or the attorney should control the case is the important issue of whether the attorney possesses the ability to satisfy the client's persistent demand for reassurance and support. Clients expect their attorneys to be their impassioned advocates, analogous to a legal mercenary fighting their personal battles against sinister adversaries. Lawyers, however, must be able to strike a balance between offering practical and objective advice, while still appearing to be ardent supporters of the client's interests. This dual role becomes difficult when the attorney anticipates that the most responsible legal advice may run counter to the client's aspirations. The client, upon learning that he or she may not be able to accomplish stated goals, may turn angrily on the attorney who will be personally blamed for this failure and even be threatened with dismissal. At the very least, clients do expect lawyers to be emotionally supportive, and, even if this service may be derisively referred to by most lawyers as hand-holding, it is a critical element of client handling. James Freund summarizes these unpopular, yet necessary, obligations with refreshing candor: "He [the client] may want you to answer questions, to reassure him that what he's doing makes sense, or just serves as a sounding board. But hey, man, that's what he pays you for! He's entitled! You may think it's not the highest and best use of your valuable time, but don't tell that to *him*. If it weren't for his ilk, you'd probably be out selling insurance."[49]

Cost of Legal Services

The cost of legal services is of obvious paramount concern to both client and attorney. Not only are there a wide variety of fee charging methods but each method may in turn be affected by additional factors such as the type of client or the specific legal problem being resolved. The following list of client categories based on economic status was compiled by Countryman and Finman in their analysis of the legal profession and illustrates the profound influence exerted by the client's economic status upon the fee:

1. Legal aid cases: typically treated without fee as a public service/ pro bono responsibility.
2. Lawyer referral cases: clients of moderate means who can pay a fee although not the customary one.
3. Regular clients who will pay the customary fee.
4. Wealthy individual clients to whom the services rendered have added value because of the increased risks involved.
5. Corporate clients who are able to deduct the legal fee as an operating expense for income tax purposes.[50]

The most frequently used fee-charging method is on the basis of time spent: typically assessed on an hourly basis, although it is often computed down to fractions of an hour. The amount charged per hour varies greatly according to the professional status of the attorney and the capacity of the client. For a beginning attorney or junior associate in a large firm the fees are at the bottom end of the spectrum and might be as low as $50 to $75 dollars per hour. As one moves up the scale toward the more senior partners in prestigious firms, the hourly rate may climb to over $300. Experienced individual practitioners and lawyers in modest-size firms can be expected to charge between $75 and $200 an hour. A prospective client needs to inquire not only as to the hourly fee but the estimated length of time needed to resolve the legal problem. Clients contemplating litigation should realize that given the lengthy amount of time expended on these types of cases, they may be facing staggering legal fees.

A second method is the establishment of a standardized charge for a specific type of legal problem. Transactions such as probating a will or assisting in the sale of real estate are common legal problems where lawyers can readily anticipate how much time they will be required to spend. Thus, the fee is established as a percentage of the dollar amount involved in the representation. In many cases, for example, lawyers charge 1 percent of the contract price for the purchase price of vacant land. Where there are economic items of great regularity and lesser total amounts, it is common for there to be a set fee. These include simple or uncontested divorces, leases, and landlord-tenant disputes. The charging figure is determined by customary practices in a particular area as well as the degree of competition among rival attorneys vying for a limited number of clients.

A fairly recent innovation in fee arrangements, used primarily in personal injury cases, is receiving a percentage of the amount recovered by the plaintiff. This is popularly referred to as a contingency fee. It has become very controversial both because of its likely contribution to the filing of frivolous suits, thus jamming the courts, as well as causing attorneys to seemingly earn astoundingly high fees for little work and thereby taking an unnecessarily large amount of money away from the injured party. In order to limit potential abuse, contingency fees in personal injury cases are limited by state law in many jurisdictions. A sliding scale of permissible percentages usually begins at 50 percent for the first one or two thousand dollars recovered and down to about 25 percent for larger amounts, with most lawyers typically receiving one-third of the plaintiffs' award. Although contingent fees are now being used in adjacent legal fields, such as contract and debt recovery as well as real estate condemnation and workers compensation claims, for the overwhelming bulk of legal work the contingent fee approach is inapplicable.[51]

For those individuals and organizations who have frequent and continued use of legal services, they often pay a fixed retainer for a calendar period, although unusual or unexpected legal problems are usually excluded from the retainer coverage. These retainer fees are often paid either through monthly or quarterly installments, with an annual fee predicated upon the amount of legal services performed in previous years. It is a gamble by both parties since an underestimate means an excessive amount of work for the firm without the normal compensation. The major advantage for both parties is the predictability of the income, especially for those lawyers with weighty operating expenses. Clients also have valued this method because it controls the amount of fee exposure during a set period of time.

Two final methods, having the fees fixed by court and charging whatever the traffic will bear, are both rather self-explanatory and require only a cursory description. Courts have the power to determine and award fees to lawyers in many situations. These may range from cases involving class action suits for environmental issues to the legal affairs of infants and incompetents. It is very difficult to find a unifying theme to these cases other than the court's decision that it is in the public's best interest that the court control the awarding of the fee.

Many lawyers resort to the long-established method of simply tailoring the fee and services to the client's ability to pay. Because clients generally assume that "you get what you pay for," they are susceptible to paying exorbitant fees. Thus, the more a client pays the better he or she assumes the lawyer's performance will be. A high fee is also a reliable indicator of an attorney's exalted position within the legal community (although there are many exceptions to this presumption). In my research on criminal lawyers, one Philadelphia attorney exhibited the callous aspects of this fee-setting method when he stated: "Anyway, the family obviously had little money, but I said if they could get $4000 together, I'd take the case. They paid me fifty dollars a week and I knew it was coming right out of their food budget. But hell, if I hadn't taken it, I wouldn't have had a food budget."[52]

Most criminal lawyers actually are more concerned with the seriousness of the case and the expected length of time it will take (i.e., whether or not it will go to trial) than the ability to pay. Another Philadelphia lawyer, Charles Peruto, offers his somewhat humorous "Hmmmmmm" method of fee charging based on these other two factors:

You come in. You sit down. I'll ask, the charge was a serious charge?

Yeah, Mr. Peruto, it was a serious charge.

Hmmmmm. Well did they catch you in the act or did they catch you later?

They got me right there.

Hmmmmm. Did you make a statement? Did you confess?

Yes, I told everything to the cops.

Hmmmmm. You take a look at their faces when they tell you the story. They're looking for some glimmer, some ray of hope, something—and you're just hmmmmming. It's about $1500 a hmmmmm.[53]

Regardless of which method of collection is used, lawyers appear to be charging very high fees, and clients are continually trying to devise strategies for reducing their legal expenses. Eight years ago an article in *Newsweek* stated that although precise figures are hidden, best estimates are "that major companies spend about 15 cents on their lawyers for every one hundred dollars in sales. If that guess is accurate the legal tab adds up to 2.5 billion dollars for the Fortune 500."[54] A more recent study by David Trubek and associates for the *UCLA Law Review* concluded that current litigation costs are so high that they may be simply too costly for both the litigants and society. Blame for the excessive costs was placed on "the complexity of procedures, the unchecked adversarial zeal of attorneys, and biases of the existing fee schedule."[55]

Efforts to develop feasible ways for both individuals and businesses to reduce their costly legal expenses have generated a plethora of possible alternatives. The following advice from attorney Albert Podell offers a range of strategies designed to reduce legal costs:

Don't see your lawyer until you've put the facts of your case on paper. It saves interviewing time and helps the lawyer get started quicker. It also saves you the cost of having the lawyer's notes transcribed.

Remember that you will be charged for every minute, so do not contact your lawyer without first preparing a list of everything you need to discuss.

Keep track of the actual time spent on each phone call or meeting. If you only talk for a few minutes but are billed for a half-hour only pay what you owe and inform your lawyer of the mistake.

If your case calls for more than 20 hours of research, have your lawyer write out the precise legal questions. Then ask your local law school's placement office to recommend a student to pour over the records. Depending on the school and the student's class rank you'll pay $6 to 12 an hour— about one-tenth what a law firm charges to have the work done by a junior associate.

You can often find copies of legal documents (e.g. "deeds or incorporation papers, hospital records, verification of addresses of witnesses to subpeona") at local government offices such as the county clerk's office or the municipal building.

If your lawyer requests information . . . furnish the material promptly. The lawyer's meter runs each time you have to be reminded to send it.[56]

Recent Developments in Fees and Services

This concluding section on lawyer-client relations will examine four recent developments in the attempt to improve the delivery of legal services, with particular emphasis on combatting the problems caused by rising legal fees. The first problem area is contingent fee contracts, a method of fee collection that, as already mentioned, has recently troubled both the courts and legislatures. The intractable weakness in such an arrangement is that the lawyer's self-interest may easily come between himself and his client, affecting not only the size of his fee, but how he conducts the case, that is, his or her willingness to accept a settlement offer. In order to curb possible abuses, several jurisdictions have granted the courts power to engage in the limited regulation of contingent fee arrangements. One of the best examples of an extensive and seemingly viable system of controlling this problem is the New Jersey Supreme Court's Rule 1:21-(7c), which establishes the following graduated scale of maximum permissible contingent fees:

50 percent on the first $1000 recovered

40 percent on the next $2000 recovered

33.3 percent on the next $47,000 recovered

20 percent on the next $50,000 recovered

10 percent on any amount over $100,000[57]

A second problem area closely related to the extensive use of contingent fee practices in this country is devising some way to discourage frivolous lawsuits by plaintiffs who have little to lose. Other nations have solved this problem by requiring the losing party to pay the winner's legal fees, in addition to whatever else the court assesses in the judgment. This solution has not been well received in most states because of its perceived chilling effect on all lawsuits—legitimate as well as frivolous. England has dealt with this dilemma by limiting the amount of the award to only those costs found necessary and proper for the successful completion of litigation.

The federal government has recently made a slight move toward dealing with this problem with the passage in 1964 and 1976 of legislation that allows for the prevailing plaintiff in most civil rights actions to be entitled to recover a reasonable fee from the losing party.[58] Alaska is the only state presently experimenting with a rule requiring losers to pay winner's legal fees, but according to the state bar association, it has not been very successful, and the state bar has called for its repeal.[59]

A third effort to improve the delivery of legal services to a wider group of potential clients, many of whom may not be able to afford legal representation, is the development of a prepaid legal services plan. Similar to an insurance policy, middle-class citizens through the payment of modest amounts are guaranteed subsidized legal representation. Wisconsin experimented with such a program in the 1960s—it was entitled Judicare—but unfortunately proved too expensive to sustain beyond its first few years of operation. A major weakness in the prepaid legal service concept is its inability to utilize the prestigious lawyers of well-established firms. Joseph Bartlett, in his critical book entitled *The Law Business: A Tired Monopoly*, notes that law firms have ignored the prepaid plans causing them to lose precious respectability in the eyes of the public.[60]

The final, and most far-reaching, proposal for improving the delivery of legal services to a broader range of potential clients is the controversial concept of mandatory pro bono. Fashioned after the medical profession's obligation to treat any sick individual without regard to capacity to pay, several states have been debating the plausibility of requiring lawyers, as part of their professional obligation, to perform a required number of free hours of legal assistance. Missouri, in fact, was successful in forcing a young attorney to defend an indigent in a criminal trial or face being disbarred.[61] Although many state and local bar associations do give lip service to their professional obligation to provide legal representation to the economically disadvantaged, the reality of available pro bono assistance is almost nonexistent. Individual firms and individual attorneys within those firms may dedicate a small percentage of their time to pro bono work, but even this small subset of the profession would likely join their professional colleagues in opposition to making such charitable activities mandatory. Even if a program of mandatory pro bono work was implemented, it could be expected to have only a limited impact on improving the availability of legal services needed by our nation's indigent. In closing, one must remain rather pessimistic concerning the ability of any or all of these reform measures discussed in this section to provide a perceptible improvement in either the quality or availability of legal services.

SPECIALIZATION AND CERTIFICATION

Just as the medical profession has witnessed the demise and near extinction of the general practitioner, so has the legal profession experienced a similar trend as nearly all attorneys conduct specialized practices. The

ABA's Special Committee on Specialization has defined a legal special-ist as "a lawyer who develops and maintains an expertise in a field of legal doctrine, a legal skill or function or a type of client sufficient to distinguish him from his fellow lawyers."[62] The committee goes on to explain that there are many different types of specialization and provides the following list of examples:

1. Specialization by field of legal doctrine: income tax, antitrust, zoning.
2. Specialization by legal skill: litigation, will drafting, labor negoti-ating.
3. Specialization by particular client: corporate house counsel, fed-eral agency, regulatory commission.
4. Specialization by trade or legally significant segment of society: hospital administrators, meat packing, oil and gas production.
5. Specialization by nonclient institution that dominates a field of practice: Securities and Exchange Commission, Internal Reve-nue, local trial court.[63]

In many ways the movement toward specialization in the legal pro-fession has been influenced by similar societal, economic, and techno-logical forces that have shaped an analogous development within the medical profession. Although general legal practitioners may still be found in small towns, the overwhelming majority of lawyers have de-cided to specialize. A recent California survey found that two out of three lawyers in that state considered themselves specialists, and four out of five lawyers who were members of firms with more than ten iden-tified themselves as specialists. An Illinois survey discovered that for even those lawyers calling themselves general practitioners, the major-ity went on to state that they also had one or more specialties.[64]

The most common explanation for the remarkable growth in special-ization has been the increasing complexity of society and corresponding growth of governmental regulations. The result has been an exponential growth in not only the amount of law but its complexity as well, which has made it increasingly difficult to keep up with legal developments in more than a select few areas of the law. The following statement by two Illinois attorneys offers an excellent explanation of why this trend to-ward specialization has been so inexorable: "New developments, proce-dures and problems in every field of practice are generated continuously by the courts, legislatures, and administrative agencies and special bar groups. Many popular and active fields of legal practice did not even exist forty years ago. The volume of current material in the form of ad-vance sheets, services, synopses, summaries, articles, journals, and the like is so numerous and voluminous that no practitioner can possibly read it all. It is unrealistic to expect any modern lawyer to stay abreast of all the developments in all areas of the law or to be competent in all fields of general practice."[65]

As a result of the remarkable growth in specialization, there has developed in recent years a growing debate within the legal profession over the necessity for certifying lawyers as being competent specialists in designated areas of the law. Many lawyers oppose any proposed regulation finding potential dangers to both the consumer and practitioner. Jerome Hochberg studied the certification issue and concluded that "these programs construct new and formidable barriers to free and open competition in the market for legal services. They reduce the supply of lawyers in critical areas, which will, if the medical specialities provide any analogy, lead to higher fees charged, not lower ones."[66] Richard Zehnle is also critical of the certification reform and writes that

> if the general public is presently baffled by the question of securing competence will it be in a better situation once lawyers are permitted to list "specialities" after their names, with only a minimum of control by some official state body? Even presuming the unqualified good will of all attorneys in scrupulously listing only real primary fields of interest, will not some subsequent disappointments of clients be inevitable? And will not these disappointments invariably lead to a further lack of trust in lawyers whose reputation has already been tarnished—rightly or wrongly—by events of recent years? . . . How will state bar associations insure the competence of those they permit to designate themselves as specialists? Here, the problem of precisely how one assesses competence leaps to mind. May not an examination simply reflect the aptitude and willingness of an unimaginative and uncreative attorney to memorize factual data successfully?[67]

Despite these criticisms, the legal profession and state bar committees across the country have stated a belief in the necessity for devising certification programs. State programs presently range from simple designation plans in which lawyers may self-designate their specialties to rigid certification programs requiring peer review and formal examination. Randolph Rollins explains the necessity and desirability for these programs by arguing that they "will serve the public by providing greater access to the legal services they need through reliable information about specialists. Secondly, it will diminish danger of the public being mislead by unregulated advertising. Thirdly, it will encourage lawyers to achieve higher standards of lawyer excellence as a condition to being certified as a specialist."[68]

Probably the most fundamental issue facing any certification plan is its definitional standard for specialization. The Virginia criteria have served as a model for many other state programs and are presented here:

1. Substantial practice in the specialty for 5 years.
2. Participation in an average of 15 hours of continuing legal education per year over a 5-year period.
3. Confirmation by others: affidavits from professionals who are familiar with the work of the applicant.
4. Written work product, prepared substantially by themselves.
5. Additional standards, including exams for certain specialties.[69]

Although individual state plans do contain a variety of provisions and requirements before certification can be granted, Richard Zehnle, after analyzing a large number of diverse state programs, believes that they do have the following set of common features:

All of the plans are voluntary and spell out two important limitations: (1) No attorney is prohibited from practicing in any field by the fact that he is not a specialist in that field; (2) Specialization in one field does not deprive an attorney of his right to practice in other fields in which he may not be specialized. Further all plans make a provision for revocation by the board of the recognition of specialization, with the right of appeal for the attorney; the precise mechanics of revocation and appeal vary. Finally, the professional and ethical problems involved in widespread referral of clients by general practitioners to specialists are confronted. Solutions proposed are mainly that a specialist may render to a client no wider service than that for which he was recommended unless (1) he receives approval from the attorney who first recommended the client or (2) he notifies the referring client by mail.[70]

Pointing toward the future of specialization and certification, with a growing number of lawyers entering practice, and competition heightened by the relaxation of previous prohibitions against lawyer advertising, it seems both inevitable and most prudent that a national plan for defining and measuring specialist competence be implemented. As Hagglund and Birnbaum point out in their recent study of legal specialization, only through the adoption of widespread standards can the profession ensure accountability to the public.[71]

LAWYER DIVERSITY: FOUR EXAMPLES

The final section of this chapter will present a series of brief sketches of various legal specialists. These cursory glimpses into the diversity of the legal profession will permit the reader to appreciate the wide-ranging issues covered by lawyers as well as gaining some insight into the unique professional styles demanded by each specialty.

The Private Criminal Lawyer

Although this is a legal specialty engaging a very small percentage of the bar (estimates from my national study found only 10,000 to 20,000 lawyers who accept criminal cases more than occasionally and only an additional 5000 employed by public defender organizations, this is compared to approximately 600,000 members of the bar),[72] it is a specialty the public views as the apotheosis of the profession. Despite the serious economic difficulties currently being experienced by criminal lawyers, they nevertheless continue to be depicted in movies and television as the most glamorous and exciting legal specialty.

Based on my detailed examination of this legal specialization (I interviewed nearly 200 criminal lawyers in nine cities), the following group of unique professional qualifications were discovered. Although several of these were applicable to only criminal law specialists, it is interesting to note that the first two are clearly endemic to all trial attorneys. In fact, most of the criminal law specialists preferred to be characterized as litigators who were equally adept in a courtroom whether they were handling a negligence, matrimonial, or criminal matter.

The first requirement for the successful criminal lawyer is to be both an extrovert in the courtroom while exercising extremely cerebral skills in preparation for this performance. Most individuals are unable to combine the often contradictory skills of public and private competence. The sharply contrasting working environment of the office and the courtroom intensifies this dichotomy. In the solitude of his or her office, the criminal lawyer is a pensive strategist. Within a short time however, he or she returns to the convivial courthouse setting where the criminal lawyer must be able to exhibit a winning personality before judge and jury.

The second is the need to be both an adroit negotiator with the prosecution while also maintaining a reputation of a feared courtroom adversary. Experienced prosecutors are not troubled by the inconsistency of a defense attorney trying to wheedle an acceptable plea bargain one moment and then trying to destroy the prosecution in open court the next. Most criminal lawyers believe that both legal skills are mutually complementary and facilitate one another. The feared adversary is more likely to be an effective plea bargainer. If defense lawyers were not thought to be worthy courtroom opponents, their negotiating effectiveness would likely be diminished.

A third characteristic is the difficulty in earning a decent income. Several criminal lawyers who I interviewed commented that the very clients whose fees were most lucrative, such as white-collar and organized crime figures, were often the least desirable on a personal basis. The upper-middle-class and corporate defendants were often described as being the least cooperative, most belligerent, and stingiest in terms of fee payment. The organized crime defendants could be counted on to pay, but the taint of associating with such individuals usually means IRS audits, grand jury appearances, and persistent complaints from more law abiding civil law clients. The recent U.S. Supreme Court decision in *Caplan and Drysdale* v. *U.S.* (No. 87-1729) (June, 1989) offers further evidence of the complicated problem of fee collection in criminal cases. The Court decided for the first time that the government can seize the assets of a criminal defendant before trial without considering whether the individual will retain sufficient funds to hire a defense lawyer. The federal law authorizing the seizure is applied primarily in racketeering and drug cases. The ABA and other lawyer groups reacted strongly against the decision, charging that the defendants' Sixth Amendment rights to counsel were seriously undermined, a position verbalized by Justice Blackmun in his dissenting opinion.[73]

The fourth unique professional difficulty facing the private criminal lawyer is the complex problem that also troubles many trial lawyers: maintaining a lofty reputation while continuing to practice in virtual isolation. As noted earlier in this chapter, a lawyer's reputation is his or her most precious asset, yet it is generally the product of hearsay, gossip, and only an occasional bit of empirical evidence. Consequently, it is no wonder that so many defense lawyers become somewhat paranoid concerning what is said about them. The problem is exacerbated by the fact that so much of what the lawyer does—plea bargaining with the prosecutor, meeting with the judge in chambers, dealing with a client—occurs beyond the public purview. Rarely will a judge, prosecutor, or client comment about what occurred during these private encounters. Nevertheless, within a short time a reputation mystically evolves that may mark the attorney for the duration of his or her professional life.

The Divorce Lawyer

Similar to the private criminal lawyer, the divorce lawyer suffers from economic hard times as well as declining professional status. With the popularity of no-fault divorce legislation in nearly every state, as well as the increasing role for nonlawyers in mediation and reconciliation efforts, divorce specialists declare themselves to be in the throes of a serious economic decline. Some states, such as California, have even gone so far as to eliminate the need for *any* courtroom appearance in no-fault divorce cases not involving children. With society alarmed by the high rate of divorce (nearly one out of every three marriages failing), lawyers, who are viewed as having too much of a vested financial interest in ensuring that the contesting parties do not reconcile, have been replaced by social workers, psychologists, and other trained professionals who are both more highly motivated and better trained to mediate between the parties and make an optimal effort toward reconciliation.

Turning to the question of status, Joseph Goulden explains:

> Few citizens who have professional contacts with divorce lawyers think kindly or highly of them. One reason, of course, is that the issue under contention—the dissolution of a marriage—is not a very happy occasion. But divorce lawyers bring much of the general opprobrium upon themselves. . . . Judge Paul Alexander of Toledo, Ohio, who has heard thousands of divorce cases during three decades on the bench, feels that divorce lawyers are produced by a sort of reverse Darwinism—a survival of the unfittest that is responsible for the greed and corruption he sees in divorce practice. Indeed, Judge Alexander accuses lawyers of pushing people into divorces that were unwanted, unnecessary, and undesirable.[74]

In a recent study (1986) William Felstiner and Austin Sarat found that one of the primary jobs of the divorce lawyer is to educate his clients and prepare them for the upcoming legal struggle. This is an important tasks for two reasons. First, most individuals undergoing a divorce are going to be very emotional and therefore have a difficult time objectively comprehending their legal problems. Second, this is also likely to be the first time that these parties have been participants in a lawsuit. Sarat and Felstiner explain that the lawyer attempts to educate clients about the requirements of the legal process and to socialize them into the role of client. The authors clarify this function by writing: "A heavy dose of cynicism helps the client realize that he/she is enmeshed in a system ridden with hazards, surprises and people who may be out to get him/her."[75]

Although written over 25 years ago, Hubert O'Gorman's book, *Lawyers and Matrimonial Cases,* still stands as the most complete examination of this specialty. O'Gorman described the major professional dilemma facing divorce lawyers in the following terms: "When they [matrimonial attorneys] are obligated to uphold laws whose deficiencies they acknowledge and lament, they represent clients whose problems they are expected to solve without violating laws or professional ethics."[76] O'Gorman notes the unique impact the emotionalism of the client's problem has on his or her relationship with the attorney. Divorce lawyers are urged by clients to become extremely partisan, which can easily cross over into vengeance. Additionally, because of their stressful situation, clients may also make demands on their attorney for emotional support; demands that may frequently extend beyond acceptable levels of professional interaction with one's client, and can reach the point where the lawyer has become a substitute spouse.

Sixty percent of the attorneys interviewed by O'Gorman acknowledged the necessity for initially exploring the possibility of reconciliation before preceding with a matrimonial suit. Nevertheless, O'Gorman concludes that "the legal training that a lawyer receives and its application in the lawyer-client relationship tend to minimize the chances of reconciliation occurring. Even when opposing counsel try to reconcile their clients, they do so without adequate professional preparation and within a context where each is held responsible for only his own client's interest."[77]

The Negligence (Personal Injury) Lawyer

Similar to the matrimonial and criminal lawyers just discussed, a personal injury attorney also suffers from low professional prestige. Nearly all of these three groups of specialists operate within either a solo practice or in association with a small law firm of less than ten attorneys. Although a negligence suit typically involves a defense attorney representing an insurance company whose policy protects the defendant, this discussion of personal injury lawyers focuses only upon the plaintiff's attorney who has initiated the suit on behalf of the injured party.

The leaders of the organized bar, often members of large corporate law firms, have been extremely critical of the negligence bar and established professional codes aimed specifically at what they perceived to be unwarranted abuses of accepted norms of conduct. The major criticism of personal injury attorneys is the belief that they engage in "ambulance chasing"—a derogatory term intimating unethical behavior in attempting to solicit clients. Jerome Carlin, in his study of private practitioners, defined ambulance chasing as "the activity of plaintiffs' lawyers who earnestly seek after or solicit the legal business of injured parties apparently qualified to claim compensation for their injuries. The object of the solicitation process is to sign the injured party to a contingent fee contract entitling the lawyers to a fixed percentage of any amount paid to the injured party, in return for legal representation."[78] Kenneth Reichstein completed a case study of the efforts of bar associations to control these errant negligence attorneys and concluded that they were disapproved of by the "high status" lawyers from large corporate firms for the following reasons: (1) personal injury solicitation leads to unfair competition; (2) some use client perjury to win weak cases; (3) they pass their "chasing" expenses on to their clients; and (4) they engage in package dealing in which several settlements are negotiated at the same time resulting in unethical trade-offs with the insurance.[79]

Despite this rather negative stereotype, the general public regards negligence lawyers fairly positively. Much of their professional mystique and admiration is likely associated with their supposed financial success through winning multimillion-dollar lawsuits on behalf of an unfortunate individual. Although the cases involving seven-figure settlements represent a very small fraction of negligence lawsuits, they still contribute to the layperson's perception of personal injury lawyers. Successful and highly publicized negligence attorneys, known for sensational courtroom tactics and earning exorbitant fees, have assisted in developing this glamorous image for their speciality by forming an association entitled "The Inner Circle of Advocates." Membership into this elite group is restricted to only those attorneys who have won at least $1 million in a damage suit. This group meets once a year to discuss successful litigation techniques. Outgoing President James Boccardo of San Jose, California, describes what transpires at their annual meetings: "We invite people to teach us—doctors, scientists, physicists, engineers, people versed in product liability. . . . We study graphic techniques, techniques in taking movies, in analyzing each frame, checking certain color tests. . . . We educate each other on up to date lore, availability of experts, trial techniques, what insurance carriers are doing, making sure everybody knows what is going on around the country."[80]

Although the overwhelming number of negligence cases involve lawsuits of less than $1000 and are settled prior to trial, in recent years a new category of negligence case has emerged that involves complex cases with multiple parties and has created a new breed of personal injury specialist. These are described as "mass-disaster" legal experts and are referred to in a recent *ABA Journal* article as the "New Elite Plaintiff Bar." These attorneys have been created by such recent lawsuits as Agent Orange, Dalkon Shield, Asbestos, Rely Tampons, and Benedicton. The article notes that these cases involve thousands of clients, are national in scope, and raise complex scientific questions of causation and legal responsibility. To be successful the new mass-disaster attorney must be able to manage what amounts to mini law firms, marshalling the resources of diverse lawyers with varying talents and large egos. The legal and managerial skills are likely to push these multimillion dollar cases against the frontiers of science and law.[81]

The Washington Lawyer

The Washington Lawyer is a unique legal specialist not only because of the types of activities in which he or she is engaged but also because it is geographically limited to our nation's capital. Joseph Goulden's examination of this unusual and powerful group of attorneys was captured in his book entitled *The Superlawyers*. The book offers the following definition of this legal specialty: "The Washington lawyer is an important figure in contemporary America because he is often the interface that holds together the economic partnership of business and government. In the decades following the New Deal, at a pace sharply accelerated during the 1960's, some Washington lawyers directed a counter-revolution unique in world economic history. Their mission was not to destroy the New Deal and its successor reform acts, but to conquer them, and to leave their structure intact so they could be transformed into instruments for the amassing of monopolistic corporate power."[82] Joseph Califano, himself a Washington lawyer and founding partner in one of the city's most prestigious firms, offers another view of the specialty that further clarifies its unique position within the legal profession: "Unlike his brother at the bar in other cities across the nation, his [the Washington lawyer] private practice steps on the brass rail of public policy every time he has an expense account luncheon. Whether he represents private, public or governmental interests, this attorney in a very real sense operates at the interface between public and private interest and is an active participant in the exercise of government power."[83]

Not every lawyer who practices in the capital qualifies as a Washington lawyer under the definitional requirements just presented. At least half of the city's attorneys work for the government, and another sizable group practice the traditional forms of private law and assist the citizens of the District of Columbia in their more mundane legal problems. Several Washington lawyers actually live elsewhere, but fly the shuttle from New York with such regularity that they qualify.

Goulden and most other observers of the Washington scene agree that whatever the total number, Washington lawyers have been increasing at a rapid rate since the 1960s. Many large corporate firms from New York and other large cities have opened branch offices in Washington with a permanent staff of attorneys familiar with the local legal culture. Lee Loevinger in his 1970 article "A Washington Lawyer Tells What It's Like," indicates that the growth of this group of specialists has paralleled the "ever-broadening scope of federal influence and the growth in size of the federal bureaucracy, and the increasing technicality and complexity of governmental intervention in the economy."[84]

Exactly what does the Washington lawyer do? It is obvious that he or she does not perform the basic legal functions described earlier such as litigating, negotiating, or drafting. He or she also does not represent the typical client that has thus far been described. Joseph Califano in the following quote offers a concise description of the basic functions of the quintessential Washington lawyer:

> He often represents not merely an individual client, but an entire industry or combination of clients: the sugar growers, the environmentalists, the oil industry, the Federal Housing Administration. The Washington lawyer rarely litigates cases; rather he tries to appoint judges. Instead of writing to his Congressman, he seeks to deliver a majority on the committee. He doesn't complain that his household goods were damaged in transit; he is after a certificate of permanent authority to move your household goods. The Washington lawyer is both counselor and lobbyist; he spends much more time and energy on Capitol Hill and in the halls of the Federal Trade Commission than in any courtroom.[85]

Washington lawyers are not without legal skills, but they are able to combine these abilities with their thorough familiarity of the corridors of power located in various governmental agencies. Their knowledge of Washington's power centers and access points impress and attract corporate clients from all over the world. For the successful Washington lawyer it is clearly a case of both "what they know as well as who they know!"

Like so many individuals who inhabit the shadowy corridors of the federal government, Washington lawyers have a poor public image. They are described as lobbyists with law degrees or simply influence peddlers capitalizing on past favors and future promises. Serving special interests, which often appear antithetical to broader societal concerns, these attorneys are contemptuously viewed by many Americans as "not practicing law so much as exerting political or personal influence."[86]

Although Goulden and other observers of the Washington legal scene believe that the negative connotation is unjustified, most would still agree with Joseph Califano when he notes that

> the model of the adversary system is not easily engrafted upon the different forums in which the Washington lawyer operates. The adversary system serves us best when all participating sides are supported by vigorous advocacy in open confrontation. In Washington, the lack of formal confrontation

and the imbalance of forces often results in a pale ghost of protest where a healthy clash of public and private interests should have been. Until all sides—and especially the public interest—are adequately represented, it is incumbent upon those representing privileged dominant interests to assume a special measure of responsibility. When the lawyer representing large corporate interests is pitted against an overworked understaffed public interest group or underequipped government body, the responsibility for integrity should be greater.[87]

There are obviously many other legal specialties that are equally interesting and unique. The field of law has expanded to cover all of the problems society continually is able to invent. Examples of recent fields of law that have followed such societal impetus include entertainment law, environmental law, sports law, and mass-disaster law. As noted earlier, the four specialties selected for discussion in this concluding section were chosen primarily because they seem to be of the greatest public interest and are most frequently involved in highly publicized litigation.

NOTES

1. Maureen Cain, "The General Practice Lawyer and the Client: Towards a Radical Conception," *International Journal of the Sociology of Law* 7 (1979): 331.
2. James C. Freund, *Legal-Ease: Fresh Insights into Lawyering* (New York: Harcourt, Brace, Jovanovich, 1984), 42.
3. Mark McCormack, *The Terrible Truth About Lawyers* (New York: Beech Tree Books, 1987), 258.
4. Ibid. p. 259.
5. Freund, *Legal-Ease*, 43.
6. Paul B. Wice, *Criminal Lawyers* (Beverly Hills, Calif.: Sage Publications, 1978), 29.
7. Wice, *Criminal Lawyers*, and Paul B. Wice, *Chaos in the Courthouse* (New York: Praeger Publishing, 1985).
8. Martin Mayer, *The Lawyers* (New York: Harper & Row, 1967), 30.
9. Charles Lasky, "The Essentials of a Successful Trial Advocacy," *The Practical Lawyer* 6 (1960): 89.
10. Louis Nizer, *My Life in Court* (New York: Pyramid Books, 1963), 114.
11. McCormack, *Terrible Truth About Lawyers*, 252.
12. Ibid. p. 253.
13. Vern Countryman and Ted Finman, *The Lawyer in Modern Society* (Boston: Little, Brown, 1966), 20.
14. Murray L. Schwartz, *Lawyers and the Legal Profession* (Indianapolis: Bobbs-Merrill, 1979), 172.
15. Mayer, *The Lawyers*, 42.
16. Ibid.
17. McCormack, *Terrible Truth About Lawyers*, 256.

18. Joseph Goulden, *The Superlawyers* (New York: Weybright and Talley, 1972), 71.
19. Mayer, *The Lawyers*, 56.
20. McCormack, *Terrible Truth About Lawyers*, 251.
21. Quintin Johnstone and Dan Hopson, Jr., *Lawyers and Their Work* (Indianapolis: Bobbs-Merrill, 1967), 110.
22. Wice, *Criminal Lawyers*, 121.
23. James C. Freund, *Lawyering: A Realistic Approach to Private Practice* (New York: Law Journal Seminars Press, 1979), 219.
24. Wayne D. Brazil, "Observations by Chicago Lawyers About the System of Civil Discovery," *American Bar Foundation Research Journal* (Spring, 1980): 222.
25. Laura Saunders, "Pretrial by Ordeal," *Forbes*, 8 October 1984, 105.
26. Ibid.
27. Mark Dombroff, "Checklist for Trial Countdown," *National Law Journal*, 13 March 1989, 15.
28. Wice, *Criminal Lawyers*, 171.
29. Donald Vinson, "What Makes Jurors Tick?" *Trial* 24/6 (June, 1988): 62.
30. Ellen Hopkins, "Jury Roulette," *New York Magazine*, 12 December 1983, 65.
31. Ibid.
32. Charles Traylor, Proceedings of the Denver Criminal Law Institute at the University of Denver Law School, 1974.
33. J. D. Reed, "They're Playing up to the Jury," *Time*, 1 August 1988, 70.
34. F. Lee Bailey and Henry Rothblatt, *Fundamentals of Criminal Law Advocacy* (Rochester: Lawyers Cooperative Publishing, 1974), 305.
35. Nathan Cohn (ed.), *3rd Criminal Law Seminar* (San Francisco: Central Book Co., 1973), 39.
36. Wice, *Criminal Lawyers*, 192.
37. Freund, *Lawyering*, 217.
38. Stephanie Goldberg, "Playing Hardball," *American Bar Association Journal* 73 (July, 1987): 48.
39. Ibid.
40. John Call, "Psychology in Litigation," *Trial* (March, 1985), 44, 46.
41. Bertram Hartnett, *Law, Lawyers, and Laymen* (New York: Harcourt Brace Jovanovich, 1984), 119.
42. Paul Wice, "The Private Practice of Criminal Law: Life in the Real World," *Criminal Law Bulletin* 14/5 (September–October, 1978): 386.
43. Robert W. Denney, "Responsible Attorney Brings Results," *National Law Journal* (February 20, 1989): 19.
44. Freund, *Lawyering*, 141.
45. Hartnett, *Law, Lawyers, and Laymen*, 211.
46. McCormack, *Terrible Truth About Lawyers*, 83.
47. Ibid. p. 84.
48. Carl J. Hosticka, "We Don't Care What Happened. We Only Care About What is Going to Happen: Lawyer-Client Negotiations of Reality," *Social Problems* 26 (1979): 602.
49. Freund, *Lawyering*, 156.
50. Countryman and Finman, *Lawyer in Modern Society*, 148.

51. Hartnett, *Law, Lawyers, and Laymen*, 103.
52. Joel Moldovsky, *The Best Defense* (New York: Macmillan, 1975), 142.
53. Wice, *Criminal Lawyers*, 113.
54. Aric Press with Susan Agrest, Peggy Clausen, and Diane Camper, "The Highest Legal Fees," *Newsweek*, 24 August 1981, 71.
55. David Trubek with Austin Sarat, William Felstiner, Herbert Kritzer, and Joel Grossman, "The Costs of Ordinary Litigation," *UCLA Law Review* 31 (October, 1983): 122.
56. Don Dunn, "How to Keep Legal Fees Somewhere Within Reason," *Business Week*, (August 24, 1987) p. 91.
57. "Recent Developments in Attorney's Fees," *Vanderbilt Law Review* 29 (1976): 710.
58. Dan B. Dobbs, "Awarding Attorneys Fees Against Adversaries," *Duke Law Review* (June, 1986): 435.
59. Andrew J. Kleinfeld, "Alaska: Where the Loser Pays the Winner's Fees," *The Judges Journal* 24 (Spring, 1985): 53.
60. Joseph Bartlett, *The Law Business: A Tired Monopoly* (Littleton: Fred Rothman, 1982), 31.
61. *Wolff* v. *Ruddy* 617 S.W. 2d. 64 Mo. (1981).
62. *Legal Specialization*, American Bar Association Special Committee on Specialization, Monograph No. 2 (1976), 3.
63. Ibid.
64. Alvin Essau, "Specialization and the Legal Profession," *Manitoba Law Journal* 9/3 (1979): 361.
65. Ibid.
66. Jerome Hochberg, "The Drive to Specialization," in *Verdicts on Lawyers*, ed. Mark Green and Ralph Nader (New York: Crowell, 1976), 121.
67. Richard H. Zehnle, *Specialization in the Legal Profession: An Analysis of Current Proposals* (Chicago: American Bar Foundation, 1975), 27.
68. O. Randolph Rollins, "The Coming of Legal Specialization," *University of Richmond Law Review* 19 (Spring, 1985): 496.
69. Ibid. p. 489.
70. Zehnle, *Specialization in the Legal Profession*, 22.
71. Clarence E. Hagglund and Robert Birnbaum, "Legal Specialization: The Need for Uniformity," *Judicature* 67/9 (April, 1984): 442.
72. Wice, *Criminal Lawyers*, 29.
73. Linda Greenhouse, "Supreme Court Backs Seizure of Assets in Criminal Cases," *New York Times* (June 23, 1989), A8.
74. Joseph Goulden, *Million Dollar Lawyers* (New York: Putnam, 1978), 33.
75. Austin Sarat and William Felstiner, "Law and Strategy in the Divorce Lawyer's Office," *Law and Society Review* 20 (1986): 126.
76. Hurbert O'Gorman, *Lawyers and Matrimonial Cases* (New York: Free Press, 1963), 30.
77. Ibid. p. 150.
78. Jerome Carlin, *Lawyers on Their Own* (New Brunswick, N.J.: Rutgers University Press, 1962).
79. Kenneth J. Reichstein, "Ambulance Chasing: A Case Study of Deviation and Control Within the Legal Profession," *Social Problems* 13 (1965): 3.
80. Paul Bernstein, "The Million Dollar Men of the Inner Circle of Advocates," *Juris Doctor* 8/2 (February, 1978): 44.

81. Diane Wagner, "The New Elite Plaintiffs Bar," *American Bar Association Journal* (February 1, 1986): 44.
82. Goulden, *The Superlawyers*, 5.
83. Joseph Califano, Jr., "The Washington Lawyers: When to Say No," in *Verdicts on Lawyers*, ed. Mark Green and Ralph Nader (New York: Crowell, 1976), 189.
84. Lee Loevinger, "A Washington Lawyer Tells What It's Like," *George Washington University Law Review* 38/4 (May, 1970): 533.
85. Califano, "Washington Lawyers," 189.
86. Loevinger, "Washington Lawyer," 538.
87. Califano, "Washington Lawyers," 194.

Chapter
5

Legal Ethics and Regulating the Profession

The previous chapters have depicted the complex and challenging professional life of America's lawyers. Although the intellectual and monetary rewards derived from the practice of law are noteworthy, there can also be a downside to its rigorous professional demands. This chapter explores efforts of the legal profession to guarantee the American public that it is meeting these challenges competently and morally. The opening section of the chapter will review the efforts of the bar to develop and implement codes of professional conduct. Succeeding sections will focus on client-related ethical issues, profession-related ethical issues, and the negative impact of professional tensions on the lawyer's private life.

PROFESSIONAL REGULATION: AN OVERVIEW

Like members of several other professions, lawyers appear to face an increasingly dissatisfied public. Their displeasure is the product of what they perceive to be a marked decline in professional competence as well as an even more upsetting slippage in the moral character of lawyers. To the credit of the legal profession, it has on several occasions been among its own most severe critics. Former Chief Justice Warren Burger has focused special attention upon trial lawyers, who he believes are inadequately trained and have been largely responsible for creating the currently "low state of American trial advocacy and a consequent diminution in the quality of our entire justice system."[1] The chief justice also urged the profession to deal more effectively with "uncivil and ill-mannered lawyers" who believe "that the zeal and effectiveness of a lawyer depends on how thoroughly he can disrupt the proceedings or how loud he can shout or how close he can come to insulting all those he encounters including the judge."[2] How is the profession to correct such abuses? Burger and others propose a special licensing system for trial lawyers that will not only eliminate incompetent advocates but will also elevate ethical standards.

The legal profession has been aware of the necessity for instituting a viable mechanism for developing and enforcing a code of conduct that can raise the attorney's level of performance and thereby regain the public's confidence. The American Bar Association (ABA) through both its national and state organizations has worked throughout this century to devise a workable system of disciplinary proceedings that can assure the public that they can depend upon the legal profession for a diligent and committed program of self-regulation. Unfortunately, the evidence appears to indicate that the profession is either unwilling to control its membership or the problem has expanded beyond the capability of its present disciplinary structure.

Why has the problem of professional discipline continued to evade resolution? Is it merely a lack of willpower or are there certain structural defects in our American legal system that contribute to the problem? Critics answer affirmatively to both sides of the question. Jethro Lieberman in his book *Crisis at the Bar* states his belief that the adversary system is certainly a contributing factor as lawyers become more committed to the needs of their client than the best interests of the larger society. According to Lieberman, lawyers are viewed by the public as "hired guns" who will engage in questionable ethical behavior if it serves their client.[3] Kurt Bulmer, a Seattle attorney who is a member of the ABA Professional Committee, also believes the adversary system is a major influence on the perpetuation of professional disciplinary problems. Bulmer states that " 'dishonest lawyers are by and large being disciplined around the country. But what people usually criticize are sharp practices, cutting corners. And the fundamental problem there is that our adversary system is designed to get lawyers as close to the edge as possible.' "[4]

Given the inherent problems raised by the adversary system, it is even more imperative that the legal profession develop workable disciplinary proceedings to curb excesses. Although many courts and bar associations have chosen to strengthen existing systems of professional self-regulation, it is disappointing to note that many lawyers have attempted to simply deal with the cosmetic issue of improving their public perception. These lawyers complain that they need to reshape their image and instead of trying to raise their standards of professional performance have opted for utilizing public relations firms to improve their standing with the public. Lieberman critiques this rather short-sighted approach in the following statement:

> It is entirely conceivable that the bar has come, through steady incantation, to believe its own lies. If so, its failure to see that lawyers have been engaging in their hypocrisies in full public view all along is understandable. And if lawyers do believe in the fiction that their rules are in the public interest, it is equally understandable why they find it mysterious that their reputation has sunk so low. But that does not alter the facts. It is the bar, not the public, that must bend in the end. The image cannot change until the underlying reality changes, until the lawyers come to their senses, lose their overweening pride, and devote themselves to rules that will serve the public before they serve themselves.[5]

Let us now turn to a closer examination of some of these rules and the difficult task of their effective implementation.

Model Rules of Professional Conduct

The American legal profession has always been concerned with maintaining a high level of professional conduct. Beginning in the eighteenth century, lawyers were required to take an oath of office promising to uphold elevated standards of professional responsibility. These oral traditions of the profession were transformed into a written format in the 1880s by Judge George Sharswood of Pennsylvania who attempted to educate young lawyers as to "The Aims and Duties of the Profession of Law." This treatise became the inspiration for the American Bar Association's first Code of Ethics, which was passed in 1887. This document contained 56 canons that more closely resembled a code of etiquette than professional ethics. It warned that lawyers should be punctual (canon 6), should not display temper (canon 7), should uphold the honor of the profession (canon 8), and should not stir up prejudice against the profession (canon 9).[6]

Although this initial effort by the ABA to devise a list of hortatory rules promoting an improved self-image for the legal profession was widely acclaimed and supported, in reality it offered little assistance to those wishing to improve the quality of professional behavior. In an attempt to deal more directly with professional regulation, the ABA revised the canons throughout the twentieth century with the latest body of model rules appearing in 1983. In addition to the recurring problem of ambiguity, the canons appeared schizophrenic in nature, representing two distinct professional traditions: brotherhood of the bar and laissez-faire for the consumer. Lieberman found that these early codes "asserted a need for lawyers to cooperate with one another but assumed that clients would act in a dog-eat-dog fashion toward each other and allowed lawyers to act on that assumption."[7] Legal historian Jerrold Auerbach was also critical of the early efforts of the ABA to protect its social economic position from the growing number of "lower-class lawyers"—the sons of immigrants who began practicing law in urban areas early in the twentieth century. The organized bar characterized these fledgling big-city solo practitioners as immoral and unprofessional and charged them with being engaged in shyster activities. The ABA's canons, therefore, prohibited such activities as advertising and soliciting, practices far from the common behavior of corporate firms whose clients were more interested in avoiding litigation than stirring it up.

It was clear by the 1960s that the canons were in drastic need of revision. During the preceding decades numerous amendments were added, accompanied by a continuing body of oracular interpretations by the ABA's Committee on Professional Ethics and Grievances.

In 1969 the ABA completed its most systematic revision of the code. The new document was entitled the Code of Professional Responsibility and proposed three categories of norms: general concepts, exhortations, and disciplinary rules. The rules are actually a group of administrative regulations that could be readily adopted by local legal authorities and would have the binding effect of law. In fact, the code was adopted in nearly every state. Geoffrey Hazard, in his treatise on legal ethics, organized the code into the following categories:

1. Rules regulating competition among lawyers (advertising, solicitation, etc.), which are subsumed under the rubric of assisting the legal profession in its duty to make legal counsel available.
2. Rules regulating competition from outside the profession. The substance of these rules is that lawyers should prevent nonlawyers from doing anything that is the "practice of law."
3. Rules requiring a lawyer to practice competently.
4. Certain rules having to do with lawyers who hold public office, whose substance is that a lawyer should not use public office for the benefit of private clients or take bribes.[8]

Geoffrey Hazard notes that the codes also deal with three problem areas: (1) confidentiality (What facts learned by a lawyer should be treated as secret and from whom and under what conditions may secrecy be lifted?); (2) conflict of interest (When and to what extent are lawyers prohibited from acting because of a conflict of interest between their clients or between themselves and clients?); and (3) prohibited assistance (What kind of things is a lawyer prohibited from doing for a client?).[9]

It is clear that the code has not sufficiently eliminated the problems of ambiguity and vagueness plaguing earlier versions, although slight improvements have been made. What is even more serious, however, is the inability of even the most recent efforts to decide whether the purpose of the code is to be an inspirational guide for the profession or the solid basis for disciplinary action when the conduct of a lawyer falls below the required minimum standards outlined in the disciplinary rules.[10]

Critics of the code agree that the true test of its worth is in the degree that it moves from uttering mere exhortation to the operation of a viable enforcement mechanism. Let us now turn to the various mechanisms of enforcement to learn not only how they are designed but even more significantly how effective they are as vehicles for effective self-regulation.

Mechanisms of Regulation

Professional behavior of lawyers is regulated by both informal and formal controls. Informal controls are generally reserved for the less serious problems but on occasion can be influential in even grave instances of misconduct. The major informal control affecting a lawyer's behavior is the knowledge that as a consequence of misconduct his or her professional reputation will be damaged. As noted in the previous chapter, an attorney's reputation is the major selling point to potential clients. Once the legal community begins to circulate a negative evaluation of an attorney's professional conduct, the economic implications will be both immediate and severe.

Closely related to reputation are the general economic principles of the marketplace that clearly indicate that it is in the attorney's best financial interests to avoid engaging in questionable behavior. Raymond Marks and Darlene Cathcart clarify the close relationship between these factors when they write: "Professional good will depends on general community reputation and closely related thereto, reputation among the buyers of legal services. Potential clients will credit the tales of dissatisfied clients even if grievance committees do not. Dissatisfied clients, whether sophisticated or not, can harm reputations: thus there will always be some market check on the nature of services rendered. Just how much remains uncertain."[11]

A third informal control that can be extremely effective is the law office. Similar to disciplinary boards for doctors within hospitals, the large law firm possesses formidable means for controlling the behavior of its partners and associates. A recent article in the *ABA Journal* pointed out that generally larger firms are able to catch potential gross misconduct before it becomes actualized. Hazard noted in the article that even more basic to controlling the misconduct in these large firms is the lengthy process of selecting partners. Hazard writes that " 'a lawyer doesn't get to be a partner in a big firm without surviving a number of years of scrutiny. Many attorneys leave during this trial period, precisely because these attorneys or the firm, decide that they can't perform adequately under the pressures of that practice.' "[12]

A final element of informal control is simply the lawyer's desire to avoid formal disciplinary procedures by a bar association or judicial agency. With the possibility of formal sanctions hanging over the attorney's head, he or she is more willing to informally dispose of the problem or complaint through an acceptable settlement with the complaining party. As disciplinary boards have been more rigorous in their resolution of client complaints, and are perceived to be dispensing harsher sanctions in an increasing number of incidents, attorneys are more motivated toward settling their problems prior to referral to a disciplinary board.

If these informal controls are unable to convince an attorney to either change behavior or negotiate a settlement with the complainant, then the problem must be resolved formally. Since lawyers rarely complain to disciplinary agencies about other lawyers, and judges are equally reluctant to utilize these formal proceedings, the overwhelming majority of complaints are initiated by clients. The disciplinary boards almost never investigate a possible incident of lawyer misconduct without first receiving a specific complaint. Occasionally a crusading journalist uncovers an unpleasant example of an attorney's malfeasance or incompetence, but these are isolated and often well-publicized exceptions.

Despite the variation among the disciplinary boards in terms of their procedures and resources, certain generalizations can be made. The initial complaint is usually directed to either a state grievance board or a state or local bar association. Nearly all of the work is handled by volunteers. Most boards attempt to dispose of the complaint informally at an intake hearing prior to the formal filing. If the complaint cannot be disposed of at intake, an investigation is conducted by the staff and a recommendation as to the validity of the charges will be made to the disciplinary agency. In less serious cases, the agency can utilize informal arbitration or privately admonish the offending attorney without public notification. In the more serious cases, where the attorney faces the possibility of suspension, disbarment, or public reprimand, the case is turned over to a judicial agency that will review the factual investigation and then rule on the attorney's conduct, either exonerating or punishing. Although the degree of centralization, procedural vigor, and staff resources vary greatly among states in the operation of their disciplinary boards, Marks and Cathcart have surveyed the nation and offer the following general observations:

1. The process is controlled by members of the bar. The legal profession has zealously resisted lay or even legislative intervention in the disciplinary process.
2. The emphasis is on procedural informality and discipline by "conscience of peers." The private bar has seemed unable or unwilling to define and exercise its full supervisory potential, particularly when judging a colleague's competence.
3. The process is essentially decentralized. Most disciplinary work is done locally, either by screening out complaints, holding initial hearings, or performing an informal arbiter role for minor complaints.
4. The process stresses secrecy. The expressed policy of the bar is to keep hearings secret in order to protect the "unjustly accused lawyer."[13]

One of the major problems with the disciplinary boards, given the wide variety of procedures and personnel, is the inconsistency in the type and seriousness of the sanctions imposed upon erring attorneys. The ABA has recently developed a set of standards that it hopes these boards will consider before imposing serious sanctions such as censure, suspension, or disbarment. The following is a list of these factors that are considered by state agencies before sanctioning an attorney:

1. The duty violated
2. Lawyer's mental state
3. Actual or potential injury caused by the misconduct
4. Existence of mitigating or aggravating factors
   a. Prior disciplinary record
   b. Dishonest nature
   c. Personal/emotional problems
   d. Good faith effort to make restitution
   e. Multiple offenses
   f. Pattern of misconduct
   g. Interim rehabilitation[14]

The New Jersey Disciplinary Review Board has often been recommended as a model program. In 1983 the state established through an order from its supreme court both a regionalized system of disciplinary review boards as well as an Office of Attorney Ethics (OAE). The OAE has jurisdiction to investigate and prosecute complex ethical matters as well as responsibility for all cases where a lawyer is a defendant in a criminal proceeding. Finally, it administers the Supreme Court's Random Audit Compliance Program, which supervises and conducts continued reviews of trust and business accounts ensuring that lawyers are following mandated recordkeeping practices.

The statewide program for controlling attorney conduct in New Jersey is a three-tier operation.

1. There are 17 regionalized district ethics committees organized along county lines, composed of both laypersons and lawyers. After a complaint is filed, this committee may either determine (a) that no unethical conduct occurred and dismiss; (b) there was unethical conduct, but it was of a minor nature and recommend a private reprimand; or (c) that it was a serious sanction and file a presentment against the attorney recommending public discipline.
2. At the next level is the Statewide Disciplinary Review Board composed of six attorneys and three laypersons. It hears appeals from individuals whose complaints were dismissed by a district committee. It also receives all recommendations for public and private discipline. After hearing oral argument, it can either dismiss the complaint, issue a private letter of reprimand, or recommend more serious discipline to the state supreme court. All proceedings are private and confidential.

3. The top tier is the New Jersey Supreme Court, which hears oral argument in the most serious disciplinary cases. Its proceedings are public, and it has the capacity to impose the most severe sanctions, that is, disbarment or suspension.[15]

New Jersey's system represents a recent evolution in disciplinary responsibility by state and local bar associations to share their control over lawyer misconduct with the state judiciary and other public agencies. This decision to divest or at least share a portion of the responsibility for lawyer discipline with the judiciary has been a major point of contention and discussion among bar associations across the country, although there has been a clearly discernible trend toward relinquishing some control over the previously lawyer-dominated process. Pressure from a concerned public as well as feared consequences from a continued negative professional image have coerced the bar into loosening its grip over disciplinary matters. Media charges of covering up as well as the skyrocketing costs of maintaining disciplinary boards have also convinced the lawyers to relax their control.[16]

One final innovation in grievance procedures of very recent vintage is the plan in both Florida and Texas to increase the public disclosure of attorneys facing disciplinary sanction. *The National Law Journal* reports that under the proposed Texas plan, grievance committees could no longer maintain secrecy over disciplinary proceedings while the announcement of penalties is pending. Additionally, a new commission would replace juries to review cases and determine sanctions. In Florida the state bar has approved a proposal to allow disclosure of an attorney facing possible discipline, regardless of the ultimate outcome once a probable-cause hearing has been completed.[17]

Assessing the Damage: Trends in Lawyer Misconduct

After reviewing the mechanisms for dealing with complaints of lawyer misconduct, it is necessary to answer the critical question of exactly how many lawyers are acting unprofessionally and ultimately facing disciplinary action. (This section also considers the type and incidence of the various forms of attorney misconduct.) It is nearly impossible to accurately assess the number of incidents where lawyers have been accused of misconduct. In a large number of instances the client does nothing about the problem. If the client does take action, it is most likely to result in an informal type of settlement in which no public record is maintained. Thus, it is in only the most serious cases where attorneys are either publicly censured, disbarred, or suspended that researchers are provided with empirical evidence clarifying the rate of incidence. Lawyer-sociologist Jerome Carlin concluded that "only about 2 percent of the attorneys who violated generally accepted ethical norms were even processed by disciplinary machinery."[18] Table 5.1, from research conducted by Eric Steele and Raymond Zimmer on the effectiveness of legal regulation, illustrates why so few clients take action against their

Table 5.1   WHAT CLIENTS THOUGHT THEY
COULD HAVE DONE ABOUT
ATTORNEY PROBLEMS

Don't know	20
Hire another attorney	12
Go to bar association	1
Nothing—just bad judgment	2
Watch more closely	1
No response	5
Nothing you can do	2

Source: Eric Steele and Raymond Zimmer, "Lawyers,
Clients and Professional Regulation," American Bar
Foundation Research Journal (1976): 958.

attorney when they perceive a lack of competence or some related type of misconduct.

Turning to the more serious incidents, which comprise only a small percentage of the total number of misconduct cases, an infinitesimal percentage of lawyers are involved in disciplinary action. In 1972, 357 lawyers, or roughly one-tenth of one percent of the nation's 380,000 practicing attorneys, were disciplined. In New York State, where there were 50,000 lawyers in 1974, disciplinary action (reprimand, censure, suspension, or disbarment) was taken against a total of 810 lawyers between 1957 and 1972, which averages out to approximately 50 per year, a very small figure but consistent with the national estimates.[19] Moving into more recent times, the *San Francisco Examiner* revealed that in California, where one out of every seven American lawyers practices, there were only 18 disbarments and 34 resignations with charges pending out of 7,981 complaints in 1985. The newspaper also discovered an additional complication in the California disciplinary procedures: the snail-like pace it took for the discipline complaints to be processed. The *Examiner* discovered that it averaged three and a half years—not counting supreme court delays—for a guilty attorney to be disciplined, while 4000 misconduct complaints were currently under investigation by the state bar more than 6 months after they had been filed.[20]

Table 5.2 provides a state-by-state examination of lawyer discipline. These figures are the result of a 1986 survey by the ABA Center for Professional Responsibility and offer a fitting conclusion to this discussion on empirical data concerning lawyer misconduct.

What are these incidents of attorney misconduct and why do they occur? Before presenting a typology of client complaints, it is important to inquire into the cause of these client-attorney problems. Research by Marks and Cathcart conclude that the greatest single cause of complaints was a breakdown in communication between lawyer and client. They described the typical case as involving a low- to middle-income client

Table 5.2   STATE-BY-STATE LAWYER DISCIPLINE

State	Resident Lawyers	Estimated Complaints Received by Agency	Number of Lawyers Privately Sanctioned	Number of Lawyers Publicly Sanctioned
Alabama	6,899	880	48	35
California	90,292	8,574	19	166
Colorado	12,717	908	77	20
Hawaii	3,453	300	24	9
Indiana	11,306	840	13	30
Maryland	13,715	1,397	9	39
Minnesota	14,460	1,233	106	31
Montana	13,222	913	51	25
Virginia	11,000	474	28	41
Wisconsin	10,472	1,147	74	45

Source: David O. Weber, "Still in Good Standing." Reprinted with permission from the *ABA Journal,* the Lawyer's Magazine, published by the American Bar Association (November, 1987): 60.

with little or no previous contact with lawyers who has had a misunderstanding with his attorney.[21] A report from the Chicago Bar Association added a second major cause of complaints: disappointed clients who were unsuccessful in their lawsuits and vented their anger and frustration on their attorneys.[22] Table 5.3 presents a fairly comprehensive listing of client complaints and their relative frequency. The information is from the Zimmer and Steele study of professional regulation completed for the American Bar Foundation.

Although a large portion of complaints appear to be caused by either disgruntled clients who were unsuccessful litigants or a breakdown in communications where both lawyer and client may bear at least partial responsibility, a third view of causation places greater blame on the attorney. The ABA Survey of the Legal Profession determined that approximately half of all complaints could be classified as either fee related or growing out of charges of unbusinesslike practices. This latter category includes such problems as neglecting to answer correspondence, failing to take action by a promised date, and neglecting to keep the client informed.[23] The survey estimated that 15 percent of attorney disbarments were the result of neglect, that is, failure to meet general professional obligations to the client. Money-related offenses (conversion, comingling, and misappropriation of funds) accounted for an additional 14 percent with 11 percent resulting from the commission of a felony.[24]

Who are the attorneys committing these unprofessional acts and finding themselves facing disciplinary action? It seems that they come disproportionately from solo practices and small firms. They have been described as being "boxed in by the lethal combination of case overload, insufficient office support, financial pressure and emotional isolation."[25]

Table 5.3   FREQUENCY OF VARIOUS
             PROBLEMS EXPERIENCED BY
             USERS OF LAWYERS

Clients reporting problems	16.3%
Type of problem	
Lawyer not capable	3.6%
Lawyer made mistakes	3.4
Lawyer didn't follow instructions	4.1
Lawyer pressured to settle	3.1
Lawyer didn't communicate	8.5
Lawyer didn't work promptly	9.6
Lawyer didn't work hard	7.1
Lawyer stole money/property	0.5
Lawyer dishonest	1.2
Lawyer fees excessive	7.1
Clients reporting no problems	83.7

Source: Eric Steele and Raymond Zimmer, "Lawyers, Clients and Professional Regulation," *American Bar Foundation Research Journal* (1976): 917.

Ethics expert Geoffrey Hazard goes on to describe these high-risk, beleaguered attorneys as being professional loners: " 'If they run into trouble, they have no one to turn to. As a result, if they sense trouble, they try to evade it. It starts with the lawyer not knowing what to do. Then the client gets upset, and then the lawyer avoids the client.' "[26] Also contributing to their greater likelihood of client-related trouble, the small firms practice what appears to be "high-risk" specialties such as domestic relations, which can easily develop acrimonious relations between client and attorney. These conclusions do not preclude large law firms from experiencing serious client problems, but large firms seem much more capable of quickly disposing of the "rotten apples" and keeping the entire incident from public scrutiny.

Critique of Disciplinary Procedures

If there is one point of consensus concerning the effectiveness of the legal profession's efforts at self-regulation, it is in both the public and the bar's agreement that the current system is not working very well. The critique reaches not only defects within the code itself but in its flawed implementation through the numerous disciplinary agencies across the country. Former Supreme Court Justice Tom Clark chaired a special ABA committee looking into the problem and concluded that "after three years of studying lawyer discipline throughout the country, this Committee must report the existence of a scandalous situation that requires the immediate attention of the profession. With few exceptions, the prevailing attitude of lawyers toward disciplinary enforcement ranges from apathy to outright hostility. Disciplinary action is practically non-existent in many jurisdictions; practices and procedures are antiquated; many disciplinary agencies have little power to take effective steps against malefactors."[27] This stinging rebuke delivered by such a respected jurist did prompt aggressive efforts to not only rewrite the code of ethics but to also improve the enforcement capabilities of local disciplinary agencies. Although attempts at improving professional regulation are still ongoing, a loud and persistent chorus of criticism continues to be directed at the inadequacies of self-regulation.

One of the most frequent complaints concerning the Code of Ethics is its inability to attain the proper level of generality. Stated more simply, the code is too ambiguous to provide lawyers a useful guide in resolving ethical dilemmas. Tony Amsterdam finds that the rules of professional conduct " 'provide lawyers with as much guidance in their work as a valentine would provide a heart surgeon.' "[28] In a less amusing, but more balanced evaluation, Theodore Schneyer acknowledges that the new model rules are an improvement over the vagaries of the earlier canons, but they still offer only a blueprint that requires long-term, overly subjective interpretive efforts by a frequently divided body of supposed experts. Schneyer believes that the new rules may be "better written with fewer internal inconsistencies but still fail to provide the necessary level of specificity."[29] The result, he believes, will be a continuing demand by lawyers for interpretive assistance from professional organizations who can unravel and clarify the code's prohibitions.

A second area of criticism involves the code's emphasis on wrongdoing with scarce attention to the more basic issue of competence. This emphasis may help convince the public that the bar is regulating itself by proceeding against the most serious cases of professional misconduct but neglects the broader issue of competent legal services, which affects a much larger segment of the profession's clientele. Marks and Cathcart urge the profession to step away from overconcern with the fault notion and the severity of notion issues that currently dominate the debate. Instead, they would encourage lawyers to recognize three basic guidelines in determining their professional behavior: (1) obey the laws of the community, (2) adhere to the rules of conduct of the profession, and (3) practice law competently.[30] A final undesirable side effect of this overemphasis on punishing wrongdoing is the continuing increase in the severity of sanctions so that their use is limited to only the most extreme cases. As Eric Schnapper has recently commented: "A punishment that strips the offender permanently, or for a limited time, of the ability to make a living is one from which even the most vindictive judge would ordinarily shrink."[31]

The third criticism is concerned with a much more pragmatic issue than the first two, which represent broader, systemic weaknesses of the code. Nevertheless, it raises a point of grave concern to major groups within the legal profession and weakens the overall effectiveness of the entire document. This is the inability of the code to reach ethical problems occurring in the law firm or in shared-practice situations. Only the misconduct of individual attorneys is covered by the code, indicating not only a possible bias against solo practitioners but the creation of a major gap in the public's protection. Critics of the code and resulting disciplinary procedures believe it is aimed at catching only the small fish while large-firm practitioners can move beyond its purview. Washington solo practitioner Sol Rosen believes that "the good ol' boy factor influences the bar to go after minority lawyers and individual practitioners more than lawyers of big firms and from major ethnic and religious backgrounds because the big firms control the bar."[32] It is disappointing to note that these charges are remarkably similar to the conclusions reached by Jerome Carlin 20 years earlier in his studies of the bar in Chicago and New York.[33] Garbus and Seligman's review of professional sanctions reached similar conclusions, caustically commenting that "the fat cats" who dominate the bar associations and construct the codes of behavior are simply unwilling to go after their colleagues at the top of the profession. The result has been the "transformation of judicial politics into a sleazy system of self-protection under which the leaders of a local bar assume the grave mantle of self-regulation and moral leadership and then wink at most improprieties they encounter."[34]

The fourth, and final, criticism to be discussed is the failure of the code to deal with problems related to the lawyer's function as adviser. Because of the nearly total emphasis of the code on problems related to advocacy, many critical aspects of the lawyer's counseling relationship with the client have been nearly entirely ignored. Louis and Harold Brown recently discussed the importance of the advising role and its ethical implications noting that "the preventive law advisor stands in the position of the final and authoritative legal decision-maker for the client both in the planning of transactions and the doing of future acts."[35]

Given the amount of recent attention directed at improving the quality of legal services, why has the level of performance continued to fall short of professional standards? One response to this question relates to the inherent problem facing any profession wishing to raise its level of performance as well as its ethical standards. Eric Schnapper described the intrinsically perplexing problem of teaching legal ethics as being analogous to convincing the general public to be polite on the subways or be kind to their children. It is simply something that cannot be easily or effectively either taught in school or enforced by third parties such as bar associations.[36] Schnapper and other analysts believe that the local legal culture of a particular community is of much greater import than a set of abstract generalizations listing standards for ethical performance. Geoffrey Hazard of Yale explains that not merely the geographic diversity but the very heterogeneity of the profession itself has caused the failure to establish any type of workable consensus over questions of acceptable conduct.[37]

A second reason for the unsatisfactory state of professional regulation is rooted in the very nature of the American legal system in which lawyers are conditioned through the adversary process and the pressures of advocacy that rules are not to be taken seriously but are rather challenges to one's creativity and courage. Jethro Lieberman sees the inevitable problem developing in attempting to convince lawyers to be more respectful toward ethical proscriptions as he writes that "the only secret that the lawyer really possesses about the law is that no one can ever be certain of what law is."[38] By continually dwelling in a professional world where conflicting interests and subjective values constitute the essence of his or her vocation, the possibility of a truly ethical lawyer is, according to one respected critic, an impossibility.[39]

The third reason for the inability of the legal profession to effectively regulate its professional conduct is simply the basic difficulty of any group being sufficiently altruistic to correct its own behavior without outside provocation. There is an obvious conflict of interest whenever certain members of the profession attempt to control and possibly sanction their colleagues. The realization that "the shoe may soon be on the other foot" creates an inevitable chilling effect upon the rigorous enforcement of any type of self-regulation system. Deborah Rhode writing in the *Texas Law Review* summarizes this dilemma in the following quote: "No matter how well-intentioned and well informed, lawyers regulating lawyers cannot escape the economic, psychological, and political constraints of their position. . . . By abjuring outside interference, professionals can readily become victims of their own insularity, losing perspective on the points at which fraternal and societal objectives diverge. No ethical code formulated under such hermetic constraints can be expected to make an enduring social contribution."[40]

The obvious answer to the serious problems derived from the continued attorney domination of the regulatory structure is to permit the lay public the opportunity to play a greater role. It is an unbridgeable conflict of interest that has grown too great for even the best-intentioned members of the profession. There must be a clear understanding among lawyers that disciplining errant attorneys is a "public problem," not a private one. Perhaps the clearest evidence of the flawed commitment of the bar to its own regulation is the paucity of resources devoted to disciplinary agencies. In addition to underfinancing, these agencies operate in a shroud of secrecy, moving cases along at a snail's pace through a labyrinth of procedural rules designed to confound and discourage most potential complainants. Thus, the entire operation of these disciplinary agencies charged with enforcing the professional code of behavior is heavily biased in favor of acquitting the attorney with as little embarrassment to the profession as possible. In closing this discussion of the many defects in the present system, the following recommendations by Seligman and Garbus are both logical and necessary: "Create an agency independent of the state and local bar associations, composed of a minority of lawyers and a majority of laymen, to establish and enforce standards of integrity and competence. Such a panel would possess both the ability and the independence to examine ethical questions long ignored by the legal profession."[41]

Whistle Blowers

Even if disciplinary agencies are restructured with increased public involvement and the codes of behavior are improved through clarity and breadth, lawyers still must be willing to participate in these proceedings if they are to be effective. Recent efforts to amend the code to include a requirement for lawyers to report professional misconduct ended in failure and raised doubts as to the likelihood that the bar is truly committed to aggressive self-regulation. Without an impetus from their peers, will attorneys possess the courage to risk professional chastisement? Given the general reluctance of most individuals to inform, and the special place of client confidentiality in the lawyer's professional code, one must be quite pessimistic about relying on the possibility of lawyers testifying against one another, even though they are strongly encouraged to do so by their professional associations. Gerald Lynch in his study of "The Lawyer as Informer" concludes that "the ABA's frank recognition that the Code's broad reporting requirement has proved to be unenforceable suggests that in balancing intraprofessional loyalty against even an explicit command to inform, lawyers have acted no differently than other citizens. Lawyers have generally determined that awareness of another lawyer's wrongdoing does not automatically impose a moral duty to inform."[42]

Critics of the self-policing aspect of the legal profession's code believe that it will work only when there is a perceived threat of public intervention. Is the public sufficiently frustrated and angered by the present failure of the disciplinary agencies to improve the quality of legal performance? Since so few members of society use lawyers on a regular basis and given the amorphous nature of most consumer-based pressure groups, it is unlikely that the legal profession will experience the necessary amount of public concern to change its ways.

ENSURING LEGAL COMPETENCE

The initial section of this chapter discussed the efforts of the legal profession to define, control, and punish attorney misconduct. The analysis moved from a brief review of the Code of Professional Responsibility through a critique of the profession's seemingly ineffective mechanisms for disciplining errant attorneys. Now let us move from an examination of the types of activities a lawyer should *not* be doing to discussion of the desired level of professional skill the public should expect from a practicing attorney. Therefore, this section shifts its focus to the broader issues of measuring and defining legal competence, determining how often attorney performance slips below the acceptable levels, and what reforms are presently being attempted to elevate these levels of performance.

Defining and Measuring

There are no objective measures or tests of lawyer's competence. Individual impressions collected in relatively casual conversations, reflecting unstated standards are disparate to the verge of worthlessness.[43]

The opening quote from Judge Marvin Frankel reflects the frustration of so many leaders of the bar who have been engaged in a relentless pursuit to construct a workable operational definition of legal competence. Competence is an idealized goal of the legal profession, but like so many similar sought-after objectives, such as equality, fairness, and access, it is a concept that has varied meanings that further complicate the likelihood of its actualization.

Deborah Rhode in her discussion of the "Rhetoric of Professional Reform" notes that demands for increased competence have been a continual feature of legal reformers for several decades. She explains that the most recent vocalized concern over the issue developed in 1970 "when Chief Justice Warren Burger asserted that between one-third and one-half of the lawyers appearing in serious cases were not really qualified to render fully adequate representation. Although the empirical basis for that assertion remained undisclosed, other commentators from all points on the ideological spectrum offered similar assessments and various committees convened to consider appropriate responses."[44]

The ABA has been one of the most dogged groups attempting to resolve the difficult problem of defining legal competence. Through their Code of Professional Responsibility, the ABA offered the rather cryptic standard that competence requires "preparation adequate to the circumstances."[45] Additionally, the association's Model Rules of Professional Conduct attempted to clarify the concept further by "requiring the legal knowledge, skill, thoroughness, and preparation reasonably necessary for the representation."[46] To ensure that a lawyer is representing his or her client competently (as provided in canon 6), the model rules have recently added DR 6-101, which attempts to clarify the specific requirements of competent representation by stating that a lawyer will not be acting competently if he or she:

1. Handles a matter that he or she knows or should know that he or she is not competent to handle without associating with a lawyer who is competent to handle it.
2. Handles a legal matter without preparation adequate to the circumstances.
3. Neglects a legal matter entrusted to him or her.[47]

The courts have also been interested in developing a workable definition of competence since they are frequently called upon to decide if a litigant has received "effective assistance of counsel." This requirement is especially critical in criminal cases where the defendant is required by the U.S. Supreme Court to have his or her Sixth Amendment guarantees of right to counsel provided in a competent manner. American courts have traditionally used "the mockery of justice" standard, which originated in the 1945 case of *Diggs* v. *Welsh*,[48] although amended in 1970 when the federal courts declared that "in order for a prisoner to succeed in a claim of ineffectiveness, it must be shown that the entire proceedings were a farce and a mockery of justice."[49] There continues to be confusion and divided opinion among the various federal circuits as to exactly what degree or standard of proof is necessary to establish incompetency of counsel. About the only point of agreement is that the mockery of justice standard is no longer workable. Presently, most of the federal courts appear to be relying upon objective standards that emphasize the specific actions of the attorney rather than the overall conduct of the trial.[50]

The competence issue assumes greater significance in the American legal system than in most other nations because of our reliance on the adversary system. This system makes the implicit assumption that it is both fair and functional because each party is represented by a competent counsel. Critics of the system, including such respected jurists as Justice William Brennan and federal judge David Bazelon, have charged that the appellate courts have papered over the incompetency question, at least as it pertains to criminal defendants. Both judges believe that this has occurred because most courts have "a natural disinclination to set aside verdicts, particularly where the defendant is believed guilty. . . . They fear that after every unsuccessful defense the cry of incompetent counsel will be heard and the courts will be flooded with petitions."[51]

The problem of defining competence is also complicated by two additional factors. First, the practice of law is extremely diverse, requiring an equally varied range of skills. To be able to draft a single abstract formulation that can adequately encompass such a heterogeneous profession appears virtually impossible. The task of conceptualization grows even more difficult as one attempts to apply it to actual circumstances.

What type of evidence must be presented to a court in order to convince a judge or jury that a lawyer has performed incompetently? As Deborah Rhode points out: "Any such assessment would require detailed monitoring of every facet of a broad sample of cases, a process that poses substantial problems of cost, confidentiality and counterfactual speculation."[52] And, as a final note, most critics note that incompetence is more a factor of attitude and motivation than the absence of specific cognitive skills.

Despite the rather gloomy prognosis just presented, the legal profession continues to search for ways to effectively evaluate the performance of attorneys. Douglas Rosenthal in his comprehensive study of the topic lists the following approaches to evaluating competence:

1. Measure competence by the training a lawyer receives and exhibits in a proficiency examination.
2. Determine the lawyer's status in the legal community such as is done by the Martindale–Hubbell law directory.
3. Evaluate competent performance in terms of successful and unsuccessful outcomes, for example, amount of money clients recover in personal injury claims.
4. Evaluate in terms of minimal standards such as by the ABA or the courts (Note, however, that the judiciary has failed to presently arrive at a common standard for defining negligence).
5. Develop a more systematic and detailed specification of what lawyers actually do when they serve clients and develop critieria for how well each activity is performed.

It would also necessitate some degree of professional evaluation by peers. (It is the final approach that I believe offers the best hope for the future resolution of this difficult problem).[53]

A further examination of proposals designed to heighten professional competence will be presented at the conclusion of this section. Let us now turn to the question of how many attorneys are currently being charged with acts of incompetence. The trends and types of legal malpractice will therefore be our next topic.

Malpractice Realities: Trends and Types

In the first section of this chapter we examined the problem of misconduct among lawyers. This is behavior that is in violation of the profession's Code of Responsible Conduct, and although it is usually initiated by client complaints, it is primarily a type of self-regulation attempting to punish and correct purposeful attorney misconduct. The discussion of malpractice and incompetence in this section examines a slightly different aspect of errant behavior by attorneys. Some clients who believe they have been harmed by their attorneys' incompetence choose to sue their lawyers for malpractice rather than, or possibly in addition to, reporting the complaint to the organized bar for a possible sanction. Although the extreme punishments of disbarment or suspension from practice are very serious and can be economically crippling, they occur so rarely and fail to provide the complaining client with a monetary award, the typical client is much more likely to initiate a malpractice lawsuit against an attorney, hoping to be financially rewarded for any damages suffered.

The most comprehensive analysis of legal malpractice claims is a recently completed five-year study by the ABA's Standing Committee on Professional Liability. Its preliminary report issued in 1987, based on 30,000 claims between 1981–1986, indicated that most malpractice suits arise in the areas of personal injury (25 percent) and real estate (23 percent). Figure 5.1 illustrates the complete picture of the origins of malpractice claims. The "other" category includes criminal law, personal injury (defendant), business transactions, worker's compensation, and securities. The study found that two-thirds of all malpractice claims against lawyers were either dismissed or resulted in no payment to the complainant. Twenty percent of the plaintiff clients negotiated for payment without going to trial while an additional 12 percent received payment following a lawsuit. The highest payments were found in personal injury (plaintiff) cases, with the lowest level in criminal and family law.

A second study, conducted by the National Malpractice Data Center, reviewed 18,500 malpractice claims during the early 1980s and offers a fairly complete breakdown of the types of lawyer errors resulting in malpractice claims (see Table 5.4). The largest group of specific errors fell within the category of failure to calendar properly. This typically meant that the lawyer either failed to know a deadline, failed to calendar a deadline, or failed to react to the calendar. These various claims may be categorized into the following four broad types of errors: administrative areas (26.2 percent), client relations (15.6 percent), substantive errors (14.5 percent), and alleged intentional wrongs (10.7 percent).[54]

A final statistical point in the discussion of malpractice claims is their meteoric rise in recent years. Although the empirical evidence on a national scale is lacking and rather impressionistic at best, most states

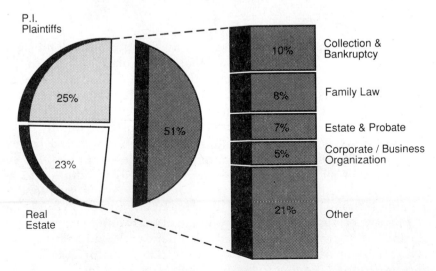

Figure 5.1 Origins of malpractice claims. [*Source:* William Gates, "Charting the Shoals of Malpractice." Reprinted with permission from the *ABA Journal*, the Lawyer's Magazine, published by the American Bar Association (July, 1987): 64.]

are reporting significant increases in malpractice actions. Louisiana, for example, from 1974 through 1976, reported annual jumps in cases from 200 to 500 to 1700 during this three-year period.[55] These figures proved quite alarming to trial lawyers who found themselves disproportionately involved in malpractice problems. A conference of litigators explained their special vulnerability in the following terms: "In no other area of the legal profession is there the potential for client dissatisfaction as there exists to those in trial and appellate practice. Since in every law suit one of the parties must lose, 50% of the clientele almost automatically become basically unhappy with the result of the case."[56]

Why have malpractice claims increased so dramatically in recent years? Their growth should come as little surprise since the overall amount of litigation, both civil and criminal, has also expanded so greatly during this same period. Many scholars believe that citizens today are more inclined to utilize the courts to enforce all of their rights whenever an injustice is perceived. Darrell Havener, a Kansas trial lawyer, concluded that Americans have adopted an "entitlement theory," which he describes as a belief that "if anything happens to me that is untoward, that jeopardizes my right to enjoy, unencumbered, my life the way I am used to, I'm entitled to something, to compensation of some kind." Havener goes on to explain that recently the entitlement theory has been joined with a growing need for holding lawyers to increased accountability: a belief in a "no risk ethic with everyone wanting assurance of what's coming to him or her and someone to blame, and who's responsible if things go wrong."[57]

Table 5.4   SOURCE OF CLAIMS BY SPECIFIC ERROR OR MISCONDUCT

Percentage	Type of Error
10.66	Failure to calendar properly
9.35	Failure to obtain client's consent or to inform client
9.16	Failure to know or properly apply the law
8.81	Inadequate discovery of facts or inadequate investigation
8.44	Planning error in choice of procedures
6.96	Failure to know or ascertain deadline correctly
5.04	Error in public record search
5.03	Failure to file documents where no deadline is involved
4.79	Failure to follow client's instructions
4.72	Procrastination in performance of services/lack of follow-up
3.99	Malicious prosecution or abuse of process
3.61	Failure to react to calendar
3.47	Fraud
3.39	Conflict of interest
12.58	All other

Source: William Gates, "The Newest Data on Lawyers Malpractice Claims." Reprinted with permission from the *ABA Journal,* the Lawyer's Magazine, published by the American Bar Association (April, 1984): 80.

Are lawyers suffering disproportionately in comparison with other professions in this recent onslaught of malpractice claims? David Haughey studied this interesting question, and after comparing the malpractice experience of lawyers and doctors, found that although legal actions have recently gained ground, they still lag far behind the malpractice suits involving doctors. His article discusses the degree to which lawyers do have a favored position and offers several explanations, the primary one being that "doctors' errors result in bodily injury or death and claimants can always hope for a large award. An attorney's mistake is more likely to result in a limited loss of money or property."[58] Many of the lawyer's activities require him or her to make an informed professional judgment whose propriety and degree of correctness fall into a gray area. Finally, it is often difficult to show how the error led to a specific loss on the part of the client. These difficulties are summarized in the following statement from *American Jurisprudence*, a legal encyclopaedia defining the generally accepted national norms on this issue:

> If an attorney acts in good faith and in an honest belief that his acts and advice are well founded and in the best interest of his client, he is not held liable for a mere error of judgment. A fortiori, an attorney is not liable for an error in judgment on points of new occurrence or of nice or doubtful construction, or for a mistaken opinion on a point of law that has not been settled by a court of last resort and on which reasonable doubt may well be entertained by informed lawyers. And an attorney has no liability when he follows a decision of the highest court of his jurisdiction and the decision is later reversed by the Supreme Court of the United States.[59]

Reform Measures: Elevating Levels of Competence

Given the alarming increase in incidence of legal malpractice claims and the resulting negative publicity for the legal profession, there has been a determined effort by the organized bar to develop a series of programs designed to upgrade the competence of practicing attorneys. It had been previously hoped that judicial review of attorney performance could serve as a vehicle for addressing, and possibly correcting, the competence issue. Judge Irving Kaufmann, however, reflects the accepted wisdom on the futility of the judicial role in treating the problem. He recognizes the increasing frequency of claims of inadequate representation being raised in his courtroom, and pessimistically concludes that "postconviction review alone is not likely to improve the quality of legal representation. Appellate judges are presented with a cold record and do not have the benefit of witnessing the conduct of the trial counsel in action. . . . A reviewing court's only powerful weapon is the ability to reverse a conviction, but the threat of appellate sanctions at some remote date is unlikely to alter a lawyer's current performance."[60]

What can be done to upgrade professional performance? Although there have been a variety of proposed reforms, the persistent cry for outside intervention into the problem appears to be the most critical avenue to pursue. By developing independent institutions to assist in a meaningful reassessment of the various strategies for identifying and redressing the problem of declining competence, the bar will be offering visible proof to the public of its sincere desire to resolve the malpractice dilemma. Lay participation will not only permit the bar to gain a clearer understanding of the public's concern over the issue of attorney competence but will also improve the quality of the regulatory mechanisms.

Another reform is to require attorneys to undergo periodic recertification throughout their professional careers. Although extremely unpopular with large segments of the legal community, recertification has gained limited support from a small group of reformers. Since it would require attorneys to expend time and money in order to prepare for the exams as well as raise the traumatic possibility of failure, many lawyers are adamant in their opposition to these programs. Douglas Parker, a strong advocate of certification exams for specialists, points to their successful use in the accounting and medical professions, but he is a lonely voice in his endorsement of this reform.

Susan Martyn does an excellent job of reviewing the entire range of reforms designed to elevate the competence of practicing attorneys in her article entitled "Lawyer Competence and Lawyer Discipline: Beyond the Bar." As the title infers, she places a great deal of emphasis on outside participation and the necessity for lay involvement. Among the proposals discussed are (1) model peer review, where a lawyer competency review board would formulate general competence criteria, remedial programs for individual lawyers, and evaluative training materials for competence appraisal; (2) mandatory continuing education where not only attendance but some type of testing would be required (this is currently being done in nine states); (3) ensuring that all grievance procedures are given expanded publicity so as to ensure greater deterrence value; and (4) a formalized mentor system modeled after the Minnesota "buddy system" in which inexperienced lawyers can seek help and guidance from experienced attorneys who have volunteered their services.[61]

How soon can one expect improvement? How quickly will these various reforms be implemented across the country? Most students of the issue remain pessimistic and probably nod in agreement with Deborah Rhode's careful and somewhat negative assessment:

> Without a fundamental rethinking of the premises and practices of bar governance, the prospects for substantial reform remain limited. No licensed vocation is well situated to assess the points at which public and parochial interests diverge. If the history of other professions is any guide, the most significant efforts to upgrade quality and efficiency will come through external pressure, whether from government or private intermediaries such as management corporation or insurance companies.[62]

BASIC PRINCIPLES GOVERNING LAWYER-CLIENT RELATIONSHIPS

In the previous sections of this chapter, the overall efforts to regulate the professional behavior of lawyers were examined by reviewing the code of professional responsibility, the mechanics of self-regulation, and the related topics of competence and malpractice. This section will focus on a narrower and more personalized aspect of a lawyer's professional life: his or her personal relationship with clients and the range of ethical problems that commonly arise. Although the lawyer-client relationship may give rise to a plethora of problems, this section will examine the following four major issues, which represent the most pressing aspects of this topic: (1) lawyer-client confidentiality, (2) conflict of interest, (3) difficult clients, and (4) excessive fees.

The Confidentiality Question

The basic rule of confidentiality requires lawyers to keep everything secret that they learn either from or about clients, except if the client will be aided by the disclosure. The rule obligates lawyers to both refrain from testifying in court as well as refusing to reveal the information in any other context. This also refers to two types of confidential matters: information obtained *from* the client during the course of lawyer-client relationship and information *about* the client that might prove to be detrimental or embarrassing. The necessity for the strict maintenance of confidentiality between lawyer and client is based primarily on its necessity for ensuring that the client will be willing to disclose as much as possible to his or her attorney. If the client fears the attorney cannot be trusted to keep any communications secret, the lawyer's effectiveness as an advocate is compromised. *McCormick's Handbook on the Law of Evidence* succinctly explains why the promise of confidentiality is so important to everyone's best interests: "Claims and disputes which may lead to litigation can most justly and expeditiously be handled by practised experts, namely lawyers and such experts can act effectively only if they are fully advised of the facts by the parties whom they represent. Such full disclosure will be promoted only if the client knows that what he tells his lawyer cannot be raised over his objection, be extorted in court from the lawyer's lips."[63]

As might be expected, there are a number of exceptions to the lawyer-client confidentiality requirement. Bruce Landesman summarizes the three major instances when an attorney is allowed to reveal information learned from or about a client: (1) when it concerns a client's intention to commit a crime and may be useful in preventing future wrongdoing; (2) when it is necessary in order to collect his or her fee; and (3) when it is necessary to assist in the defense of an accusation of wrongful conduct against the lawyer.[64]

An additional issue that is presently a matter of debate within the profession involves the lawyer's obligation to reveal the client's intention to commit perjury. Monroe Freedman and the Association of Trial Lawyers (ATL) believe that the lawyer in both civil and criminal cases should be required to assist the client even if the client insists on presenting perjured testimony. On the other side is the ABA, whose Kutak Commission proposes the required disclosure of client dishonesty, charging that the lawyer whose client commits known perjury on the witness stand is under an explicit obligation to correct the perjury. Norman Lefstein, a long-time student of the client perjury issue in criminal cases has tried to construct a middle position between the ABA and ATL positions by first of all stressing that the lawyer must have actual knowledge that the client plans to lie. He recommends that the lawyer placed in this most difficult situation should not escape by simply withdrawing from the case but should first attempt to convince the client not to testify falsely. If the defendant still insists on taking the stand against the lawyer's advice, Lefstein recommends the use of the "narrative approach." This permits the lawyer to avoid questioning the client directly in the regular manner but instead to invite his or her client to make a statement to the court in a narrative fashion. The lawyer, however, is urged not to argue the defendant's tainted version of the facts to the jury or repeat the false testimony in the closing argument.[65]

It is crucial to effective lawyer-client relationships that there be an understanding that everything said will be kept secret. Without the guarantee of confidentiality the lawyer would find it nearly impossible to obtain truthful information from a client. Clients, especially when defendants in criminal cases, are embarrassed by the truth and may not want anyone, not even the lawyer, to learn the ugly facts about their involvement in criminal activities. Even with the promise of confidentiality, many attorneys still have a difficult time convincing their clients to be truthful. Trial attorneys I have interviewed generally thought that a liberal discovery procedure that permitted access to police reports, witness statements, and other relevant data was the most effective device for pressuring the client into being more candid. As one Los Angeles criminal lawyer commented: " 'Hopefully this will jog the client's memory or at least let him know that you know a great deal about his case, and that he had better disclose the rest so as to ensure the best defense possible.' "[66]

Conflicts of Interest

A second trouble spot plaguing the relations between lawyers and clients is conflict of interest problems undermining the attorney's dedication to a client's best interests. The Code of Professional Responsibility explains the conflict of interest principle in the following terms: "Neither [a lawyer's] personal interests, the interests of other clients, nor the desires of third parties should be permitted to delete his loyalty to his client."[67] In order to ensure that this loyalty is preserved, a lawyer is prohibited from acting for a client when his or her "professional judgment" might be influenced by personal interests or the interests of other clients whom he or she also represents.

The necessity for protecting the client through the conflict of interest rule is directly related to the vulnerability of the client and the great potential for harm possessed by the ill-intentioned attorney. A recent *Harvard Law Review* article on the conflict of interest issue clarifies the necessity for the rule by stating: "Although the lawyer is often thought to be a mere extension of the client's own will, contributing simply a developed knowledge of the contents and procedures of legal institutions, the intimacy of the relationship between lawyer and client, the importance of the goals that the client asks the lawyer to help him achieve, and the extent of the lawyer's power to act within the legal system mean that the lawyer is capable of doing immense harm to, as well as good for, the client."[68]

Geoffrey Hazard of Yale, in his discussion of conflict of interest in his book on professional ethics, lists three primary examples of conflict of interest situations. The first, and most common, arises out of business transactions between lawyer and client. Although there are many permissible types of business transactions such as corporate ventures and real estate deals, the potential for abuse by an avaricious attorney to take advantage of a client creates a risky situation. A second type of conflict may develop when a lawyer serving one client is paid by another individual whose interests may not be wholly compatible with those of the first client. It appears almost impossible for the attorney to be able to equitably "serve two masters." The attorney can be too easily prejudiced in favor of serving one of the two clients, which is likely to place the other one in a disadvantaged position. A third type of conflict may be created as a result of the merger of the first two categories. This situation occurs with the representation of two or more clients when the clients' interests conflict. As noted with the confidentiality rule, a lawyer can only represent both clients when it is clear that adequate representation of each one's interests can be guaranteed and each client willingly consents to the situation after being fully apprised of all possible implications of dual representation and its impact on the attorney's ability to render independent professional service to each client.[69]

As a closing point, it is interesting to examine the unique case of government lawyers whose varied clientele raises complex conflict of interest problems. Jack Weinstein examined the ethical and political problems faced by these attorneys and was intrigued by several aspects of their difficult situation: "(1) the deep political dimension that almost all important government legal questions have; (2) the necessity of integrating the government's law office with other government departments and (3) the difficult problems of judgment and ethics created by the government lawyer's multiplicity of clients."[70] In comparison to the private lawyer, who is only concerned with doing what is best for a single client, the government attorney can be torn in many directions, playing to several competing interest groups, often at odds with one another. The attorney working on urban renewal must be responsive, for example, to not only the business interests of the city but be equally sensitive to the angry citizens who may be displaced and lose their neighborhood as a result of the economic development. Additional pressures from the mayor, city council, labor unions, building contractors, and community groups can all contribute to the creation of a nearly impossible situation.

Dealing with a Difficult Client

Must a lawyer be professionally obligated to serve every client who requests representation? What can the attorney do to withdraw legal services once he or she discovers that the client's behavior makes competent representation impossible? The current position of the ABA's professional regulations would be to answer the first question negatively, making it quite unlikely that there would be any sanctions for declining to represent a client. The ethical ramifications of refusing to represent a repugnant individual were recently debated by several law professors and the following represents a synopsis of their conclusions: First, Charles Wolfram argued that lawyers have a duty to rescue those in need and that duty extends to those in legal need. This may include helping those who are morally disreputable if the client's claim is legally just, socially important, and morally compelling, and if the need for the particular lawyer's services are pressing. Alan Donagan advocates a second position that is in disagreement with Wolfram's rather altruistic conclusion. Donagan fails to find a professional responsibility to represent immoral clients. His view of the adversary system, however, means that a lawyer is morally permitted to take such cases if the client's belief in the legitimacy of his or her cause is held in good faith. A third view is presented by Murray Schwartz, who proposes a different solution. He argues that lawyers must reject immoral civil representations since lawyers are morally accountable for the ends they serve. If a client is continually turned down, he or she can have the court assign an attorney. This collection of views by these three esteemed professors indicates to the reader both the complexity of the issue and the wide diversity of acceptable resolutions.

Moving beyond this rather esoteric discussion of whether lawyers should represent ideologically reprehensible clients is the more common problem of what a lawyer should do about a client who becomes unpleasant and difficult to counsel. Stanley Clower has written a volume on this topic, commenting on not only when to refuse these potentially troublesome cases but also offering some clues as to how to identify them. He advises lawyers to simply look to their caseload, finances, and the client's personality as obvious clues. He concludes his discussion with the familiar refrain, although difficult to scientifically operationalize, of "trusting your instincts." The following anecdote from one of Clower's colleagues serves as an example of this rather generalized piece of advice:

> This well-dressed, articulate man came to me with a damages claim against a local car wash. He carefully documented the "pre-wash" and "post-wash" conditions of his BMW, with photographs and all. Despite an apparently strong case, I felt uneasy about something. But I accepted the case anyway, on a contingency basis.
>
> During depositions, the lawyer for the car wash's insurance carrier documented the client's scam: the records showed that he had presented his "foolproof" damages case on several occasions to several different businesses. I left the depositions muttering to myself: I knew something was wrong. I should have trusted my gut reaction.[71]

One of the most interesting sections of Clower's book was his observations on how to identify a problem client. He composed the following list of client characteristics and warns attorneys that if their clients possess two or more they are likely to be difficult and constant complainers:

1. Owes money to many other lawyers
2. Fails to make regular or appropriate payments
3. Talks only negatively about previous legal help
4. Doesn't listen well
5. Has a holier than thou attitude
6. Continuously has unrealistic expectations
7. Can't seem to follow advice
8. Complains about almost everything in life
9. Does not accept reasonable solutions to complaints he or she has issued.[72]

A unique twist to the problem of difficult clients arises in the situation facing in-house corporate counselors who may be asked by their employers to commit what they believe to be unlawful acts. The lawyer faces two options: either quit outright or be fired without any legal recourse. For those attorneys who were hopeful that they could successfully oppose a possible unlawful command by charging the corporation with a wrongful termination suit, the 1986 case of *Willy* v. *Coastal Corporation*[73] arising out of Texas dashes their hopes and appears to grant corporate employers absolute protection in firing employees regardless of the fact that they were terminated for refusal to implement an illegal command. (Donald Willy claimed that he had been fired from his job as in-house corporation counsel after he required his employer to comply with various state and federal environmental laws. He sued, alleging wrongful termination, but his complaint was dismissed for failure to state a claim.)

Excessive Fees

The final client-related problem examined within this section, excessive fees, is probably of greatest import to the client. The entire process of setting fees and establishing criteria for determining a proper amount often defies logic and befuddles both attorneys and clients alike. Martin Mayer partially explains the confusion by noting that the amount a lawyer charges may be unrelated to the time spent or the apparent importance of the service rendered. He writes that "easy jobs command high fees. It is amazing how much money a lawyer will think he is entitled to for just writing a letter, and hard jobs are done for relatively little money such as labor lawyers who will sit endless nights in negotiations and write incredibly detailed contracts as part of the services due under a modest monthly retainer."[74]

The ABA's Code of Professional Responsibility offers little guidance to attorneys who wish to set proper fees that will not be viewed as excessive. Although the code does present the following list of factors that lawyers should consider in estimating their fees, their overall effect does not provide a workable, reliable formula for setting reasonable fees: (1) time and labor, (2) customary fee charged in that locality, (3) monetary value of the matter for which the service is provided, (4) preemption of other business because of possible conflict of interest, (5) urgency of the matter, (6) nature and length of the professional relationship with the client, (7) experience and reputation of the lawyer, and (8) whether the fee is fixed or contingent.[75]

Canon 2 of the code deals with the fee problem in rather vague terms by stating in its narrative section entitled "Ethical Considerations" that lawyers should not charge more than a "normal" fee. And while this is supposedly clarified in the corresponding disciplinary rule, which prohibits lawyers from "entering into an agreement for, charge, or collect an illegal or clearly excessive fee," the fuzzy terminology continues to make effective enforcement illusory. The code does, however, try to be a little more specific when it states that "a fee is clearly excessive when, after a review of the facts, a lawyer of ordinary prudence would be left with a definite and firm conviction that the fee is in excess of a reasonable fee."[76]

The tautological nature of these definitions offers little help to either the aggrieved client or the local grievance committee who has jurisdiction over such problems. While a few states do attempt to arbitrate fee disputes, the disciplinary agencies and grievance committees will only become involved if the fee is so exorbitant that it exceeds the limits of the most expensive attorney within the jurisdiction. These agencies and committees rationalize their reluctance to intervene, according to Marks and Cathcart, because of "the difficulty in assessing the worth of an individual lawyer's services and the problems inherent in applying objective criteria to intangible value judgments."[77] The ABA, in what would appear to be a somewhat inconsistent reversal of its position in the Canon of Ethics, supports this noninterventionist position by stating that "an attorney has the right to contract for any fee he chooses so long as it is not excessive . . . and this Committee is not concerned with the amount of such fees unless so excessive as to constitute a misappropriation of the client's funds."[78]

Given the lack of professional guidance and resources devoted to assisting clients who believe they have been victimized by excessive fees, a few states have established programs to assist clients in mediating fee disputes with their attorneys. The Minnesota program serves as a model for aiding clients, even when the attorney is unwilling to join. A panel, appointed by the bar association, holds a hearing to determine a fair fee for the service rendered. The panel will then offer expert testimony *against* the lawyer in court if the dispute reaches a civil suit by presenting evidence about the profession's specific view of a reasonable fee in the disputed matter.[79] A second strategy for dealing with excessive fees has been the successful legal challenge to minimum fee schedules that establish artificially high charges while statutorily eliminating competition. These schedules were declared to be unconstitutional and in violation of the federal antitrust laws in the case of *Goldfarb* v. *Virginia State Bar*.[80] The Goldfarbs were forced to pay a set fee in a real estate transaction and successfully challenged the procedure in the U.S. Supreme Court. Despite this legal victory, informal fee fixing continues in most areas and is nearly impossible to stop. A third tactic has been for many laypersons to simply turn away from using lawyers entirely and attempt to handle their problems in such areas as bankruptcy, divorce, and probate through the use of do-it-yourself kits. State bar associations rigorously oppose these threats to their economic well-being, but the popularity of the kits seems to be growing. Although all three reform alternatives are growing in popularity among disenchanted laypersons, the legal profession's response has been tepid at best, with large segments of the legal community exhibiting outright hostility toward several of these measures. It is especially upsetting to the more socially conscious members of the bar to discover that those laypersons who are most likely to suffer most frequently from the excessive legal fees may also be the group least capable of effectively challenging the profession's control over this issue.

PROFESSION-RELATED ETHICAL CONCERNS

In addition to the more narrowly defined ethical dilemmas facing individual attorneys, there are also the broader moral conundrums troubling the entire legal profession. This section will briefly examine four of these issues, introducing the reader to a select group of important ethical problems: (1) advertising and solicitation, (2) excessive aggressiveness, (3) the immoral attorney or "hired gun," and (4) mandatory pro bono.

Lawyer Advertising

The traditional position of the organized bar has been in firm opposition to lawyer advertising. The ABA believes that "competitive advertising would encourage extravagant, artful, self-laudatory brashness in seeking business and thus could mislead the layman."[81] This would, it is feared, inevitably produce unrealistic expectations from clients who would soon become cynical and distrustful of the entire profession. Ward Reynoldson sees the danger spreading from a disillusioned public into a debasement of the entire legal process and writes that soon "the solemn forums for the litigation of cases whose lawyers resemble carnival barkers at the door scarcely can avoid being viewed as carnivals, or at least, places where justice is bought and sold, as in any marketplace."[82]

The general public and segments of the legal profession termed "mavericks" by the organized bar object to this traditional view. Advertising from their perspective is a critical reform facilitating the wider delivery of legal services to citizens of modest means. Not only will it provide more Americans with increased opportunities for obtaining legal representation, but their choice of attorney will be made more intelligently, and the increased competition can be expected to further reduce costs.

The turning point in breaking up the organized bar's nearly total ban on lawyer advertising occurred in 1977 with the U.S. Supreme Court's decision in *Bates* v. *State Bar of Arizona*.[83] The Court ruled that the Arizona Bar Association's prohibition against advertising violated the First Amendment rights of a legal clinic that took an ad in a local newspaper offering their legal services "at very reasonable prices" and went on to specify that uncontested divorces were $175 plus $20 for the filing fee. The Supreme Court limited legal advertising to only those "routine legal services." The justices appeared to be influenced by a *Legal Needs of the Public Survey*, which discovered that 48.7 percent of the public strongly agreed with the statement that people do not use lawyers because there is no way of knowing which attorneys are competent to handle their specific legal problem.[84] The majority opinion stressed that not only were individuals in need of information about the nature and availability of legal services, but also that they were generally capable of understanding the problem.

What have been the consequences of the historic *Bates* decision? According to Harry Stumpf, the case has done little to clarify the use and limitations that can be applied to legal advertising. As a fallout from the decision, many state bar associations have revised their rules on the subject, rendering the advertising even more difficult than before. Nevertheless, a 1986 poll by the ABA did find that the percentage of lawyers who advertise has increased sharply in recent years, moving from approximately 3 percent in 1978 to nearly 24 percent seven years later.[85]

Because of the narrowness of the holding in *Bates* and the continued position by influential leaders of the organized bar, the dispute over lawyer advertising continues. One of the basic charges against permitting advertising is that it is expensive and will invariably drive up the costs of legal services. Research by Muris and McChesney in 1979, however, found that legal advertising lowered the costs of legal services without adversely affecting its quality. They concluded that "advertising increases the volume of services a lawyer can expect to sell. Greater volume in turn allows greater specialization in production, more effective use of systems management and the substitution of paralegals and capital for lawyer inputs."[86]

Two additional feared consequences of legal advertising—a startling increase in the amount of litigation (especially frivolous and unwarranted suits) and a decline in the quality of legal services—also appear to be unfounded. Hearings before the ABA's own Commission on Advertising, which has been carefully monitoring the problem since the *Bates* decision, concluded that there has been no evidence that advertising has led to unwarranted litigation. The commission also found evidence that quality need not decline and were satisfied to hear from economist Charles Beard that the quality of legal services in general can be expected to increase because advertisers will not be able to recoup their costs unless their services satisfy their clients. Deceptive advertising, resulting in one-time customers, will soon prove to not be a cost-effective way of practicing law.[87]

One should not become overly sanguine about the ability of advertising to quickly eradicate the problem of providing access to competent legal services to an increasingly broader base of potential clients. Yet it is a small step, and its brief experience has shown that none of the dire predictions have actually materialized such as declining quality or increasing prices.

Excessive Zeal: "Rambo Litigation"

As noted throughout this book, one of the most unique and significant characteristics of the American legal system is its adversarial nature. With a belief that justice can be best meted out in a process in which the two advocates battle before a neutral judge, it should not be unexpected that on occasion one or both of the adversaries may pursue their clients' interests with excessive zeal. Although trials and negotiations carried on in the adversarial style can be envisioned as easily advancing into unprincipled warfare between the contestants, the organized bar and the nation's judiciary have been reluctant to intervene except in the most blatant and excessive incidents. There does seem to be some recent movement toward greater willingness on the part of the judiciary to exert control in these situations and the organized bar has also begun to exhibit concern. The ABA model rules still fail to offer concrete guidance in controlling excessive advocacy, but as a result of the 1983 amendments to the Federal Rules of Civil Procedure, there is at least the pres-

ence of an enforcement mechanism.[88] Judith Maute is cautiously optimistic about the new amendments and believes that "if the rules are
rationally interpreted and strictly applied to sanction infractions, we can
expect fewer infractions."[89] Most critics still agree, however, that it is
primarily the responsibility of the trial courts to monitor instances of
outlandish aggressive advocacy and the sanctions must be appropriate
and prompt if they are to serve as an effective deterrent.

Despite the growing concern over excessive aggressiveness, there
seems to be a growing infatuation with, and an increasing number of
instances of what is popularly referred to as either "hardball tactics" or,
more colorfully stated, "Rambo litigation." Robert Saylor describes this
growing phenomenon in bellicose tactics as possessing the following
characteristics:

1. A mindset that litigation is war.
2. A conviction that it is invariably in the lawyer's best interest to
   make life miserable for his or her opponent.
3. A disdain for common courtesy and civility, thinking it will benefit an opponent.
4. A wondrous facility for manipulating facts.
5. A hair-trigger willingness to fire off unnecessary motions and use
   discovery for intimidation rather than fact finding.[90]

There is a perception, though no scientific evidence, that such tactics succeed, and many experienced attorneys argue that it is bad advocacy. Saylor explains that these colorful ploys are frequently ineffective
because they "are one-dimensional and therefore completely
predictable. . . . It is easy to set traps for him, goading him into temper
tantrums. It also lessens the force of occasional stern trial tactics. Even
if it starts as an act it eventually becomes habit and it will lock lawyers
into untenable positions and cloud their objectivity. . . . It is as likely to
turn off as many clients as it attracts."[91] Critics of the Rambo approach
also warn attorneys that the entire profession is harmed by these histrionics because they send an unpleasant message to the general public
that lawyers will resort to even the most unscrupulous means conceivable in order to defeat an adversary. Even though overly aggressive attorneys may gain an occasional advantage over more temperate and balanced adversaries, in the long run they will undermine their
professional relationships with other attorneys who will refuse to cooperate or assist them in future dealings.

The "Hired Gun": Plight of the Amoral Attorney

Closely related to the overly aggressive attorney who engages in Rambo
litigation is the broader characterization of a lawyer as an amoral individual willing to serve as a client's "hired gun." Like the Rambo litigator,
the amoral attorney is a logical outgrowth of the adversary system and

can readily be rationalized because "once the lawyer has assumed the responsibility to represent a client, the zealousness of that representation cannot be tempered by the lawyer's moral judgments of the client or of the client's cause."[92] Monroe Freedman, who is the author of the preceding quote, goes on to state that "in day to day practice the most common instances of amoral or immoral conduct by lawyers are those occasions in which we preempt our client's moral judgments!"[93]

Can an attorney following Freedman's advice be a good person and a good lawyer at the same time? The majority of lawyers would probably agree that there will be several instances during one's career where it will be very difficult to maintain both of these positions simultaneously. This will result in creating a psychological tension that can easily debilitate the most avid advocate. Obviously Freedman finds no such tension and instead agrees with the conclusion of Charles Fried, who depicts lawyers as "a special purpose friend" to his client. Fried views the lawyer as simply "someone who enters into a personal relation with you—not an abstract relation . . . and like a friend, the lawyer acts in your interests, not his own; or rather adopts your interests as his own."[94]

This rather cursory discussion of such a complex philosophical issue was intended merely to introduce the problem rather than offer an indepth analysis or propose a persuasive solution. The moral dilemma of contemporary lawyers forced to grapple with their clients' unethical problems within the confusing confines of the American legal system and guided only by the vagaries of a rarely enforced code of conduct will continue to challenge legal scholars for many years to come and generate numerous articles in professional and academic journals in the future.

Mandatory Pro Bono

On Tuesday, January 12, 1982, attorney Donald Wolff of St. Louis challenged the right of the State of Missouri to compel him to defend a criminal suspect without pay.[95] This case has sparked a growing legal controversy over whether the state or its bar association can require an attorney to perform pro bono service. Although the medical profession has long adopted the concept of "mandatory pro bono" responsibilities as an essential element in their Hippocratic oath, the legal profession is far from a consensus concerning the attorney's professional obligation to serve the public without compensation.

The Model Rules of Professional Conduct circulated by the ABA's Commission on Evaluation of Professional Standards did propose in January 1980 that the legal profession move in the direction of public service as a mandatory obligation of each lawyer. The proposal was attacked by critics as a radical change, lacking historical precedent. A few attorneys even went so far as to argue that enforcing such a responsibility would be the equivalent of professional slavery, an illegal practice forcefully prohibited by the Thirteenth Amendment. Presently, mandatory pro bono remains a highly controversial issue that has not been firmly resolved by the organized bar although there does seem to be growing support for its adoption in a limited number of states.

NEGATIVE IMPACT ON A LAWYER'S PRIVATE LIFE

The concluding section of this chapter will examine the impact of an attorney's long hours and pressure-filled professional life on his or her emotional and physical well-being. After briefly describing the stressful conditions and long hours frequently demanded by professional obligations, this section will then discuss the emotional and physical fallout resulting from these demanding conditions, followed by a brief examination of several preventive techniques that may be employed to lessen the tension level.

Long Hours and Heavy Work Load

Although there is obvious variation within the legal profession as to the length of the workday and the amount of tension inherent in each attorney's professional activities, it is generally acknowledged that most attorneys work extremely long hours, frequently immersed in stressful situations. The typical attorney works a 10- to 12-hour workday, arriving at the office between 8 and 9 to take care of minor matters and prepare for any court appearances, which usually begin at 10 o'clock. Work frequently drags on to 7 or 8 in the evening, the last few hours being a quiet time, without clients, during which an attorney can sit back and enjoy a rare contemplative moment or two. In addition to the Monday to Friday schedule, most attorneys use at least one day of the weekend to handle additional problems that are best solved in the quiet solitude of a half-empty office, undisturbed by phone calls and other annoying intrusions. This normal workweek totals 60 to 70 hours, the number rising in emergency situations, when the lawyer faces intractable deadlines. Vacations are rare, with a much needed one or two weeks off in the summer being the norm.

Labor negotiators, litigators in the throes of a trial, and young associates striving to make partner in a corporate firm can all be expected to exceed the typical workweek just presented. For the associate in fierce competition for the severely limited number of available partnership positions, 80-hour workweeks and more are commonplace. Corporate firms seem to take advantage of both the paranoia and ambition of these young associates, yet with so many burning out and dropping out of their large firms after exposure to this environment, it might be a more intelligent policy to control and moderate the race for partnership.

Why are attorneys driven to work so hard and for such long hours? Stanley Clower argues that it is the result of both their perfectionist attitude and their inability to effectively delegate work to others. Lawyers are probably more concerned with details than any other profession, for their clients demand that documents and procedures be precisely completed in order to justify their handsome fees. Attorneys feel compelled to check the work done by associates, clerks, secretaries, paralegals, and anyone else. They may delegate a task, but not the final responsibility, and this brings them continuously back into the picture. Clower describes the real or perceived situation when an attorney becomes overwhelmed by his professional responsibilities as "work overload," a vicious cycle that is depicted in Figure 5.2. The attorney suffering from work overload will typically experience attacks of panic and anxiety as well as unexpected and extreme mood swings.

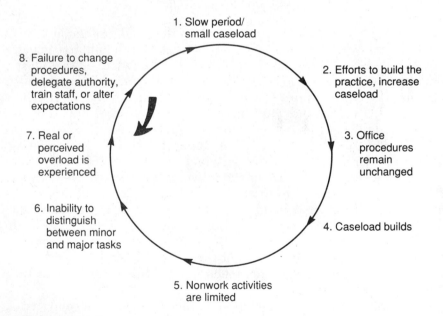

1. Slow period/small caseload

2. Efforts to build the practice, increase caseload

3. Office procedures remain unchanged

4. Caseload builds

5. Nonwork activities are limited

6. Inability to distinguish between minor and major tasks

7. Real or perceived overload is experienced

8. Failure to change procedures, delegate authority, train staff, or alter expectations

This illustration shows how easy it is to get locked into a situation of work overload. Throughout the cycle, a lawyer usually works hard and has good intentions. Once a real or perceived overload exists, it will not disappear without a change in the work system. (The lawyer is trapped between stages 7 and 8.) Eventually the lawyer may become so inefficient that clients get upset, take their business elsewhere, and advise others to do the same. The lawyer's caseload may be substantially reduced, bringing him or her back to stage 1. Unless the lawyer improves or eliminates stages 3 through 6, the cycle continues.

Figure 5.2 The vicious cycle of work overload. [*Source:* Stanley J. Clower, *You and Your Clients* (Chicago: American Bar Association, 1988), 49.]

When is the attorney about to slip into work overload? Clower believes that there are certain early warning signals that can alert an attorney to the impending crisis. Among the useful warnings offered by Clower are "irritability, headaches, other physical distress signs without known medical cause, and a sudden slump in productivity at work or home are good indicators. . . . Other people's reactions also can reveal changes in your behavior that you did not notice. If the same comments keep surfacing such as 'George, you're just not yourself lately' or 'Judy, you have looked really tired the last few weeks,' pay attention."[96]

Emotional/Psychological Consequences of Overwork

The most common term used to describe the emotional condition resulting from the overwork and tension experienced by so many lawyers is *stress*. Stress is technically defined by psychologists as any condition that requires a change or adaptation by the individual it affects.[97] The ability of people to change or adapt in the face of stressful situations is the measure of their level of mental health and what can turn stress into distress. Thomas Cory, a clinical psychologist who conducts workshops for many professional groups, including lawyers, believes that on the surface attorneys are well equipped to handle stress as a result of their rigorous educational experience. Additionally, they can expect reasonable financial rewards and status. Cory finds, however, that the reality of practice is unfortunately quite different. He offers the following lengthy list of sources of stress that appear to at least partially explain why so many attorneys suffer from this emotional condition: (1) constant pressure to keep abreast of a continually changing legal system, (2) adversarial exchanges in court and possibility of losing the case, (3) extreme competition for limited financial rewards, (4) declining prestige of the profession, and (5) frustrating interaction with clients, compounded by unreasonable demands.[98]

The result of this intense stress and tension, as it wears on attorneys for a long period of time, is to create an emotional condition currently described as "being burned out." Although this term initially referred to the point at which a missile consumed all its fuel, it is commonly used in psychology to describe someone who has succumbed to the pressure and tension dominating his or her life. The symptoms of burnout are fatigue, emotional numbness, decreased interest and satisfaction in work, and sometimes psychophysiological illnesses such as ulcers and high blood pressure.

Although all types of lawyers are readily susceptible to experiencing burnout, it is widely acknowledged that trial lawyers are especially vulnerable. John Martel, a former litigator turned novelist, who personally suffered from this type of "courtroom battle fatigue," believes that trial work "requires the expenditure of large amounts of physical and psychic energy, that leads some members of the trial bar to the nearest bar, others to ulcers, many to the relative tranquility of business law."[99] Martel believes that a large number of trial attorneys are Type A personalities, competitively driven by powerful and deep-seated emotional needs and attack their professional responsibilities with a passion and zeal that makes them ideal candidates for burnout. Even as they achieve success, the level of stress not only continues, but may actually increase over time. He explains that "maintaining this level of excellence over years can compound the stress level as emotional scar tissue begins to build. It is this duration-demand that makes the trial lawyer's game hard to play. Rarely do athletes compete at a level of consistent excellence for more than a few years. With rare exceptions, last year's stars usually give way to this year's heroes."[100] Despite the rational explanation, if you are the displaced star, the traumatic nature of the drop can be devastating and so it is little wonder that attorneys, especially litigators, suffer so commonly from this malaise.

Physical and Social Side Effects

For lawyers who are overworked and suffering from a stressful professional life that is pushing them inexorably closer to the burnout point, there may be physical and social consequences of equal significance. The incidence of lawyers who abuse drugs or alcohol and withdraw from their families and friends has been on the rise and of concern to the entire profession. Although the alcohol and drugs may provide a quick fix for an attorney striving to obtain relief from stress, it neither eliminates the cause nor improves his or her coping ability. Thus, if the abuse continues, there will likely be either a physical ailment or an emotional collapse so severe that the lawyer will be unable to continue work. How bad is the substance abuse problem among lawyers? Barbara Hinson with the South Carolina Board of Commissioners on Grievances and Discipline has researched the question and believes the problem may not be as bad as many fear, with only 4 to 5 percent of the attorneys suffering from drug or alcohol addiction (a figure fairly consistent with national statistics for the general population). She adds, however, that the numbers are on the rise and are being manifested through a growing volume of misappropriation of funds cases coming before the state board, most of which involve an underlying drug or alcohol-related problem.[101] Less optimistic about the problem is Timothy McPike of the Center for Professional Responsibility who believes the problem to be more serious and reports that the alcohol and drug treatment programs for lawyers have doubled in the past four years (1982 to 1986).

My research into criminal lawyers, a litigation specialty, uncovered a wide range of occupational hazards resulting from the enervating rigors of courtroom battles and the persistent anxiety of economic survival. Although all of these ailments should not be blamed entirely upon professional pressures, it is reasonable to conclude that an attorney's work environment does exacerbate whatever latent conditions may be festering just below the surface. It was shocking to discover the number of heart problems, stomach disorders, and cases of hypertension among the sample of lawyers interviewed. One Philadelphia lawyer explained that " 'the strains of the profession overwhelm one's physical capabilities and make a breakdown inevitable for all except those endowed with either remarkable constitutions or the common sense to slow down or switch professions.' "[102] As we have already noted, substance abuse (primarily alcoholism) and marital problems were also frequent by-products from the pressure of criminal practice. Over 40 percent of the criminal lawyers in the national sample of 200 were divorced at least once while another large group described their family life as virtually nonexistent.

What Can Be Done: Some Preventive Techniques

The most obvious, and dramatic, way to deal with the tension is simply to abandon the practice of law. A recent *New York Times* article (February 1989) by David Margolick indicated that a startling number of attorneys are doing just that. The article reported that as many as 40,000 lawyers a year are leaving the profession. Most of these disgruntled lawyers were described as being young and female, previously working as unhappy associates in large firms. Another agitated group were litigators, although corporate lawyers overall were most prevalent. As an aid in helping these disappointed attorneys make a transition into a new career, workshops are being offered such as Celia Paul's "Lawyers in Transition," which handles 100 attorneys per course.[103]

There are obviously less extreme measures for dealing with the frustrations of practicing law. We have already noted there are several early warning signs that attorneys should heed when the stress and work load begin to rise above the danger zone. One of the most common techniques for dealing with the tension is to find alternative interests outside the law. This may mean getting in better shape physically through regular health conditioning or simply becoming involved in outside interests such as playing in a band, which former litigator John Martel found was crucial in saving his sanity. Ultimately, each lawyer must find his or her own way to reduce the tension for as the noted Chicago negligence lawyer Philip Corboy stated: " 'There are no rules. Everybody's got to do it his own way.' "[104] Workshops are being made increasingly available to attorneys wishing to deal with their stress situations. They instruct attorneys in developing a number of coping mechanisms. Psychologist Cory writes that the essence of these sessions is for the lawyer to formulate realistic expectations of his or her professional and personal capabilities and limitations. He concludes that "the attorney needs to develop a definition of success based on happiness and satisfaction rather than purely on monetary gain. . . . It is crucial that the lawyer not equate losing a case with failing as a professional or a human being."[105] Former trial attorney Martel, who recently admitted to being burned out, agrees completely with Cory and emphasizes that lawyers must learn to pace themselves and even more significantly be "willing to internalize the salutory and humanistic maxim that life means you win some and you lose some. One may come up short on victories but you'll be able to live a long time."[106]

NOTES

1. Martin Garbus and Joel Seligman, "Sanctions and Disbarment: They Sit in Judgment," in *Verdicts on Lawyers,* ed. Ralph Nader and Mark Green (New York: Crowell, 1976), 47.
2. Ibid. p. 48.
3. Jethro Lieberman, *Crisis at the Bar* (New York: W. W. Norton, 1978), 166.
4. David O. Weber, "Still in Good Standing," *American Bar Association Journal* (November, 1987): 63.
5. Lieberman, *Crisis at the Bar,* 211.
6. Ibid. p. 55.
7. Ibid. p. 62.
8. Geoffrey Hazard, *Ethics in the Practice of Law* (New Haven: Yale University Press, 1978), 20.
9. Ibid.
10. Garbus and Seligman, "Sanctions and Disbarment," 50.
11. F. Raymond Marks and Darlene Cathcart, "Discipline Within the Legal Profession," *University of Illinois Law Forum* (1974): 71.
12. Emily Couric, "What Goes Wrong," *American Bar Association Journal* (October, 1986): 68.
13. Marks and Cathcart, "Discipline Within the Legal Profession," 73.
14. Cynthia Kelly, "Lawyer Sanctions: Looking back Through the Looking Glass," *Georgetown Journal of Legal Ethics* 1 (1987): 469.
15. James R. Zazzali, "Disciplining Lawyers: The New Jersey Experience," *Georgetown Journal of Legal Ethics* 1 (1987): 662.
16. Michael Powell, "Professional Divestiture: The Cession of Responsibility for Lawyer Discipline," *American Bar Foundation Research Journal* (1986): 31.
17. Gary Taylor, "Lawyers in Texas, Florida, Face Charges in Discipline," *National Law Journal* 11/28 (March 20, 1989): 28.
18. Jerome Carlin, *Lawyers' Ethics* (New York: Russell Sage, 1966), 160.
19. Garbus and Seligman, "Sanctions and Disbarments," 48.
20. Weber, "Still in Good Standing," 59.
21. Marks and Cathcart, "Discipline Within the Legal Profession," 74.
22. Ibid.
23. Eric Steele and Raymond Zimmer, "Lawyers, Clients, and Professional Regulation," *American Bar Foundation Research Journal* (1976): 968.
24. Couric, "What Goes Wrong," 68.
25. Ibid.
26. Ibid.
27. Lieberman, *Crisis at the Bar,* 200.

28. Theodore J. Schneyer. "The Model Rules and Problems of Code Interpretation and Enforcement," *American Bar Foundation Research Journal* (1980): 938.
29. Ibid. p. 939.
30. Marks and Cathcart, "Discipline Within the Legal Profession," 92.
31. Eric Schnapper, "The Myth of Legal Ethics," *American Bar Association Journal* 64 (February, 1978): 203.
32. Couric, "What Goes Wrong," 70.
33. Jerome Carlin, *Lawyers' Ethics*, and Jerome Carlin, *Lawyers on Their Own* (New Brunswick: Rutgers University Press, 1962).
34. Garbus and Seligman, "Sanctions and Disbarment," 53.
35. Louis Brown and Harold Brown, "Who Counsels the Counselor? The Code of Professional Responsibility's Ethical Considerations—A Preventive Law Analysis," *Valparaiso University Law Review* 10/3 (Spring, 1976): 476.
36. Schnapper, "The Myth of Legal Ethics," 205.
37. Hazard, *Ethics in the Practice of Law*, 11.
38. Lieberman, *Crisis at the Bar*, 208.
39. Hazard, *Ethics in the Practice of Law*, 14.
40. Deborah L. Rhode, "Why the ABA Bothers—A Functional Perspective on Professional Codes," *Texas Law Review* 59 (1987): 720.
41. Garbus and Seligman, "Sanctions and Disbarments," 57.
42. Gerald Lynch, "The Lawyer as Informer," *Duke Law Journal* (1986): 536.
43. Marvin Frankel, "Curing Lawyers' Incompetence: Primum Non Nocere," *Creighton Law Review* 10 (1977): 615.
44. Deborah L. Rhode, "The Rhetoric of Professional Reform," *Maryland Law Review* 45 (1986): 288.
45. Ibid.
46. Ibid.
47. Marks and Cathcart, "Discipline Within the Legal Profession," 67.
48. Diggs v. Welch 148 F.2d. 667 (1945).
49. Ibid.
50. "Effective Assistance of Counsel: A Constitutional Right in Transition," *Valparaiso Law Review* 10/3 (Spring, 1976): 537.
51. James L. Oaks, "Lawyer and Judge: The Ethical Duty of Competency," *Ethics and the Practice of Law*, ed. David Schroder (Englewood Cliffs, N.J.: Prentice-Hall, 1988), 189.
52. Rhode, "The Rhetoric of Professional Reform," 289.
53. Douglas Rosenthal, "Evaluating the Competence of Lawyers," *Law and Society Review* 11/2 (1976): 257.
54. William Gates, "The Newest Data on Lawyers Malpractice Claims," *American Bar Association Journal* (April, 1984): 80.
55. Darrell Havener, "A Defense Lawyer Looks at the Professional Liability of Trial Lawyers," in *Proceedings of a National Institute on the Professional Liability of Trial Lawyers* (American Bar Association, San Francisco, 1977), 11.
56. Ibid. p. 9.
57. Ibid. p. 12.
58. David O. Haughey, "Lawyers' Malpractice: A Comparative Appraisal Between Lawyers and Doctors," *Notre Dame Lawyer* 48 (1973): 888.

59. "Attorneys at Law," *American Jurisprudence* (Rochester, NY: Lawyers Co-operative Publishing Co, 1963): p. 170.
60. Irving Kaufmann, "Attorney Competence: A Plea for Reform," *American Bar Association Journal* (March, 1983): 308.
61. Susan R. Martyn, "Lawyers Competence and Lawyer Discipline: Beyond the Bar," *Georgetown Law Review* 69 (1981): 725.
62. Rhode, "The Rhetoric of Professional Reform," 290.
63. Edward W. Cleary (ed.), *McCormick's Handbook for the Law of Evidence*, 2nd ed. (St. Paul: West Publishing Co., 1972), 175.
64. Bruce Landesman, "Confidentiality and the Lawyer Client Relationship," in *Ethics and the Legal Profession*, ed. Michael Davis and Frederick Elliston (Buffalo: Prometheus Books, 1986), 364.
65. Norman Lefstein, "Client Perjury in Criminal Cases: Still in Search of an Answer," *Georgetown Journal of Legal Ethics* 1 (1987), 542.
66. Paul Wice, *Criminal Lawyers* (Beverly Hills, Calif.: Sage Publications, 1978), 116.
67. Hazard, *Ethics in the Practice of Law*, 33.
68. "Conflicts of Interest in the Legal Profession," *Harvard Law Review* 94 (1981): 1252.
69. Hazard, *Ethics in the Practice of Law*, 35, 36.
70. Jack Weinstein, "Some Ethical and Political Problems of a Government Lawyer," in *Ethics and the Practice of Law*, ed. David Shroder (Englewood Cliffs, N.J.: Prentice-Hall), 291.
71. Stanley J. Clowar, *You and Your Clients* (Chicago: American Bar Association, 1988), 35.
72. Ibid. p. 43.
73. Willy v. Coastal Corporation. 647 F. Supp. 116 Tex. (1986).
74. Martin Mayer, *The Lawyers* (New York: Harper & Row, 1967), 29.
75. Hazard, *Ethics in the Practice of Law*, 97.
76. Lieberman, *Crisis at the Bar*, 108.
77. Marks and Cathcart, "Discipline Within the Legal Profession," 79.
78. Ibid.
79. Ibid. p. 81.
80. Goldfarb v. Virginia State Bar. 421 U.S. 773 (1975).
81. Lieberman, *Crisis at the Bar*, 90.
82. W. Ward Reynoldson, "The Case Against Lawyer Advertising," *American Bar Association Journal* (January, 1989): 61.
83. Bates v. State Bar of Arizona. 433 U.S. 350 (1977).
84. Lori Andrews, *Birth of a Salesman: Lawyer Advertising and Solicitation* (Chicago: American Bar Association, 1980), 4.
85. Laura Rubenstein Reskin, "Law Poll: PR is for City Slickers," *American Bar Association Journal* (May, 1986): 53.
86. Timothy J. Muris and Fred McChesney, "Advertising and the Price and Quality of Legal Services: The Case for Legal Clinics," *American Bar Foundation Research Journal* (1979): 179.
87. Andrews, *Birth of a Salesman*, 81.
88. Judith L. Maute, "Sporting Theory of Justice: Taming Adversary Zeal with a Logical Sanction Doctrine," *Connecticut Law Review* 20 (1987): 9.
89. Ibid.

90. Robert N. Saylor, "Rambo Litigation: Why Hardball Tactics Don't Work," *American Bar Association Journal* (March, 1988): 79.
91. Ibid. p. 80.
92. Monroe H. Freedman, "The Lawyer as a Hired Gun," in *Lawyers' Ethics: Contemporary Dilemmas*, ed. Allan Gerson (New Brunswick, N.J.: Transaction Books, 1980), 69.
93. Ibid.
94. Ibid. p. 67.
95. Wolff v. Ruddy. 617 SW 2d. 64 Mo. (1981).
96. Clower, You and Your Clients, p. 51.
97. Thomas Cory, "Stress: How it Affects Lawyers and Their Clients," *Trial* (May, 1988): 55.
98. Ibid.
99. John S. Martel, "Lawyer Burnout," *Trial* (July, 1988): 62.
100. Ibid. p. 63.
101. Couric, "What Goes Wrong," 66.
102. Wice, *Criminal Lawyers*, 81.
103. Douglas Martin, "From Courtroom Wars, Battle Fatigue," *New York Times*, 20 November 1987, p. 86.
104. Ibid.
105. Cory, "Stress: How it Affects Lawyers and Their Clients," 55.
106. Martel, "Lawyer Burnout," 67.

Chapter
6

Selection and Training of Judges

*T*he first five chapters of this text have described the life of lawyers from their earliest socializing experience in law school through a description of their working environment, professional responsibilities, and finally, the strains and hardships of his or her career, which is often beset by complex ethical dilemmas. By late middle age (45 to 55), many lawyers, especially those who are either politically active or professionally successful, may opt for a radical change in their legal careers and attempt to join a rather elitist substrata of their profession—the judiciary. In contrast to most Western European nations (with the exception of England), our nation insists that our jurists be amateurs, untrained in the judicial craft prior to assuming the bench. In countries such as Germany and France, college graduates may choose to specialize in training for a future in judicial administration, working their way up from law clerk or calendar clerk to serve in a municipal trial court, and eventually, having had a distinguished prior career within the judiciary, they may wind up on an appellate court. Despite the obvious merits derived from such a protracted period of training, the United States has resolutely persisted in relying upon judicial amateurs at all levels of government from rural justices of the peace through appellate courts of final jurisdiction. It is the purpose of this chapter to first examine the various state and federal selection programs, noting not only how they work but also what impact these systems might have upon the quality of judicial performance. Secondly, this chapter will study the socialization process by which these amateur judges learn their craft and make the frequently difficult transition from advocate to arbiter.

Following the discussion of judicial selection and training found within this chapter, we will continue to examine the professional lives of the nation's judiciary, focusing on their unique working environment, their primary decision-making responsibilities, and the difficult ethical and personal problems affecting their performance. Let us now turn to a discussion of the various selection systems presently being utilized at both the state and federal levels of government.

STATE SELECTION SYSTEMS

Historical Development

Before reviewing the operation of the various selection systems used by state governments, it is necessary to briefly trace their historical development. This review may also shed light on the continuing debate over the relative merits of each system, as their respective supporters attempt to gain political supremacy and control the process. The major controversy that still rages today and appears to escape undisputed resolution is whether it is best to have a selection system designed to choose judges of the highest quality or whether it is best to have a system where the judges would be maximally accountable to the electorate. In shorthand fashion, then, we have a continuing debate between the elitists, favoring merit, and the democrats, favoring accountability.

As this brief historical review will indicate, the development of varying selection systems reflects the prevalent political attitude and ethos of the day. Prior to the War for Independence and subsequent creation of our national government, the judges in the various American colonies were appointed by the English king and expected to enforce English principles of law. These judges were selected because of their clear support of the Crown and willingness to resolve disputes from a British perspective. After the colonies gained their freedom and broke away from England to form their own state governments, a conscious attempt was made to avoid this type of executive monopoly over judicial selection. Instead the newly created 13 states developed a selection system in which judges were chosen either by the state legislature (7 states) or by a combination of governor and council (6 states).[1]

This system of legislative/executive appointment lasted until the early nineteenth century when the egalitarian spirit of Jacksonian democracy began to engulf the country, especially popular among the wave of new states joining the union during the first half of the 1800s. It was during this period that most states decided to select judges through partisan ballots, exposing them to the same degree of accountability as their counterparts in the legislative and executive branches. The politicization of judicial selection was viewed positively as a democratic process in which the wealthy and privileged classes could be prevented from maintaining control over judicial appointments. Open election meant the people could better choose one of their own to become elevated to a position on the bench, and thereby hold judges to the same level of accountability as governors and legislators.

In the early years of the twentieth century, however, there began a growing disenchantment with the existing method of judicial selection, particularly the negative influence of partisan politics. This period, often referred to as the "Progressive Era," dedicated itself to the elimination of political corruption that was thought to be especially extensive in most of our large cities but was also spreading to state capitals. Popular elections were associated with the evils of machine politics and bossism. Visions of an easily manipulated electorate, filled with the steadily increasing numbers of inexperienced immigrant voters, and a greedy political leadership rife with corruption and patronage, convinced reformers to push for the nonpartisan ballot. By 1913 Chief Justice Taft was willing to publicly endorse the nonpartisan ballot and warn the nation that there was a definite linkage between (partisan) elections and selection of demagogic judges controlling our courts.[2] During this period leaders of the organized bar at both the state and national levels joined with "good government" reformers in an effort to drive politics out of the courthouse (or at least the political views of those not in agreement with the leadership of the American Bar Association). Thus, in little more than a century the shifting political tides of our nation had come nearly full circle. The democratic impulses of the Jacksonian era were now described as "dirty politics," and the feared elitism of early Crown appointments had become reestablished and endorsed by prominent bar officials as guaranteeing a return to professional competence. The bar argued persuasively that they were in the best position to determine who should hold judgeships and were also best able to fight off the evil influence of political parties who could so easily deceive an uninformed electorate.

In attempts to find an acceptable middle ground between the elitist bar groups pushing for merit appointment and self-serving politicos endorsing partisan elections, a new group of proposals were developed by another group of reformers in hopes of best serving the public interest. This compromising innovation was presented in 1913 by the American Judicature Society, a Chicago-based law reform organization. Its new plan was to feature elements of both the appointive and elective systems in which vacancies were to be filled initially by appointment, but only after a nonpolitical nominating commission had submitted several candidate's names. After appointment, retention elections would be held several years later in which judges would run against their records rather than rival candidates.

Nearly 25 years later this plan was finally brought to life as the Missouri Nonpartisan Court Plan in which that state constructed the same type of hybrid plan designed to accomplish the seemingly contradictory tasks of obtaining higher quality judges, reducing the influence of politics, and yet still allowing the electorate to possess a form of veto power. In the 50 years since the Missouri plan was first implemented, there has been a modest trend toward its adoption, particularly in the more reform-minded states of the Rocky Mountains and far West. The most recent breakdown of the relative popularity of each type of selection system is presented in the following table, the result of a national survey by Henry Glick[3]:

Partisan elections	13
Nonpartisan elections	15
Appointment by governor	8
Appointment by legislature	2
Merit selection (Missouri Plan)	12

For purposes of simplicity and clarity, the subsequent discussion has divided the selection systems into three broad categories: elective, appointive, and merit (which in most states is actually a mixed system combining initial appointment with retention elections).

Judicial Elections

Despite the urgings of reformers and the continuing trend toward adopting merit systems, the majority of states (28) still utilize judicial elections that are divided nearly equally between partisan and nonpartisan. Advocates of electoral selection continue to stress the ability of their system to provide the much needed ingredient of accountability, which is missing from appointive and merit systems. Henry Glick, who has studied judicial elections as closely as any political scientist, offers the following group of justifications in support of the election format:

1. Even partisan judicial elections are rarely hotly contested affairs. Though many lawyers may rationalize their refusal to run for judicial office out of a fear of being involved in partisan politics, most elections actually involve minimal interference by party leaders. It is customary in many jurisdictions for the local party to simply defer to leaders of the organized bar for possible candidates.
2. The electorate is no less informed concerning judicial candidate qualifications than in any other local election. This position is supported by the research of Nicholas Lovrich and Charles Sheldon who discovered that "candidates in judicial elections could well assume that a goodly portion of their electorate is composed of self-selected interested and somewhat knowledgeable persons who pay fairly close attention to judicial elections."[4]
3. Partisan ballots seem to facilitate increased voter turnout, indirectly contributing to heightened judicial accountability. Statistics gathered by Philip Dubois in his national study of state su-

preme court elections substantiates the probable relationship between partisan elections and increased voter turnout.[5] Explanations for this correlation credit the partisan elections with providing the easiest and most direct way for voters to learn about the candidates. It is also surmised that they seem to lead to a more interesting electoral campaign, capturing the public's interest, and ultimately creating a stronger desire to enter a voting booth on election day.

4. Since many of the decisions made by judges can have important public policy implications, voters are assisted in their choice by party identification. Thus, requiring a judge to identify with a party will provide the voter with an easier mechanism for being able to classify a judge's overall political orientation.[6]

Despite Glick's rather persuasive arguments supporting partisan elections, the majority of recent research projects have been considerably less enthusiastic and has directly challenged the basic assumption that such elections are capable of holding judicial incumbents accountable. Stumpf and others have found that not only do incumbents appear to be virtually guaranteed victory, often in uncontested elections, but over half of these incumbent judges are initially appointed to an interim vacancy by the governor.[7] Atkins in his study of Florida's judicial elections concluded that if one were to define election without opposition as not being consistent with the spirit and purpose of the electoral process, then his data indicates that a majority of judges in Florida obtained their seats and were generally able to retain them without any formal evaluation by the electorate.[8]

Scholarly studies documenting the disappointingly low level of voter turnout and verifying the prevalence of voter ignorance appear to undermine the claim that judicial elections are capable of achieving a creditable level of accountability and satisfying the democratic ideal. With voter turnout usually in the 20 to 25 percent range of registered voters, several reformers and scholars have attempted to devise schemes to elevate these figures while also increasing voter awareness. Dubois in his important work on Texas judicial elections recommends that the way to raise the saliency level of these elections and stimulate voter turnout is to "allow candidates to present and debate their views on judicial policy questions and their general political and judicial philosophies."[9] McKnight and others who also studied Texas judicial elections were much more pessimistic and concluded that in their survey the electorate was found to lack the necessary information to make an intelligent voting decision that would permit the system to function properly.[10]

One of the more interesting developments in judicial elections has been the growing trend toward judges reaching the bench initially by gubernatorial appointment to an interim vacancy. The newly selected judge quickly achieves the status of "temporary incumbent" without ever having to actually participate in an election. Once the incumbent position has been obtained, the judge is virtually assured victory in subsequent elections as recent statistics show that incumbents are successful over 90 percent of the time. These studies also document the fact that in many states 40 to 50 percent of the judges were first appointed to fill an interim vacancy.[11] It is very difficult to fully understand why the process of judicial elections has taken this apolitical twist, but it seems logical to assume that the distaste of many potential candidates for partisan politics may have forced political party leaders to develop this new strategy.

In addition to voter ignorance and the inherent powers of incumbency, the "sitting judge principle" also contributes to depoliticizing judicial elections and guaranteeing incumbent victory. This principle means that there is usually an unstated, informal agreement among local bar associations and political leaders that an incumbent judge will not be challenged for purely partisan or personal reasons if the judge had done an acceptable job and is not likely to be an embarrassment in the future. Given such a broad definition of "acceptable performance," it is no wonder that so high a percentage of incumbents face little or no opposition in judicial elections.

With all that has just been said, how can an incumbent ever lose? Of course, there are exceptions, and they are most likely to occur if a judge receives an unusual amount of negative publicity either because of an extremely unpopular decision in a highly publicized case (such as approving of a radical school busing plan or forced relocation of a public housing project) or a blatant act of incompetence or impropriety in or out of court. Also, the possibility of an incumbent defeat is heightened in any jurisdiction in which there is a viable two-party contest in partisan elections. In areas of the country where such political struggles are traditionally waged, the drive for electoral victory may override the party's concern with providing lawyers an apolitical, guaranteed path to a permanent place on the bench.

Although most of our discussion of judicial elections has deemphasized the relative differences between partisan and nonpartisan ballots, it should be clarified that scheduling (that is, timing the judicial elections to concur with the more publicized national and state elections) and ballot form can clearly influence the level of accountability that each can achieve. Adamany and Dubois in their examination of Wisconsin judicial elections conclude that the nonpartisan ballot and nonconcurrent scheduling (scheduling at times other than when state and federal legislative and executive elections are held) reduced the legitimizing function of elections. This leads to a decrease in voter turnout and an overall weakening of the governance function.[12]

The final topic in our discussion of judicial elections is the nagging problem of the steadily increasing cost of campaign financing. This leads to the inevitable concern with whether certain lawyers, interest groups, or large corporations may be able to exert a disproportionate, and possibly unhealthy, influence on the outcome of these elections as a result of their sizable financial contributions. Raising campaign funds exemplifies the type of distasteful political activity that is most likely to dissuade a lawyer from considering running for judicial office, and more importantly appears to be blatantly inconsistent with their future role as an impartial arbiter of disputes. Fortunately, the results of a study of California elections discovered that campaign support is quite varied, with lawyers providing less than 40 percent of the total dollars and that in relatively small amounts. The report concluded that "campaign support was quite varied including monetary contributions from third parties and the candidates themselves, non-monetary contributions, loans and other sources. . . . It does not appear that the increasing real dollar costs of campaigns will dramatically increase the candidates reliance upon larger campaign contributors."[13]

Legislative and Gubernatorial Appointment

Ten states have chosen to have their judges appointed, two by the legislature and eight by the governor. The states opting for gubernatorial appointment are all located in New England while the two utilizing legislative appointment are both located in the South. Interestingly, all states using the appointive process were part of the original 13 colonies and have simply continued to endorse the earliest form of judicial selection.

Supporters of the appointment process believe its primary virtue is its supposed ability to eliminate partisan politics while ensuring the selection of high-quality nominees. Though critics label the appointment process "elitist" and "undemocratic," empirical evidence does seem to verify the realities of low voter turnout and general ignorance of the electorate as persistent problems plaguing most electoral systems.[14]

In the place of this inattentive and uninformed electorate, it is urged that knowledgeable groups such as local bar associations, law professors, current members of the bench, and citizen groups can advise the legislators and governors in appointing the state's judiciary. It is assumed that these groups of "experts" are better able to choose high-quality judges than a random smattering of laypersons with little knowledge or interest in legal matters. Finally, advocates of the appointive process argue that more and better quality lawyers would be willing to become judges if they did not have to subject themselves to the rigors and frustrations of an electoral campaign.

As seen throughout this discussion of judicial selection, there is little uncontrovertible evidence conclusively establishing one system's superiority over another. Each advocate can selectively construct arguments favoring his or her position, and thus we find critics of the appointive process simply turning around what we have just noted to be its positive attributes. Detractors, therefore, fear not the supposedly minimal and uninformed electorate but rather are concerned with the questionable deliberations of a select group of politicians who will be choosing those judges who may best serve their narrow aspirations, without necessarily considering the public's best interests. They (the critics) are not only fearful of the possibilities of patronage and corruption but also point to the absence of an adequate mechanism for holding the judges accountable to the public, that is, the periodic election. By failing to provide the citizenry with an opportunity to express their satisfaction (or dissatisfaction) with a judge's performance, the appointment process has omitted a critical ingredient in our democratic system.

Moving from this rather polemical discussion of the strengths and weaknesses of the appointment process, what has social science research contributed toward a better understanding of the realities of this method of judicial selection? First, it appears that the level of appointment—trial versus appellate—can often be a significant factor affecting the involvement of the governor. Nominees to appellate courts were usually personally known to the governor either through political work in the legislature or in some agency of the executive branch. Additional considerations might involve how much personal experience the governor had with the nominee outside of government, either as a fund raiser or campaign strategist.

It should be noted that sometimes these gubernatorial appointments would have to be made for symbolic or representational reasons, rather than simply rewarding a carefully chosen friend or supporter. Symbolic appointments are necessitated by political pressures from certain groups in the electorate who need to be convinced of the governor's endorsement of their goals. One of the ways a governor can tangibly indicate support of these groups is by appointing one of its members to an important position: in this case, a spot on the appellate bench. Recent examples of groups receiving symbolic appointments to the bench include blacks, Hispanics, and women. Although these appointments may be necessary to make amends for past omissions as well as being required by current political necessity, such appointments may often backfire in future elections when the governor may face an angry white middle-class electorate who has become increasingly disinterested in minority rights.

Trial court appointments do not usually permit the same latitude of choice to the governor in exercising personal preferences as in appellate appointments. In many states the legislature believes they maintain, through the tradition of senatorial courtesy, the right to influence, and if possible control, which judges are to be appointed to the trial courts within their respective elective districts. As a result of the local legislator's interest in filling judicial vacancies within his or her district, the governor often uses these appointments as a means of gaining support from critical legislative leaders. What emerges in most states is a type of patronage system for the numerous county trial courts in which the governor dispenses judicial appointments as bargaining chips with local legislators, mayors, and county party leaders. It is conceivable that judicial appointments can be held out as inducements for active party involvement. Thus, a place on the bench becomes a reasonable expectation after several years of loyal party service or considerable financial support.

Turning to the handful of states using legislative appointment, research shows that these systems are best characterized as self-perpetuating institutions in which nearly all the judges selected are former legislators. Recent studies have placed the figures at approximately 80 percent.[15] This, of course, does not prove that such a system is inherently inferior, dominated by self-serving legislators. All one can assume is that the path to judicial appointment is best taken by personal legislative experience. It should also be noted in defense of this process that former legislators typically comprise the largest category of prior vocational experience for all judges regardless of the type of selection process.

Merit Selection

Originating with the Missouri Court Plan in 1937, and presently adopted by an additional 12 states, the merit system of judicial selection attempts to incorporate the positive attributes of both elective and appointive systems. Merit selection is in reality a "mixed system" designed to select judicial candidates of high quality and eliminate the influence of partisan politics while still providing for accountability through the use of retention elections. Since its initiation, the plan has been the most popular choice for those more innovative states that have been willing to take a chance on reform and alter their methods of judicial selection.

Although each state currently using the rather complex set of procedures found in the merit system has developed several of its own unique operational twists, one can still describe the typical features found in nearly all the states. Each system employs three basic elements. First, a nominating commission comprised of representatives of the bar, bench, and general public. The members of the bar are usually selected by local bar associations, the bench by a panel of appellate judges, and lay members by the governor. (One common alternative is to have the legislature also be represented.) The nominating commission will then turn over to the governor a short list of nominees, usually between three and five. There may be, as in Missouri for example, a number of nominating commissions for varying types of courts (appellate versus trial or urban versus rural). The governor will then select his or her nominee to the vacancy, and this person will serve in office for a specific number of years, at the end of which the judge must face the electorate in an unopposed retention election. The variety of procedural formats used by merit plan systems is indicated in Table 6.1. This information was collected by Burton Atkins as part of his national study of judicial selection.

Table 6.1 STRUCTURAL COMPARISONS OF MERIT PLANS

State/City	No. of Commissions	Courts Covered	Legal Base of Plan	Purpose of Plan	Type of Election	No. of Commission Nominees
Alabama	2	Certain trial	Constitutional	Interim appointment	Partisan	3
Alaska	1	All major	Constitutional	All appointments	Retention	2 or more
Colorado	24	All major	Constitutional	All appointments	Retention	3-Appellate 2 or 3-Trial
Florida	25	All major	Constitutional	Interim appointment	Nonpartisan	3 or more
Georgia	2	All appellate & some trial	Executive order	Interim appointment	Partisan election	3
Idaho	8	All major	Statutory	Mixed	Nonpartisan or retention (depends on score)	2–4
Indiana	5	All appellate & some trial	Constitutional & executive order	All appointments	Retention	3
Iowa	113	All major	Constitutional & executive order	All appointments	Retention	3-Appellate 2-Trial
Kansas	1	Appellate	Constitutional	All appointments	Retention	3
Maryland	9	All major	Executive order	Interim appointment	Nonpartisan election	5–7
Missouri	6	All appellate & some trial	Constitutional	All appointments	Retention	3
Montana	1	All major	Constitutional	Interim appointment	Nonpartisan	3–5
Nebraska	51	All major	Constitutional	All appointments	Nonpartisan	2 or More
New York City	1	Certain trial	Informal	Mixed elections	Partisan	List maintained
Ohio	12	All major	Constitutional & statutory	Interim appointment	Nonpartisan	3
Oklahoma	1	All major	Constitutional & executive order	Mixed	Retention	3
Pennsylvania	2	All major	Executive order	Interim appointment	Partisan	3
Tennessee	1	Appellate	Statutory	All appointments	Retention	3
Utah	8	All major	Constitutional	Interim appointment	Nonpartisan	3
Vermont	1	All major	Constitutional	All appointments	None	3
Wyoming	1	All major	Constitutional	All appointments	Retention	3

Source: Burton Atkins, "Merit Selection of Judges," *Florida Bar Journal* 50 (April, 1976): 204. Copyright 1976. Reprinted with permission of the publisher.

Supporters of the merit system (best typified by Missouri's Nonpartisan Court Plan) credit this selection process with being able to chose judges of the highest quality while also excluding partisan politics. The validity of these claims is questionable since one's estimate of judicial quality is inevitably tainted by personal predilections as to make objective evaluations virtually impossible. Second, common sense along with the opinion of most legal scholars indicates that it is rather unrealistic to expect any system to be capable of totally removing political considerations from the selection process, even one as well-intentioned as the merit system. Watson and Downing, for example, in their definitive study of the Missouri plan entitled *The Politics of Bench and Bar,* conclude that not only is it naive to expect that merit selection can eliminate politics, but one of the plan's major virtues is its ability to allow a broad spectrum of legitimate audiences to have their voices heard during the selection process. They write that the plan purposefully attempts "to provide representation for four general interests concerned with judicial selection: the organized bar, the judiciary, the general public, and the state political system."[16]

If one can move beyond the sloganeering and emotional politicking engaged in by enthusiastic backers of the three major selection systems, the merit alternative may ironically be the most democratic because of its capacity to allow for such a varied collection of attentive publics to air their opinions and become involved in the process. Watson and Downing believe that the capability of the Missouri plan and other merit systems to eliminate partisan politics from judicial selection is a red herring issue and what is truly significant is whether the operation of the system allows for adequate representation of the legal, judicial, and political perspectives that are thought to be so important in determining who becomes a judge.[17] Although the merit system is far from perfect, the Watson and Downing analysis does show that these varied "attentive publics" do play a role in the selection process, although rarely of equal importance. In most states the governor and county bar associations clearly dominate the process.

Bar Polls

In several states lawyers use bar polls as a guide in helping the electorate make an informed decision in judicial elections. Presently, 30 such polls are used in states employing partisan and nonpartisan elections as well as retention elections in appointive and merit systems. These polls attempt to share with the voting public the collective wisdom of the local bar as they evaluate judges before whom they practice. The results of these polls are then made available for public consumption so the entire electorate can benefit from their professional judgment. These polls usually take one of three forms: (1) a straw poll in which lawyers are asked to select the best candidates; (2) a multiple attribute poll where lawyers rate judges on a number of distinct dimensions such as temperament, legal ability, and integrity; and (3) a general qualification board of selected lawyers rates judges according to their overall suitability for the bench.[18]

None of these various types of bar polls seems to be having much effect upon the electorate as they ponder the question of judicial competence. The polls have recently been under close scrutiny. As Errol Meidinger commented in one of the rare discussions of the topic, there must first be a better effort made to ensure that those who are doing the polling are working with reliable criteria and, in fact, do have adequate professional knowledge of the judges under review. Without this, bar polls become meaningless at best, and will likely degenerate into a popularity poll. Such polls will do more harm than good and are much worse than no poll at all.[19]

Selection Systems: How Important Are They?

As this discussion of judicial selection draws to a close, the reader is likely to still be puzzled over two very basic questions concerning the relative worth of each system: (1) Which system seems most likely to produce the highest quality judges? (2) Which system is best able to eliminate partisan politics, while still providing the maximum amount of democratic participation? Turning first to the perplexing question of choosing top-quality judges, one immediately becomes ensnarled in a semantic jungle. How are such desirable judicial traits as integrity, compassion, and impartiality to be operationally defined? These amorphous concepts are simply too elusive to fall within the parameters required by empirical research. Social scientists have studied the background characteristics and other descriptive measures of judges, but this information merely tells us which *type* of person becomes a judge in each system, not which system is choosing the best or most highly qualified judges.

The scant research that has been attempted on this first question has been fairly consistent in finding that "little evidence exists to indicate that a particular selection system produces judges with markedly different or superior credentials or that they vary on most background characteristics."[20] The few differences that were found were in such categories as type of education, type of law practice, or previous experience, and once one controlled for regional variation, even these traits lost their significance.

The second question also proved to be nearly impossible to resolve. Nearly all the research affirmed the inability of any of the selection systems to eliminate "politics" from its decision-making process. There was a modest consensus crediting the merit system with at least making slight gains toward reducing the more nefarious partisan activities while still permitting a modicum of accountability through its retention elections. As already noted, the choice of one system over another is based primarily on one's preference for either the elitist or democratic ideals. Unfortunately, neither social science research nor enlightened scholarly debate appears capable of adequately answering either of these very complex questions.

FEDERAL SELECTION PROCESS

The elevation of lawyers to the federal bench has always been studied with keen interest, although the judicial selection activities of the Carter and Reagan administrations has carried this concern to even greater heights. This intensified interest is probably the result of a combination of factors, including the lifetime tenure of each appointment, their increased national exposure, and the likelihood of deciding cases of perplexing complexity and noteworthy significance. Due to the passage of the Omnibus Judgeship Act in 1978, an unprecedented number of appointment opportunities were presented to both presidents Carter and Reagan. Let us now turn to the constitutional compromise made over 200 years ago, which has led to our current system of federal judicial selection.

Constitutional Roots

The question of how federal judges[21] were to be selected was heatedly debated and ultimately settled during the Constitutional Convention of 1787 in a fashion similar to so many of the other major separation of power controversies. The Federalists, led by Alexander Hamilton, argued for a strong central government, headed by a powerful executive who would dominate the other branches. The opposition was led by Thomas Jefferson, Luther Martin, and others who were greatly concerned with substituting one form of tyrannical leadership (the English monarch), for another, albeit an American version. These Republicans argued for a strenghtened legislative branch in which the voice of the people could be easily heard, and any attempts at dictatorial power grabbing by the executive branch could be defeated. Because the delegates to the convention were so evenly divided between these two positions, only a compromise could remove the deadlock. It was decided therefore to allow Supreme Court justices (and subsequently all lower federal court appointees) to be appointed by the president for life, but only with the advice and consent of the majority of the Senate.

The process by which federal judgeships are nominated and confirmed has remained basically unchanged since its inception. After the president has decided on a nominee, the name is turned over to the Senate, where the Judiciary Committee will conduct hearings, vote on the nominee's acceptability, and then refer it to the entire Senate, who will vote, a simple majority being required for confirmation. Despite this rather simplistic outline, the realities of the nomination and confirmation process are much more complex, and have experienced important evolutionary changes over the years. The remainder of this discussion of federal judicial appointments will examine the most recent developments in this process as well as analyzing the differences between appointment to the three different levels of federal courts: district, appeals, and Supreme.

Federal District Courts and the Role of Senatorial Courtesy

Although selection of a federal district court judge involves a wide variety of political actors, the role of the U.S. Senate and, in particular, the senators from the state where the vacancy has occurred is the most noteworthy feature of the appointment process at this level. The senators' role is enhanced if one or both are members of the president's party. Nevertheless, one must be careful not to overstate the significance of a single senator (or possibly pair of senators) since he or she really possesses only a "veto power" that is sometimes capable of blocking a presidential nominee rather than able to successfully push for a candidate, especially one that may prove objectionable to the president.

The senator may attempt to influence the president's choice of nominee, but this power must be shared with several key White House advisers and a wide range of other public and private officials who also wish to urge the selection of their preferred candidate. Within the White House, the president has shifted power over judicial selection to the Office of Legal Policy, created in 1984. This office is headed by an assistant deputy attorney general who reports to the deputy attorney general. It has also been given an independent role guaranteed by the presence of a special White House counsel for judicial selection, a post formally established in 1984. President Reagan purposefully formalized the entire process to a new level of institutionalization by also creating the President's Committee on Federal Judicial Selection. This committee is comprised of representatives from both the White House, such as the presidential counselor, the special assistant to the president for personnel, and the chief of staff, as well as the Justice Department, which includes the attorney general, the associate attorney general, and the assistant attorney general for legal policy.[22] This committee evaluates the recommendations from both the White House and Justice Department and has even on occasion generated several nominees from its own files. Sheldon Goldman has concluded that because this committee has been able to conduct its own investigations into the suitability of prospective nominees, independent of the Justice Department's inquiries, it has been able to provide the "most consistent ideological or policy orientation screening of judicial candidates since the first term of Franklin Roosevelt."[23]

The president and his or her staff will also listen to other outside groups espousing their own favored nominees. Such groups typically include the leaders of the president's political party from the state where the vacancy occurs, leaders of the state bar association, loyal local party supporters, local interest groups, and present members of the federal and state bench from the region. Once the president hears the report from the Committee on Federal Judicial Selection and has listened to representatives from the various local sources, the name(s) of one or a handful of finalists are turned over to the American Bar Association's Committee on Judicial Qualification and the Federal Bureau of Investigation. These two organizations will conduct background investigations. The FBI concentrates upon personal issues related to the nominee's emotional stability and private life. It is hoped that its inquiries will not only uncover any "skeletons in the closet" but may also provide a more thorough picture of the candidate's character. The recent embarrassment caused by learning during the Judiciary Committee hearings that Supreme Court nominee Douglas Ginsberg had been involved with drugs during his teaching days at Harvard should have been prevented by a more thorough FBI inquiry. The ABA's Committee on Judicial Qualification concentrates on the candidate's legal background and his or her professional potential for serving on the federal bench. The committee's role will be discussed in greater detail in a subsequent section of this chapter, but for present purposes, it should be noted that it is usually critical for a nominee to receive a rating by the committee of at least "qualified." (The other categories of ratings are exceptionally qualified, highly qualified, and not qualified.) The ABA investigator will speak to lawyers and judges who know the nominee and who can evaluate his or her potential for the bench. Law school professors, clients, friends, and anyone else who can shed light on the nominee's suitability will be contacted.

Once a candidate has received a clean bill of health from the FBI and a positive rating from the ABA, the president will confer with the White House staff and the Committee on Federal Judicial Selection, make a final choice, and submit the candidate's name to the Senate. At this point the Senate's confirmation responsibilities are initiated by its Judiciary Committee commencing public hearings on the nominee's qualifications. Most hearings are rather pro forma affairs that last less than a day with the nominee receiving the blessing of the committee. If, however, the Senate is controlled by the opposition party, the likelihood of a protracted set of hearings is greatly increased.

Despite reforms during the Carter administration and additional modifications during the Reagan years, a diminished power of senatorial courtesy continues to exist. In years past, when this congressional tradition was at its zenith, senators utilized what they referred to as the "blue slip device." This slip was a brief message sent by the Judiciary Committee to the senators from the state where the vacancy existed requesting either approval or disapproval of the nomination. If the slip was not returned within a week, it was assumed that no objections were being raised. Special attention was paid to the response from those senators from the president's party, although both had received the slip. The specific wording of the slip was as follows: "Will you kindly give me for use of the Committee, your opinion and information concerning the nomination of _____ . Under a rule of the Committee unless a reply is received from you within a week from this date, it will be assumed that you have no objection to this nomination."[24]

If the president and the senator of the same party and the Justice Department's Office of Legal Policy do not feel a necessity to interfere, the confirmation hearings and floor vote will usually go smoothly with the vestiges of senatorial courtesy still honored. In the small percentage of cases where neither senator is from the president's party or where the Office of Legal Policy stubbornly asserts its own choice, senatorial courtesy diminishes and presidential prerogative dominates. If the Senate is controlled by the opposition party (as occurred periodically during the Nixon and Reagan administrations) the chance of lengthy nomination hearings is greatly increased. It is at this point that the president may have to take into consideration the rival party's fervent opposition to his nominee or be willing to weather some stormy testimony at the hearings where the president's own judgment might be questioned.

President Carter also contributed to the decline of senatorial courtesy by urging the use of voluntary commissions to nominate candidates to fill vacancies within a particular state. Although this reform nearly disappeared during the Reagan years, it nevertheless seems to have strengthened the position of the White House in its ability to control the Senate during the confirmation process.

Although Harold Chase wrote his seminal work on the federal appointive process in 1972, his evaluation of the process still appears valid today as he concluded that "the federal courts are probably in pretty good shape in respect to the general quality of judges."[25] Another astute observer of the federal judiciary, journalist Nina Totenberg, reviewed the selection process four years later (1976) and offered what seems to be an even more perceptive analysis of the process and serves as a fitting conclusion to this section: "Despite the huge importance of the federal judiciary in our society, we still leave the selection of federal judges to the hurly burly of politics, both partisan and the bar. If the selection of federal judges has improved over the last two decades—and it has—it is due largely to the raised consciousness in the Justice Department and to the devoted, albeit not unselfish or perfect work of the ABA Standing Committee on the Federal Judiciary."[26]

Courts of Appeal

Senators, even from the president's own party, have usually had a great deal less influence in the selection of federal appeals court judges than during the selection of their counterparts on the district courts. This can most easily be explained by the fact that one circuit can contain several states. In the past there had been an effort to allow for the senator from the home state of the judge vacating the bench to have greater influence upon the future replacement. Reforms under President Carter, which created the rather short-lived Circuit Judge Nominating Commission, as well as the successful efforts of the Reagan administration have both worked to strengthen the hand of the White House in controlling these appeals court appointments, weakening the role of the Senate to an even greater degree.

The Carter administration's Circuit Judge Nominating Commission, despite its brief existence, could lay claim to making a vigorous effort to bring both merit selection and affirmative action to the appointment of federal judges. It was hoped that judges would be chosen by this commission without regard to traditional partisan considerations, and a persistent effort would be made to correct past discrimination against women and minority groups by elevating significant numbers of women, blacks, and Hispanics to the federal courts. In terms of satisfying the second goal, the nominating commission was quite successful as more women and blacks were named to the appeals courts than had served in their entire history. The first goal, however, of eliminating partisan politics proved to be extremely elusive. Given the inherently political nature of any selection scheme, it was quite naive and totally unrealistic to expect that by merely changing procedures one could effectively eliminate partisan considerations. Thus, the commission simply represented in the words of Larry Berkson and his colleagues who studied its operation closely, "a form of merit selection of Democrats by Democrats."[27] Their report found that "many of the panelists were chosen because of their familiarity with the Carter staff."[28]

As noted earlier, when Reagan entered the White House he quickly abolished the nominating commission and terminated the affirmative action policy. He made a careful and systematic effort to control appeals court appointments through his Office of Legal Policy and the Committee on Federal Judicial Selection. He was even willing to ignore Senate choices as evidenced in the administration's successful campaign to appoint Daniel Manion. The Senate, after a long and bitter fight over Manion's confirmation, finally squeezed out a victory for the president as Vice President Bush voted in Manion's favor to break a 49–49 tie.

The Supreme Court

Never is the president's dominance over judicial selection so clear as when he or she attempts to fill a Supreme Court vacancy. Although the president and the Committee on Federal Judicial Selection may listen to a wide range of individuals and groups each recommending their favored choice for the position, there is no doubt that the White House has the final say. As in making any federal judicial appointment, the president considers partisan politics, appeasing interest groups, and satisfying representational demands. Over time, presidents have selected justices from their own party between 80 and 90 percent of the time. More recently the consideration of representational factors has played an increasing role as various groups such as blacks, women, Catholics, and Jews have thought themselves entitled to a seat on the court. This belief first developed in 1916 with the appointment of Louis Brandeis and the ensuing demand that there was always to be a Jewish justice on the court. The tradition of a Jewish seat continued until Abe Fortas resigned in 1969 as the last Jewish justice. With Thurgood Marshall's selection in 1967 and Sandra Day O'Connor in 1981, race and gender have joined with religion to further complicate the representational variable in selection politics. David O'Brien of the University of Virginia believes that these types of considerations will continue in the future and are "likely to compete with expectations for even more ethnic representation on the court—for the appointment of an Italian, Hispanic or Asian."[29]

Beyond considerations of a candidate's party or ability to satisfy representational demands, the major factor affecting appointment to the Supreme Court is the individual's personal and ideological compatibility with the president. A president's primary goal is to pack the court with justices who can safely be expected to decide cases in a manner that is consistent with the president's legal priorities. President Reagan attempted to ensure maximum success in predicting the future behavior of his nominees by favoring the selection of justices with prior judicial experience. This allows a review of the justice's prior written opinions while sitting on lower federal or state courts. The president thus hopes to avoid being surprised by any change of character that might occur when an individual dons the black robes for the first time. All of President Reagan's nominees (including two who were not confirmed) were elevated from either federal or state appellate courts.

The experiences of presidents Eisenhower and Kennedy with appointing men who had not had any prior judicial experience and whose careers on the bench proved to be very disappointing to the presidents, were not lost on the Reagan administration. President Eisenhower once described his decision to appoint Earl Warren as Chief Justice of the Supreme Court as his greatest mistake during his eight years in office. Warren, a lifelong Republican, had been attorney general and governor of California but had never held a judicial position. Once on the court, Warren became an active leader of the liberal wing of the court, ushering in many landmark civil rights and civil liberties decisions, several of which greatly upset the president. Justice White, who also came to the Court without prior judicial experience, played an active role in President Kennedy's successful 1960 campaign and was appointed to a high position in the Justice Department just before being appointed to the Supreme Court. He also became a disappointment to the president, although not to the degree of Chief Justice Warren.

Even though the president clearly controls the nomination process for Supreme Court appointments, once a nominee is selected his or her name must then be turned over to the Senate for confirmation. Through its confirmation hearings conducted by the Judiciary Committee and ultimately through floor debate and final voting, the Senate has been able to occasionally play a significant role in the selection process. Because the Senate has been so completely shut out from the nomination process, members are capable of only exerting a negative force upon presidential selection. Thus, senators are unable to push through a candidate of their own choice (especially over the president's objection); but through their constitutionally granted role of offering "advice and consent," senators may be able to block the president's choice. This situation is most likely to occur when the president and the Senate majority represent different parties. Recent evidence of such successful confrontations were the blockage of Republican President Nixon's nominations of Clement Haynesworth and G. Harold Carswell by a Democratically controlled Senate, and the even more recent defeat of Robert Bork and Douglas Ginsberg, Reagan nominees thwarted again by a Democratic Senate.

What should be the proper role for the Senate in the conduct of its confirmation responsibilities? President Reagan and other representatives of the executive branch argued that the Senate should not introduce its own standards of acceptability for a Supreme Court justice but should defer to the president's wisdom. Confirmation hearings in the Senate should be pro forma and only when a blatant defect in a nominee's personal background is uncovered are senators justified in voting against the candidate. The Senate's inquiry should be restricted to issues relating to the candidate's temperament and integrity, not questioning ideological or political leanings as revealed through speeches, written opinions, or personal testimony at the hearings.

The Senate, however, has rejected this position as was evidenced in its refusal to confirm Robert Bork. Using a balance of powers argument, which it believes is readily apparent from a reasoned interpretation of the Constitution, as well as a number of historical precedents, the Senate challenges the president's efforts to control the entire selection process. The president, it is argued, may choose any nominee, but the Senate shares the appointment process with him or her. In exercising this responsibility to provide "advice and consent," the Senate must rely on its independent judgment of the nominee's qualifications, which includes reviewing the candidate's personal views and determining whether he or she is the type of person the Senate wishes to have on the Court. Given the lifetime tenure of the justices, all parties must be very careful in whom they approve to such a powerful and longstanding position.

Who is correct in this constitutional debate? It probably depends on one's partisan political beliefs and whether these beliefs coincide with the party controlling the White House or the Senate. In any event in the past 20 years we have seen four instances where the Senate successfully blocked a presidential nomination.

Role of the ABA's Standing Committee on the Federal Judiciary

The influence of the ABA's Standing Committee on the Federal Judiciary on the selection of federal judges at all levels has been of great interest and concern, since it is the only private and unelected institution that plays a regular role in the selection process. Why should representatives of the ABA be given the power to decide which nominees are to be designated as professionally qualified to become federal judges? Critics charge that the ABA is a conservatively biased organization, representing the interests of its corporate clients, and that it does not even fairly represent the lawyers of this nation, since more than a majority of the bar have declined membership.[30] The ABA has consistently countered such arguments by stating its belief that it does in fact represent the legal profession and possesses a unique expertise that qualifies it to evaluate a lawyer's potential for serving on the bench.

The overwhelming number of investigations conducted by the ABA committee deals with vacancies at the district court and appeals courts, although its work on Supreme Court appointments receives the most publicity. Its recommendations are accepted by the administration 99 percent of the time. In those rare instances where the committee is forced to oppose a nomination, it will present its objections publicly at the Senate confirmation hearings. The ABA investigation is typically conducted in two stages. At the preliminary or informal stage, a representative of the committee from within the judicial circuit will examine the available speeches, decisions, and other legal writing of the prospective nominee. Next, 20 to 50 confidential interviews will be held with the judges, lawyers, professors, and others who are most likely to provide an accurate evaluation of the candidate's competence, integrity, and temperament. If a clear and consistent picture emerges early in the interview process, the evaluation can soon be terminated. If however, there are conflicting judgments concerning the nominee's qualifications, additional interviews must be conducted and additional documents reviewed. At the conclusion of the informal stage, the committee member prepares a written report to the chairperson of the committee in which his or her recommendation is included. The chairperson then reviews the report, discusses it with the committee members, and sends it to the attorney general's office with the ABA's overall evaluation of either exceptionally well qualified, well qualified, qualified, or not qualified.[31]

The committee fell under heavy criticism following its approval of G. Harold Carswell, a Nixon nominee whose confirmation was eventually thwarted by the Senate. Carswell's receiving a qualified rating despite his extremely poor record on the bench and racist public remarks discredited the committee and renewed charges that it was simply the voice for corporate concerns and conservative political interests. (Carswell had been overruled by the Supreme Court more than any other lower federal court judge.) The ABA then made a conscious effort to loosen its ties to big business and right-wing political factions by appointing moderate chairpersons who promised more rigorous and objective analyses of all candidates.

THE SOCIALIZATION PROCESS

Once a lawyer has been selected to the bench, he or she soon realizes that despite the power and prestige of this new position, he or she is entering this new job untrained, and unlikely to receive more than a day or two of formal orientation. American judges, as we have previously noted, are "amateurs" who must learn their craft through a variety of formal and informal socializing processes and agents that will educate them and ease their transition from advocate to arbiter. The remainder of this chapter will examine judicial socialization, explaining its meaning, describing how it works, and studying in depth a group of Philadelphia judges as they disclose their socialization experiences.

Explaining the Concept

American judges are prime candidates for analysis by students of adult socialization. Although the majority of research into the socialization process focuses on children during their formative years, there has been much interest in the problem of "adult socialization" defined in the *Encyclopaedia of Social Sciences* as a learning process that occurs when the "individual is confronted with a new role and knows virtually nothing about what he should do. In such a case society will require new socialization."[32]

Susan Goldberg, who studied the socialization experiences of judges in the District of Columbia's Superior Court, indicates how important this learning process is to the very survival of legal institutions by writing that: "Judges must familiarize themselves with substance and procedure, case management, the norms and attitudes accepted by members of the bench and a myriad of administrative and legal procedures essential to competently assume the role of a judge in our society."[33]

It is true that nearly all American judges have shared the common experience of legal education. However, once completing law school, lawyers then specialize in divergent areas, many never venturing inside a courtroom. Exacerbating the problem to an even greater degree is the tendency to select judges, especially to the criminal bench, who are markedly deficient in courtroom and litigation experience. The problem was highlighted over 20 years ago by the President's Commission on Law Enforcement and Administration of Justice, which warned: "It is possible for a judge who the day before had made his living drafting corporate indentures to be called upon to rule on the validity of a search or to charge a jury on the law of entrapment."[34]

As a result of the overall lack of litigation experience, as well as the absence of viable orientation or training programs, newly selected judges are thrust into a rather alien environment. Students of adult socialization believe that the process may begin even before the judge officially commences his or her new professional responsibilities. Daniel Feldman offers an excellent model for tracing the development of this process. Although Feldman's study was conducted at a hospital rather than a courthouse, its applicability to the judicial scene is readily apparent. The first stage is defined as "anticipatory socialization" and occurs before the recruit enters the organization when expectations about his or her job are formed and he or she begins to receive preliminary information from the new organization or prospective employer. At the next stage, entitled "accommodation," the individual sees what the institution is actually like and attempts to become a productive member. The final stage, termed "role management," finds the recruit resolving newly emerging problems within his or her work group and beginning to mediate conflicts within the organization.[35]

The Feldman model was recently adapted to an important study of judicial socialization by Alpert, Atkins, and Ziller.[36] These authors modified the Feldman paradigm into a four-stage process that traces the judge's entire professional career. It begins with "professional socialization" before he or she becomes a judge, when a lawyer is primarily a product of earlier legal experiences, including law school. The second stage, "initiation and resolution," covers the judge's first five years on the bench where he or she typically follows an altruist or legalist orientation and begins to learn the reality of the newly accepted profession. The third stage is the "establishment period," which lasts from years 6 through 15 and has the judge adopting the role orientation of "guardian of the law." This begins a long-term process of coping and possibly redefining the role. The final stage is the "commitment period" after the judge has served 15 years and has chosen to become a legalist and guardian of the law. It is in this concluding stage that the judge experiences increased satisfaction with judicial life.[37]

The most frequently cited article on judicial socialization is by Carp and Wheeler who studied a small sample (30) of federal district judges. Their research is most helpful in describing the major types of problems faced by judges during their early years on the bench.[38] They list three major categories of socialization problems faced by new judges: legal, administrative, and psychological. Legal problems were either substantive or procedural and were usually caused by the inexperience of the judge in handling criminal cases. The administrative problems were quite unexpected and were often the most difficult to overcome. These included demands for managing a shrinking budget, reducing and controlling an expanding caseload, and resolving complicated personnel problems of their staffs. The psychological problems were summarized by the authors as being mainly "the loneliness of the office, sentencing defendants, forgetting the adversary role, local pressure, and maintaining a judicial bearing on and off the bench."[39]

Formal Training Programs

Although most judges receive only a cursory orientation to their new positions and continue to be dependent on an informal socializing process, the past 30 years have produced major efforts to improve the quality of formal judicial education. The earliest programs initiated at both the state and national level grew out of the 1956 seminars conducted by the Institute for Judicial Administration for state appellate judges. Five years later judicial education received another major boost when the ABA and W. K. Kellogg Foundation funded numerous sessions for state trial judges.

Following the success of these programs, both bench and bar supported the development of judicial education throughout the nation. By the end of the 1960s, the federal judiciary had begun its own training program in Washington, the National College of State Judges had initiated its extensive programs in Reno, and the American Academy of Judicial Education had started conducting its National Trial Judges Academy.

Beyond these early and isolated programs, a clear consensus of professional opinion had agreed on the necessity for creating and implementing a widespread program of education for all levels of judges. Standard 7.5 of the National Advisory Commission on Criminal Justice Standards and Goals exemplifies this national commitment by urging each state to "develop its own judicial college which should be responsible for the orientation of new judges and which should make available to all state judges the graduate and refresher programs of the national judicial educational organization."[40] In a recent survey (1986) of state and federal programs for judicial education completed by Mary Ann Stein for the Foundation for Women Judges, 70 programs were identified. All states except Delaware operated regular in-state programs for judges or court staff for both new or inexperienced persons.[41]

One of the most interesting programs developed in recent years is the University of Virginia's Graduate Degree Program for Judges. This program was established in 1980 and grants a Master of Laws (LL.M.) in the Judicial Process to judges (usually from appellate courts) who satisfactorily complete two successive six-week summer sessions at the law school and write a thesis under law faculty supervision. It is academic in both orientation and substance as the following curriculum clearly indicates[42]:

		Credit Hours
First Term:	Anglo-American Jurisprudence	3
	Law and Economics	3
	Theory of the First Amendment	2
	Constitutional Restrictions on Crime	1
Second Term:	Courts and the Social Scientist	3
	Law and Medicine	3
	Comparative Legal System	3
	Thesis	9

At the state level, the Illinois Plan for Judicial Education has been generally acknowledged to be one of the nation's finest programs. Illinois, which has had a totally unified court system since 1964, has been operating its program for over 30 years. In a recent article, Assistant Director Lester Bonaguro credits the use of judges rather than attorneys or law professors as lecturers in the program as a key ingredient in its success. He also urges that attendance be mandatory, that judges should come from all regions of the state, and special care be taken in the selection of relevant topics for discussion.[43]

This description of the growing number of formal judicial educational programs should not leave the reader with the sanguine impression that judges are receiving adequate training prior to reaching the bench. The reality of the situation indicates that most judges still must rely on informal socializing agents and personal initiative. Though the situation is improving, current training programs are much too brief, considering the magnitude and variety of problems facing new judges. As long as judges who lack courtroom experience are continued to be selected, the present educational efforts are likely to fall short.

Informal Training

Given the brevity and limited focus of formal orientation programs and the lack of prior litigation experience, most judges must undergo an "informal" educational process, turning to various socializing agents in their efforts to resolve the multitude of adjustment problems. Several states attempt to assist judges during this extended transition period through informal seminars and luncheon meetings with their colleagues. These sessions comprise a modest effort to provide continued assistance to the judges and serve as a more formalized aspect of their on-the-job training. Nevertheless, the primary education received by new judges once they assume the bench is through a variety of socializing agents including their fellow judges, support staff (clerks, secretaries, and bailiffs), and attorneys.

Colleagues on the bench have generally been credited with being the most prominent socializing agent for the beginning judge. This task may be accomplished through somewhat formalized seminars conducted by the presiding or chief administrative judge, but most likely it will be carried on in informal exchanges during the workday. Judge Nan Huhn from the District of Columbia's Superior Court describes this process as frequently occurring in the judge's dining room "where every day the newer judges, and a lot of the older judges go. You spend your hour there and you find out what is happening with other judges. There is also an atmosphere set by our Chief Judge that lends itself to interaction. We have gripe sessions every so often because he wants feedback."[44] A few judges complain that they feel inhibited from reaching out to their more experienced brethren, but the large majority rely primarily upon assistance from their peers.

Judges may also turn to their court staff for help in the early stages of their careers, especially in matters of administrative concern such as managing the docket. Experienced courtroom personnel may provide invaluable assistance in dealing with the sometimes overwhelming paperwork as well as clarifying obscure courtroom procedures. The judge's staff—law clerks, secretaries, court stenographers, and bailiffs—have usually been employed for several years within the local court system and can provide the necessary links to preexisting rules and regulations, many of which may be unstated folkways, that can greatly facilitate the adjustment period.

The final socializing agent frequently mentioned is the attorneys practicing within the local courthouse. They are probably the least important source of information but can occasionally provide needed advice or simply serve as a sounding board. One study discovered that many judges found attorneys to be a problem during their first months on the bench as some attorneys attempted to test the judge and see how far they could go.[45]

Despite the useful service provided by these socializing agents, it appears that the learning process is primarily a private affair in which the judge must learn on his or her own. As David Neubauer concluded: "In the end, the judges must rely on themselves. Through reading in the law library and seeking out knowledgeable persons, judges engage in self-education."[46]

First Days on the Job

In addition to problems caused by the inadequacies of local orientation and training programs, judges may also experience several other problems during their transition from advocate to arbiter. The first problem facing a novice judge, beyond initial anxiety, is the very practical situation of how to conclude his or her law practice. There is little guidance for this task other than some very vague guidelines offered by the Code of Judicial Conduct and a scattering of state statutes covering conflict of interest. Candace Goldstein, in one of the rare discussions of this topic, warns that judges must be impartial and independent and, therefore, must eliminate every possibility of reciprocal favoritism. In order to assist the judge in making a clean break with his or her law practice and legal associates, Goldstein recommends that "each state establish a committee to advise new judges on issues such as transferring cases, financial arrangements for severance, and disqualification."[47]

Before dealing with the specific legal, administrative, and psychological difficulties encountered by most judges during this period of adjustment, let us first examine the more general problem of shifting from impassioned advocate to impartial arbiter. One judge, in lamenting on the rigors of remaining neutral, reminisced fondly about the enjoyable times he had as a lawyer: "Lawyers like blondes have more fun. The biggest price judges pay is detachment. They may not lose their love for people but in their working life, they do not live that love, they implement it. The satisfactions of the office are more internal than external, more cerebral than emotional. . . . But when judges gave up being lawyers, they made the conscious choice that they wanted more meaning in their lives."[48]

The transition appears to be the most difficult for trial lawyers who are forced to control their aggressive instincts. The resulting radical alteration in courtroom style caused one judge to note that new members on the bench must be cautioned "to take the bite from their voices and the sharpness from their phrasing so as to seem to be inquiring rather than cross-examining. They have to remain both in fact and in appearance above and not participants in the battle."[49]

Even outside the courtroom a new judge's ability to remain calm and impartial may be severely tested. John Paul Ryan and his colleagues, who surveyed American trial judges, discovered that "nowhere is the tension between lawyering and judging more obvious than in negotiations. Should he be a neutral arbiter or should he try to push the parties toward disposition or settlement."[50]

A final difficulty associated with this dramatic shift to a more acquiescent role is the frustration of having to remain silent or at least under control when a judge's trained litigating instinct spurred him or her toward intervention. One federal judge commented that judges simply cannot talk back, and even though they believe they are being unfairly criticized, they must remain restrained.[51] Additionally, when judges reach an appellate court, they have even more restrictions placed upon their freedom of behavior since one of the most important parts of their responsibilities is to always give a reason for their decisions.[52]

Returning to the more specific categories of adjustment difficulties, legal problems often present the most serious challenge to the beginning judge. Especially for those judges whose legal practice rarely brought them into a courtroom, there must be a very accelerated learning process in order to grasp the mechanics of operating a court. Equally demanding is the switch from legal specialist to judicial generalist, requiring the mastery of vast bodies of substantive law in a short period of time.

Even when new judges have committed themselves to learning new areas of the law, there can be no assurance that unique, unanticipated problems will not arise while they are on the bench. Several judges have also noted that when unusual, and complex issues do develop in a case, they do not have the vast array of potential sources of information available to them as they once did when they were attorneys or law professors. Judge Edwards from Washington, D.C., described this problem as a "narrowing of the conduits of information once you reach the bench even though you need more and more information about what's going on in the world around you."[53] How can novice judges learn so much so quickly? Most studies conclude that it is usually accomplished through self-education, and, although we have already noted the assistance offered by fellow judges and court staff, it is still primarily a matter of learning by doing.[54]

A second area of concern to judges during this transitional period are various administrative problems. The major dilemma facing most judges is simply learning how to use their time wisely. Another serious problem for inexperienced judges is learning how to supervise the courtroom staff and manage the docket. These administrative and managerial tasks are very challenging because most judges come from large law firms where they rarely are forced to perform any managerial tasks. Their professional responsibilities are concentrated upon a handful of important cases at a time. They could also depend upon the assistance of a large support staff to dispose of any of the mundane or tedious administrative details that now seem to dominate a workday.

The third and final category of adjustment problems is psychological. The major psychological problem faced by most new judges is their isolation and loneliness. As one New York City judge recently commented: "When you become a judge you are absolutely more isolated. Whether it is by the Canons of Judicial Conduct or attorney perceptions, you are a pariah. Being a judge is a lonely job."[55] The realization that you are "ultimately out there by yourself" can be a rather traumatic realization, especially for judges who had been accustomed to working in a collegial atmosphere in a large firm where they could always count on their fellow attorneys for advice and support.

A second psychological difficulty noted by several judges is the unanticipated anxiety caused by the realization that their new position bestows a sometimes frightening amount of power and responsibility. One judge found that this power "was tremendous—it was my greatest astonishment—the number of decisions which had to be made in a day which affected lives."[56] As a result of this newly acquired power and prestige, another judge decried a negative side effect: "I suddenly discovered that everybody is afraid of you. Your personal life suffers a great deal. People with whom you formerly had a great deal of social contact with you find are very reluctant to invite you to their homes and that sort of thing for fear that it will be thought that they are unfairly currying favor with you."[57] Based on my interviews with over 100 judges, this precipitous decline in social life is not experienced by the majority of judges, although a slight decrease in entertaining is fairly common.[58]

In spite of all of the various problems facing beginning judges, they all do emerge from this transitional period, soon to become confident, experienced members of the bench. This discussion concludes with some comforting advice from one judge on how to survive this difficult period: "Apart from the particular warmth and effectiveness of my colleagues, I can think of two things that helped me over the past three years. The first is the passage of time. . . . I do not spend fewer hours in anguish over reaching the right result in particular cases, but it gives me some comfort that I have marked three years on the court with the law of the state intact. Second, because the process pre-supposes a mental picture of what one is doing and why one is doing it, I read extensively about the experiences of others."[59]

JUDICIAL SOCIALIZATION: THE PHILADELPHIA EXPERIENCE

As already indicated, judges receive little or no training prior to reaching the bench. Research also shows the majority of judges are ill-equipped to handle courtroom responsibilities due to their lack of familiarity with litigation, a professional specialization rarely practiced by the majority of lawyers selected for the bench. Since nearly all of these earlier socialization studies focused on either state appellate or federal judges,[60] an attempt was made to discover if a similar socialization pattern was present in a state trial court. A month was spent in the Philadelphia County (Pennsylvania) Court of Common Pleas interviewing judges in order to answer this question. Approximately 20 judges were interviewed and observed during this time period. This sample represented half of the active judges hearing criminal cases for the City of Philadelphia. The judges were randomly selected and represented all three of the court's special divisions (homicide, criminal list, and criminal calendar).

The overall conclusion reached from this month of intensive interviews and extended observations is that the judges in Philadelphia's criminal court did not suffer the same socialization difficulties described in previous studies of appellate and federal courts. Because of either inherent self-confidence, easy adaptability, or prior experience and training, these urban trial judges did not believe or act as if they had undergone any traumatic or even challenging socialization process. The remainder of this section will describe exactly what these judges did experience as they made the transition from lawyer to judge, and then attempt to explain why the Philadelphia experience appears to be so painless, particularly in contrast to the socialization difficulties described in earlier studies.

Prior Experience

The most apparent explanation for the unexpected self-confidence of the Philadelphia judges upon first taking office is most likely related to their prior legal experience. In contrast to the generally accepted belief that most judges are ill-equipped for the job as a result of their paucity of litigation experience, 80 percent of the Philadelphia judges interviewed stated that they had earlier trial experience, with over half having worked in the prosecutor's office. One of the judges had even been a law clerk in the very same court system for 20 years. Other types of legal experiences related to trial work were negligence (40 percent) and general business litigation (25 percent). Besides the large number of former prosecutors, several others had experience with the criminal justice system, as 15 percent were formerly employed in the city's prestigious public defender office, and 20 percent had experience as private criminal lawyers.

Another trend within the Philadelphia judiciary was the similarity of educational background. This, combined with the decidedly inbred nature—born and raised within the city limits—gave the court a homogeneous grouping rarely found at the appellate or federal level. It was interesting to note that even though Philadelphia's Court of Common Pleas handles both civil and criminal matters, nearly all of the judges, through a self-selection process related to their intellectual interests and previous legal experiences, have stayed within either the criminal or civil side without the expected rotation. This contrasts sharply with the federal district courts where the judges are faced with all types of cases and have no control over which category of dispute they will be deciding.

Selection Process

Despite the surprising amount of trial experience, particularly in the practice of criminal law, it clearly was the presence of political connections and activities that seemed to propel nearly all of the judges through the selection process. Common pleas judges are elected to 10-year terms and had to gain the support of the dominant leaders of the Democratic party, although a select number of "acceptable" Republicans were allowed to gain favorable backing. All judges interviewed attested to the extreme politicization of the judicial selection process.[61]

Immediately prior to running for judicial office, nearly half of the judges had held office or were actively involved in politics (according to their own self-evaluation). Several of the judges had run (usually unsuccessfully) for congressional and mayoral positions. Nearly all had sometime in their recent past maintained a moderate level of political involvement. Their activities ranged from near full-time preoccupation with politics and elections at the ward, state, and national levels to a limited participation in a few carefully chosen campaigns. Politics for most of the judges was a fascinating and important diversion toward which their formal legal careers had inevitably drawn them.

Most of the judges credited their long friendships with political leaders as being the critical factor in their good fortune but were quick to add that their professional reputation and moderate visibility on the city's social and political scene were also important reasons for their successful candidacy. The political career of one of the city's judges, Thomas A. White, was highlighted in a *Time* magazine cover story entitled "Judging the Judges" and offers convincing proof of the close linkage between politics and judicial office in Philadelphia. The article recounts that White was picked to fill a vacancy in 1977. Why? "I'm Irish," he says. "Of course I'm qualified," he hastily adds, but he matter of factly explains that the Democratic party needed an Irish judge to balance the ethnic makeup of their judicial slate. One of 16 children of an IRA member who fled Ireland, White is also a lifelong Democrat who managed to be elected to the state legislature in the Eisenhower landslide. Redistricted out of his seat in 1954 he decided to go to law school and became a criminal defense lawyer. All the loyalty was rewarded when he was backed for a judgeship by Congressman Raymond F. Lederer whom White describes as a close personal friend.[62] Although the career of Judge White is an extreme example of the possible political involvement of Philadelphia's judges prior to their election, it is nevertheless a difference in degree rather than kind.

First Days and Additional Training

The expected description of the first days on the job for new judges is usually filled with feelings of anxiety and self-doubt. The Philadelphia judges, however, recounted this memorable period as simply being a time of excitement. They generally were confident that they could handle their new responsibilities and whatever new challenges they faced could easily be surmounted through on-the-job training and informal conversations. Few judges lamented the absence of a viable orientation program although several thought that some of their colleagues could have profited from a lengthier indoctrination.

These sentiments should not be construed to imply a blasé attitude on the part of these novice judges. They were both flattered and sometimes awed by their new position and the varied perquisites to which they were now entitled. Even the idea of wearing a robe was uncomfortable at first as they strolled from their chambers to the courtroom. The bowing and scraping of city hall functionnaires is still an annoyance and embarrassment to many of them. A disappointing aspect of their new position, however, was their less than impressive chambers, located in an undistinguished office building across the street from city hall, which houses most of the courtrooms. Many judges commented that their current quarters were a perceptible step down from their former more elegant and larger private law offices.

In Philadelphia, new judges are given a two-day orientation that concentrates on administrative concerns. They are also urged to attend statewide judicial conferences held twice yearly and are designed to offer an educative component for the beginning judge as well as refresher seminars for the more experienced. These conferences were described as more social than educational experiences. The only judge interviewed who did seem to require special preparation because of his lack of legal experience was given a three-month stint in the municipal court, which handles misdemeanors and less serious cases. None of the judges interviewed had been to the National Judicial College at the University of Nevada. Most were skeptical of such programs, describing them as being social affairs with little long-term value.

Socializing Agents

Being consistent with the rest of this study's findings, the Philadelphia judges did not feel any urgency for consulting with or relying on the help of socializing agents. If a problem did arise most of the judges stated they would first turn to one of their more experienced colleagues whom they respected. The entire court of common pleas meets two or three times a year, and then only to discuss pressing administrative matters. The judges in the waiver unit, which conducts nonjury trials, meet at monthly luncheon meetings that were viewed as being informative and useful and provided a rare opportunity for the judges to interact. Outside of these meetings, new judges usually select one or two experienced judges that they personally respect and contact them privately in chambers for advice. Typical difficulties for new judges were proper drafting of charges to the jury, judicious handling of obnoxious attorneys, and aiding incompetent prosecutors.

Nearly all judges interviewed were surprised by the lack of collegiality among their fellow members of the court. There was almost no socializing outside of a few official functions. Each judge seemed to have two or three close friends among his or her colleagues but was rather disdainful toward most of the other members of the court. It was surprising to have every judge comment so negatively upon the ability of colleagues. The most typical descriptions involved the terms "lazy," "slow-witted," "inadequate," and "mediocre."

The second group of socializing agents used by judges is their court staffs. The Philadelphia judges did not emphasize the role of their staffs during their initial socialization, although they were appreciative of the many useful services that they did provide. The law clerk, usually a part-time employee with a law degree and an interest in criminal law, is the most critical member of the courtroom work group. Law clerks were frequently used to complete tedious legal research projects. Some judges offered clerk positions to outstanding law school graduates and treated it as an honorific year-long position similar to a clerkship at the appellate level. Many judges, however, simply saw the clerk as a professional aide who would remain with a particular judge for as long as they both could stand each other. These clerks occasionally worked with the judge prior to his or her reaching the bench.

Adjustments

Even though most Philadelphia judges indicated that their assuming judicial office did not necessitate any meaningful adjustments in their lives, each judge did note some particular shift in lifestyle that he or she had not fully anticipated. Almost without exception the judges stated that their social life and circle of friends did not change. If they were friendly with lawyers, both parties made a conscious effort to avoid topics that might prove uncomfortable and studiously avoided talking about pending litigation.

A few of the judges were surprised by their difficulty in abandoning their previously held adversarial role. Especially during the first months on the bench, several judges stated that they had to restrain themselves from jumping into the fray to aid an incompetent attorney. One judge had trouble stifling himself from objecting to an attorney's arguments that were drifting off the subject. Too many years as a defense attorney or prosecutor leave a mark in courtroom behavior that cannot be quickly eradicated. One judge candidly admitted that he would close his eyes in the beginning as the only way he could refrain from showing emotion. The most unusual adjustment was by one judge who felt that as a top trial lawyer he was working himself toward a nervous breakdown and he found that the pace of court life was sufficiently slow to reduce stress and lower his blood pressure.

Conclusions

As this description of judicial socialization as experienced in Philadelphia has clearly shown, the common pleas judges have generally had an easy time adapting to their new professional role. Prior work experience, especially familiarity with either litigation or the city's criminal justice system is the most obvious explanation for their easy transition. Does the Philadelphia experience directly contradict the socialization studies by Alpert, Carp, and Wheeler, and others?[63] Because these earlier studies focused on state appellate or federal courts, it is likely that the Philadelphia experience may simply be typical for urban felony courts, especially those located within a highly politicized setting.

NOTES

1. Jerome Corsi, *Introduction to Judicial Politics* (Englewood Cliffs, N.J.: Prentice-Hall, 1984), 104.
2. Ibid.
3. Henry Glick, *Courts, Politics, and Justice* (New York: McGraw-Hill, 1988), 85.
4. Nicholas Lovrich and Charles Sheldon, "Voters in Judicial Elections: An Attentive Public or an Uninformed Electorate," *Justice System Journal* 9/1 (Spring, 1984): 23.
5. Philip L. Dubois, "The Significance of Voting Cues in State Supreme Court Elections," *Law and Society Review* 13 (Spring, 1979): 775.
6. Glick, *Courts, Politics, and Justice*, 87.
7. Harry Stumpf, *American Judicial Politics* (New York: Harcourt, Brace and Jovanovich, 1988), and Burton Atkins, "Judicial Elections: What the Evidence Shows," *Florida Bar Journal* 50 (March, 1976): 152.
8. Atkins, "Judicial Elections," 153.
9. Philip Dubois, *From Ballot to Bench: Judicial Elections and the Quest for Accountability* (Austin: University of Texas Press, 1978), 250.
10. R. Neal McKnight, Roger Schaefer, and Charles Johnson, "Choosing Judges: Do the Voters Know What They are Doing," *Judicature* 62 (August, 1978): 96.
11. James Herndon, "Appointment as a Means of Initial Accession to Elective State Courts of Last Resort," *North Dakota Law Review* 38 (1962): 60; William Keefe, "Judges and Politics: The Pennsylvania Plan of Judicial Selection," *University of Pittsburgh Law Review* 20 (1959): 621; and Albert P. Melone, "Political Realities and Democratic Ideals: Accession and Competition in a State Judicial System," *North Dakota Law Review* 54 (1977): 187–211.
12. David Adamany and Philip Dubois, "Electing State Judges," *Wisconsin Law Review* 3 (1976): 731.
13. Philip Dubois, "Financing Trial Court Elections," *Judicature* 70/1 (June–July, 1986): 8.
14. Glick, *Courts, Politics, and Justice*, 88.
15. Bradley C. Canon, "The Impact of Formal Selection Processes on the Characteristics of Judges," *Law and Society Review* 6/4 (May, 1972): 579; Henry Glick and Craig Emmert, "Selection Systems and Judicial Characteristics," *Judicature* 70/4 (Dec.–Jan., 1987): 228; and Herbert Jacob, "The Effect of Institutional Differences in the Recruitment Process: The Case of State Judges," *Journal of Public Law* 13 (1964): 104–119.
16. Richard Watson and Rondal Downing, *The Politics of Bench and Bar* (New York: Wiley, 1969), 331.
17. Ibid. p. 332.
18. Errol E. Meidinger, "Bar Polls—What They Measure, What They Miss," *Judicature* 60 (May, 1977): 469.
19. Ibid.
20. Glick and Emmert, "Selection Systems," 235.
21. At this point in time (1787) the discussion focused only upon Supreme Court appointments since the lower federal courts would not be created for two more years with the passage of the Federal Judiciary Act of 1789.

22. Sheldon Goldman, "Reaganizing the Judiciary," *Judicature* 68 (April–May, 1985), 315.
23. Ibid.
24. Richard Richardson and Kenneth Vines, *The Politics of the Federal Courts* (Boston: Little, Brown, 1970), 61.
25. Harold Chase, *Federal Judges: The Appointing Process* (Minneapolis: University of Minnesota Press, 1972), 186.
26. Nina Totenberg, "Will Judges Be Chosen Rationally," *Judicature* 60 (September, 1976): 93.
27. Larry Berkson, Susan Carbon, and Alan Neff, "A Study of the U.S. Circuit Judge Nominating Commission," *Judicature* 63/3 (September, 1979): 122.
28. Ibid. p. 106.
29. David O'Brien, *Storm Center: The Supreme Court in American Politics* (New York: W. W. Norton, 1986), 66.
30. The recent work of Heinz and Laumann on Chicago lawyers indicates the significant split among lawyers who represent institutions such as corporations and those who provide defense for individuals. The latter group of attorneys, who represent the majority of our nation's lawyers, are typically not members of the ABA and opposed to many of their policy positions.
31. American Bar Association, *Standing Committee on the Federal Judiciary*, (Chicago: American Bar Association, 1977).
32. David Stills (ed.), *Encyclopaedia of Social Sciences* (New York: Macmillan, 1968), Vol. 14, 555.
33. Susan L. Goldberg, "Judicial Socialization: An Empirical Study," *Journal of Contemporary Law* 11 (1985): 425.
34. President's Commission on Law Enforcement and the Administration of Justice, *Task Force Report on the Courts* (Washington, D.C.: Government Printing Office, 1967), 68.
35. Daniel Feldman, "A Contingency Theory of Socialization," *Administrative Science Quarterly* 21 (1976): 433.
36. Lenore Alpert, Burton Atkins, and Robert Ziller, "Becoming a Judge: The Transition from Advocate to Arbiter," *Judicature* 62 (February, 1979): 325.
37. Ibid. p. 327.
38. Robert Carp and Russell Wheeler, "Sink or Swim—Socialization of a Federal District Court Judge," *Journal of Public Law* 21 (1972): 359.
39. Ibid. p. 373.
40. National Advisory Commission on Criminal Justice Standards and Goals, *The Courts* (Washington, D.C.: Government Printing Office, 1973), 156.
41. Mary Ann Stein, "Judicial Education: How Does Your State Measure Up," *Judges Journal* 26 (Fall, 1986): 28.
42. Daniel Meador, "The Graduate Degree Program for Judges at the University of Virginia," *Judges Journal* 22 (Spring, 1983): 18.
43. Lester Bonaguro, "Lawyers to Judges and Judges to Greatness: Illinois Plan for Judicial Education," *Judges Journal* 19/2 (Spring, 1980): 34.
44. "On Becoming a Judge: Socialization to the Judicial Role," *Judicature* 69/3 (October–November, 1985): 143.
45. Lenore Alpert, "Learning About Trial Judging: The Socialization of State Trial Judges," in *Courts and Judges,* ed. James Cramer (Beverly Hills: Sage Publications, 1981), 105.

46. David Neubauer, *America's Courts and the Criminal Justice System* (N. Scituate, Mass.: Duxbury Press, 1979), 169.
47. Candace Goldstein, "Becoming a Judge: Problems with Leaving a Law Practice," *Judicature* 69/2 (August–September, 1985): 94.
48. Robert Satter, "The Quality of a Judge's Experience," *ABA Journal* 65 (June, 1979): 935.
49. Ibid. p. 933.
50. John Paul Ryan, Alan Ashman, Bruce D. Sales, and Sandra Shane-DuBow, *American Trial Judges* (New York: Free Press, 1980), 136.
51. "On Becoming a Judge," 146.
52. Judith Kaye, "My Freshman Years on the Court of Appeals," *Judicature* 70/3 (October–November, 1970), 167.
53. "On Becoming a Judge," 145.
54. Stumpf, *American Judicial Politics,* 106.
55. Goldberg, "Judicial Socialization," 429.
56. Ibid.
57. "On Becoming a Judge," 146.
58. Paul B. Wice, *Chaos in the Courthouse* (New York: Praeger Books, 1985), 114.
59. Kaye, "My Freshman Years," 167.
60. Alpert, Atkins, and Ziller, "Becoming a Judge," as well as Carp and Wheeler, "Sink or Swim."
61. Previous studies of Philadelphia have also noted the significant impact that politics plays upon the city's entire criminal justice system. These include Wice, *Chaos in the Courthouse,* and *Criminal Lawyers: An Endangered Species* (Beverly Hills: Sage Publications, 1978).
62. "Judging the Judges," *Time,* 20 August 1979, p. 52.
63. Alpert, Atkins, and Ziller, "Becoming a Judge," as well as Carp and Wheeler, "Sink or Swim."

Chapter
7

The Judge's Work Environment: The Courthouse and Beyond

This chapter examines the working environment of the judge. In addition to offering a physical and social-psychological description of the courthouse, there will also be a discussion of the various members of the courtroom work group who assist the judge (i.e., law clerk, calendar clerk, bailiffs, personal secretary, and court administrator). The final section will focus on the variety of court environments, from the justice of the peace and municipal courts, which handle the least serious legal matters, to the highest level of state and federal appellate courts. The concluding section is extremely important in educating the reader to the diversity of judicial settings operating within the United States. One of the more prevalent myths held by the general public is the supposed similarity between all individuals wearing black robes and deciding legal controversies. This section attempts to dispel that shibboleth by describing the wide range of judicial environments. Let us first turn to the physical setting where judges perform their professional responsibilities: the courthouse and its impressive inner chambers.

PHYSICAL DESCRIPTION OF THE COURTHOUSE

Although one of the major themes of this chapter is to stress the diversity of judicial working environments, the physical appearances of most American courthouses are to a large degree very similar. Regardless of their geographic location or their respective level of authority, nearly all courthouses possess the same imposing facade. Representing a variety of architectural styles developed during the past two centuries, they all

present an image of stability and strength, purposefully designed to inspire awe and humility from all citizens required to use their services.
Entrance is typically gained by climbing an excessive number of steps
and by entering between massive columns and under a larger-than-life
inscription reminding all who cross the threshold of the power, wisdom,
and benevolence of the law. One might imagine that the overall effect
is to humble all litigants entering the facility, defusing their anger and
hostility. This humbling experience will continue as the court's clientele
wind their way into the interior of the building toward the equally imposing courtrooms.

For security reasons most courthouses restrict entrance to a single
door, funneling all visitors through a crowded, narrow entrance way
where once inside a police officer or bailiff will conduct a security
search. In San Francisco, where the criminal court has experienced a
number of bombings and violent demonstrations, a rather rigorous
search is conducted, first with a thorough body frisk followed by a careful inspection of all packages and briefcases. Even in courthouses permitting more open access, there will frequently be security measures
taken in front of specific courtrooms where a highly publicized trial may
attract an unusually large number of spectators. Tight controls may also
exist around a particularly sensitive office housed within the courthouse
such as an unpopular prosecutor.

Most courthouses are located near the business center of a large city
as part of the complex of governmental office buildings often adjacent to
the city hall or state capitol. They are usually distinguished from other
governmental buildings by the marbled columns supporting the already
noted enscribed mantle decrying the power and compassion of the judiciary. It has been interesting to observe in my research into the criminal
justice system that a large number of the criminal courts are located away
from the rest of the governmental offices in the center of town. Instead
they are found in dreary locales in outlying sections of the city, typically
bordering a decaying neighborhood with abandoned warehouses and vacant, trash-strewn lots. The criminal courts in New Orleans, Chicago,
and San Francisco typify such uninviting locations. The most common
reasons offered for choosing these depressing sites, which were inconve-
nient to nearly everyone, were for security purposes. These cities had
chosen to append their pretrial detention facilities to the courthouse
proper and since no one wants a jail adjacent to their backyard, especially the civic and business leaders of the community, the entire complex was moved far from view. There could also be a more subtle, psychological motivation, which I noted in my book on the urban justice
system: "One almost has the impression that the rest of the legal community as well as civic officials were fearful of contracting some type of
communicable disease if they remained in too close proximity to the
criminal courts and its undesirable clientele."[1]

The interior of the courthouse, including the individual courtrooms, continues to reinforce the sense of power designed to create a feeling of awe. Once inside the building, one usually enters a cavernous lobby covered by a high, arched ceiling, supported by more columns and frequently engraved with even more inspiring mottoes echoing the court's commitment to justice. There is an omnipresent information booth that is invariably unattended. A nearby bulletin board offers outdated clues as to what cases have been assigned to which courtrooms. In a distant corner is a newspaper stand and a nearby battery of telephones, the majority of which are out of order. Cafeterias and snack bars may be found in the basement, where lawyers and their clients nervously await their court appearances, consuming stale coffee and prepackaged sandwiches.

Moving toward the individual courtrooms, one passes through hallways painted in varying tones of institutional green or brown. As an economy move, air-conditioning is often restricted to the courtrooms and the judge's chambers, while the hallways swelter. Journalist Paul Hoffman, long-time observer of the New York judicial scene, describes this unpleasant atmosphere by writing that "the City's fiscal crisis has turned the criminal court building into a vertical slum."[2] Even within the courtroom, the 25-foot ceilings and the escalating costs of electric power undermine the effectiveness of the air-conditioning units, which seem to be operating at 50 percent capacity. Outside the courtroom, the hallways are filled with animated conversations between lawyers and their clients while concerned family members, witnesses, and nosy spectators mill about the smoke-filled corridors. Although a few of the newer courthouses, especially within the appellate and federal court systems, have set aside rooms for lawyers to converse with their clients and witnesses, most trial courts provide scarce assistance and force the attorneys to conduct business in a secluded portion of the hallway.

Once inside the courtroom, there is an immediate decrease in the decibel level and a marked improvement in air quality (not only is there the possibility of air-conditioning but a ban against smoking is rigorously enforced). Consistent with the overall imposing stature of the courthouse, the interior of individual courtrooms are also designed to impress its clientele. After passing through a series of heavy doors, one has a direct view straight ahead of the judge's elevated dais, the focal point of the entire room. Bracketed by state and national flags with additional impressive adornments behind and over his or her head (these include colorful state and federal seals, paintings of eminent jurists, and more inspiring mottoes carved between statutes of famous juristic personages), the judge sits in elevated prominence, both literally and figuratively.

In front of the judge's bench sits the court stenographer, responsible for meticulously recording all that is said while court is in session, and whose notes will eventually become the official transcript of the proceedings. To one side of the judge and at a right angle to the bench is the jury box containing sufficient seats for all jurors plus alternates. These are usually arranged in two or three rows of chairs and separated from the courtroom by a railing. On the opposite side of the room are a group of tables occupied by court clerks who assist the judge in monitoring and scheduling cases. They can be seen peeking from behind piles of computer printout and case files, trying to efficiently process the never ending flow of cases. Postponed cases, future scheduling, missing participants, and incomplete files are persistent problems facing these harassed public servants. Facing the judge are two large tables with chairs that are reserved for the opposing counsels and their clients. A wooden railing running across the width of the courtroom divides the spectator's portion of the courtroom from the working section just described. The first few rows are often reserved for attorneys and journalists with the remainder of the rows populated by an assortment of spectators, including individuals having business in the court scheduled for that day, concerned family and friends, and curious observers. In order to guarantee proper respect for the judicial proceedings, uniformed officers who are sometimes referred to as bailiffs assist the judge in maintaining order within the courtroom. Noisy spectators or inappropriate visitors (cold weather conditions can frequently entice transients and the homeless into the heated courtrooms) are quickly removed at the slightest indication from the judge. Infractions such as chewing gum loudly, reading a newspaper, dozing, or merely taking copious notes may result in removal.

This description is much more appropriate for trial courts, which have busier calendars and are housed in more modest surroundings, than appellate courts at both the state and federal levels. Although the courtroom (except for the absence of the jury box) is arranged similarly, the accoutrements in the appellate courts are much more opulent and the overall ambience noticeably more subdued and somber. Appellate proceedings are highly structured and typically involve oral arguments between counsel that may last for only a few hours. The cases often raise more complex issues of broader social and economic significance than faced by the trial courts in their harried efforts to process the thousands of cases threatening to overwhelm their limited resources.

Beyond the view of the public is the labyrinth of hallways and rooms located both behind and alongside the courtroom. It is inside these carefully controlled avenues that one finds the judge's chambers, which usually contain an anteroom or reception area where the judge's secretary sits, with additional smaller rooms for the court clerk or law assistant frequently provided. The secretary serves as a major obstacle in reaching the judge's private quarters, but access to the entire maze of hallways and offices is carefully protected by locked doorways and patrolled by armed bailiffs. The judge's private office is usually spacious but often crammed to overflowing with law books, legal memorabilia, overstuffed furniture, and miscellaneous piles of correspondence, reports, and drafts of opinions. Walls are covered by photographs, diplomas, paintings, and other personal momentos that attempt to make the room more hospitable. Judge Frank Coffin commenting on why these offices are termed "chambers" hypothesizes that "the time-honored English designation signals a hope to preserve something of the serenity, dignity and grace associated with more leisurely and reflective times. There is some substance to the hope. A judge's quarters should not be a pressure point, a rallying place for press conferences, or a command post for hectic tactical brainstorming sessions."[3]

Because a judge, especially in our urban trial courts, rarely works out of one assigned courtroom but is shifted around according to the court administrator's logistical priorities, his or her chambers may not be located in close proximity to the courtroom where the judge is currently sitting. Adding to the inconvenience is the problem caused by the recent additions to the bench that has necessitated the use of annexes to house the newly appointed judges. These buildings are usually located within a short walking distance of the main courthouse, but judges who reside in these "renovated" facilities often complain about their second-class status.

James Eisenstein and Herbert Jacob in their organizational analysis of the criminal courts believe that the physical setting of the courtroom can influence the style of interaction between members of the courtroom work group, which as we will soon see includes the judge, clerks, attorneys, litigants, secretaries, bailiffs, and anyone else having regular business before the courts. The following quote from their book, *Felony Justice*, explains the importance of these professional arrangements:

> Because only the judge among key participants has his own office in the courtroom suite, he and the other participants are thrown together much more than one might expect from a reading of their formal roles. Courtroom members spend much of their free time socializing, rather than in isolated reading or paperwork. To do paperwork or research, the prosecutor and defense counsel must retire to their offices in another part of the building or (as is typical with defense attorneys) in a separate building some distance from the courthouse. Where the clerk has no office, he spends most of his day at the courtroom table; he rarely leaves his post, because he has no locked drawers where he may secure the documents on his desk. Even when he does have a separate cubicle, he spends a large portion of his day within the courtroom, handling matters brought in by "regular" defense attorneys circulating through the courthouse.[4]

SOCIAL-PSYCHOLOGICAL DESCRIPTION

Beyond its physical characteristics, a courthouse resembles a living organism with a unique set of social and psychological attributes. We have already noted how its physical characteristics contribute to an aura of

dignity, inspiring awe and respect from all persons having business before the court. Because the judiciary lacks the power to enforce compliance with most of its decisions, it must rely upon the willing submission
of the losing party to the court's directives. Thus, the state has purposefully created an environment that will inspire respect for the court's decisions, even if they are not popular.

In addition to the obvious effort to create a sense of dignity and respect, I have always thought the courts that I have observed possessed
a striking number of social-psychological characteristics that were very
reminiscent of a traditional village. Within the confines of these courthouses, one found the judge and his or her courtroom work group operating at a high level of intimacy, highly suspicious of outsiders, and under
the autocratic control of the judge, who bore a striking resemblance to
the omnipotent village patriarch.

Turning first to the high level of intimacy found among most members of the courtroom work group, this is an unexpected sight for most
persons making their first appearance in a courtroom. Especially if someone has business before the court and is ardently contesting a dispute
with another party, viewing the apparently friendly interaction between
legal adversaries and the light-hearted badinage among most members
of the courtroom staff can be very surprising and disconcerting. Raised
on the expectation that the adversary system creates a solemn responsibility on the part of attorneys to fight aggressively and relentlessly for
their clients' best interests, it is therefore confusing to see such a convivial atmosphere.

Although the "kibbutzing" is curtailed when court is in session, it is
never completely absent. In the hallways, around the snack bars, in the
courtroom during recesses, and before and after the day's business, the
friendly joshing never seems to end. Whether this exaggerated conviviality serves as a type of necessary social lubricant to disguise actual tensions or is an accurate measure of their camaraderie is difficult to discern. Whichever purpose it serves, it is still an omnipresent style of
interaction that typified almost every courthouse visited. There were of
course variations in the general level of jocularity, with New York and
Philadelphia topping the scale and Denver and Los Angeles being the
most somber, at the opposite extreme.

A second similarity between big-city courthouses and traditional vil-
lages is their suspicion of outsiders. The legal community has always
seemed to retreat into a defensive posture behind its stylized jargon and
plethora of confusing procedures, but the criminal courts appear to take
an even more recalcitrant position toward anyone wishing to penetrate
their inner sanctum. Their paranoia is not based entirely on whimsy
since the criminal courts have borne the brunt of the public's frustration
over the rising crime rate. (Politicians have also used the courts as scape-
goats for their own inability to deal with the problem of making our soci-

ety a safer place.) The result of this external criticism is for the courtroom work group to adopt a "siege mentality" and draw together within the courthouse walls, often hiding their hostility behind nervous laughter.

This negative picture does not mean that researchers and journalists will be permanently barred from entering the inner workings of the courthouse. It has meant, however, that before one is allowed to penetrate the court's defenses, one must prove through responsible reporting and unbiased research that he or she merits the trust of the courthouse personnel. Once this trust has been established, court personnel can be as helpful and open as any public official. Again, using the village metaphor, the initial suspicion of outsiders must be worn away by tangible acts of good faith, conclusively proving one to be both reliable and trustworthy.

The nearly complete control exercised by the judge over the courtroom creates a third similarity between the traditional village and contemporary courthouse. Each judge resembles the patriarchal (or in few instances the matriarchal) head of the village or ruling family, possessing virtually dictatorial powers over all who enter his or her domain. In the courthouse, anyone who disturbs or challenges the processes of justice will be summarily removed from the courtroom. Regardless of the status or prominence of any visitor to the courtroom, once within the judge's domain, unquestioned obedience is demanded. There is no appeal from the judge's decision as he or she quickly dispatches the bailiffs to carry out personal orders. Although each city has a presiding judge who oversees the operation of all the courtrooms and can theoretically control and discipline a judge who violates professional norms, this is rarely done.

The occasional outlandish or demagogic antics of individual judges are common topics of courthouse gossip, but I have almost never witnessed a direct confrontation between a judge and lawyer or clerk where a successful challenge to judicial behavior was made. Lawyers seem to simply catalogue these judicial idiosyncracies and store them away for future use. This type of information may be useful the next time the attorney appears before a judge with a reputation for some form of unusual behavior.

The judge is clearly the most imposing and intimidating figure in the courtroom, particularly in his or her relationship to the other members of the work group. The style of judicial interaction can take various forms from aloofness to extreme gregariousness, but the judge is clearly the one who sets the tone of the relationship. The only individual consistently observed not to be intimidated by the judge is the defendant. This is especially true if the accused has had several previous experiences with the law. His or her familiarity with the justice system appears to have lessened fear and respect for all of the members of the court, including the judge.

It is amazing to observe defendants who face the possibility of very long prison sentences behaving so contemptuously in front of the judge. Their attitude is clearly reflected in both their demeanor and dress. Defendants at times seem to purposefully antagonize the judge by adopting a defiant posture, staring unconcernedly into space, or glaring toward the bench. Much of this posturing, particularly when the defendant is youthful, seems to be directed toward impressing friends and family in the audience. It is almost a symbolic assertion of independence, notwithstanding the defendant's imminent fate. Slovenly dressed, many young defendants appear to have inadvertently wandered into the courtroom. Possibly because the judges continually face so many defendants striking these disrespectful poses, there is rarely little interest in correcting their behavior. The judge may also reason that there is little need to react since sentencing responsibilities give him or her the final say in this confrontation. Another possible explanation might be that after sitting on the bench for an extended period of time, a judge is no longer shocked by such conduct and almost comes to expect it from repeat offenders.

Although the federal courts and all appellate courts maintain a more dignified atmosphere than that just described, they nevertheless also maintain similar characteristics in the complete control by the judge and pervasive antipathy toward outsiders, especially the media. Since appellate judges spend less time in the open courtroom, and more time in chambers, it can be expected that if one could penetrate the private world of the appellate courts (the judge's personal chambers), one may also find a surprising degree of relaxed interaction among most members of the courtroom staff. It may even be reasonably expected that judges, once they retreat beyond public view to their more protected quarters, are also willing to lessen their judicial posturing and engage in friendly conversations.

In one of the few successful efforts to penetrate the judge's private behavior outside of public view, Bob Woodward and Scott Armstrong described the inner workings of the United States Supreme Court in their book *The Brethren*. They were able to gain this unique glimpse into the generally sacrosanct chambers of the justices by interviewing former law clerks who were willing to provide detailed behind-the-scenes accounts of the justices' out-of-court behavior. The following anecdote from their book illustrates the type of interaction between the justices (in this case Thurgood Marshall) and their clerks: "Often Marshall would corner one of his clerks after lunch and spend hours in the special chair they reserved for him in their office. By the time he had worn out his own clerks' patience, clerks from other chambers might have wandered in for a round of the endless storytelling. But they could always leave. His own clerks had nowhere to go. . . . At one point his clerks tried piling books on Marshall's chair to discourage him from settling in for the afternoon. They underestimated their boss' stamina. . . . Finally the clerks took to hiding in the second floor office."[5]

THE COURTROOM WORK GROUP

As the caseload of the courts has expanded, judges are no longer able to single-handedly administer their case-processing responsibilities. Today, the judge must rely on a group of assistants who perform a wide range of administrative functions. Collectively, this group has been termed "the courtroom work group" and is comprised of individuals working together, each with their own delegated responsibilities and in possession of relevant skills and specialized training. Because courts perform an increasing variety of functions, the work group must provide a growing number of services. David Ozar, Cynthia Kelly, and Yvette Begue compiled the following list of tasks that the courtroom work group must presently perform: case flow management, assignment of cases, maintenance of court calendars, jury management, management of records and information, personnel management, management of courthouse facilities such as providing security, investigation of complaints concerning the court system, supervision of the work of court reporters, maintenance of public information functions with the media, and establishment and maintenance of links with community organizations interested in court performance.[6] John Paul Ryan in his comprehensive study of American trial judges stated the work group's responsibilities in simpler terms when he wrote that "judges are assisted by a variety of courthouse and courtroom personnel who work to provide security, record-keeping, general administrative management, and legal research. These lower participants do more than assist the judge, however. They also serve as sources of information and wield power. Courtroom personnel act as gatekeepers both to protect the judge and for their own purposes."[7]

Who are the individuals charged with aiding the judge in carrying out these varied responsibilities? This chapter will focus on the following six primary members of the courtroom work group who assist the judge: personal secretary, calendar clerk, bailiff, court reporter, law clerk, and court administrator. Although the majority of courts possess nearly all of these staff members, Ryan's national study of trial courts discovered that "the availability of and efficiency of courtroom personnel vary quite sharply across courts and this contributes to differences in judicial work patterns."[8] Ryan noted, as might be expected, that the number of resource staff available to a court as well as their impact upon judicial operations was directly related to the size of the court, with judges in smaller courts having the fewest resources and larger courts typically having the most.

Given the adversarial nature of the American judicial process, it is often surprising to discover the cooperative relationships existing within the courtroom setting, including not only the judge and work group but the opposing counsel as well. It is only by the skillful and cooperative efforts of *all* members of the courtroom work groups that the management of cases can proceed efficiently with optimal concern for the best interests of each member of the group. Herbert Jacob, one of the most knowledgeable experts researching the American legal system with a special interest in courtroom management, emphasizes the importance of having each member of the work group understand and conform to his or her prescribed duties in order to provide the court with the critical degree of stability. Jacob notes that each member of the team must know his or her role in order for "the routine business of the court to proceed in a quite informal fashion with many understandings that are never formally recorded but which nevertheless lubricate much of the normal work of the court."[9]

Professor Jacob continued his exploration into the organizational behavior of the courts in a major study with James Eisenstein in which they examined the criminal courts in three cities: Baltimore, Chicago, and Detroit. Their study added considerably to the understanding of the courtroom as an organized work group. They described the judge as the "linchpin" that ensures that members of the work group will coordinate their individual activities while working toward a common institutional goal. The authors summarize their analysis of work group characteristics by writing: "Courtroom workgroups are like many other organizations. They are labor-intensive, are staffed by professionals and provide services rather than products. Courtroom workgroups have an authority structure that is modified by influence relationships. . . . Although workgroups dispose of many cases during a day, they are not assembly lines. Even routine decisions involve discretion. . . . On an assembly, one worker simply relies on all the others doing their jobs; an assembly line requires few verbal or social interactions. Workgroup members must interact with one another to reach a decision."[10]

The remainder of this section will be devoted to a series of individual analyses of each of the primary members of the courtroom work group. The judge's secretary will be the first member to be discussed.

Personal Secretary

Each judge is assisted by a personal secretary who performs all of the expected secretarial functions in addition to serving as a gatekeeper and protector of the judge's privacy. In larger courts the secretary may have responsibility over a team of word processers and typists who perform the more typical secretarial tasks. The personal secretary will also be on continual guard to protect the judge's privacy as well as providing a wide range of extrajudicial services such as assisting with speeches to bar associations and community groups, as well as arranging for travel to professional conferences and seminars. Many secretaries have worked for their respective judges for long periods of time, sometimes even moving with the judge from his or her previous position at a law firm. These individuals are very conscious of their obligation to carefully screen outside interruptions. As a concluding point, nearly all judges insist that the secretary be especially sensitive to the necessity for maintaining secrecy and confidentiality. Since reporters may occasionally question the judge's personal staff about pending cases or controversial issues, it is critical that these members of the work group maintain the complete trust of their boss.

Bailiffs

The bailiff or court deputy is primarily responsible for assisting the judge in maintaining control over the courtroom, with special attention toward security and decorum. Beyond this basic task, bailiffs, may be called upon to perform a variety of other functions. In Illinois, for example, the bailiffs are members of the sheriff's department and are principally responsible for security; in Colorado law clerks act as bailiffs, calling the court to order, maintaining order in the courtroom, assisting jurors delivering files, and generally attending to the personal needs of the judge.[11] Another point of great variation among bailiffs is in their professionalism. They range from civil service appointees whose merit selection closely resembles the type of physical and mental testing process that most police officers are required to pass to the highly politicized appointment of untrained individuals whose primary qualification is a long and loyal tenure as a ward or precinct worker for the city's dominant political party. The latter situation was most obviously present in New Orleans where bailiffs are clearly acknowledged patronage positions. Despite their colorful insignia-bedecked uniforms and their impressive numerical strength, their physical appearance casts grave doubts as to their capability of dealing with any serious security problem or crisis situation.

Since most bailiffs are responsible for the general security of the courtroom as well as the judge's personal protection, it is rather surprising that they are employed during such restricted hours, being on duty only when the court is in session, which is typically between 10 A.M and 4 P.M. It is ironic, therefore, that after the courts adjourn for the day and the facility becomes increasingly less secure the bailiffs are only minimally available to offer assistance and protection. Judges frequently complain about this problem and feel especially vulnerable. Unfortunately, this problem is addressed only after a judge or court officer has been attacked.

The most prestigious bailiff in the country is Al Wong, the U.S. Supreme Court marshall who oversees the 60-person force responsible for providing security for the nation's highest court. Every courtroom visitor is X-rayed and each briefcase and purse carefully inspected. Chief Marshall Wong is also the Court's crier, announcing for all to stand when the justices enter the courtroom, and is responsible for serving as timekeeper during the restricted oral arguments.[12]

Calendar Clerks

The judge is often more dependent on his or her calendar clerk than any member of the courtroom work group. This is probably most valid at trial courts where the caseload pressures are most severe. The calendar clerk is primarily responsible for controlling the court's docket, managing the case flow, calling up the proper case, ensuring that the relevant files are available, and carefully taking notes for subsequent incorporation into the files. Depending on the specific responsibilities of a particular court, the calendar clerk may also have additional managerial tasks and liaison functions. Courts utilizing a centralized calendar, for example, frequently require their clerks to supervise the distribution of cases from the central or presiding judge, who controls the pretrial proceedings, out to the various judges responsible for conducting trials.

Although the volume of cases may be significantly smaller, the calendar clerks in appellate courts are also of critical importance to their respective judges. Appellate Judge Frank Coffin describes the office of his calendar clerk as the "nerve center" as it receives, tracks, and expedites all proceedings. Coffin identifies the unique job of one of his calendar clerks by writing: "Much of our workload, consisting of cases and questions other than those in our formal docket, arises from our clerk's preliminary scanning of each new appeal to see if all the jurisdictional and procedural requirements have been met."[13]

Beyond the clerk's technical functions in caseload management, he or she has another aspect to their job that is nearly as important. This is described as a "communications facilitator," acting not only as the central information depository but also being able to "span the boundaries" by being able to effectively reach other officials within the complex courthouse organization. Marc Gertz believes that this ability to cross courtroom boundaries and be able to interact with all of the key participants in the legal community creates a cumulative influence that can bestow a great amount of power to the calendar clerk.[14] The following excerpt from my research into urban courts reveals the critical interaction between calendar clerks and both the judiciary and legal community:

> Even though the calendar clerk may not be as influential a figure in molding the judge's behavior as once imagined, he frequently does enjoy a relatively close working relationship. Many judges have retained the same clerk for several years, although in recent years most cities assign a calendar clerk to a particular courtroom and he will serve any judge who is sitting for the requisite period of time. Where judges are able to select and retain their own calendar clerks, a warm relationship frequently develops. Because of the necessary case by case communications between judge and clerk in order to effectively monitor the docket, they inevitably act in unison and grow increasingly compatible.
>
> Lawyers also appreciate the power of the calendar clerk, for he can decide whether, if he is so inclined, to manipulate the docket. This can mean

whether you have to wait two hours or two minutes before your case will be called. Although some experienced lawyers with clout may go directly to the judge and request the favor of a speedy call, most attorneys restrict their efforts at obtaining favorable scheduling to lobbying the calendar clerk. In a few cities lawyers admitted bestowing gifts upon these clerks in exchange for a favorable place on the docket. In most instances the judge is either oblivious or turns his back on these low level machinations. As a general rule, the calendar clerks attempt to strike a happy medium between being flexible enough to accommodate a justified request, and yet rigid enough to ensure a smooth flow of cases.[15]

Finally, calendar clerks have been recently obliged to become conversant with the operation of computers as an important new tool to assist them in dealing with their expanding caseloads. While many judges drag their heels and are leery of threatening technological advances promised by these "mechanical saviors," the calendar clerks have generally been quick to recognize the great potential these machines possess in helping them control their caseload battles.

Court Reporters

Most courts still rely on the use of court reporters to maintain an official record of what is transpiring in the courtroom. This will provide a verbatim record of not only the trial but of any other adversarial proceeding. The reporters are usually state employees and are considered among the judge's personal staff. A recent article on court employees indicated that court reporters are in a unique position because in many states they are allowed to sell their transcripts to attorneys and their clients, while other jurisdictions permit them to work part-time for lawyers conducting depositions or other types of free-lance work.[16] Many laypersons are perplexed by the reliance of courts upon stenographic recording as opposed to utilizing more modern recording methods such as videotapes, but traditions die hard, and the court's basic conservative tendency has preserved the court reporter's position in nearly every courthouse in the United States.

Law Clerks

Law clerks have been frequently described at both the trial and appellate courts as providing invaluable and influential intellectual assistance to the judge. Ryan, commenting only about state trial courts, writes that law clerks "facilitate the performance of legal research tasks . . . and enable judges to produce written decisions in selected cases by doing background research and perhaps initial drafting. In small courts, law clerks assist judges in less conventional or expected ways, by facilitating their keeping abreast of changing substantive law."[17] The role of the law clerk becomes even more expanded at the appellate level where they assist the judge in the writing of opinions. In those appellate courts such as the U.S. Supreme Court, which possess discretionary control over the selection of its caseload, the law clerks have the additional responsibility of providing assistance in this selection process.

Historically, the position of law clerk was first created approximately 100 years ago when Chief Justice Horace Gray of the Massachusetts Supreme Court began the practice each year of selecting a top law school graduate to assist him in his chambers. The law clerk worked for a year aiding the justice by checking citations, correcting galley proofs of opinions, running errands, and preparing memoranda on specific questions. Although clerks today may perform a broader range of tasks, most still possess the basic responsibilities initially required. The modern view of the role of law clerk is eloquently stated by federal appellate court Judge Frank Coffin in the following quote: "In short, as a result of the preparatory work of the clerks, the judge's critical and judgmental faculties are released for action at a stage when the development of the opinion has ripened and the issues needing decision have been pinpointed. This also means that those critical faculties can be brought to bear on more issues in more cases."[18]

Most law clerks are appointed for a set period of service of one or two years, usually immediately after law school graduation. It is typically viewed as an honor and awarded to the graduates with the most distinguished law school records. A minority of courts have allowed law clerks to serve for longer periods of time, with a select few jurisdictions designing the position as a permanent career appointment. California has recently contemplated creating law clerks as career positions while Philadelphia's Common Pleas Court has allowed its judges to hire a single law clerk for the duration of the judge's tenure. Nevertheless, most law clerks, especially at the appellate level, are chosen by a specific judge who has total discretion over the appointment decision. Given the prestige of this position, it is often a stepping-stone in a young lawyer's career, leading to a lucrative appointment in the private sector or a responsible position in government. Most law clerks regard their experience as one of the high points of their professional careers and often sense an emotional letdown once they begin practicing law. These sentiments were recently echoed by Federal District Court Judge Sal Levantino of Austin, Texas, a former law clerk who commented: " 'It really ought to be at the end of your career rather than at the beginning.' "[19]

What exactly do these law clerks do? Their duties vary tremendously from simply serving as research assistants to making critical decisions in the screening process. Most commonly they are used as preliminary drafters of opinions or orders, although the amount of freedom permitted varies widely from judge to judge. Since the level of court also exerts a great influence on the range of their responsibilities, the following discussion of their functions will be broken down by the particular type of court.

Beginning first with trial courts, law clerks serve primarily as research assistants for each judge. Although most of these clerkships are for a year, it is at the trial court level when one finds nearly all of the career appointments. The career clerks often perform a wide range of additional duties beyond research, ranging from serving as messenger boys to representing the judge at social functions. Moving to the state appellate courts, M. E. Noble described their work as also being very technical, their primary function being to analyze decisions cited, thereby saving "a tremendous amount of time for their justices by eliminating cases not applicable to questions presented and through independent research find cases more directly on point."[20]

Law clerks seem to be given the greatest responsibility in the federal appellate courts. This often creates an intimate and complex relationship between the federal judge and his or her clerk. Judge Patricia Wald of the D.C. Court of Appeals is energized by each year trying to work out "the balance between the endless energy and imagination of the clerks and the perspective of the judge."[21] The federal appeals court presently uses clerks to assist the judges in distinguishing between cases that can be handled quickly and those that are more complex and likely to require more time. One recent innovation at the appellate level has been the establishment of a staff law clerk who works for the entire court instead of an individual judge. Law clerks handle a broad category of cases that can be perfunctorily processed such as the increasing number of pro se petitions from indigent defendants. The role of law clerk appears to have expanded during the past decade at the federal appellate courts as a direct result of the increasing caseload pressures. Judge Coffin writes that these pressures give the judge no alternative but to develop "a kind of intense utilization of law clerks. . . . During his [the appellate judge] time in chambers, in addition to doing the thinking, research, writing, and editing of his eight or twelve new opinions, he must also continue any unfinished business, write critiques of his colleagues' opinions, respond to their suggestions and criticisms, tend to the daily flow of administrative duties, and try to catch up on his professional reading. A yearly output of ninety or even more formal opinions by a judge, in addition to less formal memoranda opinions and orders, not by any means a rarity, is perhaps three times the output of most judges in the early 1960s."[22]

As one might expect, the most prestigious law clerk positions are found on the U.S. Supreme Court. These law clerks are often given opportunities to influence judicial policy in major court decisions. The selection of each justice's four law clerks is a personal choice among the large number of applicants who must write directly to a specific justice. There has been a recent trend toward selecting clerks who have had previous experience clerking in the lower federal courts, especially the courts of appeals, although several still come directly from law school, and their academic record still remains the major factor influencing selection. The major responsibility of Supreme Court clerks has been in helping each justice decide what cases he or she wishes to hear (stated more technically, those cases in which a writ of certiorari may be granted). Professor David O'Brien believes this is the clerk's most indispensable role because "as the number of filings each year rose, justices delegated the responsibility of initially reading all filings . . . which seek review but may be denied or granted at the Court's own discretion. Clerks then write one- to two-page summary of the facts, the questions presented, and the recommended course of action—that is, whether the case should be denied, dismissed, or granted full briefing and plenary consideration."[23]

When the justices have completed their discussion of a case, voted, and begun to compose a written opinion, several members of the court will allow their clerks to draft a preliminary opinion. The role of the law clerk during the editing and revising of subsequent drafts will vary widely from justice to justice. A recent Supreme Court reform has been the creation of a "cert pool" in which several justices designate a single clerk to prepare a memo for the mutual use of the participating justices.

Especially at the appellate court level, there has been occasional debate as to whether the clerks have been granted too much influence over judicial decisions. The problem usually involves the role of the clerk in either the decision to grant certiorari or whether a case should be given a full hearing or an abbreviated procedure. Because law clerks are used in such a variety of ways with radically different degrees of autonomy, it is difficult to conclude what their overall level of responsibility should be. Nevertheless, the issue has been receiving increased attention, and David Crump reports a new effort to provide greater guidance for law clerks by offering some type of manual for their consultation similar to the *Law Clerk Handbook* presently being published by the Federal Judicial Center. He also notes that law schools might offer courses in their curricula for future law clerks such as the one currently being used at South Texas College of Law.[24]

Regardless of their specific responsibilities, the law clerks and the judges for whom they work form unique relationships in which both parties benefit. Because the law clerk is privy to so many confidential matters, he or she can develop a level of trust that leads to a deep and long lasting bond between clerk and judge. Judge Coffin believes that in selecting a law clerk, he must try to estimate the trustworthiness of the applicant, a factor that may be of even greater importance than intelligence. He explains that

> a chambers community is nourished in an atmosphere of assured confidentiality. In an era when the public's right to know is asserted in regard to nearly every institution, it may seem archaic to value confidentiality for judicial chambers. But I see no valid public purpose served by disclosure of what goes on between judges or between a judge and his law clerks. . . . The apprehension by a judge that his every remark, be it deliberate or random,

cerebral or emotional, tentative or final, could someday gain public currency would be a corrosive force. So my first admonition and plea to my clerks is that what goes on in my chambers of any serious and professional import remains a matter of confidence for their lifetime. So far, to my knowledge, this request has been heeded.[25]

Court Administrators

One of the most significant additions to the courtroom work group has been the trained court administrator. Court executives may now be found in nearly every state and major city in the country. In a 1976 survey by Harvey Solomon of the Institute for Court Management, it was discovered that the "typical state court administrator is backed up by a staff of 14 professionals and 15 clerks or secretaries. The average budget for 1973 was $900,000. The average salary of a state court administrator is $31,000."[26] It can be conservatively estimated that in the subsequent 18 years these figures, especially for the budget, have more than doubled. The court administrators are also found at the federal level where under the 1978 circuit court executive law their role at both the district court and court of appeals was defined and expanded. At the Supreme Court there exists an administrative assistant to the chief justice who performs similar tasks.

The court administrator has been compared to the older, more established profession of hospital administrator whose primary role is to keep the facility running smoothly while doctors perform their technically demanding tasks. Court administrators assist the judiciary in battling their steadily increasing dockets and streamlining their courthouse operations. In contrast to the individual court clerks who manage the operation of an individual courtroom, the court administrator assists the presiding judge in running the entire courthouse. In many states there is a centralized arm of the Supreme Court or its chief justice. This organization oversees the operation of all of the local state court systems at the county or city level, setting statewide priorities for effective courthouse administration. The following is a list of the major responsibilities of the court administrator compiled by Burton Butler in a survey of presiding judges:

1. Fiscal management
2. Systems analysis, research, and data processing management
3. Space and equipment management
4. Liaison management with other agencies
5. Caseflow management
6. Personnel management
7. Jury and witness management
8. Public information management
9. General management of nonjudicial activities[27]

The federal courts have instituted court executives at both the circuit and district court level. Their responsibilities appear to be fairly similar to their counterparts at the state level. Professor Steven Flanders has carefully traced the 15-year history of federal court executives and believes that the group has provided great assistance to the federal judiciary. One unique aspect of the federal court executive position is its relationship to the judicial council of each circuit. Flanders explains this unusual organizational position by writing that "circuit and district executives are distinct from other federal court managers in that it is up to the incumbent and the affected courts to define the executive role in each instance, for the office is unusual in its placement, or lack of placement within the judicial hierarchy. The one placement that is clear is that the circuit executive is appointed by and responsible to the judicial council. This is typically a diffuse body however, that may have well over a dozen members and meet as frequently as twice a year."[28] The federal executive typically serves as the administrative assistant to the chief judge of either the district or circuit and must perform a wide range of functions whose general purpose is to relieve the judge of trivial and repetitive types of responsibilities. One of the major areas of assistance is the allocation of space and facilities, a time-consuming headache for most chief judges that is now the job of the court executive. Their additional tasks are similar to those of state executives (court administrators) involving budgetary, personnel, and data-gathering activities. Court administrators have emerged as professionals whose expertise in management provides much needed assistance to the judicial leadership at all levels of government. They can help resolve not only the minor technical problems that can easily grow to stymie any court system but can also lend invaluable assistance in the important broader areas of long-term planning and improved public relations.

As a closing comment, it should be noted that there are inherent tensions existing between court administrators and the judicial officials they serve. Most court administrators realize that they can be unceremoniously fired by their judicial superiors if they are perceived as encroaching on the turf of local judges or clashing over a critical issue without the possibility of compromise, or if there is simply a basic conflict of personalities that undermines the court's effectiveness.

Presiding/Administrative Judge

The one judicial officer who is most likely to be interested in utilizing the special expertise of court executives (also referred to as court administrators) is the presiding judge (who is also called the administrative judge in several jurisdictions). This judge is the specially designated leader of his or her court system and may be chosen in a variety of ways including election by colleagues on the bench, appointed by another branch of government (i.e., governor or legislature), or simply on the basis of seniority. The necessity for creating a presiding judge developed from the growing bureaucracy surrounding court systems. James Gazell found this present at all levels of government and described the phenomenon by writing: "The state supreme court is assuming the role of top management with the Chief Justice as chairman of the board of justices. . . . The appellate courts are beginning to resemble middle management. The Chief Judges of the trial courts are starting to constitute supervisory management over a labor force of judges, associate judges, magistrates, clerks, attorneys, and litigants."[29]

What are the responsibilities of presiding or chief administrative judges? Gazell notes that they face many of the same managerial problems that confront corporate as well as governmental leaders in the other branches. These include delegating authority wisely, maintaining unity of command, narrowing the span of control, avoiding excessive layering, effectively measuring output, and striking a balance between scientific management utilizing technical expertise and a human relations approach stressing psychology in the treatment of personnel.[30] Beyond the generalized responsibilities just listed, presiding judges have specific tasks related to ensuring the smooth operation of their respective court systems. Ted Rubin of the Institute for Court Management lists what he believes to be the primary tasks of these judicial leaders: (1) assign judges to various courts, (2) initiate disciplinary action against members of the bench, (3) spokesperson for bench to bar and general public, (4) preside over functions involving bench, (5) ex officio member of various committees within the court system, (6) decide administrative matters related to members of his or her court such as vacations and retirements, and (7) plan and execute continuing education projects.[31]

The most famous presiding judge in the nation is the chief justice of the U.S. Supreme Court. Although the Constitution does not bestow any special responsibilities or powers upon the chief justice, he or she has often come to symbolize the ideological posture of the entire Court. Thus one speaks of the Warren court's due process revolution and civil rights achievements or the more conservative Burger court, which followed immediately and attempted to minimize or emasculate several of the Warren court decisions. The chief justice can assume a leadership role through informal powers of persuasion although the majority of individuals who held this exalted position have not chosen to use their position in this fashion. The one clear power that the chief justice does possess is in the selection of which justice will be chosen to write the court's majority opinion, although even this power can only be exercised if the chief justice votes with the majority.

There have been several chief justices in the Supreme Court's recent history that have exhibited a variety of leadership styles. Walter Murphy discusses several of these in his book *Elements of Judicial Strategy*. One of the most interesting and active leaders of the Court was Chief Justice Taft who, following his presidency, was appointed by President Harding to head a bitterly divided Court. He immediately began "to heal the divisions in the court and to quiet the dissents that were destroying its authority."[32] Sheldon Novick describes Taft's effective leadership style in the following quote:

> The conferences were no longer acrimonious. Taft presided as if over a seminar, carefully eliciting everyone's views of every case and Van Devanter, who rarely wrote opinions but whose views were respected by his colleagues, served as Taft's deputy, mediating among the justices and negotiating changes in opinions to secure agreement. McReynolds occasionally flew off on his own, and Brandeis occasionally wrote a dissent, but these were not important defections, and even Brandeis was struggling to find a middle ground upon which to join his colleagues.[33]

At the trial court level one does not find the presiding judge exerting significant influence over the day-to-day operations of colleagues. It is true that in those courthouses using central calendars the presiding judge can use his or her assignment powers to affect the workload of fellow judges. However, beyond annoyances over assignment problems, most judges interviewed by me were rarely affected by their presiding judge. Although the position and title would appear to infer added prestige, nearly all the judges were relatively disinterested in being elevated to the position. It was viewed by many as an escape from the real job of judging—handling the complexities of litigation—and moving into a bureaucratic position dominated by administrative tedium. The following comment by District Court Judge Jack Weinstein indicates that this problem is present in the federal as well as the state court system: "If the Chief Judge is to devote a substantial amount of his time to administrative duties, how can he continue to properly attend to his case-deciding and opinion-writing functions? . . . The answer, it seems to me is that we must recognize that the duties of the Chief Judge in other areas must be reduced so that he can properly perform his administrative functions."[34]

A secondary problem, also of grave significance, is how a presiding judge may most effectively deal with colleagues. There has frequently been severe tension growing between a chief judge and his or her associates whenever the chief attempts to exercise some of the prerogatives of the position. Most lawyers who become judges are attracted by the independence and autonomy offered by a judicial post. It is, therefore, not surprising that many judges would chafe at even the mildest intrusion into their professional life from a presiding judge who they view as basically their equal. Forrest Hanna studied this problem in the Missouri judicial system as it evolved from a traditional system of judicial autonomy to a multijudge court acting under the administrative direction of a chief judge. Hanna's case study concluded that the presiding judges had two methods of pressuring their colleagues: (1) the use of a contempt of court action that was not well received and (2) the more favored approach of persuasion and reason in convincing a resistant judge to alter his or her position.[35]

Despite the intrinsic difficulties facing a presiding judge, he or she can play a critical role in ensuring that the court system is performing at a maximum level of proficiency. Federal Judge Jack Weinstein concludes this section with the following remarks concerning the important role played by the chief judge in assisting the courts toward this end: "Substantive issues and substantive difficulties can often be solved by the legislature. Only the courts can insure that they themselves operate effectively. . . . we need a head of the system dispensing justice—someone to call to account the administrative judges, and, in fact, any and all State court judges; to help initiate and implement administrative and procedural reforms; to communicate to the public, the legislature, and the executive the detailed needs of the courts; and to insure that the resources supplied by the taxpayers are put to proper use. And that person, I believe, can only be the Chief Judge of the State's highest court."[36]

VARIETY OF COURT ENVIRONMENTS

The final section of this chapter examines the variety of court environments and their possible impact on the professional life of judges. Although the layperson commonly lumps all judges together, there are major differences between the professional behavior of judges depending on the type or level of court to which they are assigned. Thus, Supreme Court justices and appellate court judges have professional responsibilities significantly different from their counterparts at the trial court level. This section will, therefore, briefly describe these various court environments with special concern over those characteristics that can create unique working conditions within each level of court. There will be a conscious effort to avoid describing the jurisdictional requirements and complex procedural rules governing the operation of these varying legal systems; these topics extend beyond the narrow scope of this volume and are worthy of entire treatises in their own right. There is likewise no attempt to describe the work of judges on these numerous courts since this topic will be more broadly discussed in a subsequent chapter of this book. This chapter will discuss the following types of judicial environments: state courts handling the lowest level of criminal and civil proceedings, i.e., misdemeanor and small claims; state trial courts; state appellate courts; federal district trial courts; federal courts of appeal; and the U.S. Supreme Court. Again, it must be remembered that the cursory discussion of each type of court environment is structured so as to allow the reader to better appreciate the wide variety of judicial working environments and the possible influence of these diverse settings upon the judge's professional behavior.

Lowest Level of State Courts

> The judge looks troubled and impatient. The lawyers look weary of their smugness. The audience looks taut and grieved. The defendants are a flow rather than individually accused personalities. They look like the collapse of Western civilization, manifest in an unending variety of forms. . . . One after another, the cases are called for arraignment. They are judged in 5 minutes or more often 30 seconds. They are heard from early in the morning until the middle of the night, every single day. And still there is always a crowd of restless cases that have been waiting for too long.[37]

This description of New York City's Municipal Court, which handles the city's thousands of misdemeanor cases, succinctly captures the "feel" of these lower courts. Their most noteworthy characteristic is the overwhelming volume of cases facing the beleaguered judge. The cases are handled quickly, with little attention to the individual defendant. This frequently results in a general disregard or at best, lack of concern, for due process guarantees. The presence of competent counsel is unusual, as many defendants waive their Sixth Amendment right to counsel with the understanding that the judge will therefore treat their case more leniently (a valid assumption in most instances). In those rare instances where a defendant wishes to exercise his or her full constitutional rights and stand trial with the required legal assistance, the judge's disapproval becomes obvious. A trial date will be set and since this may not be for another three to four weeks, the defendant will have to post bond in order to be granted pretrial freedom. Thus, for many defendants who are indigent, they face the choice of speedy justice where they waive their right to counsel or request an opportunity to have legal representation but be forced to spend the three to four weeks in jail because of an inability to raise the necessary bail.

Most defendants will make a single appearance before the judge and plead guilty at the first opportunity in order to both escape the wrath of the judge as well as to vacate the depressing surroundings. The decrepit physical appearance of the lower courts exemplify their low status within the legal system. Howard Senzel, a former employee of New York City's Municipal Court, uses his skill as a professional writer to provide the following visual description of this depressing courtroom setting: "From the ceiling, just shy of cathedral height, little clumps of plaster fall occasionally into the lights and the proceedings. . . . The velvet rope guarding access to the court leaks crumbling sponge rubber where it has split from being overhandled. Thick ridges of greasy dirt balance on the folds of the limp flag hanging behind the judge. Above the flag there is a bullet hole in the wall, right under the 'r' of 'In God We Trust'."[38]

Beyond the unpleasant working conditions and physical deterioration of the courtroom, the judges and most of the courtroom work group suffer from a feeling of inferiority, relative to the other levels of the legal system. Karen Knob and Brent Lindberg, who examined misdemeanor justice a decade ago, concluded that lower court judges suffered from "severe attitudinal deficiencies" as a result of their perceived low priority in the state's justice system.[39] As a result of these feelings and the resulting frustration, judges appeared unwilling to adhere to due process standards and were inattentive toward individual defendants appearing before them. In some lower courts judges even have gone so far as to handle several cases at one time in order to accelerate the wheels of justice and relieve their overloaded calendars. The repetitive nature of the offenses, compounded by the frequent reappearance of certain defendants (i.e., prostitutes, junkies, petty thieves) further contributed to the impetus for this turnstile system of justice.

The findings from Maureen Mileski's study of the interaction between judges and defendants in these lower courts provides further evidence of the significant impact that this environment has on judicial behavior:

1. Lower courts process defendants with striking rapidity.
2. The judge typically, but not always, apprises defendants of their legal rights. However, most apprisings are to groups rather than individual defendants.
3. The judge is less likely to apprise accused persons individually or at all in legally nonserious cases, cases where the defendants are less likely to protest their dispositions.
4. Courts sometimes sanction uncooperative attorneys by sanctioning their clients.
5. The judge rarely moralizes to or lectures defendants in the courtroom.
6. The control of crime is as much a bureaucratic enterprise as it is a moral enterprise.
7. The court is legally lenient in its dispositions.[40]

The problems of massive caseloads and inadequate resources have been facing the municipal courts for many years. In 1967, the President's Commission on Law Enforcement and the Administration of Justice documented the problem in a Task Force Report on the Courts that found one municipal court judge in Detroit handling 20,000 misdemeanors and nontraffic petty offense cases a year, while in Atlanta three judges disposed of more than 70,000 minor criminal cases in 1966.[41] The commission's major recommendation for reforming these lower courts was to unify them with the rest of the state's trial court system. Unfortunately, even in those few jurisdictions where the unification concept was implemented, the never-ending flow of cases has negated the effectiveness of the renovated court structure.

The rural counterpart to the municipal court judge is the justice of the peace. These judges, who are often without formal legal education, are primarily responsible for traffic offenses, although they may also deal with less serious criminal matters. Due to their autonomy and resulting discretionary powers, they operate in sparsely settled locales widely scattered across the countryside with little supervision. Similar to their urban colleagues, when a defendant wishes to challenge the court's ruling, an appeal can be made up to the county trial level. Because nearly all of the lower courts fail to provide a stenographic transcription or record of the proceedings, appeals are typically treated as a de novo, or new, proceedings originating at the county trial level.

Because of the suffocating volume of cases at the lowest level and its serious consequences for the quality of justice afforded individual litigants, many states have attempted to divert as many cases as possible out of the traditional courthouse and into "alternative forms of dispute resolution." Thus, disputes between neighbors, uncontested divorce proceedings, and small claims cases are being tried before either small groups of laypersons serving as volunteer judges or trained mediators who are frequently attorneys with experience in the relevant fields of law. If both parties consent to removing the dispute from the conventional judicial forum, it is then disposed of by one of these alternative procedures. Thus far these new quasi-judicial institutions have achieved only modest success in lessening the lower court's stifling caseload, but it is a new concept that may still prove effective in the future if it continues to receive the support of the bench and bar.

In concluding this brief portrait of the lower courts, we see an overwhelmed individual judge attempting to keep up with a staggering caseload, realizing that his or her efforts go largely unappreciated by both the defendants and fellow members of the bench. Given these working conditions and negative attitudes, it is not so unexpected that the defendant receives the unpleasant fallout from the judge's professional frustration.

County Trial Courts

The state trial court handles all of the criminal and civil matters not disposed of at the lowest level of courts just discussed. It is, therefore, the judicial environment most commonly used by the public, especially the nation's large middle class. These trial courts, which are organized at the county or city level, are responsible for determining initial findings of fact in all local litigation that requires their being divided into criminal, civil, family, and probate divisions. The criminal court has jurisdiction over all felony or serious cases violating state law and may also handle de novo appeals from the lower courts. The civil courts hear a broad range of legal matters ranging from business disputes through negligence, libel, and slander (basically all noncriminal matters). The family court will usually combine juvenile court with its jurisdiction over matrimonial and custody disputes, while the probate division specializes in problems associated with wills, trusts, and estates.

An individual judge sits in each of these trial courts and is responsible, with the occasional assistance of a jury, for deciding the disposition of legal disputes arising within his or her jurisdiction. Although these courts are very busy, their caseloads rarely reach the staggering proportions of the lower courts. The trial courts are also distinguished from the lower courts because they maintain a complete written record of all proceedings, which will be of critical importance if an appeal is made. Additionally, the trial courts hold a series of pretrial proceedings that cannot only drag a case out for several months, and even years, but will require the litigants to make several court appearances before a series of judges. A final point of distinction is that nearly every litigant, both plaintiff and defendant, will have the assistance of counsel, whereas many defendants in the lower courts waive their right to counsel and choose to be their own attorney. Generally speaking, the cases heard at the county trial courts involve more serious matters than are confronted by the lower courts.

The judges in the trial courts generally specialize in one of the four divisions and rarely shift areas. Even within a division, some judges prefer to conduct trials while others tend to spend the majority of their time managing large caseloads and overseeing the pretrial proceedings and conferences. In both civil and criminal cases, the judges attempt to settle as many cases as possible without a trial. The time and expense of a trial pressures judges to dispose of nearly 90 percent of their caseload through negotiated settlements. Although most judges soon tire of the bureaucratic and administrative tedium inherent in the pretrial processing of cases, they realize it is a necessary alternative to the costly trial. It also became apparent that certain judges do not have either the patience or managerial skill necessary to effectively move large numbers of cases through the pretrial labyrinth and are, therefore, by process of elimination relegated to only conducting trials.

Although the trial courts are obviously important public institutions for many Americans, they are often overshadowed by the more publicized appellate courts at both the state and federal levels. It is this lack of public appreciation, despite their obvious salience, that many students of the legal system believe should be redressed. As political scientist Kenneth Dolbeare points out: "The local trial court is one of several institutions affecting the who gets what, when, and how of local politics."[42]

State Appellate Courts

With the exception of the prosecution in a criminal case, when the losing side wishes to challenge the court's decision following a trial, the case may be appealed to a higher court that has the power to reverse the trial court's decision. On the average, between 10 and 20 percent of the trial court decisions are appealed. This makes the case-processing funnel resemble an inverted pyramid. The following statistics from the Illinois courts illustrate a typical breakdown between the trial court, intermediate appellate court, and state supreme court.

Circuit court (trial)	2,912,958 cases filed
Appellate court (intermediate)	3,020 cases filed
Supreme court	447 cases filed[43]

Illinois, like approximately half of the other states in the nation, employs a two-tier appellate process. Initially, appeals from the trial court will go to an intermediate appellate court. These were usually created in order to relieve the pressure on the higher or supreme court. In states utilizing this two-tier approach, the higher court, which is frequently, although not always, termed the "supreme court" (for purposes of consistency and simplicity the terms shall be used interchangeably within this chapter), may be given more discretionary power over its caseload. Smaller states with lighter caseloads allow direct appeal from the trial court to the state supreme court. The decision of a state supreme court is binding throughout the state and may next be appealed into the federal appellate system.

Rubin points out in his excellent volume, *The Courts: Fulcrum of the Justice System,* that the two major purposes of appellate review are to first do justice to the litigants and secondly provide for the development and growth of the law. Rubin also notes that the appellate courts may have important rule-making functions governing the operating procedures of the entire state court system, as well as assuming administrative responsibility for its overall operation. The chief justice of the state supreme court often works closely with the state court administrator to manage the entire system. This includes making critical budgetary and personnel decisions and occupies approximately a third of the chief's time.[44] There may also be several additional functions performed by the supreme court, including the operation of a statewide disciplinary board ruling on grievances against members of the state bar, membership on judicial nominating commissions, and responsibility for conducting workshops and conferences for the continuing education of the state's judiciary.[45]

Beyond the structural and procedural features of a state appellate court, it contains several features that sharply distinguish it from the trial courts and that create a unique working environment for its members. Its most significant difference from the trial court is its responsibility to rule on issues of law, not fact. The factual issues have technically already been resolved at the trial stage where a judge and jury decided which version of the facts was more convincing. At the appellate level the court is restricted to evaluating the conduct of the trial, including critical pre-trial motions, to see if the judge acted properly and ensured a fair trial in accord with constitutional and statutory requirements.

A second unique feature is that appellate court judges work in groups rather than individually. The typical intermediate appeals court utilizes a three-judge panel while supreme courts vary from five to nine members. Collegial decision making is obviously very different from the dynamics of a solitary trial judge wrestling privately with a difficult issue. In order to successfully win fellow members of the court over to their point of view, collegial appellate judges must be adroit at convincing a recalcitrant dissenter to modify his or her position and switch sides. A recent (1987) study by John Cooley on the process of appellate decision making found these judges continually striving for unanimity. They used face-to-face contacts, telephone conversations, and even carefully written letters to convince their brethren. Among the common techniques used to convince a judge to change his or her mind or remain with the majority were the following: "being courteous, arguing like hell, being stubborn, listening with respect, use peer pressure to let the dissenter know of general dissatisfaction, always provide a graceful exit, change the basis for the decision but not the decision itself, and make the first concession but don't verbalize it as such."[46]

The appellate proceeding is quite different from the trial process. The oral argument is limited to a very brief period of time, and the entire formal presentation is tightly controlled by a group of highly prescribed rules. The judges, in fact, have already reviewed the trial transcript as well as the written briefs from both adversaries, so the oral argument offers more of an opportunity for the judges to ask questions of the attorneys rather than be persuaded by their eloquence. Once the oral argument is completed, the judges move into secret session where the case is discussed and voted upon, and then the laborious task of writing the court's opinion commences. This final job of transforming the court's decision into a permanent written opinion designed to stand the test of time is clearly the appellate judge's most challenging, and often most time-consuming, responsibility.

As a final point of contrast with the trial courts, it should be noted that the cases reaching the appellate level, especially at the supreme court, are usually more complex and have broader policy implications. This is not to denigrate the importance of cases decided at the trial courts, but there is usually a self-selection process at work in which cases carried to the state supreme court are more likely to involve more significant social and political questions that require resolution by the state's highest judicial tribunal.

Federal District Courts

There are presently 94 federal district courts in the United States with approximately 600 judges and are located in every state of the union (the only exception is the district of Wyoming which includes Idaho and part of Montana). Depending on caseload, some states may have more than one district court such as New York, California, and Texas, which each have four. Again, relative to the size of the docket each district may have from 1 to 27 (Southern District of New York) judges assigned. The federal district courts are analogous to the state trial courts. They are the lowest rung of the federal judicial hierarchy. Because of their position as the originating forum for federal legal disputes, they have been termed "the shock troops of the judiciary."[47] Despite their position at the bottom of the federal system, they are a prestigious and important institution described by Joseph Goulden as conducting "damnably important business in our country. Their decisions affect how we make and spend money, where our children attend school, our neighborhood living patterns and the quality of the environment around us."[48]

As discussed in Chapter 6, the federal district judges (just as are the entire federal judiciary) are appointed by the president with the consent of the Senate for life. Although several scholars have criticized the length of such appointments, leading to arrogant behavior by senile and infirm judges, it has always been defended by its capacity to provide judicial independence from the political pressures generated by either the general public or the other two branches of government. Although appointments to the federal bench are viewed as political patronage shared between the president and senators from the party representing the state where a vacancy has occurred, they have generally produced high-quality judges. It is interesting to note that such a high percentage of federal judges (approximately 85 percent) actually come from the same state where they have been appointed. Thus, despite being members of a federal judiciary, they are also products of the "local legal culture" and may have to make a conscious, and sometimes a courageous, decision to enforce national laws in a local setting. This problem was described by Jack Peltason in his study of the 58 federal district judges who were called upon to enforce the unpopular school desegregation cases in their Southern jurisdictions immediately after the *Brown* vs. *the Board of Education of Topeka, Kansas*, decision in 1954. Peltason's book on this issue was appropriately entitled *Fifty-Eight Lonely Men*.[49]

The federal district court judge, assisted by a U.S. magistrate who performs a wide variety of pretrial tasks, must manage the steadily increasing number of cases entering the federal system. Complicating this job even more is the requirement that these judges handle *both* criminal and civil cases, thereby being forced to become knowledgeable in an extraordinarily wide range of legal fields. This contrasts sharply with the state trial courts where the judges are allowed to specialize in either criminal, civil, family, or probate matters. The federal judge's problems are exacerbated further by the fact that most of their cases are more complex than the average case appearing before a state trial court.

Like any public official charged with making difficult policy decisions, the federal district judges are not without their critics. One of the most respected, himself a member of the federal judiciary, is Richard

Posner, who offers the following list of areas of recurrent deficiency that he believes to be major flaws in the performance of federal district courts that require immediate improvement:

1. Some district judges are careless about verifying the existence of federal subject matter jurisdiction when neither party challenges the court's jurisdiction.
2. District judges sometimes are (understandably) rather insensitive to the limitations of appellate jurisdiction and to the caseload pressures in the courts of appeals.
3. Some district judges delegate too much of their authority not just to their law clerks (a problem at all levels of the federal judiciary) but to magistrates and externs.[50]

In especially complex cases or under unusual circumstances, the federal district court will form a special three-judge panel consisting of two district court judges and one court of appeals judge. These special tribunals have been limited by Congress and primarily involve either legislative reapportionment cases or litigation emanating from the Voting Rights Act of 1965 and the Civil Rights Act of 1964. Appeals from these special three-judge courts go directly to the U.S. Supreme Court.

Federal Courts of Appeal

Similar to the intermediate appellate courts at the state level, which were created to help relieve the caseload pressures on their respective supreme courts, Congress in 1891 created the federal courts of appeals to accomplish the same goal. There are presently 12 circuits in the federal system: 11 numbered circuits each containing at least 3 states and a twelfth one for the District of Columbia, an extremely busy jurisdiction due to its location at the seat of the national government. Each of the circuit courts has between 6 and 28 judges, depending on size of caseload. The entire system presently contains slightly more than 200 appellate judges.

Most of the business of the courts of appeals is generated from direct appeals from the federal district courts, although they also receive a growing number of appeals from the various federal regulatory agencies (i.e., Security and Exchange Commission, Food and Drug Administration, Federal Communications Commission, and Federal Trade Commission) as well as specialized federal courts such as the U.S. Court of Claims, U.S. Tax Court, and the U.S. Court of Military Appeals. As with most appellate courts, they resolve issues of law not fact, conduct their proceedings with highly prescribed rules limiting argumentation to brief periods of time, and issue signed opinions as to the reasons for their decision. The most unusual feature of the federal courts of appeal is that they hear cases in three-judge panels that are randomly constituted on a rotating basis. This means a constantly shifting group of coalitions forming for each case. The dynamics of working with these continually changing panels of judges can complicate the decision-making process, for it becomes extremely difficult to anticipate the court's behavior in such an oscillating environment. Appellate Court Judge Patricia Wald describes the typical workload of her fellow appeals court judges as "130–150 cases each term and as many motions; participation in 6–10 en banc cases (involving the entire circuit), author up to 40 opinions and another 20–30 memorandum opinions, consider 100 petitions for rehearing; serve on several judicial council committees and all the while strive to keep abreast of the world at large."[51]

It was initially hoped that the courts of appeals would assist the Supreme Court in overseeing the management of the lower federal courts, but this task has been steadily delegated to an allied bureaucracy of recent creation: the Administrative Office of the U.S. Courts. Somewhat analogous to the administrative office of state courts, this federal counterpart was described by Woodford Howard as maintaining "tight reins on fiscal management, housekeeping, and data collections" for the entire federal judiciary.[52]

U.S. Supreme Court

The rather cursory discussion of the U.S. Supreme Court within this concluding section of the chapter is no reflection upon the important role that it plays as the pinnacle of our nation's judicial system. The reader is reminded, however, that the limited purpose of this section is to gain an appreciation for the influence of a judicial system's unique working environment on the behavior of its judges and justices. Although the earlier discussion of state supreme courts may to some degree have covered several of the U.S. Supreme Court's most prominent features, nevertheless, because of its elevated place at the apex of our nation's judicial branch, it bears closer scrutiny. Paul Freund, long-time student of the Supreme Court, begins our discussion of this revered institution by presenting a list of its most fundamental responsibilities: (1) It resolves disputes between states. (2) It provides for the uniformity of federal law. (3) It maintains the constitutional order by determining if executive or legislative actions conform to the Constitution.[53]

Possibly the most unusual aspect of the U.S. Supreme Court's operations is its discretionary power to select which cases it wishes to hear. It is true that under its original jurisdiction as mandated in Article III of the federal Constitution, it is required to hear cases involving ambassadors and other public ministers as well as cases "in which a State is a party," but in reality there are very few cases that reach the Court falling into either of these jurisdictional requirements. For the overwhelming majority of cases, the justices have the discretionary power to select which cases they wish to hear and simply turn away the others for either lack of a substantial question or want of jurisdiction. At least four justices must desire to hear a case before it will be added to the docket for oral argument. Given the Court's time limitations, it is possible for the members to only hear between 150–200 cases a year. This means that in the past few years as the petitions to the Court have continued to grow to nearly 5000 cases, it will actually only hear 4–5 percent of them. These figures also indicate that the Court spends as much time deciding which cases it will eventually hear as deciding those cases which are granted certiorari, heard in oral argument, and finally voted upon with a written opinion usually offered.

In addition to the time-consuming task of deciding which cases it wishes to hear, the Court will devote time to the hearing of oral arguments (which typically last much more than an hour), postargument conferences where the justices discuss and vote on those cases heard during the preceding week, and finally writing the opinions for each case. It is in this final, lengthy task of opinion writing that the justices are likely to engage in the most prolonged and emotional interaction with one another. This fascinating process, which has been so effectively shielded from public view for so much of the Court's history, was recently exposed by investigative journalists Bob Woodward and Scott Armstrong in their best selling book, *The Brethren.* The book describes efforts by Chief Justice Warren Burger to lead a badly divided Court, as well as portraying the subtle coalition building of Justice William Brennan as he attempted to maximize the efficacy of the shrinking liberal wing of the Court. The volume offers a detailed examination of the Supreme Court during five of its terms from 1971 through 1975. What results is a fascinating and previously unknown glimpse into the private machinations and complex interactions among the Court's nine justices.[54]

Despite the extraordinary portrait of the U.S. Supreme Court presented by Woodward and Armstrong, the public continues to hold on to previous myths and misconceptions. Several of the present group of justices have responded to this need for improved public education by writing articles and appearing on television hoping to explain the Court's operation and behavior in more realistic terms, candidly discussing its institutional problems. Three issues that have troubled several of the justices are the public's mistaken belief that the law clerks exercise undue influence over the respective justices who employ them; second, the perception that judges do not work very hard, taking four-month vacations from June to October when the court is in recess; and finally the belief that individual justices tend to vote reflexively and cluster to tightly held voting blocks. Recent cases involving the constitutional protection afforded to those burning the flag as symbolic speech, followed by the court's at least partial dismantling of the *Roe* v. *Wade* abortion decision clearly indicates that at least on the present court, no such consistent voting block exists. Justice Powell in a recent article attempted to correct the second myth of a leisurely paced summer vacation by writing that "to be sure we do not have the burden of arguments and opinion writing [during the summer]. But major responsibilities continue throughout every week of the year. Petitions and appeals are filed at the same rate in the summer as during the rest of the year—some 70/80 a week; applications for stays and other relief continue to come in from the circuits and there is the advance study of cases already set for argument during the next term. Wherever a justice may be, petitions, memoranda from his clerks and briefs are regularly sent to him for study or action. Moreover, we remain constantly on call for emergency matters."[55] Turning to the question of the influence of law clerks, Justice Powell explains that in general they "perform essentially the same functions for justices that the ablest young associate lawyers perform for partners in a large law firm."[56]

It seems apparent that the U.S. Supreme Court is the most unique judicial environment in the nation. It brings together nine strong-willed, highly intelligent individuals to rule on the major controversies plaguing our society. They must act as a body to hear, decide, and explain how these complex social and political issues are to be resolved. This is often done after other courts and even other branches of government have failed.

It has been the purpose of this chapter to illustrate how important the judge's working environment is upon his or her professional responsibilities regardless of whether the judge is sitting in the elevated status of a Supreme Court justice or the unpleasant ambience of our nation's municipal courts. Let us now move from the working environment to the actual job performance by our nation's judiciary and attempt to understand more clearly the "art of judging."

NOTES

1. Paul B. Wice, *Chaos in the Courthouse* (New York: Praeger Publishing, 1985), 46.
2. Paul Hoffman, *Courthouse* (New York: Hawthorn Books, 1979), 8.
3. Frank Coffin, *The Ways of a Judge: Reflections from the Federal Appellate Bench* (Boston: Houghton Mifflin, 1980), 67.
4. James Eisenstein and Herbert Jacob, *Felony Justice* (Boston: Little, Brown, 1977), 42.
5. Bob Woodward and Scott Armstrong, *The Brethren* (New York: Simon and Schuster, 1979), 197.
6. David T. Ozar, Cynthia Kelly, and Yvette Begue, "Ethical Conduct of State Court Employees and Administrators," *Judicature* 71/5 (February/March, 1988): 163.
7. John Paul Ryan, Alan Ashman, Bruce D. Sales, and Sandra Shane-DuBow, *American Trial Judges* (New York: Free Press, 1980), 101.
8. Ibid. p. 115.
9. Herbert Jacob, "Criminal Courts as Organizational Phenomena," quoted in *The American System of Criminal Justice*, ed. George Cole (N. Scituate: Duxbury Press, 1975), 328.

10. Eisenstein and Jacob, *Felony Justice*, 37, 38.
11. Ozar et al., "Ethical Conduct," 165.
12. Richard Williams, "Supreme Court of the United States: The Staff That Keeps it Operating," *Smithsonian Magazine* (January, 1977): 38.
13. Coffin, *The Ways of a Judge*, 74.
14. Marc Gertz, "Influence in Court Systems: The Clerk as Interface," *Justice System Journal* 3/3 (Fall, 1977): 30.
15. Wice, *Chaos in the Courthouse*, 51.
16. Ryan et al., *American Trial Judges*, 165.
17. Ibid. p. 115.
18. Coffin, *The Ways of a Judge*, 69.
19. David Crump, "Law Clerks: Their Roles and Relationships With Their Judges," *Judicature* 69/4 (December/January, 1986): 236.
20. M. E. Noble, "The Law Clerk," *Trial Judges Journal* 7 (October, 1968): 4.
21. Patricia Wald, "The Problem with the Courts, *Trial* (June, 1984): 31.
22. Coffin, *The Ways of a Judge*, 70.
23. David O'Brien, *Storm Center: The Supreme Court in American Politics* (New York: Norton, 1986), 129.
24. Crump, "Law Clerks," 70.
25. Coffin, *The Ways of a Judge*, 73.
26. Harvey Solomon, "The Rise of the Court Executive," *Judicature* 60/3 (October, 1976): 114.
27. Burton Butler, "Presiding Judges' Role Perceptions of Trial Court Administrators," *Justice System Journal* (Winter, 1977): 181.
28. Steven Flanders, "Court Executives and Decentralization of the Federal Judiciary," *Judicature* 70/5 (February/March, 1987): 174.
29. James A. Gazell, *State Trial Courts as Bureaucracies* (Port Washington: Dunellen Publishing, 1975), 25.
30. Ibid. p. 26.
31. Ted Rubin, *Courts* (Pacific Palisades: Goodyear Publishing, 1976), 187.
32. Sheldon Novick, *Honorable Justice* (Boston: Little, Brown, 1989), 344.
33. Ibid. p. 346.
34. Jack B. Weinstein, "The Role of the Chief Justice in the Modern System of Justice," in *Judicial Administration: Text and Readings*, ed. Russell Wheeler and Howard Whitcomb (Englewood Cliffs, N.J.: Prentice-Hall, 1977), 144.
35. Forrest Hanna, "Delineating the Role of the Presiding Judge," *State Court Journal* 10/2 (Spring, 1976): 20.
36. Weinstein, "Role of the Chief Justice," 148.
37. Howard T. Senzel, *Cases* (New York: Viking, 1982), 2.
38. Ibid. p. 3.
39. Karen Knob and Brent Lindberg, "Misdemeanor Justice: Is Due Process the Problem," *Judicature* 60 (April, 1977), 423.
40. Maureen Mileski, "Courtroom Encounters: An Observation Study of a Lower Criminal Court," *Law and Society Review* 5/4 (May 1971): 473.
41. The President's Commission on Law Enforcement and Administration of Justice, *Task Force Reports: The Courts* (Washington, D.C.: Government Printing Office, 1967), 31.
42. Gazell, *State Trial Courts as Bureaucracies*, 5.
43. Rubin, *Courts*, 125.

44. Ibid. p. 138.
45. Ibid. p. 139.
46. John Cooley, "How Decisions Are Made in Appellate Courts," *The Judges Journal* (Spring, 1987): 2.
47. Joseph Goulden, *The Benchwarmers* (New York: Weybright and Talley, 1974), 2.
48. Ibid.
49. Jack Peltason, *Fifty-Eight Lonely Men* (New York: Harcourt Brace, 1961).
50. Richard Posner, *The Federal Courts* (Cambridge: Harvard University Press, 1985), 225.
51. Wald, "Problem with the Courts," 31.
52. J. Woodford Howard, *Courts of Appeals in the Federal Judicial System* (Princeton: Princeton University Press, 1981).
53. Paul Freund, "The Supreme Court," in *Talks on American Law*, ed. Harold Berman (New York: Vintage Books, 1961), 71.
54. Woodward and Armstrong, *The Brethren*.
55. Lewis Powell, "Myths and Misconceptions About the Supreme Court," *American Bar Association Journal* 61 (November, 1975): 1344.
56. Ibid.

Chapter
8

The Art of Judging

One of the most commonly held myths about judges is that they spend most of their time trying cases. As shown in Chapter 7, there are many different types of judges who operate in significantly diverse working environments. Not only does each type of court require the judge to perform specific tasks unique to that environment, there are also a number of broader judicial functions that all members of the bench are required to perform. The following is a list of these basic judicial functions suggested by John Paul Ryan and his colleagues at the American Judicature Society included in their comprehensive study of the American judiciary:

1. Adjudication
2. Administrative duties
   a. Internally: running the office and chambers
   b. Externally: managing the caseload
3. Negotiation
4. Research and opinion writing
5. Community relations[1]

It is believed that the mastery of these five judicial tasks may lead a judge to conclude that he or she has achieved some degree of success in the "art of judging," the overall topic for this chapter. Professor Zachariah Chafee attempted to explain this "art" by stating: "While in the art of judging, legal power is much, it is not all, but that the important residuum in the equipment of a judge is the desire to understand human life

Table 8.1   TYPES OF JUDGES AND THEIR VARIED FUNCTIONS

	Lower Court	Trial Court	Appellate Court
Adjudication			
a. Pretrial	20% (a and b)	40% (a and b)	5–10% (c)
b. Trial			
c. Oral argument			
Administrative duties			
a. Internal (office)	5	5	5
b. External (caseload)	65	30	25
Negotiation	5	10	—
Research and writing	—	10	50
Community relations	5	5	10

as well as embalmed legal experience. Judges should keep in continuous fruitful contact with the changing social background out of which controversies arise."[2]

It should be noted that judges working in diverse types of courts, i.e., trial versus appellate, are likely to devote varying amounts of time to the different tasks, thus a municipal court judge may spend most of his or her time managing the caseload while an appellate judge devotes the majority of his or her workday to research and opinion writing. Based on observations and interviews of over 100 judges during the past 20 years, as well as a review of the literature, Table 8.1 offers an estimated percentage breakdown for the three major types of judges in terms of how much time they spend on each of these tasks. These are rather rough approximations whose main purpose is to provide a visual and quantified measure of the relative time spent on these various responsibilities.

NATURE AND VARIETY OF JUDICIAL FUNCTIONS

The opening section of this chapter will examine each of the basic judicial functions suggested by the Ryan research. Subsequent sections will provide a more detailed examination of pretrial, trial, and appellate responsibilities.

Adjudicative

As noted earlier, the general public believes that the adjucative function is the judge's quintessential professional responsibility, and in fact dominates his or her workday. Although laypersons may badly overestimate the amount of time that a judge devotes to the conducting of trials, it is a very important part of the job. Legal scholars frequently describe this task as the "umpireal function" where the judge sits as a neutral arbiter between the contesting adversaries. Judge Marvin Frankel explains the intrinsic difficulty of maintaining a neutral position in an article entitled "The Adversary Judge." Frankel writes that the essence of the judge's adjudicative role is impartiality and detachment. Judge Frankel continues his explanation by writing: "Much of the script, cues and setting of the courtroom drama support the judge in performing his role as impartial arbiter. But there are pressures in different directions—the very nature of our accepted trial procedures generates forces that work against the judge's efforts to be neutral and detached. These conditions have a tendency to embroil the judge in the battle, to enlist him as an ally or to identify him as an enemy."[3]

In order to fully comprehend the judge's adjudicative responsibilities, it is important for them to be viewed in their broadest context: all of the time spent in a courtroom, not only trying the case but also all of a judge's pretrial activities. The adjudicative function should also include appellate courtroom activities such as those associated with oral arguments and even encompassing the private conference room discussion where cases are debated en banc, votes taken, and written opinions assigned.

Although a judge may spend a great deal of time in the courtroom managing the caseload, the adjudicative function has the narrower focus of the judge making decisions concerning the merits of the case. Thus, scheduling responsibilities are managerial or administrative while the deciding of pretrial motions, the conducting of a trial, or the listening to oral arguments are all adjudicative behaviors directly relevant to the ultimate resolution of a legal dispute. (A more detailed examination of the judge's pretrial and trial responsibilities will be offered in the subsequent sections of this chapter.) As Table 8.1 indicated, it is estimated that lower court judges, and to a greater degree trial court judges, spend nearly half of their time on adjudicative tasks while their appellate counterparts rarely devote more than 5–10 percent of their time to adjudicative functions (primarily hearing oral arguments with some time devoted to postargument conferences).

Administrative/Managerial

Trial judges spend nearly as much time on administrative tasks as on their adjudicative responsibilities. Laymen who are unfamiliar with the judicial process are usually surprised by the large amount of time expended by judges on administrative matters. But as Table 8.1 indicates, managerial functions even account for a large portion of the appellate judge's time, especially on a Supreme Court, which has the discretionary power to limit its caseload. Members of the U.S. Supreme Court, for example, use most of their supposed summer vacation from June to October deciding which cases they wish to hear during the next term.

Administrative tasks at the trial level primarily involve the cooperative efforts of both the judge and his or her calendar clerks to schedule and process as many cases as possible, being sure that all necessary parties and documents are present in court at the required time. A secondary managerial responsibility of all judges is supervising the courtroom work group. Each judge must make fiscal and personnel decisions affecting the work group, which includes personal secretaries, calendar clerks, law clerks, interns, bailiffs, stenographers, and court administrators. Functioning almost as the head of a small law firm, the judge must make decisions concerning the promotion, vacations, work schedules, hiring, firing, and disciplining of the courtroom work group. The judge's ability to make these managerial decisions in such a way as to promote office morale can have an immediate impact on how well the group performs its various administrative tasks. Given the rising caseloads and shrinking resources, it is obvious to most judges that it is imperative that they sharpen their managerial and leadership skills in order to achieve maximum results with minimum material.

One of the major difficulties in making our judicial system function more smoothly has been the traditional failure of judges to recognize the importance of their managerial responsibilities. Not only are judges attracted to the bench mainly because of the anticipated enjoyment of conducting trials, but as lawyers, they are not trained in or even required to develop administrative skills. (The office manager or personal secretary is continually relied upon to handle the minutae of law firm administration.) As Judge Hubert Will explains: "Judges are not, as for centuries they were believed to be, primarily referees. . . . Rather they are the superintendents of the production of justice and their responsibilities begin when a case is filed."[4] In his article on the art of judging, Judge Will stresses that if a judge is "to promote justice he/she must assume supervision of a case early. They must carefully oversee their dockets, expedite discovery, and provide impartial third part intervention to settle cases."[5]

The judges have also been among the last professional group to adopt the recent technological advances of the computer age to the problems of courtroom management. Paul Cotter convincingly describes the plight of the contemporary judge facing a complex case without computer assistance: "Pleadings, endlessly filed and endlessly amended make it difficult to track issues. Exhibits by the gross somehow must be organized systematically, marked in an order that doesn't break down over the course of the trial and must be easily found at a moment's notice. At trial, testimony given last month but relevant to today's witness or ruling must be located. The judge required to issue a written decision may have as much as 20 shelf feet of transcripts."[6] When this explosion of information is compounded by a full docket of hundreds of such cases, one begins to sense the awesome administrative task facing contemporary judges at nearly all levels of our legal system.

Negotiation

The third major function performed by judges is negotiation. This task results from the caseload pressure on trial court judges to move cases along. By assisting both adversaries in settling their dispute without going to trial, judges can expedite the processing of the dispute while also saving the system the costly expense of a trial. The judge's role in the negotiation process can take a variety of forms ranging from the informal, subtle suggestion that both sides should discuss the possibility of settling the case to a more formal position in a pretrial conference with the judge actively pressuring the attorneys to reach a negotiated settlement. Negotiations occur primarily at the trial court level and are a critical part of both the civil as well as the criminal processes, although greater publicity is given to plea bargaining between the prosecutor and the defense attorney in the criminal courts. Therefore, Albert Alschuler's typology of negotiating roles for judges is nearly as relevant to civil case negotiation as to criminal case plea bargaining, the actual focus of his research. Alschuler believes that judges may assume one of the four following negotiating styles:

1. The judge does not engage in negotiations, leaving it entirely up to the attorneys (especially the prosecutor).
2. The judge does not explicity play a role in the negotiations, but through a consistent pattern alerts both sides to the advantages of early settlement and the disadvantages to the defense attorney of severe sentences for his or her client following trial conviction.
3. The judge participates actively in pretrial negotiations but does not make specific promises as to what the ultimate sentence or decision will be.
4. The judge actively participates in the negotiating process and is willing to offer specific benefits in exchange for a pretrial settlement.[7]

According to a study by John Paul Ryan and James Alfini of plea bargaining in major American cities, the trial judge generally plays an important role in helping to fashion these negotiated settlements, although they admit that much variation exists that may be caused by either the judge's perception of his or her negotiating skill or whether the jurisdiction has imposed a rule prohibiting or discouraging judicial participation.[8] From my travel across the nation observing judges in 15 urban criminal courts, more than half of the judges opted for Alschuler's third role of informally participating in the negotiation process while the remaining judges were roughly divided between actively participating with specific promises or merely encouraging plea bargaining by consistently offering less severe sentences in cases not going to trial.[9]

How do litigators feel about the judges becoming actively involved in pretrial negotiations? Many judges are hesitant to play an active role because of a belief that the parties involved do not wish to see them participate in the settlement process, but according to research by Charles Craven, most litigators "desire aggressive judicial participation in the settlement process."[10] I believe it is crucial for the judge to assist in developing innovative settlement, especially when the litigants have reached an impasse and appear to be locked into positions that may exclude a reasonable resolution. Craven writes that "judicial conciliators can encourage the exploration of other formulations in a non-threatening manner which does not require either advocate to make any overt concessions."[11] The major problem feared by attorneys occurs when the trial judge also serves as a mediator. Lawyers are apprehensive when a judge's negotiation efforts fail; the judge may harbor some resentment against one or both of the attorneys for obstructing efforts to successfully settle the case. The simple solution recommended by Craven and others is to have the scheduled trial judge select another judge to conduct negotiations with a guarantee that confidential disclosures made during the negotiations will not be divulged to the trial judge.

Despite the heavy publicity given to the judge's role in plea bargaining efforts in the criminal courts, the negotiation function is also a critical part of the judge's job in civil proceedings. Herbert Kritzer believes that the judge's role as a negotiator in civil litigation has expanded dramatically in recent years "reversing a forty year trend toward turning control of the litigation process over to the parties and their representatives."[12]

Research and Opinion Writing

Although Table 8.1 indicates that trial judges may spend a small amount of time on research and opinion writing (estimated at 10 percent), it is at the appellate level where judges devote approximately half of their workday to this task. For trial judges their research and opinion writing responsibilities are related to resolving pretrial motions. In criminal cases this often involves motions to suppress evidence that may have been illegally or unconstitutionally obtained, while civil court judges frequently handle motions seeking to settle discovery problems between the contesting parties. Judges at all levels have law clerks to assist them in the research necessary to respond properly to the issues raised by these motions, but it is generally conceded that judges will write the final draft of any opinion.

Since appellate justices spend so much of their time on opinion writing, they are often assisted by more than one law clerk whose responsibilities may range from the most basic research and citation checking to writing initial drafts of the judge's opinion. The U.S. Supreme Court currently allows each justice to utilize four law clerks (a more complete analysis of the job of law clerks is offered in Chapter 7). Judge Frank

Coffin, a federal appellate court judge, has recently written a thoughtful volume discussing his professional responsibilities and describes his job as following a "cycle of work" that involves the following stages:

> I read (or scan) briefs alone, usually at night.
>
> I talk over each case with my clerks, one of whom has given particular attention to it. I make notes of our colloquy.
>
> I listen to oral argument in court and ask a few questions.
>
> I confer with my fellow judges late in the day after the argument.
>
> I research, discuss, and draft an opinion in chambers or discuss, edit, and redraft the first draft of a clerk.
>
> I circulate my draft to my colleagues and respond to their suggestions; when they circulate their drafts I propose changes to which they respond.[13]

Since most appellate courts operate with a number of judges sitting en banc, the opinion writing process is complicated further (as was pointed out in Judge Coffin's description of his "work cycle") by having to consider the position of other members of the majority coalition, in addition to the judge assigned the task of actually authoring the majority opinion. In order to obtain a consensus among members of the majority, a preliminary draft is circulated. There is pressure to work out any disagreements since it is possible for a recalcitrant judge to change his or her position. In a close decision this shift could transform the majority into a minority. It is more common, however, for a disgruntled judge on the winning majority to simply write a "concurring" opinion that clarifies the specific reason for reaching his or her decision, a reason that may be quite distinct from the arguments offered within the majority opinion. It is also common for members of the losing side to write a "dissenting" opinion arguing why they disagreed with the majority's decision.

Community Relations

All judges appear to reserve a small amount of their time for public relations or as most judges would prefer to call it "public education." Even within the judiciary, at each level, there is significant variation among the judges as to their willingness to engage in any type of extrajudicial activities. Presiding judges, who generally believe it is part of their responsibilities to represent the judiciary before the general public as well as in dealing with other branches of government, are the court officers most likely to devote time to this task. The active role played by Chief Justice Burger as spokesman for the Supreme Court and vocal critic of the nation's legal system serves as an excellent example of a jurist actively playing this role. His critique of the ineffectiveness of the nation's trial attorneys was a crucial factor in bar associations reexamining the training and competence of these legal specialists.

Most judges are reluctant to be as outspoken as Chief Justice Burger. They believe that such public statements may lower the professional dignity of judges and place them too close to the political arena. Close association with either political party or a specific public issue may threaten to undermine the required independence and objectivity expected from the judiciary, especially in those jurisdictions where judges are elected on partisan ballots. Some judges, nevertheless, do believe they should attempt to elevate the status of their profession and educate the public as to the realities of the nation's justice system. One Indiana judge, for example, who believes in the necessity for raising the awareness of the public about the courts, has a radio show every Friday morning where he spends 25 minutes answering questions about the courts and the local legal system.[14] Even judges who are concerned with educating the public are careful never to discuss any aspect of a case presently pending in their courts. They are also reluctant to present their opinions on issues that are likely to arise in future cases. By having one's ideas concerning various issues preserved in speeches and articles, it casts doubt upon the judge's open-mindedness when cases focusing on related problems appear in his or her courtroom. In order to avoid the possibility of appearing less than completely objective, many judges simply prefer to keep their opinions to themselves and remain silent.

This discussion has briefly reviewed the major functions of American judges. It is obvious from this discussion that the judges at different levels of the justice system may emphasize some tasks more than others, and that even within a particular court, the judges may be given different responsibilities that would also necessitate a varied allocation of time among these functions. In the subsequent sections of this chapter, a more detailed examination of the judge's craft will be presented as the pretrial, trial, and appellate responsibilities are analyzed.

PRETRIAL RESPONSIBILITIES

As we have already noted, approximately 90 percent of the cases filed in our civil and criminal courts fail to reach the trial stage and are instead resolved during the pretrial period. Our trial courts recognize this reality and devote a significant amount of personnel as well as space to the processing of cases during the pretrial period. Most litigants will make numerous appearances before a judge during this period in which the court will be making critical decisions affecting the resolution of the overwhelming majority of cases initially filed in their jurisdiction. The three major responsibilities of a judge during the pretrial period are as a case manager, negotiator, and facilitator of discovery.

Managerial Responsibilities

Turning first to the judge's managerial responsibilities, there is a generally accepted belief that there are certain managerial principles that should be followed if a judge is to effectively control his or her calendar.

First, the judge must take early control of a case and maintain close supervision throughout the entire pretrial period. Second, the judge must schedule each court date within the shortest time possible. In order to achieve this a judge may have to adopt a rather inflexible attitude toward attorneys who may be pressuring the bench for repeated postponements. Most attorneys rely upon court delays as a way to balance their overcommitted schedules that may include more cases than they can handle, especially if several have trial dates within close proximity. Many clients, most commonly defendants in both criminal and civil cases, who are in no hurry to go to trial also wish to delay litigation as much as possible. The judge, therefore, needs to take a firm stand on frivolous requests for continuances and excuses for being unprepared. However, in order to be reasonable and fair, the judge must recognize the legitimate problems faced by attorneys and clients and be willing to be accommodating if their requests have merit and do not place either of the litigants at a serious disadvantage. A fourth principle, recommended by Paul Connolly, is that the judge maintain calendar integrity. Connolly explains that "the court is under the same obligation as the attorneys to act diligently and to schedule court events expecting that they will happen on time."[15]

The judges, as we discovered in Chapter 7, are assisted in their case managing responsibilities by several members of the courtroom work group, in particular calendar clerks, law assistants, and secretaries. Despite this assistance, it is obvious to even the casual courtroom observer that some judges are simply more adept at processing a large volume of cases in an efficient manner than are others who may be better suited to the slower, more tedious task of trying cases. Judges with certain managerial skills are usually selected by the chief judge to handle the pretrial proceedings such as arraignments, preliminary hearings, settlement conferences, and motions court. Judges assigned to the trial division would usually be responsible for one or two trials per week depending on the complexity of the case. Judges usually remain assigned to either the pretrial or trial division for most of their tenure on the bench, developing reputations as adroit case managers or as rarely reversed trial judges. Occasionally judges from the overworked pretrial division are given an annual one- or two-month "vacation" to sit in the slow-paced trial division as a break from the chaotic action.

Once a judge is identified as an effective case manager, an accolade earned by only a handful of judges in each jurisdiction, he or she is "rewarded" by having an increasing number of cases diverted into his or her courtroom. This dubious honor results in either the judge burning out prematurely or simply becoming increasingly careless and impersonal in the handling of individual cases. Administrative or presiding judges need to better train *all* the judges as to effective managerial techniques rather than overwork the few who bring well-developed administrative skills directly to the bench.

There is a dark side to speedy case processing that is frequently raised by judges and scholars who believe there has been a panicky, overconcern with the managerial skills of judges. They voice a fear that due process guarantees of a fair trial are lost in the unbridled enthusiasm for reducing court delay through rapid case movement. Judges must be able to strike that difficult balance between being an efficient case manager while still ensuring that individual litigants will always receive a fair and complete legal hearing, regardless of the crushing caseload pressures.[16]

Negotiating Settlements

Whether operating a civil or criminal court, a judge is frequently called upon to negotiate pretrial settlements. Many judges gain reputations for their skillful management of the negotiation process. One judge described the necessity for responsible behavior in negotiating sessions in the following terms: "When a judge participates in plea bargaining . . . he must be particularly careful not to abuse the power of his office. He must not manipulate. He must not cajole. He must not threaten. For if he does any of these things, the judge not only destroys the value of the bargain but also undermines the integrity of the criminal justice system."[17]

Judges maintain a variety of attitudes toward negotiated pretrial settlements, although most acknowledge its necessity in controlling escalating caseloads. Each judge, depending on his or her attitude as well as negotiating skill, develops a special style of conducting settlement discussions, although the local court customs can also modify practices. A former judge herself, Marie Provine, has studied the varied styles of judicial intervention in the settlement process and constructed the following typology:

1. Personal participation (by judges) in conferences or other settlement-oriented procedures.
2. Selective referral (by the judge) to settlement procedures administered by others inside or outside the court structure.
3. Judicial support for across-the-broad referral programs and systemwide rules designed to change the stakes for litigants and thereby encourage settlement.
4. Design and implementation of court-annexed settlement procedures of the types noted here.[18]

In my own observations of judges and their management of pretrial negotiation, I found most judges carefully avoiding pressuring the defendant into a plea agreement. Typically, the judge and both attorneys would conduct a side-bar conference where the various possibilities would be discussed. The client would be left behind at a nearby table, a few yards to the rear. After the discussion was concluded, the attorney would go back and present the various possibilities to the client. This included the prosecutor's position, and the judge's attitude toward what the prosecutor was offering. The defense counsel would soon return with the client's decision. Once the defendant accepted the plea bargain, all of the parties would gather before the bench for the formal arraignment. Most judges disliked this charade where the judge asks the defendant to reassure the court that no promises have been made in exchange for the plea and that he or she was not coerced into this decision by his or her attorney. Despite the objectionable nature of this oft-repeated scenario, judges and attorneys realize it is a necessary procedure in order to avoid future charges by the defendant that he or she was unwittingly duped into waiving the right to a trial by pleading guilty.

Although the working out of a plea bargain as just described is a calm exercise in negotiation, rarely reaching the level of adversarial confrontation envisioned in the idealized criminal court process, only a few cities allow for more lively negotiations. These usually occurred in the judge's chambers and developed into hotly contested arguments. In Chicago, for example, where plea bargaining appeared both forthright and formalized, the judge played an active role in hammering out an agreement. As one of the Windy City's criminal judges said in a recent interview in which he was justifying his plea bargaining practices: "He [the defendant] takes some of my time—I take some of his. That's the way it works."[19]

Although the bulk of discussions and analyses of the negotiation process focus upon plea bargaining in the criminal courts, it must be remembered that pretrial settlements also constitute the norm in civil courts as well. As federal District Court Judge Hubert Will recently instructed a group of new judges: "In my experience, more than 95% of all civil cases are disposed of before trial." He went on to add that he thought this was a highly desirable occurrence since a realistic view of most cases shows there is some merit on both sides. Therefore, a freely negotiated compromise is likely to provide the optimal degree of justice.[20]

Given the omnipresence of negotiated pretrial settlements within our nation's justice system, it is obvious that judges and their staff must develop effective techniques in implementing their negotiating responsibilities. Table 8.2 shows the wide array of techniques recommended by both judges and attorneys for settling cases. It is apparent from the multiplicity of techniques available that judges are able to select a strategy that is most consistent with personal overall style of judicial craftsmanship and the selected form of judicial intervention.

Herbert Kritzer has also studied the issue of the judicial role in pretrial negotiations and, after reviewing national surveys of both state and federal judges, developed a list of ten activities that judges can employ to promote settlement:

- Setting and holding to a firm trial date early in the litigation (obviously this can also simply speed a case to trial).

Table 8.2   TECHNIQUES SELECTED BY JUDGES AND ATTORNEYS

Technique	Percent of Judges Who Would Use Technique	Percent of Attorneys Who Want Technique Used
Pressure the ill-prepared attorney.	15	22
Ask both lawyers to compromise.	56	46
Offer alternative proposal not thought of by lawyers.	53	63
Call a certain figure reasonable.	29	27
Bring the client to the conference.	24	30
Point out, to the client, the strengths and weaknesses of his or her case.	13	24
Require a settlement conference even though one is not mandated by court rules.	62	67
Channel discussion to areas that have the highest probability of settlement.	58	61
Speak personally with the client to persuade him or her to accept.	4	5
Suggest a settlement figure to the client.	5	8
Argue logically for concessions.	47	52
Downgrade the merits of the stronger case and/or the demerits of the weaker.	8	6
Analyze the case for the lawyer.	23	16
Note to the lawyer the high risk of going to trial.	39	18
Note for the client, the rewards of pretrial settlement.	20	27
Offer advice to a lawyer.	7	10
Talk to each lawyer separately about settlement.	26	42
Set an inexorable trial date.	29	24
Inform the attorneys as to how similar cases have been settled.	61	61
Suggest a settlement figure after asking for lawyers' inputs.	42	49

Source: Dale Rude and James Wall, Jr., "Judicial Involvement in Settlement: How Judges and Lawyers View It," *Judicature* 72(3) (October–November, 1988): 177.

- Refusing to grant postponements or recesses—once the day of the trial has been reached—to discuss settlement, unless the case takes an unexpected turn.
- Assessing the costs of empaneling a jury against parties or counsel who unreasonably delay settlement until the day of trial.
- Initiating settlement discussion once the parties have had an opportunity to evaluate the case.
- Discussing previously tried cases during settlement discussions as a device to put the current case in a better perspective.
- Undertaking an insurance-like analysis of liability and damages during the settlement discussions.

- Suggesting a fair settlement figure during settlement discussions.
- Including the actual parties in the settlement discussions (along with the attorneys).
- Meeting separately with each side to explore the possibilities and terms of settlement.

   In addition, the judges alone were asked about their use of four specific techniques for expediting the processing of cases:

- Conducting a preliminary pretrial conference shortly after the case is filed.
- Establishing a time schedule to regulate and expedite the discovery process.
- Placing limits on the scope, duration, and extensiveness of discovery without waiting for requests for such action from the parties.
- Holding regular hearings or conferences to monitor the progress of the case.[21]

Many judges, scholars, and court administrators have studied the settlement process in recent years, and the result has been a plethora of new reforms geared toward ensuring that the litigants receive an equitable treatment while the court is permitted to resolve the dispute in an expeditious manner. Charles Craven of George Washington University Law School has written extensively on the topic and urges that judges should attempt to provide gentle but persistent encouragement during the early stages of litigation when the parties are most open-minded. If there appears to be an initial hostility toward negotiation by one or both of the parties, the judge must endeavor to establish meaningful communication. If this fails, separate sessions could be considered in which the judge must promise to keep the confidences shared by both sides during private conversations. Judge Hubert Will has formulated another interesting innovation described as a type of modified minitrial (He terms this his "Lloyds of London" technique) in which he asks both parties to "analyze their controversy from the perspective of an insurance company representative. Following their narrative presentations, summarizing their respective positions, each side is instructed to objectively assess the likely trial result if the controversy is not amicably resolved. . . . The judge then multiplies each side's projected probability that the plaintiff would prevail by the likely award each has predicted would be obtained if the plaintiff were to win."[22] If the parties continue to remain opposed to judicial settlement, the judge may have to bring in an impartial court-appointed expert. This, of course, can only be done if both parties agree.

   How successful have all of these various reforms and innovations been? William McDonald of Georgetown University's Institute for Criminal Law and Procedure recently completed a national study of pretrial negotiation reforms in the criminal courts and concluded that the last 20 years have "succeeded in making pleas more intelligent and insuring that defendants get the deals they thought they were going to get. . . . In short, the expanded plea-taking procedures have made guilty

pleas far more informed than they once were and minimized the possibility of broken, misleading, or misconstrued promises."[23] McDonald,
however, is not overly sanguine and reminds readers that despite all of
these new techniques and the improved judicial supervision, plea bargains still have an inherent coercive character and have on occasion deprived a defendant of due process guarantees when a trial might have
resulted in an acquittal.[24]

Making Discovery Work

The final pretrial responsibility to be discussed is the judge's control
over the discovery process. Discovery is a process used in both civil and
criminal courts that requires the contesting parties to share certain basic
information with each other. This typically includes the list of witnesses,
critical documents, and the major charges and countercharges to be
raised. Current courtroom procedures do not resemble or even permit
Perry Mason's dramatic ability to bring in last minute witnesses or hidden pieces of evidence that are miraculously uncovered and rushed into
court in the final moments of the trial. Discovery, like pretrial negotiations, is designed to expedite the resolution of disputes by allowing both
parties to view the strength of their adversary's case. Once everyone has
a clearer sense of what type of opposition is to be faced and a more realistic appraisal of the likelihood of victory, the parties can engage in more
meaningful negotiations.

The responsibility of the judge in overseeing the discovery process
is to facilitate the exchange of information. By ensuring that both sides
receive the necessary documents and other critical paperwork, the judge
not only contributes to more expeditious settlement of the dispute but
also assists in leading the case toward a more just and equitable resolution. The task can often be quite challenging when one of the parties
wishes to delay or harass his or her adversary by requesting unnecessary
information that may take lengthy amounts of time and energy to com-
pile. One federal judge urges his colleagues to adopt a 20-question rule,
which limits the number of interrogatories (discovery requests) to 20 before requiring the permission of the court. He feels that because of the
continual abuse by attorneys of the discovery process, judges must carefully control discovery motions unless the parties certify in writing they
have met, have resolved some disagreements, and are at an impasse on
those that are the subject of the motion.[25]

TRIAL RESPONSIBILITIES

Even though a small percentage of civil and criminal cases are ultimately resolved through a trial, these cases are nevertheless the major
focal point of our justice system. Additionally, those disputes reaching

the trial stage are often the most complex and important cases entering the legal arena. These are more likely to involve more serious crimes, more highly publicized contestants, greater amounts of money, and issues of heightened public concern. Thus, it is in those few cases reaching the trial stage that we can best view the judge performing his or her traditional function of sitting as a neutral arbiter between the adversaries, ensuring that the procedures are followed and that justice is done. Let us now examine the major responsibilities of the judge during a trial. (This discussion will emphasize general tasks, purposefully avoiding an overly legalistic examination of the various procedural technicalities.)

Dealing with Attorneys

The most persistent and challenging responsibility of the trial judge is to be able to calmly sit in the center of an adversarial struggle between two aggressive attorneys and maintain an impartial and objective stance. Defense attorney Henry Rothblatt correctly advises the trial judge that he must "not only be totally indifferent as between the parties but he must also give the impression of being so. He must scrupulously avoid any conduct which may give the appearance or impression that he is not totally unbiased."[26] Because American judges reach the bench without any specialized training (see Chapter 6), it is often quite difficult for many judges to unlearn the role of advocate, which has been inculcated into his or her professional behavior since graduation from law school. Judges must quickly be able to repress those adversarial instincts that may have been successful attributes during their earlier courtroom achievements. For several judges interviewed, this transition was a difficult task and involved a persistent and conscious effort. One East Coast judge confessed that the process took several years. During his early years on the bench, he remembered beginning to rise unconsciously from his chair, with the intention of making an objection to one of the attorney's remarks. Fortunately, he always regained his composure before actually embarrassing himself, but his court clerk asked him several times why he stretched and stood up so many times during the course of a trial.[27]

Frustrating the judge's efforts to remain impartial in the treatment of the competing attorneys is the aggressive and often abrasive nature of the trial advocate. It is difficult for a judge not to grow upset with a lawyer whose stalling tactics disrupt his or her ability to control and hopefully unclog the congested calendar. Many judges forget that the attorney's primary responsibility is to the client and not to the promotion of an efficiently run courtroom. Confrontation between judge and attorney is not only to be expected but is often necessary if the lawyer is to satisfy professional obligations to his or her client. (The dimensions of this issue are discussed in Chapter 5.)

A further complication in the judge's efforts to maintain impartiality is when one of the advocates appears to be incompetent, and threatens the client's chances for a possible victory. Is the judge to simply sit back and observe the proceeding without intervention? How badly must an attorney falter before a judge will be compelled to short-circuit the adversarial proceedings and come to the assistance of an inept lawyer? Most judges believe that resolving the perplexing questions associated with incompetent attorneys is among the most difficult facing any trial judge. As the number of lawsuits initiated by disgruntled clients charging their attorneys with incompetent representation or simply malpractice has increased meteorically in recent years, trial judges are becoming more prudent in exercising their supervisory responsibilities.

Judges develop a variety of strategies to aid an inept attorney, short of asking him or her to resign from the case. The most common method is simply for the judge to call the attorney up to the bench for a "side-bar" conference and inform him or her that there is a need to upgrade the performance. These conferences occur in hushed tones along the bench or even behind it. If a jury is in session, they will be ordered to leave the courtroom in order to eliminate the possibility of the judge's comments being overheard. If the judge believes a more protracted discussion is necessary, he or she will declare a brief recess and adjourn with the attorney to chambers.

I found judges to vary significantly as to the quality of help and advice they were willing to offer an erring attorney. Approximately half of the judges observed would merely issue a vague warning to the attorney that he or she was straying off the point, omitting some vital elements, or simply failing to convince the bench (and in all likelihood the jury as well) of whatever point he or she was striving to make. Several judges, however, would be more specific and offer clues as to what must be done in order to get the case back on track and at least preserve a slight chance for victory. A few judges were observed offering concrete suggestions as to avenues to explore and issues to raise, although it was always as a recommendation and never an order. Most typically this assistance was couched in the phrase "I suppose you are going to ask this or that" and expect that even the densest attorney could take the hint. Occasionally a judge who wished to avoid the delay of a side-bar conference and had confidence in his or her ability to control the courtroom would beckon an attorney close to the bench and in hushed tones offer advice directly without a formalized break in the proceedings. A few judges would simply try to ask counsel questions that would help him or her return to the proper direction for subsequent inquiries.

The interaction between judges and attorneys seemed most strained not by their behavior in the courtroom but their inability to appear in court on time and be prepared to go to trial. The attorneys simply tried to keep too many cases active at the same time. The most firmly etched memory from my years of court watching is the frustrated judge, barking at his bailiffs to try and find attorney "X" who was just there a minute ago. This attorney, who had slipped out of court 10 minutes earlier while the judge was trying to locate a missing witness, was quickly scurrying up to another courtroom, three flights up, in order to check on a presentencing hearing already scheduled for the same afternoon. After a half hour the attorney sheepishly wandered back into the courtroom, but somehow the arresting officer, a crucial witness, had now disappeared. With the defense attorney and the police officer out of the courtroom, the prosecutor decided it would be a golden opportunity to get a cup of coffee back in his office and catch up on the morning gossip. Therefore, 15 minutes later when the police officer and the defense attorney reappeared, the prosecutor was chatting with his colleagues several courtrooms away. After an hour, when everyone was assembled before the judge, the court clerk noticed that critical paperwork, such as a prior arrest sheet on the defendant, was missing from the case file and another postponement (delay) would be necessary. Similar scenes, reminiscent of a Marx Brothers comedy routine with disappearing and reappearing actors, were observed repeatedly in every courthouse visited. The inability to gather all the requisite participants in a courtroom at the appointed time and prepared to initiate proceedings was one of the most frustrating events in the judge's nerve-wracking day. Despite the regularity of their occurrence, all judges were visibly upset by these delays whenever they happened in their courtroom.

Despite the judge's frustrations over attorneys' professional imperfections and impatience with substandard performance, the general wisdom is to offer the attorney wide latitude in his or her courtroom behavior before intervening. Henry Lummus offered the following advice to trial judges 50 years ago, and it remains an accepted guideline for judges to follow: "A judge should be patient even with dull arguments. . . . A moderate degree of mental slowness or apparent slowness, gives time for reflection, avoids snap judgments and prevents parties from complaining that they were dismissed unheard. . . . A judge should give counsel reasonable latitude, especially in cross-examination. The bearing of every question cannot be made clear to the judge without making it all too clear to the witness. Opportunity must be given to weave apparently useless strings into a net from which the witness cannot escape."[28]

Dealing with Juries

One of the major responsibilities of the trial judge is to ensure that the jury is given a full and fair presentation of the facts and an understandable and uncomplicated exposition of the law.[29] The complicated interaction between judge, jury, witnesses, and opposing attorneys is best described by experienced trial judge Bernard Botein who characterized the judge's role as a type of traffic cop, giving stop and go signals to all of the parties. Complicating the trial judge's performance is the fine line between the various opportunities where he or she is required to speak to the jury and the unprofessional interference with the jury's efforts to reach an independent decision.[30] The following is a brief list of several instances where the judge is usually obligated to instruct the jury: (1) upon selection to the jury panel for the week, (2) before the voir dire, (3) after the jury is sworn in for a case and is about to hear the opening argument, (4) "charging the jury," that is, offering assistance or instructions to the jury to aid members in their deliberations, and (5) just prior to its discharge. Additionally, there are many more occasions when the judge is permitted to communicate with the jurors. These opportunities are part of the judge's discretionary powers to ensure that the defendant receives a fair trial and often take the form of warnings or cautions to the jurors.

There are also several instances when the judge must issue an admonition to jurors in order to assist them in their struggle to reach an appropriate decision. The most common examples of such judicial warnings are (1) urging objectivity, (2) prohibiting any outside communication, (3) warning against speculation or being in personal knowledge of information not offered in evidence, (4) forbidding the reaching of an early verdict (or by lot or chance), and (5) warning against deciding who you believe *should* win.

Probably the most important jury-related task performed by the trial judge occurs at the conclusion of the trial when the jury is charged, that is, given final instructions by the judge to assist them during their deliberations. Although a few cynical judges believe that the instructions are an exercise in futility since the jurors are likely to go off and decide the case according to their already firmly established convictions, most judges spend a great deal of time and care in fashioning this final set of instructions. Judges and court administrators have continually attempted to improve the quality of these charges, which must deal with such difficult questions as clarifying the burden of proof, weight of evidence, credibility of witnesses, and form of the verdict. Given the length and complexity of most instructions, there has been a recent trend toward having the judge present the charge in writing rather than the traditional manner of simply reading it in open court. Even as the jury is deliberating, the judge must remain in close proximity in order to provide additional instructions or clarify those already offered.

A final problem for the judge is determining how long the jury should be permitted to deliberate before declaring a mistrial. There is no national standard recommending a specific period of time, but given the expense and inconvenience of a retrial, most judges err on the side of caution and offer the jury every chance possible to reach a decision. When a jury does return without a verdict, the judge will carefully question all of its members as to their inability to agree on a verdict.

Thus far the interactions between judge and jury have been either acceptable or obligatory. There are occasions, however, where trial judges exceed these limits and engage in questionable acts of communication with the jury. The judge, through gestures, facial expressions, and other forms of body language can subtly and often unintentionally "speak" to the jury and influence jurors' behavior. Jurors look to the judge as their instructor and guide. Even beyond the formal instructions offered by the judge at certain required stages, the members of the jury can be observed looking toward the judge for clues as to their proper interpretation of events transpiring before them. The most common example of this type of communication occurs when a witness is being examined by one of the attorneys. The jury continually looks to the judge to see how he or she is reacting to the testimony. So slight a movement as the judge allowing his or her eyes to close can convince some jurors that the witness should not be believed. One judge candidly admitted that jurors are "putty in our hands," and he thought he could influence their decision by a wide range of barely detectable behaviors that would never be reflected in the stenographer's official court record and therefore not perceptible to appellate judges. Expressing disbelief at certain testimony or sagely nodding one's head as if in agreement can exert a powerful influence on a jury that is virtually impossible for an opposing attorney to overcome. It is because of this immense power, commented a New York judge, that "we have an especially high burden to preserve the image of impartiality."[31]

Many judges attempt to self-consciously prohibit the jury from gaining insights into their inner feelings. Some described themselves as maintaining a "stony silence" or a listless demeanor. Only one judge I interviewed felt that his capacity for influencing jurors was overrated and modestly stated that "jurors don't seem particularly interested in my reactions and seemed to go their own way regardless of my desires."[32] He added that he was further convinced of his limited efficacy by chatting with jurors after a case had ended to see why they reached a particular decision. Although a firm believer in the ability of juries to reach the proper decision, the judge also felt that the group dynamics occurring within the jury room were much more significant than their perceptions of the judge's desires.

Although most judges generally agree that juries do a good job and are quite conscientious, most members of the courtroom work group, especially the contesting lawyers and their nervous clients, are unable to predict with any degree of certainty what will be the ultimate outcome of their deliberations. There is a general consensus among trial judges that juries often reach the proper conclusion or at least an acceptable one given the facts of the case, but it is often for the wrong reason. As experienced Federal District Court Judge Charles Wyzanski pointed out: "My thirty years of experience lead me to believe that you cannot, no matter what your experience, safely predict the outcome of case in a trial court with a jury."[33]

Anyone visiting a trial is likely to be fascinated with the social-psychological dynamics of jury behavior. Because so much of the trial is slow-moving and repetitive, jurors can be seen daydreaming, dozing, flirting, or a range of other activities diverting their attention away from the testimony. Nevertheless, the judge seems able to muster their energies at the critical points of the trial when they must be attentive. This appears to be one of the critical capabilities that a good judge must possess. He or she can bring jurors back from the far reaches of their daydreams and fantasies without influencing the direction of their decision. A chemistry can be developed in which a jury relies upon the judge to provide subtle, unobtrusive signals alerting it to critical testimony.

Judges frequently view their contact with jurors as an excellent opportunity for educating a small segment of the public on the operation of the courts. Judge Bernard Botein would bring eight to ten jurors into his chambers after a trial and hold an informal conference in order to learn how these laypersons felt about the quality of justice being dispensed by the local courts. Other judges have been observed continually disrupting the trial in order to clarify or emphasize something that was occurring for the benefit of the jury. These judges believe that by serving on a jury, an individual is entitled to become a more enlightened citizen, at least in terms of his or her understanding of how the American legal system operates.

Searching for the Truth

In those trials conducted before a judge without the presence of a jury, the judge is faced with the difficult task of weighing the evidence presented by each of the contesting attorneys and solitarily deciding which version of the truth is most convincing. Such perplexing questions as the credibility of witnesses and the reliability of physical evidence must be resolved by the trial judge sitting in isolation. How is a single individual able to unravel the legal and factual conundrums caused by conflicting precedents, ambiguous statutes, and directly contradictory testimony? Who or what is to be believed?

Why have we given the trial judge such a difficult job? Judge Marvin Frankel believes it is an inherent defect in our adversary system of justice. He explains that the adversary process "often achieves truth only as a convenience, a by-product or an accidental approximation. The business of the advocate, simply put, is to win if possible without violating the law. His is not the search for truth as such . . . the truth and victory are mutually incompatible for some considerable percentage of the attorneys trying cases at any given time."[34] Frankel is rather pessimistic in how to overcome adversary excesses and raise the truth-finding potential of our system, although he does weakly recommend greater intervention by the judge during the trial as well as better training for the attorneys as beginning steps.

Other judges, such as Irving Kaufmann, believe that their colleagues on the bench must recognize the inherent difficulty in their task and realistically adjust to being placed in the center of a "tortuous process of balancing compelling and conflicting inequities."[35] Justice Benjamin

Cardozo, who was also troubled by the omnipresent uncertainty under-mining his professional responsibilities, explains in the following quote how he eventually came to terms with the problem:

> I was much troubled in spirit my first years upon the bench, to find how trackless was the ocean on which I had embarked. I sought for certainty. I was oppressed and disheartened when I found that the quest for it was fu-tile. I was trying to reach land, the solid land of fixed and settled rules. . . . As the years have gone by, and as I have reflected more and more upon the nature of the judicial process, I have become reconciled to the uncertainty because I have grown to see it as inevitable. I have grown to see that the process in its highest reaches is not discovery, but creation.[36]

Kaufmann agrees that such uncertainty is inevitable but goes on to ratio-nalize its positive attributes: "This decisional anguish reflects the dy-namic nature of the judicial process. Certainty is a close affiliate of stag-nation . . . the law serves as a vibrant and capacious vehicle for social advancement, capable of accommodating the variegated demands posed by an ever more sophisticated society."[37]

Judges cannot simply ponder the difficulty of resolving continuous conundrums that arise in their courtrooms in a detached, philosophical posture. They must descend into the reality of the perplexing cases be-ing argued before them, making as much sense as they can from the clash of biased, incomplete, and contradictory evidence being presented. When asked how they finally decide the difficult issues of fact, many judges state they are forced to rely on their intuition and experience. Some judges explain this as their "judicial hunch." Judge Frank Coffin went so far as to describe the judge's ability to actually "smell the truth": "I like to think that one of the things a judge develops over time is a judicial nose. Such an organ is exquisitely sensitive, if not allergic to both strong and faint odors that the briefs exude. The judicial nose, if it is to serve its possessor properly, must distinguish between the scents that are merely unpleasant and those that signify the presence of some endemic disease or weakness."[38]

The judicial hunch is developed after many years on the bench and is a combination of cautious cynicism, past experience, and clear com-prehension of legal standards. How many judges possess such a keenly developed sense of the truth? It was interesting to find that in my inter-views with trial judges across the country, nearly all were confident of their own ability to intuitively sense the truth, but were extremely skep-tical that the majority of their colleagues possessed a similar capability.[39]

Keeping Track of the Proceedings

Since trials may extend into several weeks duration, judges are often faced with the difficult task of keeping track of these protracted proceed-ings. The judge must be able to not only effectively monitor current proceedings but also be able to remember what transpired previously in an ongoing case. This can be of critical importance in charging the jury or in his or her own search for the truth. Nearly every judge devises some type of system of note taking, in addition to the official record kept by the court stenographer. I observed several judges who were compulsive note takers and would accumulate a copious personal record of the trial. One judge found that it was an excellent ploy for keeping sufficiently busy so as to not unintentionally distract the jurors. Another judge used his extensive note taking as a guise to sustain his interest in the trial, which can become extremely boring and repetitious. He remembered from law school that he could stay awake and pay closer attention in class by trying to take down as much as possible, and he easily transferred such a pattern of behavior to the courtroom as an antidote for judicial fatigue.

A current topic of interest to judges concerned with keeping an accurate record of the trial is the use of videotapes to replace or complement the court stenographer's notes. Most judges favored the present stenographic system, fearing that videotaping would inhibit the jurors and interfere in some way with the sanctity of the courtroom and the fair administration of justice. A vocal minority of judges interviewed were in favor of videotaping and pointed to its successful adoption in several jurisdictions (Florida and Alaska were the most commonly noted for operating successful videotaping programs). These judges thought that too many significant features of the trial were not being captured within the stenographic transcript. Inflections of voice, body language, and other physical gestures could only be preserved on videotape.

Despite its seeming importance, few legal commentators have addressed the topic of judicial note taking. Bernard Botein in his important work, *Trial Judge,* briefly describes the variety of note-taking techniques: "Some develop their own shorthand, others laboriously outline everything, some synthesize it down to a few sentences, remembered informally."[40] Botein reminisced how his own notes became briefer as the years passed—a trend paralleled in all of the judges interviewed. The other important commentator on the subject of a trial judge's notes is the respected former federal Judge Harold Medina. He believes that "the number one menace is the judge who thinks his memory is so good that notes are a mere waste of time."[41] He urges each judge to develop a proficiency in note taking so as to be able to succinctly capture the important points of a trial and exclude the irrelevant minutiae. He believes the notes are critical if a judge is to offer a worthwhile charge to the jury. This charge should be a fair and accurate summary of the conflicting versions of the facts as given by the witnesses and a full and comprehensive statement of the rules of law governing the case. Medina's note-taking style was to keep notes for a single day on a page or two in a loose-leaf binder. Occasionally he would signal the court reporter to mark a page of their stenographic record so that when a recess was taken, he could write out the exact words used by a witness.[42]

Sentencing

The most difficult task facing a criminal court judge is sentencing a defendant. Although trial judges may have a variety of reasons for this belief, it is clear from my interviews as well as the research of others that this is their most challenging responsibility, producing the highest level of anxiety. Judges are aware of the horrible conditions awaiting defendants sentenced to penal institutions just as they are cognizant of the generally ineffectiveness of the probation alternative. Compassionate judges are aware of the inability of either form of sentence to adequately prevent the defendant from returning to society even more embittered and more committed to a continued life of crime.

Complicating the emotional strain under which judges must reach sentencing decisions is the increasing public outcry against the supposed leniency of their decisions. The mass media, concerned citizen groups, local politicians, and members of the law enforcement establishment such as police and prosecutors have all been united in their criticism of judicial sentencing. The police and prosecutors, in particular, have been most vocal in their disparaging remarks. The judges realize that the police and prosecutors may be partially motivated in the negative comments by a desire to shift the spotlight away from their own crime-fighting inadequacies, but the public appears convinced that the judges and their ineffective sentencing decisions are primary reasons for the breakdown in society's ability to control crime and keep their local neighborhoods safe.

Judges are frustrated in their ability to carry out their sentencing responsibilities because of the frequently inadequate information available to them concerning the defendant's background. One judge termed the sentencing process a "calculated gamble . . . and an impossible job," for which he felt very poorly prepared and especially handicapped by the very limited information available.[43] A Colorado judge explains the isolated nature of the sentencing decision by complaining: "Who can a judge talk to about these things—there's nobody. Other judges don't help—they can give you advice but then they're wounded if you don't take it—no one can help you."[44]

Despite all of the difficulties inherent in the sentencing process, judges are still responsible for making their decisions. What then are the factors a judge does consider in attempting to resolve these sentencing decisions? Most judges begin with an inquiry into the defendant's background to see if the present criminal activity has followed a discernible trend of antisocial behavior, or is clearly an aberration in an otherwise law-abiding life. Unfortunately, many defendants do not easily fall completely within either category. If they did exhibit such clear-cut patterns, the judge would have a fairly easy time with the sentencing decision. Those defendants with consistent patterns of criminal behavior would be sent to prison and those who have committed an isolated act would receive probation. Many defendants, however, are more likely to have had an earlier criminal record but only involving less serious property crimes. Others may have a conviction for a felony, but it could have occurred many years earlier, perhaps when he or she was a juvenile. During the intervening years, the defendant may have had a clean slate.

Judges also consider a defendant's previous opportunities for rehabilitation. If the defendant seemed to be making a sincere effort in putting his or her life back in order, a second or third chance may be offered. On the other hand, when a defendant has failed to take advantage of opportunities the court has offered in the past such as a drug program, vocational training, or psychiatric counseling, the court is more likely to give up on the defendant and sentence him or her to prison. The attitude and motivation of the defendant as manifested through his or her track record in these rehabilitative programs is of crucial significance to the judge. It appeared in most instances where defendants were to receive prison sentences (when they were not clearly mandated by statute due to the serious nature of the crime) to be the most persuasive factor in the judge's decision. The defendant was thought to have insulted the court by the refusal to take advantage of this earlier, generous opportunity for a second chance.

Judges are willing to read character references on behalf of the defendant as submitted by the defense attorney, but the facts of the presentence report concerning the seriousness of the present offense, the defendant's past criminal record and willingness to participate in previous rehabilitative programs combine to provide the most critical information influencing the judge's sentencing decision. The prosecutors usually attempt to counter the defense attorney's plea for leniency with an equally unrealistic recommendation stressing the necessity for protecting society from sociopaths such as the defendant. Most judges, particularly those sentencing large numbers of defendants after accepting a guilty plea, are unmoved by the posturing of both prosecution and defense, and generally adopt a reasonable compromise.

Obviously, not all sentencing decisions are of equal difficulty. Most judges acknowledge that they often have an easier time sentencing white-collar and middle-class defendants because of a greater empathy and heightened sensitivity as to how the anticipated punishment will influence future behavior. Martin Levin found this to be true in his study of Pittsburgh judges who were willing to "stand apart from the law and to act as a buffer between it and the middle class person they were sentencing."[45] Judge John Barth (a pseudonym for a Midwestern judge studied by James Simon) points out, however, in the following confession that sometimes even the sentencing of a middle-class defendant can be an agonizing experience:

> Why do I care about Lowell Evans? I'd like to think it's because I'm such a decent compassionate human being. But I know that's not quite an accurate analysis. Face it Barth. You're a prisoner of your own middle class values and Lowell Evans is somebody you can relate to. He's not a rapist or thief or murderer. No, Lowell Evans is a man who has tried to make an honest

wage for himself and his family all of his adult life. He's had anxieties like most other blue and white collar workers. . . . And he made a mistake. But it's a mistake I can understand and empathize with. There may be a double standard in my courtroom, but it's not based on class distinctions. I'll give both poor and middle class defendants who are threats to the law-abiding community equal time in prison. Lowell Evans is different. It doesn't matter whether he's poor or middle class. He's no threat to the rest of us. So I'll fight to keep him out of prison.[46]

In order to avoid the possibility of rendering an inappropriate sentence—either overly punitive or inadequately severe—due to a judge's heightened emotional state, members of the criminal bench are warned to avoid sentencing while experiencing extreme mood swings. A Colorado judge warned that "the ideal judge, whose mood never changes does not exist. You get tired or pressed and there's not a damn thing you can do about it. A judge is not a machine. What you have to do is realize that you're in a mood. I never sentence out of mood. I deliberately try to get 'up' for sentencing."[47]

Despite the cautionary advice just offered, it is virtually impossible for a judge to be able to consistently sentence defendants in a rational, mechanical fashion without being affected by psychological forces over which he or she has little control. Canadian criminologist John Hogarth, a respected expert on sentencing practices, concluded his most recent study with the sobering reminder that "it is a human process and subject to all the frailties of the human mind. Judges rearrange the facts to fit the type of sentence they use habitually and that most sentencing variations have little to do with the details of the crime and everything to do with the judge's perceptions."[48] Psychiatrist Willard Gaylin has also examined the dynamics of sentencing and agrees with Hogarth that "each [judge] has a point of view, a set of standards and values, a bias which will color and influence his decisions. . . . We act from what we are and we are what we have endured as well as what we have been taught."[49]

The previous quotes indicate the highly individualized nature of judicial sentencing decisions. Although some defenders of judicial independence may argue that judges need this discretion in order to intelligently and compassionately tailor each sentence to the individual situation, the general consensus in recent years has been to be critical of the disparities that have resulted. Thus, the public, which has grown increasingly upset over what it perceives to be a growing tendency toward leniency, has now added the charge of inconsistent and irrational sentencing propensities in which both the defendant and society are being penalized. Defendants arrested for the same crime are seen to receive divergent sentences. The judges defend such variation on the basis of their obligation to individualize each sentencing decision, considering unique factors that relate to the specific needs of the defendant.

Within the past decade the majority of state legislatures have responded favorably to this public clamor and have increased the severity of sentences while reducing the discretionary power of the judge by creating determinant rather than indeterminant sentences. With determinant sentences, once a defendant is found guilty of a particular crime, the judge *must* sentence him or her to a narrow range of minimum and maximum years or months. Additional restraints on the judge's sentencing choices may be determined by whether the defendant has prior felony convictions, whether these convictions involved violence, whether a gun was used in the current offense, whether the victim was a senior citizen, or whether heroin or some other dangerous drug was used or sold in large quantities. If any or a combination of these factors are present in the defendant's case, then the judge is directed to alter the sentence as dictated by each of these special circumstances.

Judges object to the reduction of their sentencing power because of its inhibiting effect on their ability to reach what they believe to be a just disposition. Confident of their expertise, educated by their experience, judges believe that they can only reach an intelligent sentencing disposition by being allowed to consider a wide range of mitigating factors concerning the defendant's background and any unusual aspects surrounding a particular crime. It is by being able to ponder the wide range of factors and being able to utilize a variety of sentencing alternatives that judges can effectively fit the disposition to the crime *and* the defendant. This particularistic style of sentencing was an outgrowth of penal reforms dating back to the 1920s and reflects the need to treat each defendant as an individual. Thus, the presence of disparities between individuals charged with the same crime was not a problem to be lamented, but rather a reflection of the judge's recognition of the unique circumstances in each case and a testimony to the judge's perspicacity and care.

The judges themselves have attempted for several decades to reform their sentencing practices. They were clearly aware of the public sentiment against their brethren. Their reform efforts have involved both educative and institutional reforms that have been geared primarily toward resolving the disparity question. The educative reforms are typified by the development of sentencing institutes such as the popular National College of Judges in Reno, Nevada. These programs are usually one to two weeks in duration and attempt to show judges how differing personal perspectives can influence their sentencing decisions. Hypothetical case histories of defendants are distributed to the judges in attendance and each must impose his or her own sentence and then explain it to colleagues. The judges quickly comprehend how their personal backgrounds and individual personality influences their ability to impose a particular sentence. The institute believes that by educating judges as to the divergent opinions held by their colleagues, they will be more careful in the future to control personal prejudices affecting their professional behavior. Whether these institutes can have long-range effects upon a judge's sentencing proclivities has never been conclusively established. Critics of these programs believe they are more of a busman's holiday, and the many diversions of Reno serve to undercut the capability of such institutes to significantly alter judicial behavior.

Other reforms such as sentencing councils and appellate review of sentences have also attempted to reduce unwarranted disparities by developing procedures designed to enroll larger numbers of judges in supervising each other's sentences, and in some instances requiring written justifications. The sentencing council is a procedure whereby several judges of a multijudge court meet periodically to consider what sentences should be imposed in pending cases. It is a procedure used primarily by federal district courts. Its primary advantage is that it shows the participating judges their differing sentencing practices and then offers a forum in which these differences can be debated and a consensus formed. The most bothersome aspect of the councils is that the judges meet prior to the sentencing hearing. This means that the sentencing judge, who has final responsibility for the sentencing, may have his or her objectivity impaired by the council's earlier discussions.

Although we have always allowed appellate review for sentences that failed to conform to statutory limits, nearly one-third of the states do not permit appellate review on the merits of the sentence. Additionally, a growing number of states have interpreted their general review statutes to grant such authority for appellate review. Usually this review is conducted by the regular appellate division, although a handful of states have created special courts staffed with experienced judges solely for the purpose of reviewing sentences. Several judges interviewed were upset by appellate review and sentencing councils, viewing these reforms as an indication of the lack of faith by their colleagues in their ability to reach an appropriate disposition. It was believed to be another example of the trial court judge losing power as a result of public frustration over the rising crime rate. It was especially upsetting since it was fellow members of the bench who wilted under public pressure. It was expected to cause even greater tensions between trial and appellate judges, although the actual number of such appeals is miniscule and rarely successful. Since these reforms are still in the embryonic stages and affect only a minority of jurisdictions, it is premature for both judges and critics to offer conclusions as to the long-run consequences of these reforms.

One final attempt at improving the consistency and certainty of sentencing has been the use of sentencing guidelines. These guidelines limit the judge to sentence within a required set of boundaries and were modeled after guidelines used by parole boards as an aid in determining whether certain prisoners should be granted early release. The approach has subsequently been applied to the sentencing process and is used in several states as well as by the federal courts. The federal guidelines were created in 1987 by Congress and implemented by the U.S. Sentencing Commission. Most of the sentencing guidelines offer the judge a range of possible sentences depending on the seriousness of the crime and the criminal history of the defendant. A typical guideline structure is presented in Table 8.3, with the recommended periods of incarceration (by months) listed within each cell of the matrix. As with all of the reform efforts, the sentencing guideline alternative is also imperfect. Critics such as Norval Morris believe it possesses serious methodological flaws and offers "a false precision of that which by its very nature can never be precise."[50]

APPELLATE RESPONSIBILITIES

Following the completion of the trial where the critical factual issues have been resolved, and one side emerges victorious, the losing party may wish to appeal the decision. In both the state and federal systems, an appellate division exists to examine the performance of the trial court. The appeals court is empowered to review the proceedings to determine if there were significant errors of law committed that would necessitate overturning the original decision or at least ordering a new trial to correct specific errors. Chapter 7 described the work environment of appellate courts whose collegial style of decision making contrasts sharply with the individualized pattern of judging found at the trial level. This concluding section of Chapter 8 will describe the unique group of professional responsibilities facing appellate court judges beginning with their selection of cases and preparation for oral argument.

Preparing for Argument and Selecting Cases

An appellate court will begin its review of a case when its members receive legal briefs from the contesting parties as well as a complete transcript of the lower court's entire proceedings. Before the appellate court sets a date for oral argument, its members must first carefully analyze all of these materials and make a threshold decision as to whether or not they have jurisdiction over the issues raised by the litigants. Next, in state supreme courts and at the United States Supreme Court, there will have to be a decision as to whether the case raises a significantly important issue necessitating their accepting the case. Once the court agrees that a case is within its jurisdiction and decides to hear the dispute, a date will be set for oral argument before the entire court. Judge Frank Coffin of the federal court of appeals describes the process of preparing for oral argument in the following statement:

> By the middle of the third week of a typical month, the briefs for our next session of court arrive in several heavy cartons. Although my clerks and I are working away on opinions from earlier sessions, we know that we have

Table 8.3 MINNESOTA PRESUMPTIVE SENTENCING FORMAT[a]

Severity Levels of Conviction Offense[b]		Criminal History Score						
		0	1	2	3	4	5	6 or more
Unauthorized use of motor vehicle Possession of marijuana	I	12c	12c	12c	15	18	21	24d
Theft-related crimes ($150–$2500) Sale of marijuana	II	12c	12c	14	17	20	23	27 25–29
Theft crimes ($150–$2500)	III	12c	13	16	19	22 21–23	27 25–29	32 30–34
Burglary-felony intent receiving stolen goods ($150–$2500)	IV	12d	15	18	21	25 24–26	32 30–34	41 37–45
Simple robbery	V	18	23	27	30 29–31	38 36–40	46 43–49	54 50–58
Assault, 2nd degree	VI	21	26	30	34 33–35	44 42–46	54 50–58	65 60–70
Aggravated robbery	VII	24 23–25	32 30–34	41 38–44	49 45–53	65 60–70	81 75–87	97 90–104
Assault, 1st degree Criminal sexual conduct, 1st degree	VIII	43 41–45	54 50–58	65 60–70	76 71–81	95 89–101	113 106–120	132 124–140
Murder, 3rd degree	IX	97 94–100	119 116–122	127 124–130	149 143–155	176 168–184	205 195–215	230 218–242
Murder, 2nd degree	X	116 111–121	140 133–147	162 153–171	203 192–214	243 231–255	284 270–298	324 309–339

[a]Boldface numbers within the grid denote the range within which a judge may sentence without the sentence being deemed a departure.

[b]First-degree murder is excluded from the guidelines by law and continues to have a mandatory life sentence.

[c]One year and one day.

[d]The dark heavy line is the dispositional line. Above the line indicates probationary sentences (OUT), under the line indicates sentences of incarceration (IN).

Source: Reprinted by permission from page 492 of Criminal Justice by Joel Samaha. Copyright 1988 by West Publishing Company.

to make time to prepare, for my way involves a two step approach to a case before I mount the bench to hear argument: reading briefs and then discussing them with my clerks. . . .

Each of my three clerks takes a third of the briefs and a pile containing copies of all is reserved for me. The clerks' task is to read their briefs with some care and report to the rest of us what the case is about, what the key issues are, where some of the major problems lurk, and what questions might usefully be asked at argument . . . I suspect that most judges prepare by having their clerks prepare a "bench memorandum." This is a typed memorandum that can be quickly read or reread at the bench; it contains salient facts, issues, contentions, and some thoughtful insights and questions from a clerk.[51]

Judges vary in how carefully they read all the briefs and appendices. Federal Judge Harold Medina candidly admits that several of his colleagues do no read them at all, relying entirely on their law clerks while others will read them very carefully. Medina even noted a small number who simply glance at them to quickly discern the major points and will then rely primarily on the opinions of the lower courts to clarify most critical issues. Medina himself chooses to read each brief before hearing oral argument because it assists him in framing questions for the attorneys. Medina explains that "not infrequently there will be something on which I would like one of the lawyers to give a supplementary brief explaining certain authorities or something that he has not put in the briefs already filed."[52]

One interesting innovation attempted by an Illinois appellate court is to have a selected judge be responsible for a pre-oral-argument memorandum. This court, similar to the federal courts of appeal, has a number of three-judge panels randomly selected by a computer with one member designated as the lead judge who will work with his or her law clerk on this memo, which the other judges will utilize. Although all judges do review the briefs, they do not have the time to read the trial records, which can reach enormous lengths. Despite the value as a time-saving device, one Illinois judge was concerned with becoming overly dependent on the lead judge and his or her law clerk who are assigned to a particular case.[53]

Oral Argument

In contrast to the original trial, which can be a lengthy, protracted contest involving countless witnesses and lasting several months, the oral argument at the appellate level is a rather abbreviated, highly proscribed proceeding that is commonly completed within a few hours. The major reason for the brevity and tight control exercised over appellate arguments is their narrow focus on only issues of law. The perplexing issues of fact, which had to be determined after hours of competing testimony from experts and witnesses from both sides, have already been resolved and the appeals court is only being asked the more basic legal question of whether the trial proceedings satisfied the required constitutional and statutory standards.

Appellate court proceedings also contrast with the trial court in that the original court is controlled by a single judge whereas the appellate courts may have anywhere from three to nine judges sitting together, all jointly responsible for listening to and finally resolving each dispute. If these groups of judges did not tightly monitor the oral arguments, they would be unable to review the large number of cases appealed to their respective courts each year. The U.S. Supreme Court, for example, received approximately 5000 cases in 1988 and was able to hear only 175. Given its time constraints and lengthy period of time necessary for the arduous task of opinion writing, the highest federal court is unable to hear more than 200 cases per year, no matter how many thousands of appeals arrive.

Most appellate court judges would agree with Judge Coffin who does not believe that the oral argument yields very valuable dividends. He writes that a few positive things do occur such as "some facts falling into place and the context is better understood. Some issues drop out of the case and new ones appear that no one has yet thought about. . . . Counsel occasionally make concessions as to facts, claims, or law which may profoundly affect the outcome, the approach, or the scope of appeal."[54] From observing appellate courts at both the state and federal levels, it appears obvious that the oral argument is a rather perfunctory proceeding in which the contesting attorneys are given a brief opportunity to debate the major issues of their case with members of the appellate court. The appellate judges appear to be thoroughly versed in the legal issues and frequently have already decided how the dispute should be resolved. The oral arguments therefore are often used as an opportunity for individual judges, through their interrogation of the attorneys, to convince their nonaligned colleagues on the bench to join their side of the argument. Attorneys who naively hope to use their oral presentation as a last-ditch effort to persuade judges to change their minds as a result of their eloquence and brilliance are invariably frustrated by the constant interruptions by judges wishing to make their own points.

Postargument Conferences

Shortly after the oral arguments are completed, the appellate court will hold a conference to discuss and decide the cases just heard. These conferences may be held at the end of each day of oral argument or, more commonly, on the last day of the week. At one U.S. court of appeals, the three-judge panel has chosen to meet at the end of the day around 3:30 to discuss the five to seven cases heard that day. The discussions are conducted rather informally with no set protocol and were equated to a "Quaker meeting where speaking occurs as the spirit moves. This means very little colloquy in some cases, hours of talk in others."[55] Another federal appeals judge noted that his court moved much more slowly. No discussion was allowed until every judge on the panel had prepared and circulated a written memo expressing his or her views on the case and tentative voting decision. The actual conference would then be scheduled the following Wednesday or Thursday and the presiding judge would hold all the earlier written memos on each case and would know those cases where there existed a strong difference of opinion that might require a lengthy discussion. He would then guide the judges through their discussions of all the cases "arguing backwards and forwards, backwards and forwards and reaching a decision as to what they want to do."[56]

The U.S. Supreme Court appears to have the most formalistic procedures for its conferences, probably caused by the number of cases, their complexity, and significance that, if uncontrolled, could extend for days. In fact, we shall see it is during the opinion-writing phase where preliminary drafts are circulated that justices often enter into a protracted debate with one another concerning the resolution of thorny issues within the opinion. The conference is held in a modest-sized room to which only the justices are admitted. They usually meet on the Friday of each week following oral arguments. They are allowed to bring only a small notebook into the room in order to record their votes. The chief justice begins discussion of each case, and the remaining members of the court are allowed to speak in descending order of seniority. Following the discussion, the vote is taken, which proceeds in ascending order of seniority with the most junior member of the court voting first. The reason for this reversal is to ensure that the youngest justices will not be unduly influenced by how the more senior members vote, as well as avoiding placing the youngest justice in the critical position of casting the deciding vote in a 4 to 4 decision. Each case is decided by majority vote. Justices recuse (withdraw) themselves from cases in which they conceive of the possibility of a conflict of interest. When a justice has had previous service in the Justice Department as solicitor general or attorney general, it is likely that there will be several occasions during the first few years on the court when he or she will have to withdraw from a case.

After the vote has been completed, the next step is the assignment of the majority opinion. If the chief justice is on the winning side, he or she can choose either to write the opinion or assign it to another member of the winning side. If the chief justice is not on the winning side, than the most senior member (in terms of service on the court) can either write the majority opinion or assign it to another justice. Some believe the assignment power can be important in determining the subtle drift of the opinion and influence its future impact. The majority opinion, however, is a difficult assignment for it must state the reasons for the court's decision in a manner that is acceptable to all of the other members of the winning side. If the opinion does not prove acceptable to one of the majority judges, it must either be rewritten or lose the vote, and in a close vote risk a reversal of the opinion. Because the majority opinion must satisfy a number of justices who may hold sharply divergent reasons for reaching a similar conclusion, the result can be a choppy and confusing opinion.

Writing the Opinion

The majority opinion of the court, which expresses the reasoning behind the appellate court's decision, is often a difficult and time-consuming process, especially where other members of the winning coalition possess strong ideas about how the opinion should be written. Although there is continual debate over the role of the law clerks in the formulation of these opinions, it is still the individual justice who must take ultimate responsibility for what is said. Writing the opinions is also challenging at the appellate level because of the complexity and importance of each case. The legal controversy would not have reached this level of tribunal if it were a simple issue, easily resolved. Judge Irving Kaufmann explains the problems of opinion writing in stating that "a judge is bound to follow case law; yet he must be prepared to distinguish or deviate from it, for each new factual variation demands a ward past authority. Moreover many appeals present questions that are only slightly different, if at all, from those that have come before. . . . The challenges arise when the facts are not replicative from those in cases past, when the precedents are pregnant with ambiguity or conflict, or the case presents a combination of the two. No statutory or common law rule points the way to an inevitable."[57]

We return again to the words of Judge Frank Coffin who provides one of the most honest and lucid descriptions of the process of appellate opinion writing in the following rather lengthy quote:

> As the writing progresses, as the necessary but grubby work of building a foundation is finished, my interest, excitement, and speed increase. As I write on the issues, I try to put as fairly and strongly as I can the contention that I shall rule against. Sometimes, while writing, I will have a new thought. If after I roll it about in my mind a while, it seems to have flaws, I'll write it down. Sometimes the next day I will see its unsoundness or my law clerks will. Sometimes, however, the thought survives. More often than not, the thought will be an effort to say how our decision makes broad and enduring policy sense and how a contrary decision would not do so, if applied generally.
>
> After four or five hours of steady work—with the foundation laid, the issues stated, and innumerable little decisions made as to sequences, what authorities to use and what to leave out, tone and nuances—I find my pen flying over the pages. Speed at this point is a built-in stimulant to succinctness. I am now eager to finish and more easily reject excessive refinement. Or, if a footnote is needed, I shall mark the gap and leave it for the morrow. The result is a shorter draft than I would have made without impatience.

Sometimes my clerks, writing during office hours, not sensing the pressure that comes from knowing that sustained writing time is a rare and precious commodity, will present me with a long, heavily footnoted draft that I would never have the time to construct. Then my job is to winnow, shear, simplify. But with my drafts, their job is to see if flesh should be added to the bones.[58]

If a judge is on the winning side and wishes to explain his or her personal reasons for deciding the case, and yet has not been selected to write the majority opinion, he or she may still express personal views in a concurring opinion. Concurring opinions often focus on a particular aspect of the case that the judge believes was of significant import, but was not sufficiently emphasized in the majority opinion. It is conceivable in a complex case where the judges are having a difficult time reaching a consensus, each member of the winning side could write his or her own opinion (one majority and the remainder being concurring).

Judges who wind up on the losing side (also referred to as the minority) can also express their reasons in a dissenting opinion. These opinions usually do not directly attack the majority opinion but are attempts at explaining why they disagree and present an alternative resolution of the issues. Because the membership of the appellate courts is constantly changing and different historical periods can also influence a court's view of a problem, it is very possible that earlier dissenting opinions may, after the passage of time, eventually become the majority view of a subsequent court. A noteworthy example of this phenomenon is John Marshall Harlan's dissenting opinion in the Supreme Court's 1896 case of *Plessy* v. *Ferguson*, which established the doctrine of "separate but equal." Fifty-eight years later in *Brown* v. *Board of Education of Topeka Kansas*, Harlan's dissent was adopted by the winning side and was quoted throughout Chief Justice Earl Warren's majority opinion.

Appellate judges nearly all believe that the task of opinion writing is their most challenging responsibility. Not only must they operate under severe time constraints because of heavy caseloads, but their views must be shared first with their colleagues on the bench and then with the general public. The publication of a judge's personal and hopefully carefully reasoned opinion puts a great deal of pressure on him or her. The logic and wisdom of one's reasoning will be scrutinized by other appellate court judges both in one's own jurisdiction as well as across the country, in addition to legal scholars, bar associations, and the concerned public. John Dawson clarifies the significance of appellate opinions by explaining their ability to provide a continuity so necessary in our nation's common law system. Without the guidance and stability offered by written opinions, Dawson foresees a system that would be "confusing and apt to seem unjust for the same problem to be decided different ways merely because the decisions are made at different times or between different people. For the persons affected by decisions, consistency is an important virtue, not only because it permits prediction but because it seems more fair."[59]

Probably the most unique feature of the appellate bench is its collegial nature, and, as we have already noted, this has an important impact upon opinion writing. Even before judges circulate their opinions among other members of the court, their writing is influenced by what one judge refers to as "anticipatory collegiality," which he defines as an "instinctive and unself-conscious sensitivity to one's colleagues sensitivities."[60] Once a draft has been completed, it is then sent to the other justices on the majority who will respond either formally in writing or informally in a casual visit to each other's chambers for a discussion. As a result of these encounters between members of the winning coalition, a majority opinion is written that is acceptable to all. In contrast to the trial judge who makes rulings independently and without the necessity for consultation with other judges, the appellate judge must be able to engage in the art of compromise. David Shapiro explains further that the effective appellate judge "must have a sense of when to settle for less than his heart's desire, either in writing his own opinion or in joining someone else's."[61] Shapiro is quick to point out, however, that the collegial pressure to compromise should not force a judge "to make or join in a statement that does not represent the judge's views and that will mislead the opinion readers as to what those views are."[62]

Although appellate courts usually have a presiding judge or chief justice, his or her responsibilities are primarily administrative and do not disrupt the overall sense of collegiality. The appellate judges must operate as an intimate group at close quarters, and individual members of a court are bestowed with equal authority. Since membership on the appellate bench tends to be of rather long duration (the federal bench and many state supreme courts are appointed for lifetime tenure), the judges usually grow very close regardless of differences in judicial philosophies and political beliefs. Occasionally, however, the pressure of coerced intimacy between unfriendly colleagues can erupt into ugly scenes such as the anti-Semitic barbs that Justice McReynolds directed toward Justice Brandeis or Justice Frankfurter's comment that one of Justice Black's opinions "almost made him puke."[63] Appellate judges share a common responsibility to produce the careful judicial review of all cases and controversies appealed to their court. Federal Judge Harold Medina summarizes the essence of this unique collegial life found within appellate courts when he notes how the judges "learn to live together and work together, rub shoulders and have their spats and happy times, each striving to find his own little place in the sun, adjustments are made, friendly intimacies and courtesies multiply and the law thrives mightily."[64]

As a closing point, one must be careful not to overstate the influence of the collegial atmosphere, thereby underemphasizing the importance of the personal beliefs and predilections of the individual appellate judge assigned responsibility for writing the court's majority opinion. Even Judge Medina was quick to note after his discussion of the wonder of the collegial atmosphere, that there are significant differences between the judges that are not surmounted or controlled by their cooperative endeavors. He explains that "these differences in the personalities of appellate judges are like differences in points of view on life and things in general. Naturally some are more conservative than others, some like administrative duties, some are more interested than others in helping to make the law grow and adjust itself to changing times and mores."[65]

NOTES

1. John Paul Ryan, Alan Ashman, Bruce D. Sales, and Sandra Shane-DuBow, *American Trial Judges* (New York: Free Press, 1980), 6–8.
2. Zachariah Chafee, "Economic Interpretations of Judges," *The Inquiring Mind* (New York: Da Capo Press, 1974), 265.
3. Marvin Frankel, "Adversary Judge," *Texas Law Review* 54 (March, 1976): 469.
4. Hubert Will, "The Art of Judging," *Trial* 21 (October, 1985): 79.
5. Ibid.
6. B. Paul Cotter, "When the Electronic Judge Meets the Electronic Lawyer," *The Judges Journal* 27/2 (Spring, 1988): 3.
7. Albert Alschuler, "The Trial Judge's Role in Plea Bargaining—Part I," *Columbia Law Review* 76 (November, 1976): 1061.
8. James Alfini and John Paul Ryan, "Trial Judge Participation in Plea Bargaining," *Law and Society Review* 13 (Winter, 1979): 479.
9. Paul B. Wice, *Chaos in the Courtroom* (New York: Praeger Publishers, 1985), 137.
10. Charles B. Craven, "When Parties Can't Settle: Mediation Techniques Every Judge Needs to Master," *The Judges Journal* 26/1 (Winter, 1987): 4.
11. Ibid. p. 7.
12. Herbert Kritzer, "The Judge's Role in Pretrial Case Processing," *Judicature* 66/1 (June–July, 1982): 28.
13. Frank Coffin, *The Ways of a Judge* (Boston: Houghton Mifflin, 1980), 79.
14. James Richards, "Radio Justice," *The Judges Journal* 21/2 (Spring, 1982): 20.
15. Paul Connolly, "Why Do We Need Managerial Judges," *The Judges Journal* 23/4 (Fall, 1984): 34.
16. As already noted in Chapter 6, the selection of judges from large law firms in which they invariably had little or no managerial responsibilities only exacerbates the problem.
17. James F. Simon, *The Judge* (New York: David McKay, 1976), 203.
18. Marie Provine, "Managing Negotiated Justice: Settlement Procedures in the Courts," *Justice System Journal* 12/1 (Spring, 1987): 94.
19. Daniel Holt, "The Justice Machine," *Newsweek*, 8 March 1971, p. 29.

20. Will, "The Art of Judging," 81.
21. Kritzer, "The Judge's Role in Pretrial Case Processing," 31.
22. Craven, "When Parties Can't Settle," 9.
23. William McDonald, "Judicial Supervision of the Guilty Plea Process," *Judicature* 70/4 (December–January, 1987): 215.
24. Ibid.
25. Will, "The Art of Judging," 79.
26. Henry Rothblatt, "Prejudicial Conduct of the Trial Judge in Criminal Matters," *Criminal Law Bulletin* 2 (September, 1966): 3.
27. Wice, *Chaos in the Courthouse*, 120.
28. Henry Lummus, *The Trial Judge* (Brooklyn: Foundation Press, 1937), 22.
29. Bernard Botein, *Trial Judge* (New York: Simon and Schuster, 1952), 185.
30. Ibid. p. 188.
31. Confidential interview with New York City Supreme Court judge in summer of 1980.
32. Report to Governor Carey by the Executive Advisory Committee on Sentencing, *Crime and Punishment in New York* (Albany, 1979), 22.
33. Charles Wyzanski, "An Activist Judge: Mea Maxima Culpa," *Georgia Law Review* 7 (1973): 208.
34. Marvin Frankel, "The Search for Truth: An Umpireal View," *University of Pennsylvania Law Review* 123/5 (May, 1975): 1037.
35. Irving Kaufmann, "The Anatomy of Decision-Making," *Fordham Law Review*, 53 (October, 1984): 15.
36. Benjamin Cardozo, *The Nature of the Judicial Process* (New Haven: Yale University Press, 1949): 166.
37. Ibid.
38. Coffin, *The Ways of a Judge*, 103.
39. Wicc, *Chaos in the Courthouse*, 124.
40. Botein, *Trial Judge*, 26.
41. Harold Medina, "Trial Judge Notes: A Study in Judicial Administration," *Cornell Law Quarterly* 49 (Fall, 1963): 1.
42. Ibid. p. 3.
43. Simon, *The Judge*, 139.
44. Donald Dale Jackson, *Judges* (New York: Atheneum, 1974), 201.
45. Martin Levin, *Urban Politics and the Criminal Courts* (Chicago: University of Chicago Press, 1977), 123.
46. Simon, *The Judge*, 136.
47. Jackson, *Judges*, 214.
48. Ibid. p. 372.
49. Willard Gaylin, *Partial Justice* (New York: Alfred Knopf, 1974), 162.
50. Norval Morris, "The Sentencing Disease: The Judge's Changing Role in the Criminal Court Process," *The Judges Journal* 18 (Summer, 1979): 50.
51. Coffin, *The Ways of a Judge*, p. 81.
52. Harold Medina, "The Decisional Process," *Bar Bulletin of New York County Lawyers Association* 20 (1962): 95.
53. "Interaction and Decision-making on Collegial Courts: A Panel Discussion," *Judicature* 71/6 (April–May, 1988): 341.
54. Coffin, *The Ways of a Judge*, p. 110.

55. Ibid. p. 110.
56. Medina, "Decisional Process," 97.
57. Kaufmann, "Anatomy of Decision-Making," 12.
58. Coffin, *The Ways of a Judge*, 159.
59. John P. Dawson, "The Functions of a Judge," in *Talks on American Law*, ed. Harold Berman (New York: Vintage Books, 1961), 21.
60. Coffin, *The Ways of a Judge*, 181.
61. David L. Shapiro, "In Defense of Judicial Candor," *Harvard Law Review* 100 (February, 1987): 743.
62. Ibid.
63. James F. Simon, *The Antagonists: Hugo Black, Felix Frankfurter and Civil Liberties in Modern America* (New York: Simon and Schuster, 1989), 18.
64. Harold Medina, "Some Reflections on the Judicial Function at the Appellate Level," *Washington University Law Quarterly* (1961): 149.
65. Ibid.

Chapter
9

The Strains and Hardships of Judging

*F*rom the perspective of the general public, the professional life of a judge is perceived to be one of high status and privilege. Selection to the bench becomes a wonderful, challenging conclusion to one's legal career. It is an opportunity to apply years of professional experience to society's problems, reaching out to troubled individuals in search of justice. This chapter begins with a brief discussion of the positive aspects of the judging profession, and the remainder is devoted to a detailed examination of the various strains and hardships presently affecting the professional lives of the nation's judiciary. It will be a penetrating, and slightly depressing view of the chaotic working conditions and pressurized atmosphere that undermine the efforts of so many of our judges. It is true, as we have noted in Chapter 7 that there is a significant diversity among the varied levels of judges from the lowest municipal courts through the highest appellate courts. Thus, judges operating at the lower end of the judicial spectrum in crowded trial courts are much more likely to be suffering from the professional difficulties discussed in this chapter, but even the Supreme Court justices will also experience similar problems, albeit in a relatively less exaggerated form.

BEGINNING ON A POSITIVE NOTE

Despite the emphasis in this chapter on the negative aspects of a judge's professional life, this initial section will concentrate upon the positive side of this challenging position. Most judges, in moments of candor, will admit that they generally do enjoy the deferential treatment they often receive, especially by members of their courtroom work group. It is nice to have door opened and crowded hallways suddenly become passable as judges move through the courthouse. The loyalty of the staff, extending from the courtroom bailiffs to the secretaries and law clerks, is another factor contributing to the judge's feeling of power and prestige. Even though sociologists inform us that the status of judges, particularly at the local level, has declined over the past few decades, most judges believe their professional status is still elevated and most of the legal community remains both envious and respectful.

A second aspect of their position that nearly all judges find attractive is the intellectual challenges that they continually face. Regardless of the level of court, most judges are excited by the constantly changing nature of the legal conundrums facing them each day. How could they most effectively balance the demands of society for security and order with the equally compelling personal freedoms guaranteed by the Constitution? How can they choose between the need to provide stability and consistency in their decisions by strict adherence to established legal precedents while still allowing for the law to evolve and grow into a competent mechanism for deciding contemporary issues? How were the subtle and changing rhythms of the Burger and Rhenquist courts to be interpreted in light of the earlier Warren court decisions? Complicating the judge's job even more has been the case law explosion at both the state and federal courts that has driven judges and their law clerks (as well as most of the legal profession) into law libraries, seminars, workshops, and other information services that will allow them to stay current. Judges realize that the basic reason for their very existence is to serve as the legitimate means by which society's and individual's controversies are resolved.

A third attraction of the judiciary is more altruistic and emphasizes the challenging objective of serving the community through application of legal skills. Judges frequently state a sincere belief in their capacity to reach a just and fair decision. Beyond the intellectual powers that one may apply to a case, many judges think they possess the compassion and common sense to consistently reach equitable decisions. Although the intellectual challenges were exciting and quite demanding, judges speak more frequently of the importance of their role in protecting individual interests while guaranteeing the rule of law. There appears to be a general sense of confidence in their ability to penetrate the thorny legal issues complicating a controversy brought before them, and be able to resolve the dilemma fairly.

The final attraction stated by most judges, especially those at the appellate level, is to be able, through one's decisions and opinions, to leave a living legacy of their time on the bench. This was a precious opportunity to be able to create a tangible record of achievement, especially in such a critical public institution as the courts. Their decisions would not only affect those individuals who were directly involved in litigation but would also be preserved for generations of future lawyers and judges as a permanent testimony to their wisdom and compassion.

THE MOST COMMON COMPLAINTS

Despite the positive feelings just described, nearly all judges are troubled by a wide variety of problems diminishing the quality of their professional lives. This section of the chapter will examine the common complaints that extend from a perceived loss of professional status to such tangible and somewhat mundane concerns as inadequate compensation and unpleasant working conditions. Table 9.1 presents a list of the most frustrating aspects of being a judge according to a national survey conducted by Ellen Rosen and indicates not only the diversity of problems but also their relative salience to individual members of the judiciary.

Decline in Status: Negative Public Perception

Although according to recent sociological research on the relative status of numerous professions, the judiciary ranks near the top, there is nevertheless a perception among many jurists that their profession's prestige is on the decline. As noted in Chapter 1, according to studies by Donald Treiman, judges score very high, reaching five points above the rest of the legal profession, although there was significant variation between levels of judges with a Supreme Court justice scoring eight points higher than a municipal court judge. Especially for judges at the trial courts, public opinion polls critical of their professional performance tend to

Table 9.1 MOST FRUSTRATING ASPECTS OF BEING A JUDGE

1. Heavy workload and administrative problems	30%
2. Unprepared and unequal lawyers	16
3. Child custody and matrimonial cases	8
4. Delays	7
5. Feeling isolated	6
6. Sentencing	5
7. Inadequate pay	3
8. Low public perceptions	3
9. Difficult decisions	3
10. Other	15

Source: Ellen Rosen, "The Nation's Judges: No Unanimous Opinion," *Court Review* 24(4) (Fall, 1987): 5.

validate the perceptions among judges that their work is not only unappreciated by the general public, but in the area of criminal law, they are held at least partially responsible for the problem. Even appellate judges, especially in the more visible supreme courts, can sense the public's strong disapproval, not only in decisions affecting the rights of person's accused of crimes, but in the civil rights field where affirmative action and school busing decisions are most unpopular.

The public has long been able to separate its feelings toward the institution of the courts, which remains quite positive, with the much more negative attitude toward the specific decisions of individual judges. This seemingly paradoxical situation was most apparent over 50 years ago during the unsuccessful court-packing plan of President Franklin Roosevelt. Despite the public's strong disapproval of the Supreme Court's series of decisions declaring various New Deal laws unconstitutional, they were even more upset when the president attempted to tamper with the basic structure of this sacrosanct institution. FDR's scheme was viewed as an unconscionable politicization of the judiciary, which should remain above the political fray.

The anger of the citizenry today is directed primarily at the criminal courts whose inability to reduce the escalating crime rate is a source of intense frustration. Other agencies responsible for the administration of our nation's criminal justice system—the police and correctional officials—are more than happy to use the courts as a scapegoat for the rising crime rates, thereby escaping further scorn. Politicians, likewise, are also willing to shift the blame to the courts rather than take responsibility themselves. Criminal court judges are correct in pointing out that their narrow responsibilities are limited to adjudicating those cases brought to them by the police and prosecutors, and they have no ability or power to affect those very basic social problems that are most closely related to perpetuating urban crime (i.e., economic, educational, and family conditions). Nevertheless, the public remains unconvinced, and continues to endorse the simplistic, inaccurate, and even irresponsible accusations against the judicial system for its role in the crime problem. The judges may intellectually understand that the public's sentiment is based on misinformation and distortions as well as a failure to grasp the complexities of the etiology of crime, yet no one enjoys being disliked, and many judges are frustrated by their inability to elevate the public's confidence in their performance.

Monetary Frustrations

Moving to a much more pragmatic complaint, nearly all judges believe that they are not only unappreciated but clearly underpaid. When Mary Volcansek-Clark surveyed Florida judges as to why they might consider joining the bench, she discovered that financial factors were one of the

primary reasons inhibiting their desire to become judges. Seventy percent of the judges she interviewed believed that they had suffered a loss
of income as a result of moving to the bench.[1] Interviews by Isaiah Zimmerman, a Washington clinical psychologist, concluded that "while to
most of the population the average judicial salary may appear comfortable, the self-image of judges place them more within the ranks of highly
paid federal and state executives. Living with such discrepancies produces stress."[2] One trial judge after four years on the bench told Dr.
Zimmerman that given the high cost of living and the reluctance of legislative bodies to raise judicial salaries to keep up with his escalating
expenses, he contemplated early retirement and returning to private
practice.[3]

The national statistics on judicial salaries during the past decade
bear out the angry claims by judges that their compensation is lagging
behind inflation. When compared to top attorneys whose real income
grew by 9 percent from 1974 to 1984, the nation's judges had their incomes decline by 15 percent.[4] Table 9.2 presents the national figures
for state supreme court justices, which further supports this depressing
trend.

Judicial salaries range from $40,000–50,000 a year in southern states
to approximately $100,000 in the federal court system and several East
Coast and West Coast states. Although state appellate court systems may
earn more than their trial court counterparts, it is rarely a significant difference. Many judges complain about having to take a severe cut from
their private practice income once they join the bench, with average loss
estimated to be approximately 50 percent. Most of the younger judges
interviewed complained that the differential between their judicial salary and their earning capacity as private practitioners was growing wider
with each passing year. Exacerbating the financial pressures were the
educational expenses being faced by the majority of judges who had col-
lege-age children and could expect to be facing six to eight years of paying hefty tuitions. Additionally, judges have financial commitments such
as home mortgages that were incurred prior to their new financial situation.

Several of the judges I interviewed were cynical about the supposed
enormity of financial losses suffered by their colleagues as a result of
joining the bench. These judges thought that a large number of their
brethren had not been financially well off prior to becoming a judge, and
had actually received an increase in salary as a result of their new position. These judges were frequently the products of a highly politicized
system of judicial selection and received their appointment as a result
of many years of loyal party service. They had likely held bureaucratic
positions within city government that paid a modest salary. If they did
have an association with a law firm, it was usually in name only. Their
legal work was more likely business-related, typically in the area of real

Table 9.2 PERCENT CHANGE IN SUPREME COURT JUSTICES' SALARIES ADJUSTED FOR INFLATION

State	17 Years 1967–1984	10 Years 1974–1984	5 Years 1979–1984
Alabama	5	35	13
Alaska	1	-12	8
Arizona	-5	-15	-15
Arkansas	-13	-6	-1
California	-11	-18	-11
Colorado	-8	-15	-3
Connecticut	-32	-18	8
Delaware	-18	-22	-11
Dist. of Columbia	-5	-10	-2
Florida	-36	-11	-3
Georgia	-23	-24	-8
Hawaii	-36	-22	-17
Idaho	-24	-25	-13
Illinois	-36	-25	-10
Indiana	-33	-21	-21
Iowa	-11	-12	-13
Kansas	6	0	14
Kentucky	-7	-13	4
Louisiana	-14	-16	-17
Maine	-21	-19	-9
Maryland	-33	-24	-6
Massachusetts	-23	-17	0
Michigan	-32	-19	-8
Minnesota	-20	-15	-13
Mississippi	0	-18	-10
Missouri	4	9	1

State	17 Years 1967–1984	10 Years 1974–1984	5 Years 1979–1984
Montana	-7	-14	-10
Nebraska	-12	-13	-9
Nevada	-10	4	-9
New Hampshire	-23	-23	-6
New Jersey	-19	-23	-3
New Mexico	-8	-7	5
New York	-34	-37	-18
North Carolina	-22	-18	-7
North Dakota	-4	-9	-4
Ohio	-9	-19	-7
Oklahoma	15	-6	2
Oregon	-27	-21	-23
Pennsylvania	-34	-27	-3
Rhode Island	-27	-19	-9
South Carolina	-5	-5	-3
South Dakota	-3	4	5
Tennessee	5	-21	-21
Texas	-9	-9	-6
Utah	-3	5	-3
Vermont	-25	-22	-4
Virginia	-4	-20	-6
Washington	-23	-10	-4
West Virginia	-21	-20	1
Wisconsin	-9	-19	-3
Wyoming	24	0	-1
U.S. Supreme Court	-18	-20	-2

Source: Thomas Marvell, "Judicial Salaries: Doing Work for Less Pay," The Judges Journal 24 (1) (Winter, 1985): 37.

estate or insurance, and rarely amounted to incomes approaching that which they currently earned on the bench.

How many judges have actually suffered significantly as a result of joining the bench? How many have profited from this move? These questions are almost impossible to answer. What can be concluded, however, is that a large proportion of our nation's judges perceive themselves as being underpaid. When judges do believe that they are not being sufficiently compensated and are thereby relatively deprived, their attitudes can have negative repercussions on their job performance. It seems quite plausible that judges who complain most about their salaries are least likely to devote themselves unselfishly to their professional responsibilities.

Working Conditions

The deteriorating conditions of so many of the courthouses described in Chapter 7 have a deleterious effect on judges and their courtroom work groups. These declining physical conditions combine with equally depressing problems of crowded calendars, inadequate staffing, and ineffective security to serve as a constant reminder to the judge of his or her questionable professional status. The clogged toilets, overflowing trash cans, graffiti-scarred walls, and inoperative or barely functioning heating and cooling plants are just a few of the problems present in the courthouses that make the judges so discouraged by their working environment.

Even more troublesome to most judges than the depressing physical setting was their vulnerability to physical attack as a result of the absence of a viable security system. Although there have been only a limited number of judges and their staff members who have actually been victimized, the number of incidents (ranging in seriousness from verbal abuse to actual assaults) appear to be increasing, and the threat of future assaults is a constant topic of conversation and an omnipresent fear. The security problem becomes most serious in the late afternoon and evening when the limited number of bailiffs are reduced even further to only a skeletal crew. With the chambers hidden from public view by a labyrinth of connected hallways, judges are especially vulnerable to attack when they attempt to leave the building in the evening. Many courts, especially those located in deteriorating neighborhoods, will provide an armed escort for the judge through the building and out to his or her car. Criminal court judges feel particularly vulnerable to attack from unhappy, vengeance-seeking defendants.

The reader must remember that this depressing picture applies mainly to state trial courts located in urban areas. Nearly all of the state appellate courts, rural trial courts, and the federal courts are housed in much more impressive surroundings, safer and more compatible with the public's preconceived notion of how a courthouse should appear.

Administrative Tedium

Even more than their physical surroundings, most judges are much more troubled by the endless attention to administrative details that seem to dominate their professional lives. Most individuals are attracted to the bench in order to "do justice," try cases, and resolve challenging legal issues. Therefore, when they become overwhelmed by ever-increasing bureaucratic demands, they become quite frustrated. The administrative problems become even more serious and persistent due to the irritating lack of cooperation that frequently plagues judges as they frantically try to collect missing documents, temporarily absent attorneys, and forgetful or confused witnesses. One recently retired southern judge captured the sentiments of many of his colleagues by commenting that he was so busy with administrative trivia that he had no time to think. He felt he was becoming more of a clerk and less of a judge.[5] Aggravating the judges even further is the recent demand for accountability in which administrative and presiding judges require members of the bench to maintain a time sheet in which they must record how each hour of the working day is spent, including reporting the length of their lunches. One eastern city carried the accountability phenomenon to its farthest extreme by requiring their judges to explain each 15 minute segment of the day—a task that deeply angered every member of the city's judiciary.

The problems in sloppy coordination and erratic communication has severely handicapped judges in their ability to process cases, especially during pretrial stages where massive backlogs are most likely to occur. These communication and coordination problems have worsened to the degree that it appears that approximately every other case must be postponed or delayed because of some missing person or document.

Judges do appear to be able to exercise a limited degree of influence in reducing the number of postponements. This may be accomplished either by gaining a reputation as a no-nonsense judge who will consistently penalize anyone failing to appear in his or her courtroom at the required time or the judge becomes a person who is willing to drive both himself or herself and the staff unmercifully in a never-ending struggle to control the docket and ensure the prompt appearance of all parties. Judges who adopt either of these styles, and particularly the latter, run a strong risk of antagonizing their personal staff as well as the courtroom work group. These tensions can cause the other actors to become uncooperative or recalcitrant and eventually be counterproductive. Thus, the abrasive judge, striving for courtroom efficiency may be less successful in his search than a more complacent judge who works through a pile of cases in a relaxed and friendly manner.

The court administrator is the public official whose position was created to assist the judge tackle these burdensome tasks. The powers of the administrative judge and those of his or her assistants varies significantly from city to city, but generally one expects this official to be held accountable for controlling the behavior of his or her management specialists. It is ironic, that despite the fact that these administrative officials were developed for the purpose of aiding the judiciary with their managerial expertise, they have, at least in the opinion of most judges, made judges' professional lives more miserable by appreciably increasing the amount of tedious paperwork that must be completed.

The administrative judges and their staffs are likely targets for the frustrated judges who are drowning in files, records, and miscellaneous documents. Also, because the court administrators are technically responsible for the working conditions, including the deteriorating physical plant and vanishing professional amenities, they are blamed for all of the problems that upset the judges. As the minor irritations continue to mount, and begin to multiply in both frequency and severity, the hostility of the judges also begins to escalate. When the air-conditioning system malfunctions during the same day that the photocopying machine breaks down and a law clerk is mugged in the bathroom, the judge is likely to designate the Office of Court Administrator as the primary cause for all of these woes.

An administrative judge is able to survive in this nerve-wracking environment by utilizing a "stick and carrot" method of dealing with the judges. He or she makes them cognizant of the autocratic potential for making their lives pleasant or miserable. The administrative judge's power to control which chambers a judge may be assigned, which courtroom will he have, who will be her bailiffs—these are all critical factors affecting the quality of the judge's professional existence. It may, therefore, behoove the judge to cooperate with the presiding or administrative judge as much as possible, for the alternative may lead to a very unpleasant tenure on the bench. Since all judges receive nearly the same salary in a specific jurisdiction, their only way of indicating their relative superiority would be in their possession of a better office or more stylish courtroom.

As a closing note, the judges themselves do seem to contribute to this administrative chaos and are not entirely blameless. Their prior experience as attorneys, assisted by a handful of loyal clerks and secretaries, has not prepared them for the massive and detailed administrative responsibilities presently facing them. Scheduling cases, dealing with various public bureaucracies, shuffling an endless flow of records and documents are all tasks that most judges never had to previously confront. The isolated efforts to deal with these administrative problems through increased use of computers as well as additional training for the staff does not seem an adequate response to so deep-rooted a problem.

Undesirable Media Attention

With few exceptions most of our nation's judges wish to escape the attention of the mass media. When a judge does make the evening news, regardless of whether it is a favorable or unfavorable incident, the typical reaction is to continue to remain aloof, shunning all publicity. A recent survey of Wisconsin judges by Robert Drechsel did discover, however, a growing number of judges willing to assist journalists and provide information to the public, but the majority still remain a passive news source and may be criticized for indirectly contributing to the problem of an uninformed public—at least in law-related matters.[6]

Most judges are successful in their efforts to avoid the media's spotlight. They accomplish this by refraining from making judgments that can upset and possibly outrage the public such as releasing a person accused of a heinous crime on a very low bail just because the accused has strong family ties in the community. Judges acknowledge the power of the media and generally agree with one Philadelphia judge who told me that the local newspaper *(The Inquirer)* "can really do a number on you if they want to."[7] Not all judges are "camera/media shy." Several, who are described by their more cautious colleagues as egomaniacs, grandstanders, or simply engaging in political careerism (striving to build public support for a future move to higher political office), may actively seek the ear of the press, appearing on radio and television shows as well as willingly offering their views to newspaper reporters. One midwestern judge justified his excessive interest in media attention by describing himself as a judicial educator who had an obligation to better inform the public.

An especially sensitive area of media coverage that troubles most judges is the possible impact such reporting could have on potential jurors. Research by Ralph Frasca discovered, however, that despite these fears, "the conditions necessary for media coverage to prejudice jurors to the extent that they are unable to decide a case based on courtroom evidence are likely to occur in only one of every 10,000 cases."[8] Many judges and court administrators are skeptical of Frasca's findings and there has been a movement toward assisting judges in the handling of highly publicized trials involving media attention. As a general guideline, Bernard Meyer instructs judges that in a publicized case, they must first communicate with both contesting parties what is required to ensure a fair trial. Meyer warns that "only when both sides understand the needs and rights of the other will each side respect and try not to infringe therein. Each case involving appreciable publicity is somewhat unique and judges must frame specific orders for that particular case."[9]

A related issue is the quality of court reporting and the resulting level of public knowledge concerning the operation of the legal system. There appears to be a broad consensus among judges and social scientists that the quality of media coverage of the courts is relatively meager and superficial. Robert Drechsel, who has written extensively on judges and the mass media, believes that this unfortunate situation has developed as a result of the lack of journalistic resources, newspaper space, and air time. He also believes that many journalists lack legal expertise, and even though those reporters covering the U.S. Supreme Court for the major newspapers and magazines may be relatively well trained, reporters at the trial court level are lacking in both experience and legal knowledge.[10] Ethan Katsh found that even at the highest level, coverage by the major television networks was rather sporadic. He explains this limited coverage as a function of the Court's schedule of handing down decisions in clusters on one or two days during a week, although he also believes that television's emphasis on the visual and concrete may undermine its ability to cover abstract concepts such as court decisions.[11]

Political Involvement

Most judges object to the necessity of having to become involved in politics as part of their selection to the bench. Several lawyers interviewed who practiced in locales where the judicial selection process was highly politicized refused to consider moving to the bench because of the required political campaigning. The judges with the strongest animosity toward coerced involvement into local politics were usually those who had previously practiced in large, prestigious law firms and were novices to the political arena. The political rallys, fundraisers, and closed-door strategy sessions were all despised diversions from their primary goal, which was simply to decide cases and serve their city. Whether the selection process was by election or appointment followed by retention elections, the judges were still required to participate in the political process and interact with the local party leadership. A more complete discussion of the role of politics and its influence on judicial selection is presented in Chapter 6. At this point the reader need only be aware that political involvement represents for the large majority of our nation's judiciary one of the more unpleasant aspects of obtaining and maintaining a position on the bench.

Lonely Isolation

Because trial courts are controlled by individual judges sitting in isolation, each judge is forced to perform his or her professional responsibilities without the assistance of colleagues. Even in appellate courts, the majority of a judge's time is spent in chambers removed from both colleagues and courtroom work group. For judges who are by nature gregarious and enjoy the conviviality of law practice in a large firm, becoming a judge can be a lonely experience. Isaiah Zimmerman believes that judges are especially prone to bouts of loneliness and explains that they are part of one of the few professions that is "required to divest themselves of long-held personal associations at the peak of their career. . . . Social life with members of the local bar, membership in associations and clubs, seats on boards have to go or at least be reconsidered."[12] Not all judges believe that appointment to the bench necessitates such a radical loss of social life, but it is agreed that judges must be more guarded in their conversations, even at purely social events.

Stress

When asked what it takes to be a good judge, an eastern judge interviewed in 1980 quipped: "Ten valiums and some good bourbon."[13] His tongue-in-cheek response was an obvious reference to the great amount of stress felt by many judges. After reviewing the numerous complaints catalogued in the preceding section of this chapter, it is clear that a judge's job can be extremely stressful. Stress has been defined as a "nonspecific response to outside demands. As demands increase the body and the mind re-organize continually to cope with them. Eventually, under chronic conditions of overload, the efficiency of that coping process becomes marginal and the quality of work and personal life is threatened."[14]

In recent years psychologists and physicians have begun to recognize that judges as well as other "achieving professionals" are increasingly prone toward stress. Bernard Suran explains that high-powered professionals such as judges share a set of psychological characteristics that appear to drive them toward premature "burnout."[15] This group of supercharged professionals share an exaggerated need to control their environment as well as the events that touch their lives. Suran concludes his analysis by finding that these stress-prone professionals are driven toward "high intellectual perfectionism, denial of feelings and interpersonal needs, all factors combining to leave them extremely susceptible to psychological distress."[16]

Beyond their shared problems with other highly motivated professionals, judges appear to be even more prone to stress because of various pressures endemic to their professional responsibilities. Zimmerman suggests the following list of significant stress-producing factors inherent in judicial careers: lonely transition, social isolation, financial pressure, lack of feedback, information and topic overload, midlife passage stress, and little control over caseload and clientele.[17] Many of the factors listed by Zimmerman parallel the list of complaints discussed earlier in this chapter. Robert Showalter and Daniel Martell have also studied the roots of judicial stress and agree with Zimmerman that the problem seems to grow out of frustration with the inability to control the work situation. They believe the constantly shifting intellectual demands of the chaotic working conditions is clearly the preeminent factor pushing judges beyond the limits of their psychological coping mechanisms. Similar to Zimmerman, Showalter and Martell list the judge's social isolation, the large and unpredictable workload, declining public respect, and the perplexing uncertainty in appellate law as being the major sources of judicial stress.[18]

Despite the seemingly obvious stress-producing nature of the judge's professional responsibilities and working conditions, only recently have mental health professionals and the judiciary itself begun to address this problem. An example of the growing awareness of this issue is the formation in 1983 of the National Judges Health-Stress Research Project, which is a joint endeavor by the Institute of Law, Psychiatry and Public Policy of the University of Virginia and the American Academy of Judicial Education. Its major purpose is to examine relevant personality variables, clinical symptoms, stress levels, and health-related outcomes as reported by surveyed judges.[19] This project and others attempt to identify the early signs of stress, noting which types of judges are most prone to suffer, and finally to develop techniques to manage or reduce the stress. The National Judges Health-Stress Research Project identified stress-prone judges as possessing Type A personalities, which demonstrate the following traits: (1) a belief that he or she can control or influence the events of daily living, (2) an ability to feel deeply involved in or committed to the activities of his or her life, and (3) the anticipation of change as an exciting challenge to further development.[20] Their high-stress judges usually possessed the following group of symptoms within the three general areas of healthy functioning: cognitive, psychological, and interpersonal:

1. Cognitive symptoms: trouble concentrating and difficulty in making decisions.
2. Psychophysiological symptoms: disturbed digestive functions including nausea, pains in the chest, difficulty breathing, feeling of being agitated or tense and difficulty falling asleep or a pattern of fitful sleep.
3. Interpersonal symptoms: uncharacteristic outbursts of temper, frequent arguments, a sense of not feeling close to significant others, and a feeling of self-consciousness when in situations that normally require some level of social interaction.[21]

Clinical psychologist Zimmerman provides another series of early warning signs of judicial burnout that, although similar to the National Research Project just discussed, offers additional assistance in identifying these troubled judges: poor memory for recent events, a blunting of sensitivity and empathy for others, an unfounded egocentric self-confidence, a feeling of disconnection from others, general cynicism and feelings of despondency, chronic fatigue, headaches, insomnia, excessive drinking, lowered resistance to infections and reduced sexual drive.[22]

What happens if a judge ignores the early warning signs or refuses to take the advice of concerned friends, colleagues, and family members? The likelihood for early retirement based on medical disability looms as a distinct possibility although most judges suffering from stress can usually develop techniques for at least temporarily coping with the problem. Nevertheless, it is a serious problem, and if it is allowed to reach extreme proportions can result in tragedy as in the case of Judge Frank Kinney of the Connecticut Superior Court. After suffering a fatal heart attack in 1988, Judge Kinney's widow brought an action against the State of Connecticut charging that her husband's working conditions literally drove him to his premature death. (He was 53 years old at the time of his fatal heart attack.) As reported in the *New York Times* by David Margolick, Judge Kinney, who was an administrative judge responsible for keeping the state's burgeoning felony caseload moving, found his days "filled with prosecutors, defense lawyers, clerks, secretaries, job applicants, policemen, court reporters and other judges. Nights he would bring home his battered brown briefcase . . . and spend another 3 to 4 hours in the basement office he had fashioned out of his children's old playroom. It resumed the next morning as he made his oatmeal; thousands of cases were systematically reviewed, charted, tracked. Judge Kinney took a vacation once in 1971. Whenever he was urged to take another, he invariably laughed or shrugged his shoulders. Who else he asked would do the work."[23]

Hopefully Judge Kinney is a rare and extreme example of the stress and burnout phenomenon, but it does affect a sufficiently large number of judges to force the profession to begin developing accessible and effective stress reduction programs. The National Health-Stress Project report noted earlier recommends that judges can best reduce stress through prudent nutrition, a well-defined program of planned relaxation and exercise, and the development of a unified philosophy of life.[24] Bernard Suran, a professor of clinical psychiatry, has also studied the problem of psychological stress among judges and other professionals and believes that if diagnosed in time, it need not distract or deter judges from a healthy and successful career. Suran's specific recommendations for the problem include (1) a public information campaign that shapes attitudes about psychological disability within the membership, (2) provisions for treatment prior to disciplinary action, and (3) the institutionalization of mental health liaisons and consultation services for every case of judicial disability involving psychological problems.[25] The section on judicial stress concludes with a personalized prevention plan proposed by Isaiah Zimmerman (see Box 9.1).

MAINTAINING ORDER IN THE COURTROOM

One of the most challenging responsibilities of a judge during the time spent in the open courtroom is maintaining the proper level of order and decorum. Judges must deal with emotional outbursts from lawyers, litigants, and courtroom spectators. Although the reported incidence of such outbursts appears quite minimal, it is nevertheless of constant concern to most judges. From my years of courtroom observations as well as the more authoritative Dorsen report, only a small number of incidents were discovered. Norman Dorsen and his associates from the Bar

Box 9.1 PERSONAL BURNOUT PREVENTION PLAN
By Isaiah M. Zimmerman

Select only *one* action from each track: then undertake
all four actions together over a two-week period.

I. Professional Track (Choose only one)

1. Discuss your thoughts and feelings about your work with your closest
   friend and your spouse.

2. Resign from one committee or board.

3. Read one book in a totally unfamiliar field or topic.

4. Ask a respected law professor or colleague to critique a sample of your
   recent writing.

5. Tell several close colleagues that you are going through a period of important personal reassessment. Do not be apologetic, defensive, or humorous about it.

II. Personal Track (Choose only one)

1. Meditate, pray, or simply relax, with eyes shut, for a brief period each
   day.

2. At home, finish one house-repair or gardening project.

3. By telephone, "visit" and chat with three friends you have not seen for
   a long time.

4. Ask your spouse to be the initiating and active partner in sex and affection
   for two weeks.

5. Go through your family photo albums. Think about the course of your life
   and discuss it with your family.

III. Physical Track (Choose only one)

1. Do an alternating tensing and relaxing exercise for three minutes, twice
   each day.

2. After medical consultation, start light jogging, rapid walking, or swimming
   daily.

3. Arrange not to be disturbed, and take a short nap daily in the office, or
   as soon as you come home.

4. Cut out all sugar and salt in your diet, limit coffee, tea, and liquor to one
   drink a day.

IV. Administrative Track (Choose only one)

1. Exchange your briefcase for a larger in-basket and take no work home.

(continued on page 304)

Box 9.1 (continued)

2. Take an hour off each week to visit around your courthouse and get acquainted with the people who work there. Show an active interest in their jobs and problems.

3. At the end of each day, take 15 minutes to talk the day over with your whole staff and go over plans for the next day.

4. Find funds and time for a course or workshop not directly related to your work: a "mini-sabbatical."

5. Invite your administrative staff to two "brainstorming" sessions (one week apart) where no ideas will be criticized during the session.

It is suggested that the above program, or a similar concept, be carried out once every six months as a form of personal renewal and as an "early warning system." The value inherent in such an approach is that no matter how heavy the work at the court gets, the quality and liveliness of one's personal life must not yield to the pressures involved.

Association of the City of New York discovered that after sending out questionnaires to 4600 trial judges throughout the United States, only 107 judges reported a total of 112 cases of disorder in their courtrooms. These incidents occurred most frequently during serious criminal cases although a surprising number of divorce proceedings were noted. Seventy-four of the cases involved criminal defendants (13 of whom were later found to be mentally disturbed), and 17 were spectators and 8 were attorneys. The court dealt with these disturbances by issuing contempt citations (32), warnings (24), binding and gagging a defendant (17), removal from the courtroom (13), declaring a mistrial (1), and clearing the courtroom (1).[26]

Litigants and their supporters in the courtroom are most likely to present behavior problems for the judge. Their unacceptable courtroom conduct ranges from passive disrespect and noncooperation to isolated emotional outbursts and repeated interruptions requiring physical restraint or removal. The large majority of incidents involve passive disrespect and related, less severe forms of noncooperation. In the criminal cases I have observed, the frequency of defendant disrespect was so common that many judges appeared barely cognizant of the defendant's contemptuous attitude. It is puzzling to many first-time observers to view defendants behaving so disrespectfully at arraignments and presentencing hearings where it is obviously a very inopportune moment to antagonize a judge who is in the process of determining whether or not the defendant will face incarceration (and if so, for how long). It was very normal for youthful defendants, in particular, to flaunt their disrespect toward the court by assuming slouching postures, uttering unintelligible grunting responses to questions from the judge, and casting sullen glances toward the bench.

Earlier research by Jaros and Mendelsohn in Detroit's recorders court[27] clearly supports the premise that judges will penalize defendants who appear disrespectful in their courtrooms (and conversely reward those defendants who have the sense to try and placate the judge by exhibiting remorse and respect). Why then do defendants persist in this masochistic ritual? One can only imagine that there must be some strong belief in the necessity for maintaining a "macho image" in front of friends and spectators in the courtroom. Deference to the court may be equated with weakness in their distorted social education, and no sign of weakness is to be shown, even if it is sure to cause serious personal hardship. Some defendants may also believe, along with the general public, in the continual leniency of the courts, and in a revolving door system of justice in which the courts never seem willing to treat their case seriously. These defendants fail to realize that as they become older and their crimes become more serious, the court's patience will run out, and they will face a lengthy prison term rather than the expected probationary sentence they received in previous encounters.

Judges, as was just noted, do have a range of sanctions available to them when facing disruptive behavior in their courtrooms. When the litigants are the source of trouble, judges are first inclined toward using preventive strategies such as issuing a warning or negotiating a solution. If, however, the defendant continues to misbehave, he or she may also face the more serious reprimands of being held in contempt of court. Courts distinguish contempt at two levels; it may either be civil or criminal or direct versus indirect. (Direct contempt occurs in the presence of a judge, and indirect occurs outside the courtroom and usually involves failure to comply with a court order. Criminal contempt is distinguished from civil because it involves a possible term of incarceration, and the latter is limited to some type of monetary fine or sanction.)

Attorneys may also be disciplined by the judge because of their misbehavior. These infractions include making disrespectful remarks to the judge, disobedience of proper court procedures or orders, utilizing purposefully obstructionist or dilatory tactics, or repetitive or excessive argumentation. The judge carefully evaluates whether the attorney is intentionally engaging in one of these forms of misbehavior or simply being unintentionally overzealous in advocating a client's interests. If the latter, most judges will simply warn the erring attorney. When a judge, however, believes that the lawyer acted intentionally (and repeatedly), there are a wide variety of sanctions available extending from contempt citations to discipline by the local bar association to suspension of the right to practice.

Most judges are reluctant to use their contempt power except in the most extreme cases. It is generally believed by most judges that if a colleague exercises the contempt power with any degree of regularity, he or she is demonstrating a serious weakness in both judicial temperament as well as an inability to control the courtroom. Despite the rarity of its usage, the contempt power is a frequently debated topic among judges and law professors interested in the administration of justice. The major problem with the contempt power is its potential for abuse because it has never been clearly defined and as Dan B. Dobbs wrote in the *Cornell Law Review*, "it has the potential power to invade without predetermined limits the private lives and behavior of those within the court's decree. This kind of power, often used wisely and within the appropriate limits is so subject to abuse that any society based on law needs to know its limits."[28] Francis Homan echoes this concern and writes that "the weapon of contempt in the hands of an unprincipled judge is deadly. You can appeal these contempt citations but what action lies against a judge who slanders or libels counsel during the course of a trial or unjustly finds him guilty of contempt—not very much."[29]

If the contempt power of the judge is to be controlled, it is obvious that the first area of reform lies in the necessity for having legislatures clarify the massive confusion and uncertainty presently surrounding its usage. The remedy could be provided through clear-cut statutory guidelines. A second area of reform is in the need for providing clearer procedural protections to individuals facing contempt charges. It seems rather obvious that the current process whereby the judge acts as both prosecutor and jury is unacceptable. Third, it is strongly suggested that judges should first resort to alternative methods of control or discipline before resorting to the issuance of a contempt citation. The Dorsen report on courtroom conduct published under the direction of the Association of the Bar of the City of New York recommends the following list of preventive measures that a judge might consider in lieu of the more serious contempt order:

1. Make known the ground rules that all participants will be expected to follow.
2. Reassure the defendant that all his or her rights will be respected.
3. Sever offenses or defendants if he believes that the large number of participants has reached a point unfair to particular defendants or prejudicial to the order of the proceedings.
4. Issue clear warnings, outside the presence of the jury, promptly after the first instance of disruptive conduct, advising a defendant what the consequences of further disorder will be.
5. With discretion, call a brief recess to cool off a potentially explosive situation.[30]

In closing this section on the role of the judge in maintaining order within the courtroom, it should be remembered that even though the frequency of misbehavior may be rare, it is of great concern and salience to the judiciary. Judges, as one would expect, are sensitive to their own vulnerability and therefore are greatly concerned with their ability to effectively defend against challenges to their authority. Now let us move on to the critical issue of judicial misconduct and what can be done about it.

JUDICIAL MISCONDUCT

One of the most perplexing issues related to judicial behavior is the problem of misconduct. This section will first attempt to discern how serious a problem it actually is, then move on to examine the different forms of judicial misconduct, concluding with a description of the mechanisms for monitoring errant behavior and the range of sanctions available to these disciplinary institutions.

How Serious a Problem: Its Frequency and Significance

Attempting to systematically assess the amount and seriousness of errant judicial behavior is an extremely difficult problem, hindered by both practical and methodological obstacles. John Culver and Randal Cruikshank in their analysis of judicial misconduct enumerate three of these impediments. First is the public's unwillingness to believe that respected judicial officers would betray the public trust through malfeasance. When combining the insulation of the judiciary with the public's ignorance of its day-to-day professional activities, even unpopular judges are able to easily evade public scrutiny and criticism. Second, lawyers who are the very group who are most knowledgeable about judicial misconduct, and even most likely to be directly affected by errant behavior, are also least willing to come forward and report any transgressions. Herman Schwartz explains the bar's reluctance to complain publicly by writing that "no matter how discourteous or prejudicial a judge may be, bar associations rarely deny an endorsement to a sitting judge. One reason for the silence is the fear that such criticism might jeopardize their livelihood—they may have to appear before these guys in the future."[31] Third, when judges are involved in some type of embarrassing situation, they are usually allowed to retire for "personal or health" reasons before the media publicly discredits them. Permitting voluntary retirement also ensures that the judge will not lose his or her pension rights which would be reduced if a judge is removed from office by a disciplinary commission.[32]

Despite these serious obstacles, Culver and Cruikshank were able to systematically analyze the extent of judicial misconduct and concluded that (1) more judges are now being disciplined than in the pre-1960 period while a significant number of judges are resigning under investigation; (2) the disciplinary procedures are more realistic and more workable than previous methods; and (3) public visibility affects discipline with the trial courts being more susceptible to complaints than appellate judges. There is general agreement that since the establish-ment of judicial disciplinary commissions, which began in the early 1960s in California and New York and have now spread to 37 additional states, there has been a perceptible increase in both the number of com-plaints as well as the number of judges disciplined. Nevertheless, there is still strong public support and regard for the judiciary, and, if there is an increased number of incidents of judicial impropriety, the evidence suggests that the bench is no less tainted than other professions. Addi-tionally, the absolute number of instances remains small and are primar-ily of a less serious nature.[33]

The largest number of problems clearly seems to be in the lower courts. According to one study, it was estimated that approximately half of the 15,000 magistrates and justices of the peace sitting in lower courts are unfit for service.[34] This shocking estimate is consistent with esti-mates by the President's Task Force on the Courts in 1967, which re-ported that lower courts attract less competent personnel. Many states appear to acknowledge this problem and have been actively attempting during the past decade to raise the qualifications for individuals selected to lower court positions, with special emphasis on eliminating the previ-ous use of lay magistrates. Alan Alschuler in his review of courtroom misconduct believes that the primary reasons for the high rate of judicial misconduct in the lower courts, beyond the questionable competence of the judges, is the absence of any real threat of appellate review as well as the impossible caseloads facing these tribunals. Alschuler also ex-plains that in those rare instances where the judge's conduct is reviewed by an appellate court, there appears to be a strong reluctance to punish a colleague, and if the members of the appellate court do choose to repri-mand one of their brethren, it is usually done privately with as little public notice as possible.[35]

In order to obtain a better understanding of current trends in judicial misconduct, let us briefly review some recent research. Table 9.3 is from a study of disciplinary commissions by Jolanta Perlstein and Nathan Goldman that combines the reports from several jurisdictions and offers a fairly detailed look at the variety and frequency of incidents. It indi-cates that the majority of problems (56.4 percent) resulted from in-court conduct while conflicts of interest and off-the-bench activities account for the overwhelming number of remaining incidents (33.8 percent).

Annual reports from the New York Commission on Judicial Conduct reaffirm the national survey by Perlstein and Goldman. After dismissing nearly two-thirds of their 600 complaints as being either frivolous or out-side their jurisdiction, the commission concluded that by far the greatest number of remaining cases involved ticket-fixing charges against lower court judges.[36] The most authoritative inquiry into the misconduct of federal judges was completed by Collins Fitzpatrick who reviewed the 1987 Annual Report of the Administrative Office of the U.S. Courts,

Table 9.3   REPORTED CASES OF MISCONDUCT HANDLED BY
COMMISSIONS BY NATURE OF ACTIVITY

Nature of Activity	Number of Cases	Percentage
In-court conduct	*117*	*56.5*
Failure to perform	35	16.9
Lack of decorum, rudeness	25	12.1
Ticket fixing	21	10.1
Abuse of power, corruption	20	9.7
Ex parte hearing held	16	7.7
Conflicts of interest or appearance thereof	*36*	*17.4*
Direct conflict of interest	12	5.8
Political activities	14	6.8
Practicing law	10	4.8
Incapacity	*6*	*2.9*
Alcoholism	3	1.5
Senility, old age	3	1.5
Off-bench activities	*34*	*16.4*
Criminal cases	22	10.6
Private activities	12	5.8
Miscellaneous	*14*	*6.8*

Source: Jolanta Perlstein and Nathan Goldman, "Judicial Disciplinary Commissions: A New Approach to the Discipline and Removal of State Judges," in *The Analyses of Judicial Reform,* ed. Philip Dubois (Lexington, Mass: Lexington Books, 1982): 96.

which reported that 232 judicial complaints were filed. The circuit chief judges dismissed 198, and another 35 were dismissed by judicial councils, 2 complaints were withdrawn, 8 were terminated after appropriate action was taken, and one was referred to the U.S. judicial conference (no specifics were provided as to what the "appropriate action" was).[37]

Do these statistics accurately reflect the reality of the problem of judicial misconduct? Most critics, including Fitzpatrick, believe that they badly underrepresent the actual number of instances of errant behavior. As we have already noted, attorneys are extremely reluctant to file a complaint for fear the judge might be prejudiced against him or her in a future case. Additionally, it is clear that most cases of serious misconduct are likely to be resolved by the judge's voluntary resignation or retirement, and if there is an investigation and hearing it is conducted secretly with no public notice of the final disposition.

As the preceding array of statistics indicate, it is very difficult to obtain a reliable and valid empirical description of judicial misconduct. Let us now examine the substantive nature and variety of manifestations that judicial misconduct may take.

Range of Problems

As was evident in the previous discussion of lawyer's misbehavior in Chapter 5, errant judicial conduct can also vary widely in seriousness and substance. We have noted that the preponderance of incidents cluster at the least serious end of the spectrum and commonly involve rudeness or bias. They appear to occur most frequently when judges assume an overly aggressive posture in the questioning of witnesses or comment too forcefully on the credibility and relevance of evidence or testimony. Their combined effect connotes the impression of judicial partisanship to both the litigants and the jury. The more serious categories of judicial misconduct are the result of either incompetence or venality. Although these transgressions are extremely isolated, they are usually important media events. In the post-Watergate period of heightened citizen scrutiny of public officials and their standard of morality, the media devotes a great deal of attention to any breach of the public faith, especially by the judiciary. Let us now examine some of the more prevalent forms of judicial misconduct, beginning with a discussion of the serious consequences caused by a judge lacking in judicial temperament.

Lack of Judicial Temperament   Given the chaotic conditions found in the courtroom, and the various pressures exerted upon trial judges, it is not unexpected that they may not be able to continually maintain a calm and dispassionate disposition. The frustrations of needless delays, incomplete records, insolent defendants, and incompetent attorneys all contribute to a debilitating and enervating judicial experience. Occasionally one does find a judge who does lack the necessary character traits and patience to overcome the pressures of the job. These judges can be observed exhibiting bursts of anger as their frustration drives them toward rude and abusive treatment of their courtroom work group and any other individuals who are in close proximity when their temper exceeds the boiling point.

It is indeed unfortunate that there are a few judges who are so easily driven to irrational and emotional tirades as to be clearly lacking in the requisite judicial temperament necessary for calm and dispassionate decision making. Under the American Bar Association's Code of Judicial Conduct (canon 2, which requires a judge to avoid impropriety and the appearance of impropriety in all activities, and canon 3, which requires a judge to perform the duties of the office impartially and diligently), there is an effort to address the issue of judicial temperament, but unfortunately it provides only the vaguest of idealized guidelines.[38]

The language used by a judge to address lawyers and litigants often provides the most tangible evidence of a judge lacking the proper temperament, especially to the degree required by the Code of Judicial Conduct. Incidents involving racial or sexist slurs are most likely to receive public attention and merit disciplinary action. Two recent cases reported by Yvette Begue and Candace Goldstein in their article entitled "How Judges Get into Trouble" provides excellent examples of this type of problem:

> In one case, a judge referred to a woman attorney as "lawyerette" and asked her why she wasn't wearing a tie. A few years later, at a hearing in chambers, the judge referred to another woman attorney employed by the attorney general's office as "attorney generalette." The court censured the judge for this and other conduct.
>
> In New York, a district court judge was admonished for commenting on the figure of women lawyers. In some instances, the judge suggested that the women could obtain what they were asking of the court because of their physical appearance. The comments occurred in the course of the judge's official duties but not within hearing of the general public. The discipline commission considered in mitigation the judge's good reputation and his acknowledgment that his comments were inappropriate. Further, the commission remarked that had the comments been made within the hearing of the public, a more severe sanction might have been warranted.[39]

Because judges possess such great power within the domain of the courtroom, their lack of proper temperament is often either tolerated or excused. It is also true that even the most even-tempered judge can on occasion be provoked by the chaotic conditions unfolding in the courtroom. Nevertheless, as Herman Schwartz warns in his article on "Judges as Tyrants," it is because their power verges on the absolute and because most of what they do is unreviewable, "such god-like powers ought to produce a corresponding humility but as with most mortals, power usually only breeds arrogance."[40] Let us hope that Schwartz's cynical warnings are an exaggeration.

Conflict of Interest   In order to guarantee that a judge is not influenced in his or her rulings by a chance to achieve personal gain, judges are prohibited from taking part in any case where there might be a conflict of interest. Historically, judges are disqualified from participating in any case in which they have (1) financial interests, (2) prior professional involvement in a proceeding or transaction, (3) a family relationship with a party or attorney, and (4) actual bias or prejudice against or in favor of one of the parties.[41] Canon 5C(1) of the ABA Code of Judicial Conduct specifically prohibits financial and business dealings by a judge "that tend to reflect adversely on his impartiality, interfere with the proper performance of his practical duties, exploit his judicial authority or involve him in frequent transactions with lawyers or persons likely to come before the court on which he serves."[42]

Since the conflict of interest issue, when combined with prejudicial behavior and lack of judicial temperament, undermines the very legitimacy of our legal system, disciplinary boards have been very careful to prevent even the appearance of bias or favoritism in any of these areas.

Conflict of interest problems, despite the vagaries inherent in the Canon of Ethics, are taken very seriously and dealt with severely. Marvin Comiskey and Philip Patterson in their comprehensive volume on judicial ethics and discipline note that judges have been found in violation of the conflict of interest canon in the following group of circumstances:

1. Judges are prohibited from operating or actively participating in most businesses thought to be affected with a public interest such as banks, public utilities, or insurance companies.
2. Judges can only act as a fiduciary for the estate, trust, or person of a member of his or her family, and then only if such service will not interfere with the proper performance of judicial duties.
3. Judges cannot allow any business to publicize their relationship with the judge. This would clearly be permitting the business to exploit his or her judicial position.[43]

Prejudicial Behavior   If a judge appears to be biased either for or against one of the parties in a lawsuit, the very foundations of the legal system are shattered. The most basic assumption in our nation's adversary system of justice involves the judge's role of neutral arbiter mediating between the two advocates. If the judge has decided prematurely to favor one side in a dispute, before the evidence from both parties has been presented in its entirety, the proceeding is a wasteful pretense and the legal system is little more than a sham.

Not only is the problem of judicial prejudice arguably the most serious form of misconduct, according to most analysts, it is also the most common. Contributing to the difficulty in solving the problem is the ambiguity of current standards that simply urge the judge to "avoid impropriety and the appearance of impropriety in all his activities" (canon 2 of the Code of Judicial Conduct). Additionally, as pointed out by Brian Henry and others: "It is unrealistic to expect that a judge can consciously eliminate all conduct that may violate a defendant's right to a fair jury trial. Judges are only human and naturally will react to events at trial."[44]

Albert Alschuler in his study of courtroom misconduct found that the most common form of prejudicial behavior involved the treatment of witnesses.[45] The judge was charged with either questioning the witness too zealously or commenting too forcefully on the evidence. In both examples the judge's behavior clearly favored one of the parties and exceeded the acceptable limits of required neutrality. Another recurring problem area involves the judge making pejorative remarks to attorneys during the trial. If a judge must make a critical comment, it should be reserved for a bench conference or in chambers. When a heated remark does accidentally slip out, the judge must quickly warn jurors to disregard such comments during their subsequent deliberations.

Why are these incidents of judicial prejudice so common? First of all, judges as we have continually noted are only human and are easily caught up in the emotional intensity of a trial or oral argument. A second, more disturbing explanation was offered by Schwartz who believes that many judges see themselves as the judicial arm of law enforcement and will work closely with prosecutors during pretrial proceedings. Perhaps even more significant is the fact that so many judges are themselves former prosecutors. Schwartz goes on to add that "since so many judges don't reach the bench until their later years, they have often grown increasingly conservative and less tolerant of deviance and difference, especially when it directly challenges the system in which he has done so well. And the politics surrounding the selection exacerbate his law enforcement posture even more."[46]

Corruption and Bribery Corruption and bribery represent the most serious forms of judicial misconduct. They stretch far beyond the intemperate or incompetent judge who fails to carry out professional obligations. They are clear acts of malfeasance, carried out by a venal or immoral judge. Fortunately, these transgressions are extremely rare, but when uncovered they usually become highly publicized events sometimes gaining national attention. One student of the subject, Charles Ashman, believes the problem to be rather widespread and has written a book entitled *The Finest Judges Money Can Buy,* which briefly discusses case studies of nearly 200 corrupt judges. His book contains chapters on the relationship between organized crime and the judiciary, judicial avarice, moral decadence, court jesters, and political manipulators and grafters. His compilation offers a frightening portrait, but one must realize that he is covering all federal and state judges for a 40-year period.[47]

Without minimizing the problem, nearly all research has found judicial malfeasance to be a very rare phenomenon. There can be observed on a daily basis judges losing their tempers, raising their voices, and permitting their emotions to be observed by everyone in the courtroom. This, however, seems to be much more a product of courtroom pressures rather than an abundance of unsuited, ill-tempered judges who should be relieved of their duties. Nevertheless, when incidents of bribery, corruption, or some other serious criminal behavior are uncovered among members of the bench, such as were recently reported in Chicago and Philadelphia, the entire judicial system within that jurisdiction becomes suspect. The public confidence therefore requires that when serious incidents are discovered, they are dealt with quickly and sternly.

Prohibited Off-the-Bench Activities The ABA Standards of Judicial Conduct not only address issues on the bench but are also concerned with questionable behavior off the bench. The necessity for carefully scrutinizing the off-the-bench activities of judges according to Steven Lubet is justified for the following reasons: "(1) the need to avoid the appearance of partiality or favoritism, (2) the need to maintain public confidence in the judiciary, (3) the need to ensure that judges will not be distracted by non-judicial activities and in a discrete set of circumstances, and (4) the need to maintain the separation of powers."[48] Unfortunately, the code does not provide clear guidance on this topic other than encouraging certain quasi-judicial or civic activities and to limit but not prohibit extrajudicial activities.

Critics of these judicial norms go on to explain how difficult it is to enforce such vague guidelines, which raise more questions than they answer; for example: "What constitutes conduct beyond reproach in the spheres of social relationships, business dealings, personal behavior, and intellectual expression? Should these matters be judged according to national, state, or local standards? What is the interplay between these character-oriented restrictions and the associational freedoms guaranteed by the 1st Amendment?"[49]

Although the range of undesirable off-bench conduct is quite diverse, they generally fall into four main categories: abuse of position, personal improprieties, campaign improprieties, and unprofessional involvement in civic and charitable activities. The abuse of position category can be best understood by division into three types of infractions. First and most common is the fixing of traffic tickets. When a judge is found to have been guilty of this offense, he or she faces a wide variety of possible sanctions, depending upon local precedents. In New York State, for example, where there has been an active and well-publicized campaign against such activity, judges are removed from office. In Iowa, however, where judges play a much more limited role in traffic court, a magistrate will only receive a reprimand or four-day suspension.[50] The second abuse problem is more subtle than fixing traffic cases. It is the misuse of the prestige of the judicial office in order to receive special treatment. The case of *in re Tscherhart* offers an excellent example of this type of offense. A judge had become upset at a bank's efforts to collect on a loan he had guaranteed for his son. The judge visited the bank, identified himself as a judge, and demanded special treatment. He further threatened to withdraw court funds on deposit in the bank. After the bank filed suit, he called the bank's counsel and warned him that as a judge he was "not insignificant." As a result of these actions, the judge was censured by the Michigan disciplinary commission.[51] The third abuse area is becoming actively involved in political campaigns that are unrelated to the administration of justice.

One of the most complex areas of concern, which clearly lacks the venality and selfishness of the first three categories, is the problem of judges becoming overly involved in civic and charitable activities. Candace Goldstein points out that as a general rule the ABA's Model Code of Judicial Conduct discourages fundraising on behalf of charitable organizations. Restrictions are especially severe on a judge's direct involvement in the solicitation of funds from members of the public. Nevertheless, three gray areas have emerged: (1) appearance of a judge's name and title on an organization's letterhead that will be mailed to solicit donations, (2) solicitation of memberships rather than just donations, and (3) use of judicial influence to compel charitable donations.[52] The only violation of this type of activity reported to the American Judicature Society in 1985 involved a judge who was disciplined for charitable fundraising after he had engaged in face-to-face solicitation of practicing lawyers in his chambers. The disciplinary board noted that this conduct would place pressure on any lawyer appearing before the judge who may have balked at the requested contribution.[53]

Physical/Mental Incapacity The final category of judicial misconduct could arguably be placed outside this entire discussion since it refers to medical and emotional problems suffered by a judge that may unintentionally impede his or her capability to perform the required professional responsibilities. This problem is, however, placed within the confines of judicial misconduct because we are focusing on judges who refuse to acknowledge the presence of any mental or physical handicaps despite advice or recommendations from their colleagues and concerned health professionals. Misconduct on or off the bench may sometimes be caused by a physical or mental disability such as alcoholism, senility, or any other incapacitating health problem. As with so much of this discussion of judicial misconduct, there are few guidelines for handling disability cases and little precedent guiding courts in determining whether a judge should be relieved of his or her duties.[54] Jeffrey Shaman, director of the Center for Judicial Conduct Organizations, expands on the difficulty of developing and implementing workable guidelines for misconduct cases in the following statement:

> While it is recognized that disability whether physical or psychological, should be treated with sympathy and patience, it is difficult to remain tolerant of a public official with as much responsibility and power as a judge who is not properly performing the functions of his or her office. When the judicial disability is accompanied by misbehavior as it often is, the situation becomes even more problematic. Although judicial misbehavior cannot be overlooked, to what extent should disability be considered in mitigation of misbehavior?[55]

Shaman reports that in recent years there has been a growing awareness that judges are affected by the same disabilities and afflictions that trouble other individuals. Realizing that judging is a stressful occupation, judges are likely to be even more susceptible to intense, emotional problems besetting the general population. The increasing incidence of judicial disability has become apparent to most concerned public officials who are aware of the cases of depression, alcoholism, and drug abuse being uncovered among members of the bench.[56]

It is true that nearly every state has developed provisions for handling involuntary retirement of disabled judges (or simply temporary suspension if the disability is not permanent). Despite the abundance of legislation, however, unless the disability is overpowering and embarrassingly obvious, the judges are extremely reluctant to remove one another from office simply because senility, fragility, or the possibility of a dependency problem has become increasingly apparent. Since so many of the nation's judiciary do not reach the bench until the "golden years," most are very sensitive to the unpleasant side effects inherent in the aging process. They may feel themselves on the edge of developing at least a partial medical or physical problem and therefore do not wish to be too quick to remove a colleague from office. As one Washington judge commented in an interview on the topic: "The shoe may soon be on the other foot."[57] As a closing note, the problem is most apparent in the federal courts where all of the judges (district, appellate, and Supreme Court) are appointed for lifetime tenure. Congress has recently reacted to the problem by passing in 1980 the Judicial Councils Reform and Conduct and Disability Act. (This legislation will be described in the closing section of this chapter.) Although there has been a persistent demand at the state level to enact legislation requiring the compulsory retirement of judges, most have resisted. Presently only 22 have mandatory retirement, and the age has generally been raised from 70 to 75.

The Competency Issue: Measuring Performance

The discussion of problems in judicial performance thus far has focused primarily on misconduct, which is usually contradictory to the Canons of Judicial Conduct and the statutes of each jurisdiction. An even greater problem, at least in terms of magnitude, although equally difficult to resolve, is the incompetent judge. A judge who unintentionally performs below acceptable levels of competence, conducting error-filled trials, making ill-advised decisions, and inefficiently administering the courtroom can be nearly as destructive to the overall quality of justice in a community as the rather isolated case of a judge purposefully engaging in misbehavior. It is possible that if a judge's performance reaches such a blatant level of incompetence as to qualify as "neglect of duty" or "malpractice in office," he or she can be removed from office through impeachment. This has, however, not proven to be a very effective way to deal with incompetent performance since many states require the finding of "criminality or moral turpitude" as the only conduct justifying use of the impeachment process.

Although lawyers can be sued by their clients for incompetent or negligent performance below the accepted professional standards, judges cannot be held liable for their professional behavior, regardless of its apparent poor quality. The process of appellate review is the functional equivalent of correcting erroneous or incompetent judicial performance. This review is viewed by some as an implicit evaluation of the legal soundness of trial judges and therefore an acceptable method of controlling substandard judicial performance. However, as John Paul Ryan points out in his analysis of judicial evaluation systems, judges may be reversed for a variety of reasons such as legal errors or differences in interpretation of statutes or earlier decisions. He also explains that very few cases are actually appealed, and those that are may be rather atypical and not representative of the judge's normal level of performance. For all of these reasons, Ryan concludes that reversal rates can be a very misleading measure of the quality of judicial performance.[58]

Judges, because of their unique position in our nation's political system, present a very difficult problem in terms of regulating their performance through the enforcement of professional standards. As a *New York University Law Review* article noted nearly 30 years ago:

> The problem of fixing standards requires a decision as to what society has a right to expect from its judges. On the other hand, judges are given a public trust. Virtually every decision they make requires them to choose between conflicting interests. Any factor that renders a judge unable or unwilling to do so satisfactorily undermines a basic premise of our legal system—that disputes can be settled fairly through the legal process. On the other hand, judges are human beings. Perfection is unattainable. The difficult problem is where to draw the line short of perfection. . . . The very status judges enjoy suggests the appropriateness of restraint; an unfounded accusation against an innocent judge might jeopardize his career.[59]

Despite all of the inherent difficulties in evaluating judicial performance, it is nevertheless agreed that some measure or operational definition of an acceptable level of professional competence be devised. Presently, the two primary aspects of judicial performance that are evaluated are the quantity and quality of work. Measuring the quantity usually entails examining the judge's productivity, and while it does lend itself to empirical measures, most critics agree that it is a flawed device that can be easily manipulated to mislead the public. Simply noting how many jury trials are completed or how many cases are disposed of during a calendar year indicates very little about the quality of justice found within the courtroom. A second aspect of the quantity issue is the attempt to measure how hard the judge is working, not just in terms of case outputs, but rather in the number of hours worked over a given period of time. This is also a deceiving measure and criticized as being so crude as to be meaningless. It fails to account for the intensity and quality of a judge's work product, rewarding the judge who moves at a snail-like pace but is willing to devote long hours to his caseload, which could be easily cleared by a more efficient colleague in half the time. Stott's observations after attempting to measure the performance of Colorado's judiciary clarify the weaknesses of the quantitative approach: "Many techniques exist to measure judicial activity, but the quantity of matters processed does not provide a qualitative measure. . . . Measures of activity are not meaningful measures of productivity and may have no relevance whatever to the quality of a particular judge."[60]

The second, and even more difficult aspect of judicial performance involves the attempt to measure the quality of a judge's work. Appellate reviews (which have already been discussed) and lawyer evaluations through bar polls have been the two most prevalent methods of measurement utilized to evaluate the quality of a judge's professional performance. Bar polls are typically based on the responses of a sample of lawyers within a jurisdiction providing not only an overall evaluation of a judge's performance, but may also measure his or her skill in specific areas of performance, commenting on legal ability, diligence, punctuality, judicial temperament, courtesy, and integrity. These polls are viewed skeptically in terms of their ability to provide a complete and authoritative judgment of a judge's competence. Critics note the narrow range of topics covered as well as the numerous methodological problems caused by attempting to employ empirical measures to subtle gradations of human behavior. Larry Cohen writes that the polls are usually conducted by bar associations and "tend to rate judges as lawyers see them and fail to take account for the many human criteria that effect our clients who are patrons of the system and who are most seriously affected by judicial performance."[61]

Serious efforts have recently been made to overcome the pitfalls of previous evaluation schemes. A major program has been conducted by the ABA's Evaluation of Judicial Performance Project, begun in 1983 and directed by Richard Kuh. Daina Farthing-Capowich, who has worked on this project and studied nationwide efforts to develop effective and reliable judicial evaluation systems, writes optimistically:

> Credible performance evaluation procedures are being developed in a few states, which suggests that the information necessary for improvement of the work of judges can be assembled without compromising their independence. Alaska has a full-scale process that focuses on retention, which includes public dissemination of information. New Jersey is pilot testing a program that will be administered internally and the results will be retained by the judicial system. The primary goal is the improvement of judges' performance rather than facilitation of the selection or retention processes. The District of Columbia uses a tenure commission to gather evaluative information on a judge's previous term of service and to recommend whether he or she should be retained in office for an additional term. Colorado designed a relatively elaborate process several years ago, but has not yet taken steps toward implementation.[62]

Table 9.4 offers a comprehensive portrait of these various evaluation programs with a brief summary of their major characteristics. The eleven states listed in the table are making valiant efforts to devise workable programs for evaluating the performance of their judges. The overall prognosis for the success of such programs, however, still remains rather guarded. The primary reason for the caution, beyond the plethora of methodological difficulties already noted, is the significant impact of the political context in which the judiciary must perform. As John Paul Ryan convincingly points out:

> No amount of technical, scientific, or administrative language can cloud this reality. Trial judges are public figures who are sometimes asked to make controversial rulings, decisions, or sentences. In so doing, judges create images—positive or negative—in the minds of those who may be measuring or evaluating their performance. Individual judges become classified or stereotyped as liberal or conservative, soft on criminals, anti-union, underminers of the family structure, or whatever. This, in addition to the usually known political party affiliation of judges, creates a store of images that can overwhelm the best intentioned efforts at objective evaluation, to say nothing of less well-intentioned efforts.[63]

Code of Judicial Conduct

Throughout earlier portions of this chapter reference was made to various canons from a Code of Judicial Conduct approved by the ABA and adopted by 47 states (either by statute or court rule). The present code was created in 1972 and replaces an older ABA document, entitled the Canons of Judicial Ethics. The 1972 version takes a broader view of judicial regulation than its 1924 predecessor, which emphasized "moral posturing and generalized exhortation . . . and contains primarily specific regulations and restrictions. It divides its coverage of judicial performance within three broad conceptual areas: judicial, quasi-judicial, and extra judicial."[64]

The following is a summary of this document's major canons and offers the reader a clear sense of its overall direction and style:

Canon 1: A judge should uphold the integrity and independence of the judiciary.

Canon 2: A judge should avoid impropriety and appearance of impropriety in all his or her activities.

Canon 3: A judge should perform the duties of his or her office diligently and impartially.

Canon 4: A judge may engage in activities to improve the law, the legal system, and the administration of justice.

Canon 5: A judge should regulate his extrajudicial activities to minimize the risk of conflict with his or her judicial duties.

Canon 6: A judge should regularly file reports of compensation received, quasi-judicial, and extrajudicial activities.

Canon 7: A judge should refrain from political activity inappropriate to the judicial office.[65]

Table 9.4 CHARACTERISTICS OF EXISTING AND PLANNED JUDICIAL PERFORMANCE EVALUATION PROGRAMS

State	Judicial Selection Method[a]	Term	Judicial Retention Method	Term	Purpose of JPE Primary	Purpose of JPE Secondary
Alaska	Judicial Council recommends two or more for gubernatorial appointment; governor selects	Until next election: not less than 3 yrs[b]	Nonpartisan election	4–10 yrs[c]	Retention	Under review[d]
Connecticut	Gubernatorial nomination for legislative appointment	8 yrs[f]	Judicial Review Council recommends to governor, governor recommends for legislative reappointment	8 yrs	Improve performance	Assignment Judicial education Increase public confidence
District of Columbia	Nominating Commission, President appoints, U.S. Senate confirms	15 yrs[g]	Varies depending on rating[h]	15 yrs	Retention	None
Louisiana	Nonpartisan election	6 and 10 yrs[i]	Nonpartisan election	6 and 10 yrs[i]	Improve performance	Assignment Public education[j] Judicial education[k]
Navajo Nation	Appointed by Tribal Council	2 yrs	Reappointed by Tribal Council	Life	Improve performance	Judicial education

State						
Nebraska	Nominating Commission for gubernatorial appointment	3 yrs	Nonpartisan election	6 yrs	Retention Improve performance	Retention
New Jersey	Gubernatorial appointment	7 yrs	Gubernatorial reappointment	Life[l]	Improve performance	Assignment Judicial education[m] Retention
New Mexico	Partisan election	6 and 8 yrs[q]	Partisan election	6 and 8 yrs[q]	Under review	Under review
Oregon	Nonpartisan election	6 yrs	Nonpartisan election	6 yrs	Under review	Under review
Vermont	Nominating Commission: governor appoints, Senate confirms[r]	6 yrs	Automatic unless General Assembly removes	6 yrs	Improve performance Judicial education	Under review Retention[s]
West Virginia	Partisan election	8 and 12 yrs[t]	Partisan election	8 and 12 yrs[t]	Under review	Under review

[a] Berkson, Beller, and Grimaldi, *Judicial Selection in the United States: A Compendium of Provisions.* Chicago: American Judicature Society, 1981.

[b] Applies to the supreme court, court of appeals, and superior court. Judges of the district court serve until the first general election which is more than one year after appointment.

[c] Supreme court, 10 years: court of appeals, 8 years: superior court, 6 years: district court, 4 years.

[d] Additional purposes under consideration include improved performance, judicial education, and assignment.

[e] Quantitative and narrative.

[f] Applies to the supreme court and superior court.

[g] Applies to the court of appeals and superior court.

[h] If the Commission on Judicial Disabilities and Tenure finds the judge to be "exceptionally well qualified" or "well qualified," the judge is automatically reappointed. A judge rated as "qualified" may or may not be nominated for reappointment at the President's discretion. A rating of "unqualified" bars a judge from reappointment.

[i] Appellate judges serve 10 years and trail court judges serve 6 years.

[j] Public education is viewed as a limited but useful by-product of judicial performance evaluation.

Table 9.4 CONTINUED

| | JPE Program Structure | | | |
| | Data Collection Methods | Respondents | Dissemination | Information Disseminated |
State				
Alaska	Questionnaires[e] Interviews with judges Review public records Public hearings Review audio and written records of proceedings Sentencing data	Attorneys Peace and probation officers Evaluated judge Public	Evaluated judge Judicial Council Lieutenant-Governor Registered voters	Survey data and comments All Summary Summary
Connecticut	Questionnaires	Attorneys Appellate judges Administrative judges Jurors	Evaluated judge Chief justice State court administrator	All All All
District of Columbia	Informal discussions Interviews Bar polls Letters Read opinions Court records	Court personnel Evaluated judge Attorneys Laypersons Court personnel Other judges	Administrative judge President Senate Public Evaluated judge	Summary Full dissemination to all
Louisiana	Questionnaires	Attorneys Judges Media Bailiffs Court clerks Probation and parole officers Law professors D.A. investigators	Evaluated judge Louisiana Judicial College Supreme court Judicial administrator Public	All Aggregate plus education responses Assignment aggregate and education responses Assignment responses Aggregate data
Navajo Nation	Questionnaires	Attorney advocates Jurors	Under review	Under review

State	Method	Respondents	Recipients/Dissemination
Nebraska	Questionnaires	Attorneys	Evaluated judge .... All Public .... Summary
New Jersey	Questionnaires Objective measures[n]	Attorneys Jurors Assignment judges Appellate judges[o]	Evaluated judge .... All Judicial Education Unit .... Summarized Assignment judge .... Other dissemination under review[p] Chief justice Governor
New Mexico	Under review	Under review	Under review
Oregon	Under review	Under review	Under review
Vermont	Questionnaires	Attorneys Court personnel Jurors Litigants Informed external agency personnel	Evaluated judge .... All Administrative judge .... All
West Virginia	Under review	Under review	Under review

[k]The draft of the final report does not specify judicial education as a purpose; however, it is clear from the report that relevant data will be collected and used for this purpose.

[l]Serves during good behavior.

[m]It is possible that data may be used for reappointment purposes at the chief justice's and governor's discretion.

[n]Objective measures collected routinely by the AOC will also be reviewed.

[o]It is possible that additional respondents will be added later. See text for detail.

[p]Others listed will receive some evaluation results; however, the extent and form of the information to be received are still under review.

[q]General jurisdiction court judges serve 6 years while appellate judges serve 8 years.

[r]Except probate judges, who are elected.

[s]This may be added as a purpose once the program is implemented successfully on an internal basis.

[t]Supreme court justices serve 12 years; circuit court judges, 8 years.

Source: Daina Farthing-Capowich, "Developing Court-Sponsored Programs," State Court Journal 8 (Summer, 1984): 28.

Given the broad direction offered by these professional guidelines, they can be expected to provide scant guidance for puzzled or wayward judges. They do, however, provide a foundation for discussions focusing on the parameters of judicial performance and provoke lively debate at professional conferences. Recent interest in the code has emanated from Judge Lois Forer's published comments arguing for an additional canon directed at the topic of judicial responsibility. She wishes to encourage judges to become more active whistle blowers when they observe problems in their courtroom that are not apparent to the litigants.[66]

Institutions and Sanctions for Disciplining Judges

In earlier discussions of judicial misconduct, we have focused primarily upon the substantive nature of the various problems judges may face that could possibly result in disciplinary action. In this chapter's concluding section we will examine the procedures and institutions used to discipline judges and the range of sanctions available to them.

Although impeachment has long been considered the primary (and in several states the only) method for disciplining a judge, there has in recent years developed a range of alternative options. The following list compiled by Marvin Comiskey and Philip Patterson indicate the current group of available sanctions:

1. Removal by the executive branch.
2. Legislative removal by impeachment.
3. Legislative removal by joint resolution of both houses.
4. Removal by the governor on address by both houses of the legislature.
5. Removal during a judge's term of office by recall election.
6. Removal by defeat in regular elections at the end of a judge's term of office.
7. Removal or discipline by a court in proceedings initiated in the courts.
8. Removal or discipline by disbarring or disciplining judges in their capacities as a member of the bar.
9. Removal or discipline in a proceeding initiated before permanent disciplinary commission or special disciplinary tribunal.[67]

The final alternative listed by Comiskey and Patterson, sanctions by a disciplinary commission, has replaced the historic impeachment process as the most common type of sanctioning procedure. Impeachment has become less popular due to its lengthy and partisan nature. Culver and Cruikshank report, for example, "that the average impeachment proceeding consumes some 16 days although some have lasted as long as 6 weeks. Moreover, there are no real procedural safeguards for the accused. . . . Perhaps most damaging, impeachment is a mechanism of last resort for dealing with the most unfit judges; there is no provision for correcting minor improprieties."[68]

Because of the inadequacies of the impeachment process, as well as the growing public concern over a perceived decline in judicial performance, a movement developed during the 1960s and 1970s to construct alternative mechanisms for disciplining judges. The major thrust of this movement was to establish state commissions to receive complaints concerning judicial misconduct, and after investigations and hearings were conducted, to recommend the appropriate action. The earliest discipline commission was formed in New York State in 1947, but the California Judicial Qualifications Commission created in 1960 has served as the most popular model for other jurisdictions. The California commission is composed of five judges appointed by the state supreme court, two lawyers appointed by the state bar association and two laymen appointed by the governor. The commission has a permanent staff with the use of outside investigators. It can act on its own initiative in a wide range of cases. Albert Alschuler in his study of courtroom misconduct discovered that in 1972 the commission received approximately 100 complaints. Two-thirds of the complaints were settled by the staff. The commission has been fairly successful in resolving disciplinary matters quietly and informally. Only 3 cases were referred to the state supreme court, and 50 judges resigned while their cases were under investigation. Alschuler concludes that "the California experience has demonstrated that a commission system can be effective in disciplining judges for abusive courtroom behavior. Nevertheless, one may have an uneasy feeling about a regime that emphasizes confidentiality, accomplishes its results primarily through backroom settlements, and that is dominated by members of the elite professional group that it is designed to control."[69]

Perlstein and Goldman report in their national study of judicial disciplinary commissions that three basic types have emerged. The most popular is the one-tier system used by 35 states. The investigation of complaints and recommendations to the state supreme court are delegated to one body. Although it appears to be very efficient, critics charge that it lacks sufficient due process safeguards The second type is the two- or multitier system utilized in 8 states. It divides the screening and investigating functions from the recommending responsibility by creating at least two separate institutions. The third system used by only four states is termed the "commission-legislature alternative." It delegates to the commission the responsibility for recommending discipline short of removal to the highest court of the state, while the removal power remains with the legislature.[70]

The federal government, which bestows lifetime tenure to all members of the judicial branch, has for many years relied solely on impeachment as its sole form of disciplinary sanction. This was changed in 1980 with the passage of the Judicial Councils Reform and Conduct and Disability Act. Presently, any complaints concerning a federal judge are reviewed by the chief judge of the appropriate judicial circuit who can either dismiss it or refer it to a judicial council comprised of district and appellate judges. This council may then either censure or reprimand the judge, selecting public or private notice. The judge is permitted to appeal the censure before sanctions can be imposed to a three-member panel of the Judicial Conference of the United States. Collins Fitzpatrick, attempting to analyze the significance of this new federal disciplinary commission, especially as reflected in an annual statistical report that showed only one case referred to the Judicial Conference and 95 percent of the complaints dismissed by either the circuit chief or judicial councils, offers the following cautious advice:

> One might look at these statistics and conclude that the federal courts are in very good shape because there are not very many problems. One might also look at these statistics and surmise that the judiciary is not taking its responsibilities seriously enough because there are certainly more problems than nine a year in the entire country.
>
> The cold statistics do not report the extent of the problems on the bench, nor do they report the extent of the judiciary's corrective actions in dealing with these problems. Why are there not more formal complaints? First, attorneys are often reluctant for fear the judge might be prejudiced against their current or future clients. While there has always been a reluctance by attorneys to petition for a writ of mandamus against a particular judge, there seems to be even more reluctance to file a judicial misconduct complaint. This reluctance similarly limits attorney complaints to the Judiciary Committees of Congress and would limit complaints to any proposed institution. The reluctance of active attorneys to complain is endemic to a system such as ours in which due process requires that the judge be informed of the identity of the complainant.[71]

Stephen Burbank, who has spent a great deal of time studying the evolution of the Federal Judicial Discipline Act believes that the major weakness of the act is its failure to adequately publicize the findings of misconduct. Without adequate public disclosure, the act, according to Burbank, poorly serves the best interests of the public by failing to create the requisite sense of judicial accountability.[72]

In addition to the confidentiality issue, which is found not only at the federal level but in several state systems as well, is the equally important procedural problem of penalizing judges who appeal disciplinary sanctions. Daniel Brooks believes that many judicial disciplinary systems are violating due process rights of the judges by having them face the possibility of enhanced punishment if they choose to appeal the original recommended sanction. He concluded his assessment of the problem with the warning that "the new efficient model of judicial accountability can be administered with excessive zeal," and questions whether "this retaliatory procedure does not run afoul of the due process clause of the 14th Amendment."[73]

How much judicial misconduct is really occurring within our nation's justice system. Culver and Cruikshank conclude that it is nearly impossible to answer this question with any degree of accuracy due to the numerous practical and methodological obstacles that deflect such inquiries. The authors believe the difficulties in accurate assessment persist because of the following problems which have been so difficult to resolve:

> First, while the public may abhor the conduct of a magistrate, there exists a mystique surrounding the judicial office that numbs retaliatory action. In spite of whatever unpopularity their office manifests, most judges are invisible enough to avoid being voted out of office. Second, the legal profession is a closed profession and those best situated to observe judicial misconduct are those most reluctant to report it—lawyers and other judges. Third, mindful of the notoriety which accompanies judicial scandals, many judges opt to retire for "personal" or "health" reasons before media publicity discredits them. Voluntary retirement also ensures pension rights, which can be restricted if a judge is removed from office.[74]

As a closing note to this chapter and without attempting to minimize the seriousness of the topic, nearly all research has concluded that judicial malfeasance is a very rare occurrence. Nevertheless, when a judge does begin to exhibit a pattern of behavior that threatens his or her legitimacy as a neutral arbiter and compassionate dispenser of justice, it is critical that action be taken. Even if these instances remain rare, they serve to undermine the credibility and efficacy of the entire judicial system. The public expects and demands its judges to be not only fair but to also give the appearance of such behavior. Anything less will seriously weaken the public's confidence in our nation's legal system.

NOTES

1. Mary Volcansek-Clark, "Why Lawyers Become Judges," *Judicature* 62 (October, 1978): 175.
2. Isaiah Zimmerman, "Stress: What it Does to Judges and How it Can Be Lessened," *The Judges Journal* 20/3 (Summer, 1981): 7.
3. Ibid.
4. Thomas Marvell, "Judicial Salaries: Doing More Work For Less Pay," *The Judges Journal*, 24/1 (Winter, 1985): 37.
5. Confidential interview with recently retired Washington, D.C., criminal court judge during July, 1980.
6. Robert Drechsel, "Uncertain Dancers: Judges and the News Media," *Judicature* 70/5 (February–March, 1987), 264.
7. Confidential interview with an eastern judge conducted during June, 1980.

8. Ralph Frasca, "Estimating the Coverage of Trials Prejudiced by Press Coverage," *Judicature* 72/3 (October–November, 1988): 169.
9. Bernard Meyer, "The Trial Judge's Guide to News Reporting and Fair Trials," *The Journal of Criminal Law, Criminology and Police Science* 60 (September, 1987): 287.
10. Drechsel, "Uncertain Dancers," 266.
11. Ethan Katsh, "The Supreme Court Beat: How Television Covers the U.S. Supreme Court," *Judicature* 67/1 (June–July, 1983): 11.
12. Zimmerman, "Stress: What it Does to Judges," 6.
13. Confidential interview with a New York City Supreme Court judge during June, 1980.
14. Zimmerman, "Stress: What it Does to Judges," 5.
15. Bernard Suran, "Psychological Disability Among Judges and Other Professionals: Some Causes and Cures," *Judicature* 66/5 (November, 1982): 185.
16. Ibid. p. 188.
17. Zimmerman, "Stress: What it Does to Judges," 6–9.
18. Robert Showalter and Daniel Martell, "Personality, Stress and Health in American Judges," *Court Review* 23/3 (Summer 1986): 11.
19. Robert Showalter and Daniel Martell, "Personality, Stress and Health in American Judges," *Judicature* 69/2 (August–September 1985): 83.
20. Ibid. p. 86
21. Ibid. p. 85.
22. Zimmerman, "Stress: What it Does to Judges," 9.
23. David Margolick, "At the Bar," *New York Times*, 6 April 1989, p. B5.
24. Robert Showalter and Daniel Martell, *Judicature*, p. 85.
25. Suran, "Psychological Disability," 191.
26. Norman Dorsen and Leon Friedman, *Disorder in the Court* (New York: Pantheon, 1973), 6.
27. Dean Jaros and Robert Mendelsohn, "The Judicial Role and Sentencing Behavior," *Midwest Journal of Political Science* 11 (1967): 471.
28. Dan B. Dobbs, "Contempt of Court: A Survey," *Cornell Law Quarterly* 56/2 (January 1971): 282.
29. Francis G. Homan, Jr., "Abuse of Attorneys by Judges," *Cleveland—Marshall Law Review*, 14 (January 1965): 86.
30. Dorsen and Friedman, *Disorder in the Court*, 257.
31. Herman Schwartz, "Judges as Tyrants," *Criminal Law Bulletin* 7 (March, 1971): 132.
32. John Culver and Randal Cruikshank, "Judicial Misconduct: Bench Behavior and the New Disciplinary Measures," *State Court Journal* 2/2 (Spring 1978): 4.
33. Ibid.
34. Howard James, *Crisis in the Courts* (New York: David McKay, 1968): 4.
35. Albert Alschuler, "Courtroom Misconduct by Prosecutors and Trial Judges," *Texas Law Review* 50 (April 1972): 688.
36. Yvette Begue and Candace Goldstein, "How Judges Get into Trouble," *The Judges Journal* 26/4 (Fall, 1987): 12.
37. Collins Fitzpatrick, "Misconduct and Disability of Federal Judges: The Unreported Responses," *Judicature* 71/5 (February–March, 1988): 77.

38. "ABA Code of Judicial Conduct," *Judicature* 69/2 (August–September, 1985): 77.
39. Begue and Goldstein, "How Judges Get into Trouble," 11.
40. Schwartz, "Judges as Tyrants," 131.
41. Marvin Comiskey and Philip Patterson, *The Judiciary: Selection, Compensation, Ethics, and Discipline* (New York: Quorum Books, 1987), 67.
42. "ABA Code of Judicial Conduct," 79.
43. Comiskey and Patterson, *The Judiciary*, 171.
44. Brian Henry, "Prejudicial Judicial Communications," *Trial* 24/8 (August, 1988): 54.
45. Alschuler; "Courtroom Misconduct," 685.
46. Schwartz, "Judges as Tyrants," 132.
47. Charles Ashman, *The Finest Judges Money Can Buy* (Los Angeles: Nash Publishing, 1973).
48. Steven Lubet, "Participation by Judges in Civic and Charitable Activities: What Are the Limits?" *Judicature* 69/2 (August–September, 1985): 69.
49. Steven Lubet, "Beyond Reproach: Ethical Restriction on the Extra-Judicial Activities of State and Federal Judges" (Chicago: The American Judicial Society, 1984), 7.
50. Begue and Goldstein, " "How Judges Get into Trouble," 12.
51. Ibid.
52. Candace Goldstein, "Fundraising by Judges," *Court Review* 24/(1) (Winter 1987): 8.
53. Lubet, "Participation by Judges," 73.
54. Begue and Goldstein, "How Judges Get into Trouble," 12.
55. Jeffrey Shaman, "Guidelines for Cases Involving Judicial Disability," *Judicature* 69/2 (August–September, 1985): 110.
56. Ibid.
57. Confidential interview with a Washington, D. C., judge, August, 1980.
58. John Paul Ryan, Alan Ashman, Bruce D. Sales, and Sandra Shane-DuBow, *American Trial Judges* (New York: Free Press, 1980).
59. "Remedies for Judicial Misconduct and Disability: Removal and Discipline of Judges," *New York University Law Review* 41 (1966): 150.
60. E. Keith Stott, Jr., "A Proposal to Evaluate Colorado's Judges," *Colorado Lawyer* 9 (1980): 7.
61. Peter Costas, "How Shall We Judge the Judges," *Connecticut Bar Journal* 49 (1975): 140.
62. Daina Farthing-Capowich, "Developing Court-Sponsored Programs," *State Court Journal* 8 (Summer, 1984): 27.
63. John Paul Ryan, "Evaluating Judicial Performance: Problems of Measurement and Politics," in *The Analysis of Judicial Reform*, ed. Philip Dubois (Lexington: Lexington Books, 1982), 131.
64. Steven Lubet, "Beyond Reproach," 4.
65. "ABA Code of Judicial Conduct," 77.
66. Lois Forer, "When Judges Should Be Whistle Blowers: Ethical Obligations of the Judiciary to the Public," *The Judges Journal* 27 (Summer, 1988): 6.
67. Comiskey and Patterson, *The Judiciary*, 149.
68. Ibid. p. 110.

69. Alschuler, "Courtroom Misconduct," 694.
70. Jolanta Perlstein and Nathan Goldman, "Judicial Disciplinary Commissions: A New Approach to the Discipline and Removal of State Judges," in *The Analysis of Judicial Reform*, ed. Philip DuBois (Lexington: Lexington Books, 1982), 94.
71. Fitzpatrick, "Misconduct and Disability of Federal Judges," 282.
72. Stephen Burbank, "Politics and Progress in Implementing the Federal Discipline Act," *Judicature* 71/1 (June–July, 1987): 15.
73. Daniel Brooks, "Penalizing Judges Who Appeal Disciplinary Sanctions: The Unconstitutionality of Upping the Ante," *Judicature* 69/2 (August/September, 1985): 97.
74. Culver and Cruikshank, "Judicial Misconduct," 4.

Recommended Readings

CHAPTER 1

American Bar Association. *A Review of Legal Education in the U.S.* Chicago: American Bar Association, 1984.

Carlson A. and C. Werts. *Relationship Among Law School Predictors.* Princeton: Educational Testing Service, 1976.

Carrington, Paul and J. Conley. "The Alienation of Law Students." *Michigan Law Review* 75 (1977): 887.

Cramton, Roger C. "Change and Continuity in Legal Education." *Michigan Law Review* 74 (1976): 1161.

Gillers, Stephen (ed.). *Looking at Law Schools.* New York: Taplinger, 1977.

Halpern, Stephen. "On the Politics and Pathology of Legal Education." *Journal of Legal Education* 32 (1982): 383.

Kennedy, David. "How the Law School Fails." *Yale Review of Law and Social Action* 1 (1970): 71.

Menand, Louis. "What is Critical Legal Studies? Radicalism for Yuppies?" *New Republic* (March 17, 1986): 20.

Nelson, Robert. "The Changing Structure of Opportunity: Recruitment and Careers in Large Law Firms." *American Bar Foundation Research Journal* (1983): 109.

Reisman, David. "Some Observations of Legal Education," in Arthur Sutherland's *The Path of the Law.* Cambridge: Harvard University Press, 1968.

Shaffer, T. I. and Robert Redmount. "Legal Education: The Classroom Experience." *Notre Dame Lawyer* 52 (1976): 190.

Shanfield, Stephen and Andrew Benjamin. "Psychiatric Distress in Law Students." *Journal of Legal Education* 35 (1985): 65.

Stevens, Robert. *Law School: Legal Education in America from the 1850's to the 1980's.* Chapel Hill: University of North Carolina Press, 1983.

Stover, Robert. "Law School and Professional Responsibility." *Judicature* 66 (1982): 194.

"Symposium: New Directions in Legal Education and Practice." *Denver Law Journal* 50 (1974): 389.

Turow, Scott. *One L: Inside Account of Life at Harvard Law School.* New York: Penguin Books, 1977.

Zemans, Frances and Victor Rosenbloom. "Preparation for the Practice of Law." *American Bar Foundation Research Journal* (1980): 1.

CHAPTER 2

Abel, Richard. *American Lawyers.* New York: Oxford University Press, 1989.

Abel, Richard. "The Transformation of the American Legal Profession." *Law and Soceity Review* 20 (1986): 53.

Carbon, Susan, Pauline Houlden, and Larry Berkson. "Women on the State Bench." *Judicature* 65 (1982): 286.

Curran, Barbara. "American Lawyers in the 1980's: A Profession in Transition." *Law and Society Review* 20 (1986): 19.

Curran, Barbara. *The Lawyers Statistical Report: A Statistical Profile of the U.S. Legal Profession in the 1980's.* Chicago: American Bar Foundation, 1985.

Eich, William. "Gender Bias in the Courtroom." *Judicature* 69 (1985): 339.

Epstein, Cynthia. *Women in the Law.* New York: Anchor Books, 1983.

Glick, Henry and Craig Emmert. "Stability and Change: Characteristics of State Supreme Court Judges." *Judicature* 70 (2) (August–September 1986): 107.

Halliday, Terrence. "Six Score Years and Ten: Demographic Transitions in the American Legal Professions 1850–1980." *Law and Society Review* 20 (1986): 53.

Jackson, Donald Dale. *Judges.* New York: Atheneum, 1974.

Liefland, L. "Career Patterns of Male and Female Lawyers." *Buffalo Law Review* 35 (Spring, 1986): 601.

Luney, Percy. "Minorities in the Legal Profession." *American Bar Association Journal* 70 (April, 1984): 58.

Mindes, Marvin and Alan C. Acock. "Tricksters, Hero, Helper: A Report on Lawyer Image." *American Bar Foundation Research Journal* (1982): 177.

Morello, Karen. *The Woman Lawyer in America.* New York: Random House, 1987.

Noonan, J. T. "Education, Intelligence, and Character in Judges." *Minnesota Law Review* 71 (May, 1987): 1119.

Pashigian, B. Peter. "The Number and Earnings of Lawyers: Some Recent Findings." *American Bar Foundation Research Journal* (Winter 1978): 51.

Rothman, Robert. "Deprofessionalization: The Case of Law in America." *Work and Occupations* 11 (1984): 183.

Ryan, John Paul, Alan Ashman, Bruce D. Sales, and Sandra Shane-DuBow, *American Trial Judges*. New York: The Free Press, 1980.

Waltz, J. R. "The Unpopularity of Lawyers in America." *Cleveland State Law Review* 25 (1976): 143.

CHAPTER 3

American Bar Association Special Committee on the Delivery of Legal Services. *Legal Clinics: Merely Advertising Law Firms*. Chicago: ABA, 1981.

Auerbach, Jerold. *Unequal Justice*. New York: Oxford University Press, 1976.

Ball, Howard. *The Federal Justice System*. Englewood Cliffs: Prentice-Hall, 1987.

Bellows, Paul. "Branches: Key to Growth." *The National Law Journal* (December 2, 1988): S-13.

Biehl, Kathy. "Going Solo." *American Bar Association Journal* (April, 1988): 68.

Brown, H. P. "The Paralegal Profession." *Howard Law Journal* 19 (1976): 19.

Carlin, Jerome. *Lawyers on Their Own*. New Brunswick: Rutgers University Press, 1962.

Eisenstein, James and Herbert Jacob. *Felony Justice*. Boston: Little, Brown 1977.

Goulden, Joseph. *The Superlawyers*. New York: Weybright and Talley, 1972.

Green, Mark. "The ABA as a Trade Association," in Ralph Nader and Mark Green (Eds.). *Verdicts on Lawyers*. New York: Crowell, 1976.

Halliday, Terrence, C. L. Cappell, and John Heinz. "Diversity, Representation, and Leadership in an Urban Bar." *American Bar Foundation Research Journal* (1976): 717.

Heinz, John and Edward Laumann. *Chicago Lawyers: The Social Structure of the Bar*. New York: Russell Sage, 1984.

Hoffman, Paul. *Lions in the Street*. New York: New American Library, 1973.

Nelson, Robert L. *Partners with Power: The Transformation of the Large Law Firm*. Berkeley: University of California Press, 1988.

Smigel, Irwin. *The Wall Street Lawyer*. Bloomington: Indiana University Press, 1973.

Spangler, Eve. *Lawyers for Hire*. New Haven: Yale University Press, 1986.

Stewart, James B. *Partners*. New York: Simon and Schuster, 1983.

Wice, Paul B. *Chaos in the Courthouse*. New York: Praeger Publishing, 1985.

Wice, Paul B. *Criminal Lawyers: An Endangered Species*. Beverly Hills: Sage Publications, 1978.

Zemans, Frances and Victor Rosenbloom. *The Making of a Public Profession*. Chicago: American Bar Foundation, 1981.

CHAPTER 4

Bartlett, Joseph. *The Law Business: A Tired Monopoly*. Littleton: Fred Rothman, 1982.

Call, John. "Psychology in Litigation." *Trial* (March 1985): 44.

Freund, James. *Legal-Ease: Fresh Insights into Lawyering*. New York: Harcourt Brace, 1984.

Goldberg, Stephanie. "Playing Hardball." *American Bar Association Journal* (July, 1987): 48.

Gouldin, Joseph. *Million Dollar Lawyers*. New York: Putnam, 1978.

Handler, Joel. *The Lawyer and His Community*. Madison: University of Wisconsin Press, 1967.

Hartnett, Bertram. *Law, Lawyers, and Laymen*. New York: Harcourt Brace Jovanovich, 1984.

Hosticka, Carl. "We Don't Care About What Happened, We Only Care About What is Going To Happen: Lawyer-Client Negotiations of Reality." *Social Problems* 26 (1979): 599.

Johnstone, Quintin and Dan Hopson, Jr., *Lawyers and Their Work*. Indianapolis: Bobbs-Merrill, 1967.

Kleinfeld, Andrew. "Alaska: Where the Loser Pays the Winner's Fees." *The Judges Journal* 24 (2) (Spring, 1985): 4.

Kritzer, Herbert. "The Dimensions of Lawyer-Client Relations." *American Bar Foundation Research Journal* (Spring, 1984): 409.

Legal Specialization. Chicago: ABA Special Committee on Specialization, 1976.

Mayer, Martin. *The Lawyers*. New York: Harper & Row, 1967.

McCormick, Mark. *The Terrible Truth About Lawyers*. New York: Beech Tree Books, 1987.

Nader, Ralph and Mark Green. *Verdicts on Lawyers*. New York: Crowell, 1976.

Nizer, Louis. *My Life in Court*. New York: Pyramid Books, 1963.

Reich, Cary. "The Litigator." *New York Times Magazine* (June 1, 1986), p. 18.

Schwartz, Murray L. *Lawyers and the Legal Profession*. Indianapolis: Bobbs-Merrill, 1979.

Trubek, David. "The Costs of Ordinary Litigation." *UCLA Law Review* 31 (October, 1983): 111.

Wice, Paul B. *Criminal Lawyers: An Endangered Species*. Beverly Hills: Sage Publications, 1978.

CHAPTER 5

Bloom, Murray. *The Trouble With Lawyers*. New York: Simon and Schuster, 1968.

Carlin, Jerome. *Lawyers' Ethics*. New York: Russell Sage, 1966.

Clower, Stanley J. *You and Your Clients.* Chicago: American Bar Association, 1988.

"Conflicts of Interests in the Legal Profession." *Harvard Law Review* 94 (1981): 1252.

Frankel, Marvin. "Curing Lawyers's Incompetence: Primum Non Nocere." *Creighton Law Review* 10 (1977): 615.

Freedman, Monroe. *Lawyers' Ethics in an Adversary System.* Indianapolis: Bobbs-Merrill, 1975.

Fried, Charles. "The Lawyer as a Friend: The Moral Foundations of the Lawyer-Client Relationship." *Yale Law Review* 85 (1976): 1060.

Gates, William. "The Newest Data on Lawyers' Malpractice." *American Bar Association Journal* 70 (April, 1984): 80.

Gellers, Stephen. *The Rights of Lawyers and Clients.* New York: Avon Books, 1979.

Haughey, David O. "Lawyers' Malpractice: A Comparative Perspective." *Notre Dame Lawyer* 48 (1973): 888.

Hazard, Geoffrey. *Ethics in the Practice of Law.* New Haven: Yale University Press, 1978.

Kaufmann, Irving. "Attorney Competence: A Plea for Reform." *American Bar Association Journal* (March, 1983): 308.

Lieberman, Jethro. *Crisis at the Bar.* New York: W. W. Norton, 1978.

Lungren, James (Ed.) "Review Symposium: The Model Rules of Professional Conduct." *American Bar Foundation Research Journal* (Fall, 1980): 921.

Morgan, T. D. "The Evolving Concept of Professional Responsibility." *Harvard Law Review* 90 (1977): 702.

Powell, Michael. "Professional Divestiture: The Cession of Responsibility for Lawyer Discipline." *American Bar Foundation Research Journal,* (1986): 31.

Rhode, Deborah L. "The Rhetoric of Professional Reform." *Maryland Law Review* 45 (1986): 288.

Rosenthal, Douglas. "Evaluating the Competence of Lawyers." *Law and Society Review* 11/2 (1976): 257.

Shroder, David. (Ed.) *Ethics and the Practice of Law.* Englewood Cliffs: Prentice-Hall, 1988.

CHAPTER 6

Berkson, Larry. "Judicial Selection Today." *Judicature* 64 (October 1980): 176.

Carp, Robert and Russell Wheeler. "Sink or Swim: Socialization of a Federal District Judge." *Journal of Public Law* 21 (1972): 359.

Chase, Harold. *Federal Judges: The Appointing Process.* Minneapolis: University of Minnesota Press, 1972.

Dawson, Richard and Kenneth Prewitt. *Political Socialization.* Boston: Little, Brown, 1969.

Dubois, Philip. *From Ballot to Bench*. Austin: University of Texas Press, 1980.

Eisenstein, James. *Politics and the Legal Process*. New York: Harper & Row, 1973.

Escovitz, Sari, Fred Kurland, and Nan Gold. *Judicial Selection and Tenure*. Chicago: American Judicature Society, 1975.

Glick, Henry and Craig Emmert. "Selection Systems and Judicial Characteristics." *Judicature* 70 (December–January, 1987): 228.

Goldberg, Susan. "Judicial Socialization: An Empirical Study." *Journal of Contemporary Law* 11 (1985): 423.

Goldman, Sheldon. "Reaganizing the Judiciary." *Judicature* 68 (April–May, 1985): 313.

Goldstein, Candace. "Becoming a Judge: Problems with Leaving a Law Practice." *Judicature* 69/3 (October–November, 1985): 139.

Grossman, Joel. *Lawyers and Judges*. New York: Wiley, 1965.

Karlen, Delmar. "Judicial Education." *American Bar Association Journal* 52 (1966): 1049.

Maddi, Dorothy. *Judicial Performance Polls*. Chicago: American Bar Foundation, 1977.

McKnight, Neal. "Choosing Judges: Do the Voters Know What They're Doing." *Judicature* 62 (August, 1978): 96.

Schotland, Ray. "Elective Judges Campaign Financing." *Journal of Law and Politics* 2 (Spring, 1985): 64.

Slotnick, Elliot. "The ABA Standing Committee on Federal Judiciary: A Contemporary Assessment." *Judicature* 66 (1983): 352.

Mary Lou Stein. "Judicial Education: How Does Your State Measure Up." *The Judges Journal* 25/4 (Fall, 1986): 28.

Watson, Richard and Randal Downing. *The Politics of Bench and Bar*. New York: Wiley, 1969.

CHAPTER 7

Barber, Suzanna. "Televised Trials: Weighing Advantages and Disadvantages." *Justice System Journal* 10/3 (Winter, 1985): 279.

"Courts and the Community." *The Judges Journal* 21/2 (Spring, 1982): 3.

Crump, David. "Law Clerks: Their Roles and Relationships with Their Judges." *Judicature* 69(4) (December–January, 1986): 236.

Gazell, James. *State Trial Courts as Bureaucracies*. Port Washington: Dunellen, 1975.

Gazell, James. "Three Principal Facets of Judicial Management." *Criminology* 9 (August, 1971): 131.

Gertz, Marc. "Influence in Court Systems: The Clerk as Interface." *Justice System Journal* 3/3 (Fall, 1977): 30.

Hanna, Forrest. "Delineating the Role of the Presiding Judge." *State Court Journal* 10/2 (Spring, 1976): 20.

Hoffman, Paul. *Courthouse.* New York: Hawthorn Books, 1979.

Howard, J. Woodford. *Courts of Appeals in the Federal Judicial System.* Princeton: Princeton University Press, 1981.

Mileski, Maureen. "Courtroom Encounters: An Observation Study of a Lower Criminal Court." *Law and Society Review* 5/4 (May, 1971): 473.

Oakley, John and Robert Thompson. *Law Clerks and the Judicial Process.* Berkeley: University of California Press, 1980.

O'Brien, David. *Storm Center: The Supreme Court in American Politics.* New York: Norton, 1986.

Ozar, David, Cynthia Kelly, and Yvette Begue, "Ethical Conduct of State Court Employees and Administrators." *Judicature* 71/5 (February–March, 1988): 163.

Posner, Richard. *The Federal Courts.* Cambridge: Harvard University Press, 1985.

President's Commission on Law Enforcement and the Administration of Justice. *Task Force Reports: The Courts.* Washington, D.C.: GPO, 1967.

Rubin, Ted. *Courts: Fulcrum of the Justice System.* Pacific Palisades: Goodyear, 1976.

Senzel, Howard. *Cases.* New York: Viking, 1982.

Wice, Paul B. *Chaos in the Courthouse.* New York: Praeger Publishing, 1985.

Williams, Richard. "Supreme Court of the U.S.: The Staff That Keeps it Operating." *Smithsonian Magazine* (January, 1977): 38.

CHAPTER 8

Coffin, Frank. *The Ways of a Judge.* Boston: Houghton Mifflin, 1980.

Cotter, B. Paul. "When the Electronic Judge Meets the Electronic Lawyer." *The Judges Journal* 27/2 (Spring, 1988): 2.

Dawson, John. "The Functions of a Judge," in Harold Berman (Ed.), *Talks on American Law.* New York: Vintage Books, 1961.

Frankel, Marvin. "Adversary Judge." *Texas Law Review* 54 (March, 1976): 469.

Kaufmann, Irving. "The Anatomy of Decision-Making." *Fordham Law Review* 53 (October, 1984): 1.

Kritzer, Herbert. "The Judge's Role in Pretrial Case Processing." *Judicature* 66(1) (June–July, 1982): 28.

Lummus, Henry. *The Trial Judge.* Brooklyn: The Foundation Press, 1937.

Luskin, Mary Lee. "Social Loafing on the Bench." *Justice System Journal* 12/2 (Fall, 1987): 177.

McDonald, William. "Judicial Supervision of the Guilty Plea Process." *Judicature* 70/4 (December–January, 1987): 203.

Medina, Harold. "Some Reflections on the Judicial Function at the Appellate Level." *Washington University Law Quarterly* (1961): 149.

Ryan, John Paul, Alan Ashman, Bruce D. Sales, and Sandra Shane-DuBow, *American Trial Judges.* New York: The Free Press, 1980.

Shapiro, David. "In Defense of Judicial Candor." *Harvard Law Review* 100 (February, 1987): 743.

Simon, James. *The Judge.* New York: David McKay, 1976.

Will, Hubert. "The Art of Judging." *Trial* 21 (October, 1985): 79.

Wyzanski, Charles. "An Activist Judge: Mea Maxima Culpa." *Georgia Law Review* 7 (1973): 208.

CHAPTER 9

"ABA Code of Judicial Conduct." *Judicature* 69/2 (August–September, 1985): 77.

Alschuler, Albert. "Courtroom Misconduct by Prosecutors and Trial Judges." *Texas Law Review* 50 (April, 1972): 687.

Begue, Yvette and Candace Goldstein. "How Judges Get into Trouble." *The Judges Journal* 26/4 (Fall, 1987): 8.

Brooks, Daniel. "Close Questions About Judicial Disability and Misconduct." *Judicature* 69/2 (August–September, 1985): 103.

Brooks, Terrence. "How Judges Get into Trouble." *The Judges Journal* 23(3) (Summer, 1984): 4.

Burbank, Stephen. "The Federal Judicial Discipline Act." *Judicature* 67(4) (October, 1983): 183.

Comiskey, Marvin and Philip Patterson. *The Judiciary: Selection, Compensation, Ethics and Discipline.* New York: Quorum Books, 1987.

Culver, John and Randal Cruikshank. "Judicial Misconduct: Bench Behavior and the New Disciplinary Measures." *State Court Journal* 2 (Spring, 1978): 3.

"Disqualification of Judges." *Oregon Law Review* 48 (1969): 311.

Dorsen, Norman and Leon Friedman. *Disorder in the Court.* New York: Pantheon, 1973.

Drechsel, Robert. "Uncertain Dancers: Judges and the News Media." *Judicature* 70/5 (February–March, 1987): 264.

Dubois, Philip. *The Analysis of Judicial Reform.* Lexington: Lexington Books, 1982.

James, Howard. *Crisis in the Courts.* New York: David McKay, 1968.

Marvell, Thomas. "Judicial Salaries: Doing More Work for Less Pay." *The Judges Journal* 24/1 (Winter, 1985): 34.

Schwartz, Herman. "Judges as Tyrants." *Criminal Law Bulletin* 7 (March, 1971): 129.

Showalter, Robert and Daniel Martell. "Personality, Stress, and Health in American Judges." *Judicature* 69/2 (August–September, 1985): 82.

Suran, Bernard. "Psychological Disability Among Judges and Other Professionals." *Judicature* 66/5 (November, 1982): 185.

Zimmerman, Isaiah. "Stress: What it Does to Judges." *The Judges Journal* 20/3 (Summer, 1981): 4.

Index